H U M A N A T U R E

HUMANATURE

Peter Goin
July, 2004

  PETER GOIN

UNIVERSITY OF TEXAS PRESS

This book was acquired and developed by the Center for American Places, Harrisonburg, Virginia, for publication by the University of Texas Press.

♾ The paper in this publication meets the minimum requirements of American National Standard for Information Sciences—Permanence for Printed Library Materials, ANSI Z39.48-1984

Library of Congress
Cataloging-in-Publication Data

Goin, Peter, 1951–
    Humanature / Peter Goin.
            p.   cm.
    Includes bibliographical references.
    ISBN 0-292-72785-2 (cloth : alk. paper)
    ISBN 0-292-72786-0 (pbk. : alk. paper)
    1. Man—Influence on nature.
2. Human geography.   3. Nature conservation.   4. Man—Influence on nature —Pictorial works.   5. Human geography—Pictorial works.   6. Nature conservation—Pictorial works.   1. Title.
GF75.G64   1996
304.2′022′2—dc20   95-36500

FRONTISPIECE: On 26 September 1991, researchers from the Biosphere 2 project sealed the airlock on a three-acre, enclosed ecological system in the foothills of the Santa Catalina Mountains north of Tucson, Arizona. Public relations information about Biosphere 2 proclaims: "Biosphere 2 is essentially an airtight structure, composed of elements from Biosphere 1, planet Earth. Like Earth's biosphere, Biosphere 2 is designed as a stable, complex and evolving system—sealed off from the outside world, yet open to electrical and solar energy as well as information exchange."

Biosphere 2 contains seven biomes: tropical rainforest (pictured here), savanna, marsh, twenty-five-foot-deep ocean, desert, intensive agricultural area, and human habitat. The ecological systems inside are designed to recycle air, water, wastes, and nutrients, maintaining the 3,800 plant and animal species as well as sustaining the biospherian crew during the time of each experiment. Two years to the day after entering Biosphere 2, the eight-person crew emerged, having lost about fifteen percent body fat.

Biosphere 2 is one of the latest versions of *humanature*.

CONTENTS

Preface   vii

Humanature   1

Notes   23

Trees   25

The Zoo   47

Beaches   67

The Mine   91

Reclaimed Land   107

The River   125

Dams   145

Wildlife   165

Acknowledgments   189

Suggested Readings   191

About the Author   192

PREFACE

For twenty-five years I have traveled throughout North America to make photographs of its landscapes. Until recently I had always accepted the notion that there is such a place as wilderness and that nature and culture, as concepts, are best represented by things wild and things human-made. Rarely, in my mind or in the collective mind of American society, had the two terms become integral parts of a larger theme.

While driving through the American South a few years ago, as I began to conceptualize this book, I came upon a weathered sign that said *virgin forest,* and I thought: If "virgin" refers to a young person known for his or her piety and sexual abstinence, then what is a "virgin forest?" Probably an old stand of mature oak and hardwood trees regal in their age and stately manner, never having endured the disgrace of clear-cut logging —trees that could offer testimony to the abiding power of the natural world, trees that could serve as proud adversaries to and survivors of human exploitation and greed. Surely this was a place in which nature ruled supreme over culture, which is the entire point of sayings such as Thoreau's "In wildness is the preservation of the world."

I turned the steering wheel in that gentle sort of way that accommodates the kind of slow bend known well to drivers in the rural South, and the car made the curve with ease. But instead of an "old growth" forest looming into sight just around the bend, the trees—every last one of them—were longleaf pine, perhaps ten years old, neatly planted in rows and nearly identical in shape, color, and height. It soon became clear that here "virgin" simply meant unharvested. On that straightaway, as I slowed down to appreciate what I had seen, outside my window the trees passed by with mathematical precision. I began to make associations to culture immediately, and began to think about stand density, rotation schedules, species-age composition, site selection and soil quality, annual growth, and corporate investors who protect their investments with proper yields and returns. This was not a place in which to experience wild nature or to comprehend the serenity of wilderness; this was plantation agriculture disguised under the banner of "virgin forest," as if to make us feel better about our real intentions and actions.

My intellectual adjustment to this reconceptualized notion of "virgin forest" —not pristine nature, but human-made physical setting—was physically jarring, as if someone had come right up to my now-parked car, asked me to step outside, and punched me in the gut just to make sure I got the point. Having lived in urban environments most of my life, I was unprepared for this realization. I had always turned to nature as a source of inspiration, just as millions of Americans had since the days of Thoreau, William Cullen Bryant, Emerson, and all the other renowned nineteenth-century romantics and transcendentalists. I had always believed in the primacy of nature—that physical intimacy with nature is a path to some sort of personal salvation and a release from the modern urban ills of stress, crime, social rigidity, and class immobility. But here amongst this "virgin forest," I was confronted not only with myself, but also with a notion that T. S. Eliot had long argued: "Behavior is belief."

And in so confronting the mirror of the self—and of the culture and society in which I was born, raised, and educated—I recognized that what I was looking at was not something isolated or rare, but something more aggressively pervasive throughout North America and the world itself. I was looking at something I now refer to as *humanature.* This book, then, is a serious look at what I found—about ourselves as human beings and about the landscapes and places we create.

"And God said, 'Let us make man in our image,

after our likeness: and let them have dominion

over the fish of the sea, and over the fowl of

the air, and over the cattle, and over all the Earth,

and over every creeping thing that creepeth upon

the Earth.' "   (GENESIS 1:26)

H U M A N A T U R E

Throughout history, people have altered the Earth's air, water, and soil in order to survive and to thrive as a species. The consequences are pervasive. In the United States, meandering rivers and their oxbows are too often dredged into channelized straight lines while remote mountain ranges, seen from thirty thousand feet above, are criss-crossed with spider webs that must be roads, preludes to questionable development. Yellow-brown haze blurs many horizons, burns our lungs, and kills the trees downwind with acidic precision. Rivers and aquifers become over-subscribed, and large cities such as Las Vegas, Los Angeles, Phoenix, and Tucson negotiate allocations for water-flow that may never materialize or be equitably distributed. Grass lawns, deciduous trees, and agricultural fields turn desert communities into replicas of other well-watered places and times. Domestic populations of dogs, cats, cows, and horses continue to replace the splendid variety of native wildlife. Once unsullied scenic areas such as Yosemite and Lake Tahoe suffer heavy burdens of tourist traffic, and campfire pollution and backpacker gridlock are common problems. High-technology logging and frequent high-fuel forest fires reduce national forests to scarred landscapes, and many national parks have become landscape zoos. Nature, if it exists in pure form at all, is under siege.

Although the Garden of Eden has been an enduring image of earthly paradise, our planet is now a contaminated garden. Frightening levels of radioactivity and millions of pounds of pesticides pollute the soil. During the 1950s and 1960s, atmospheric testing of nuclear weapons released radioactive isotopes such as iodine-131, strontium-90, cesium-137, and carbon-14 into the atmosphere. These elements were absorbed into the food chain, and their long-term effects are still ominous and unpredictable. Worldwide, the background radiation levels since the first nuclear detonation in 1945 have increased seven percent, and the overwhelming levels of radioactive contamination at the Nevada Test Site, the Hanford Nuclear Reservation in Washington State, Rocky Flats in Colorado, and the Savannah River nuclear facility in South Carolina, among others, pose a real danger to future generations.

Aridity, poor land management, and vast agricultural monocultures have reduced available arable land and have resulted in greater reliance on pesticides and chemical fertilizers to meet increased demand. Carbon dioxide levels in the air have grown approximately twenty-five percent during the last century, and this rise is not simply due to the exhaust from burning oil and natural gas. Deforestation also causes prolonged atmospheric changes. For example, although not widely reported, deforestation has resulted in an explosion of the world's termite population: there is now about one-half ton of termites for every person on Earth, and termites generate vast amounts of methane gas, which traps solar radiation. Even the flatulence of hundreds of millions of cows contributes to increased amounts of methane in the atmosphere.[1]

Water, often treated by our society as a commodity or an abstract legal right rather than the most basic physical requirement for life, has become scarce, polluted, or salinated. Rain, once an independent and mysterious presence, has become an extension of the human will and, with its chemical inducement and contamination, a depressing reminder of the scale of human arrogance and neglect. The world's oceans are treated as a vast dumping ground for garbage, sewage, oil, and even nuclear and medical wastes.

In the United States, in the span of one lifetime during the nineteenth century, loggers deforested an area the size of Europe—more than 160 billion board feet of white pine were harvested in the old Northwest of Michigan, Wisconsin, and Minnesota. And in another lifetime since 1955 the ancient forests of the Pacific Northwest have been all but obliterated, leaving at the most about four or five percent old growth as museum relics, never again to be part of a large forest. Today, machines used to strip-mine coal move 210 tons of earth every fifty-five seconds.

From the end of the sixteenth century to the end of the twentieth, the process of creating extensive agricultural lands in the United States exterminated habitats from coast to coast and decimated wildlife.

FIGURE 1: *Adam and Eve*, 1504, Albrecht Dürer. Centennial Gift of Landon T. Clay. Courtesy Museum of Fine Arts, Boston.

During the westward expansion, hunters slaughtered herds of bison numbering in the millions. And, as the millennium approaches, many other plant and wildlife species are either endangered or, like the passenger pigeon, extinct. Within the next thirty years humankind may wipe out one-fifth of the world's known species—a rate of more than one species per hour. Nine thousand species of birds survive today, yet nearly twenty percent of those species are thought to be endangered or at imminent risk of extinction.[2] We have abused our garden.

However, the belief that pollution is a problem exclusive to the modern era is one of the great misconceptions about our relationship with nature. Although soaring populations and global exploitation have greatly accelerated the impact of human activity in the latter half of the twentieth century, such concerns are not new. Anxieties about deforestation and soil erosion, for example, can be found in the literature of classical Greece, Imperial Rome, and Mauryan India, and sporadically occur in the annals of the early Spanish and Portuguese empires. The tradition of managing, altering, and spoiling the environment is not so much a human problem as it is an indication of the human condition.

Human tampering with the natural world has made Earth itself an artifact, for the process of civilization has been one of domesticating environments. Civilization advanced by overcoming nature, by converting elements within the natural world—fire, water, minerals, plants, and animals—into resources for human manipulation. According to Lewis Mumford and other scholars, the exploitation and management of nature began when the great age of hunter-gatherers evolved into the age of subsistence farmers, or when the Upper Paleolithic period (Stone Age) gave way to the Neolithic. Since the development of agriculture during the Neolithic, human beings have lived in transformed environments. For example, geographer Carl Sauer attributes the domestication of fire with the creation of most of the Earth's grasslands. The present location and composition of the planet's savannas are largely anthropogenic because of human-made fire and the subsequent grazing of livestock—from carabao and pigs in the tropics to reindeer in the Arctic, from camels, cattle, and sheep in the lowlands to yaks in the alpine zones. And there is also evidence that people may have played a role in the extinction of some of the large fauna during the late Pleistocene.

Indeed, the ever-decreasing number of plant and animal species that populate the Earth can be tied, directly or indirectly, to human influence. Surviving species are subject to ever-increasing levels of management, manipulation, and exploitation. Symbolic of the ambitious human desire to control biotic communities is the fact that many of the plants we see in shopping malls, hospitals, and office complexes are manufactured from plastic and paper. Imitation plants are often preferred because they require little maintenance, no soil, watering, feeding, pruning, replacing, or nurturing. Human-made plants can be placed any-

where regardless of humidity and light levels. They require no pesticides, and their roots do not interfere with pipes and cables. The illusion that they are "real" is often reinforced by including a select number of live plants strategically placed at eye level close to pedestrian traffic. Imitation *Ficus benjamina* trees, often designed and manufactured fifteen feet high, are made more lifelike by using real trunks cured to permanence by kiln drying. A company in Alberta, Canada, is experimenting with the "mummification" of eucalyptus and cedar trees for permanent "maintenance-free" ornamentation. Although an early attempt to place artificial plants along highways in California failed when they melted in the midday sun, more advanced, heat-resistant models are being

designed to change color with the seasons and to feature "buds" programmed to open and close at certain times and temperatures. Maintenance of these New Age plants will be limited to washing, probably accomplished by sprinklers in order to enhance the illusion that they are real.[3]

From the beginning of European expansion in the Americas, people have attempted to control biotic communities, and that effort represents what geographer Alfred Crosby calls "ecological imperialism." As soon as Europeans conquered an island in the New World, they transformed—both by design and by accident—its flora and fauna. Newcomers quickly cleared forested land of trees, which they considered obstacles to agriculture. To supplant indigenous

FIGURE 2: Clear-cut area within the Sugarloaf Mountain Recreation Area, South Carolina.

Harmful non-indigenous species in the United States

State by state distribution of some high-impact non-indigenous species

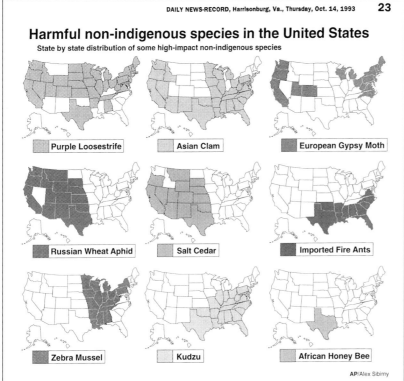

AP/Alex Sibirny

Aliens Invading U.S.

WASHINGTON (AP) — With kudzu vines crawling across the witness table, experts told members of Congress recently that thousands of foreign plant and animal varieties are pushing out native species and costing billions of dollars to control.

Congress' Office of Technology Assistance presented a 390-page report that chronicles the threat from 4,500 foreign species that have found their way into the United States.

"I'm afraid we come with bad news," project director Phyllis N. Windle told a congressional hearing. "The economic and environmental impacts are snowballing" from a wide variety of invading plants and animals, she said.

Ms. Windle and other researchers were accompanied by a jar of Asian clams, the jaws of an imported black carp and a tangle of fast-growing foreign foliage collected from a Washington, D.C., park.

The clams are clogging pipes leading to power turbines and the carp is being intentionally imported to destroy spreading foreign shellfish. But the fish, which grows up to 150 pounds, may prefer a more native diet, Ms. Windle said.

In some states, she said, foreign species make up 30 percent of plant life, and in Hawaii, it's at least 50 percent.

"The movement of plants, animals and microbes beyond their natural range is much like a game of biological Russian roulette," said the report.

Some prove beneficial, like such non-indigenous species as cattle, wheat and soybeans, which were not found in North America until they were brought in from other parts of the world.

Some die out, overwhelmed by their new environment.

But some stay, spread and even take over, like the kudzu vine that was brought in from Asia in the 1930s to control soil erosion along highways in the South and now covers trees and power lines across several states.

The invaders lurk in old tires, hitchhike aboard planes, hide in household goods and swim in the ballast of ships. They range from the brown tree snake that has wiped out nearly every native bird species on Guam to zebra mussels that have overwhelmed the Great Lakes.

The report estimated damage from 79 foreign species brought in from 1906 to 1991 at $97 billion

and said just 15 potentially high-impact plants, insects, aquatic invertebrates and other species could cause as much as $134 billion in losses over the next 50 years.

The report said 205 foreign species have established free-growing populations in America since 1980. Fifty-nine of the most recent imports are expected to prove harmful.

Based on studies by six scientists and information from 36 other experts, the report concluded that the new species are creating "a growing economic and environmental burden for the country."

It said federal and state laws are inadequate to diminish the danger and "generally, new imports are presumed safe unless proven otherwise."

Sometimes eradication efforts do more harm than good.

Chemicals used to kill millions of imported fire ants spread the damage, the report said, killing the ants' predators and leaving habitats open for the ants remaining.

The report concluded that the spread of new species is inevitable.

FIGURE 3: Reprinted courtesy of the Harrisonburg *Daily News-Record* and the Associated Press.

species, early settlers imported Old World plants and animals, adding to the local ecosystems cattle, sheep, camels, rabbits, pigeons, chickens, partridges, and ducks. Rats, of course, were inadvertently imported to the Americas on European ships. Many early explorers and whalers "seeded" remote islands with pigs to assure a supply of meat for other transient Europeans who would set anchor. The Old World also contributed grapevines, melons, pears, apples, sugar, and the peanut, as well as horses, dogs, and the honeybee. Many of these introduced plants went "wild," including turnips, mustard, mint, and chamomile. The stinging nettle, now considered a pest, was introduced along with the Old World peach and white clover.

Of the 500 farmland weeds in the United States, 258 are from the Old World.[4] The trend continues. Perhaps the most visually obvious example is an invasive, weedy vine native to Asia called kudzu (*Pueraria lobata*). Introduced from either Japan or Korea at the Philadelphia International Centennial Exhibition in 1876, it was first used in the South as a shade plant on porches and arbors. During the 1930s, in an attempt to control erosion on bare banks and fallow fields throughout the South, the U.S. Department of Agriculture paid farmers up to eight dollars for every acre they planted in kudzu. This program was so successful that in 1935 the Soil Conservation Service heralded kudzu as a "miraculous soil saver." By the mid-1940s kudzu covered more than 500,000 acres. Growing up to twelve inches a day, it became known as the "foot-a-night" vine.

Unfortunately, kudzu is extremely difficult to eliminate; it grows rapidly in nearly any kind of soil, and its roots sink deep into the earth. Georgia folklore even warns that one should keep windows closed at night to keep out the kudzu. State governments quit using kudzu along highways in the 1950s and by 1970 it was classified as a weed and money was appropriated for its eradication. By 1990 kudzu covered more than 2 million acres of forest land in the South.[5]

Considering the exponential population growth worldwide during the last half-century, the pervasive use of fossil fuels and hydroelectric power, the development of science and technology, introduction of new weaponry, and the complexity and scale of pollution, the imperative for attempting to manage the "global village" has become both inevitable and pervasive.

One of America's conservation heroes, John Muir, wrote in the *Sacramento Record-Union* on 5 February 1876 an article titled, "God's First Temples: How Shall We Preserve our Forests?" In it he suggests that government management and control are the obvious means to protect nature. While he expresses ambivalence over the interpretation of national forests as economic zones, he argues that human beings are nature's gardeners and that the selective cutting of mature trees could help keep forests "a never failing fountain of wealth and beauty."[6] In keeping with this philosophy, in May of 1908 President Theodore

FIGURE 4 (above): The caption written on the back of the photograph reads "Kudzu to be planted on severely gullied area."

FIGURE 5 (below): Rephotograph dated 21 September 1939: "Follow up picture of three-year-old kudzu planted on severely gullied land." Photo credit: Wulch, reprinted courtesy of U.S. Department of Agriculture, Soil Conservation Service.

FIGURE 6: "Eroded old field in which erosion has reached the gully stage. Durham Division, Compartment 16, Stand 21." This agricultural land in Durham, North Carolina, was bought at low cost by the Duke family (founders of Duke University) in the 1920s and turned into a now-beautiful "nature preserve" called the Duke Forest. Photo credit: C. F. Korstian, 2 March 1935. Photographs in figures 6–12 courtesy Office of the Duke Forest, School of the Environment, Duke University.

FIGURE 7: Erosion control efforts in the American South. Exact location and photographer unknown, although possibly taken by E. E. Neukom, 7 March 1934.

FIGURE 8: "Planting seedlings in furrows." Exact location unknown, but likely in North Carolina. Photograph part of a forestry and soil erosion project. Photo credit: E. E. Neukom, 9 January 1935.

FIGURE 9: "Pruning loblolly pine stand. Durham Division, Compartment 48, Stand 7." Photo credit: C. F. Korstian, 20 March 1935.

Roosevelt called a conference of governors to formulate rules for the management of forests and waterways. In his opening speech he discussed renewable resources and stated that "man can improve on nature by compelling the resources to renew and even reconstruct themselves in such a manner as to serve increasingly beneficial uses."[7] Gifford Pinchot, who was then the U.S. government's chief forester, agreed when he said that the "first principle of conservation is development."[8]

Today, many conservationists, environmental activists, landscape architects, and scientists believe in the idea of "nature" as a model for restoration efforts. The final product, however much an artifact of human design, construction, and manipulation, is always intended to appear "natural." As evidence of their success, the layperson is often unable to distinguish between a restored habitat and a natural environment, even when a forest or a beach, for example, may be a human creation.

FIGURE 10: "Timber stand improvement work in progress by Civilian Conservation Corps men, south half of experimental cutting. Durham Division, Compartment 64, Stand 10." Forest "improvement" includes trimming trees in the forests and clearing the underbrush. Photo credit: C. F. Korstian, 30 November 1934.

FIGURE 11: "Check dams and logs supporting terraces built by Civilian Conservation Corps on area up the hill just north of Pinecrest Road, looking south. Durham Division, Compartment 5, Stand 12." Photo credit: C. F. Korstian, 7 December 1934.

FIGURE 12: "International TD-6 tractor with bulldozer blade pulling a heavy Athens disc used to knock down and break up trees under pulpwood size as the first step in the control of undesirable hardwoods in this uneven-aged white oak—black oak—red oak stand. Note the heavy granite [block] wired to the disc to give additional weight. Durham Division, Compartment 39, Stand 3, Duke Forest." Photo credit: B. F. Smith, 16 November 1950.

Beaches are perpetually in motion, and constant human effort and tremendous energy must be exerted to stabilize and maintain them in their present location and condition. Because hurricanes and nor'easters cannot be diverted and tides are inevitable, the dominant method of beach management is sand replenishment and dune construction and reinforcement. At the same time, stabilization is attempted by three primary methods: building structures perpendicular to the shoreline (jetties); parallel to the shoreline (breakwaters); and, to absorb the impact of the breaking waves, building seawalls. Consequently, sea barriers, seawalls, and rock-and-debris embankments are common features along our Atlantic and Gulf coasts.

Consider the example of Miami Beach. In May of 1977 the Great Lakes Dredge and Dry Dock Company began dredging sand from the continental shelf, sucking it up to and in front of hotel bulkheads in Miami Beach. By 1980 the U.S. Army Corps of Engineers had built a beach three hundred feet wide and ten miles long and had spent more than 64 million dollars. Nearly 14 million cubic yards of sand were moved, making this the largest beach-building project in the world. More than 211,000 cubic yards of sand have to be replaced each year, and maintenance costs exceed one million dollars.[9] This is one among many such projects: there are more than 280 barriers protecting the United States coastline, and all coastal states have coastal-management plans.

The Corps of Engineers has suggested constructing artificial headlands that will create "natural" filtering mechanisms and "duplicate the success of nature" in stabilizing sedimentary coastlines.[10] As an example of this advice, in 1985 chemist Ed Garbisch of Environmental Concern, Inc., created new marshlands out of New Jersey wetlands. The project involved cutting channels in damaged wetlands and excavating the marsh so that rejuvenating ocean tides could enter. Mallard nests were established in constructed knolls, and fifty acres were seeded with spartina, a marsh grass. Coconut fiber blankets were laid onto beach dunes and American

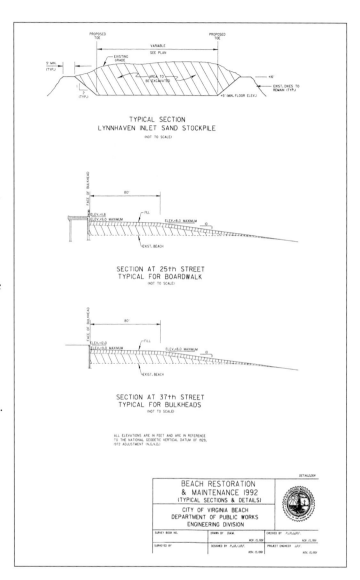

FIGURE 13: Detail of an architectural drawing for the 1992 beach restoration and maintenance plan at Virginia Beach, Virginia. Courtesy Office of Beach Management, City of Virginia Beach, Virginia.

FIGURE 14: "Sand dune encroaching upon forest. Grass planting in foreground. Currituck Sound in background. Near Kittyhawk, North Carolina." Photo credit: C. F. Korstian, 4 June 1936. Photographs in figures 14–17 courtesy Office of the Duke Forest, School of the Environment, Duke University.

FIGURE 15: "Grass planting and brush fences near Kittyhawk, North Carolina." The Civilian Conservation Corps planted this ammophilia grass in the hope it would stabilize shifting sands. Cattle grazing was still permitted, however, threatening the stabilization efforts. Photo credit: C. F. Korstian, 4 June 1936.

FIGURE 16: "Grass planting and board fences constructed along State Highway No. 344. Near Kittyhawk, North Carolina." The fences help control wind erosion. Photo credit: C. F. Korstian, 4 June 1936.

FIGURE 17: "Looking north toward sound from north side of Roanoke Island showing grass planting and brush fences built by Civilian Conservation Corps to check shifting sand." Roanoke Island, off the coast of North Carolina south of Kittyhawk, in Croatan Sound between Albemarle Sound and Pamlico Sound, is popularly remembered as the birthplace of the first white child born in the British colonies in America, Virginia Dare. The first colonizing expedition under Sir Richard Grenville and Sir Ralph Lane landed on Roanoke Island in August of 1585, but they returned to England the next year. Captain John White and another group of colonists, under the direction of Sir Walter Raleigh, arrived on the island in 1587. By 1591 the colony had disappeared.

At the colony site, now named Ft. Raleigh, a commemorative plaque at the Elizabethan Gardens proclaims: "Down the centuries, English women have built Gardens to the Glory of God, the beauty of the countryside, and the comfort of their souls. The Women of the Garden Club of North Carolina, Inc. have planted this garden in memory of the valiant men and women who founded the first English colony in America. From this hallowed ground on Roanoke Island, they walked away through the dark forest and into history." Photo credit: C. F. Korstian, 4 June 1936.

beachgrass was planted through slits cut in the blankets in an attempt to stabilize the shifting sand during periods of rain and high winds.[11] Using this method more than two hundred marshes have been re-created from Maine to Virginia. Herring and black-gulls have been reintroduced into coastal habitats and now rival pigeons and starlings in number.

The pervasive management of nature in the United States includes more than constructing beaches and wetlands. Perhaps the most apparent human effort to control nature is the management of water, particularly river systems such as the Mississippi River. The chief tributaries of the world's third-longest river system are the Missouri, Ohio, Arkansas, Tennessee, Wabash, Cumberland, Platte, and Yellowstone rivers. The size of this river system, the sheer volume of water drained from its terrain, and the frequency of dramatic, ruinous flooding reinforced demands for its control. The rapid growth of urban centers along its shores, the richness of its adjacent agricultural lands, and the river's potential as an industrial highway dictated the inevitability of human management, a principle that was institutionalized in the 1890 constitution for the State of Mississippi. One section of that document addresses in careful, painstaking detail the rules and regulations for the maintenance of a levee system along the Mississippi River. This section, Article 11, runs over eight pages and includes both technical and fiscal terms of the management compact.[12]

John McPhee's original interest in writing *The Control of Nature* (1989) was

FIGURE 18: The Kissimmee River in central Florida was a meandering river more than 103 miles long that the U.S. Army Corps of Engineers turned into a canal. (*See also* color plates on pages 126–133.)

This federal flood control project was conceived and planned between 1954 and 1960; construction began in 1961 and was completed by 1971. Photographer and exact date unknown.

sparked by his discovery of the metaphoric symbolism behind the control of the Atchafalaya River, a distributary branch of the Mississippi. In the Mississippi's deltaic plain, the river's natural process involves periodically changing course while flooding hundreds of square miles. Obviously, a free-flowing, unregulated river would wreak havoc with urban areas, industry, agriculture, and individual livelihood. Consequently, McPhee writes, the nation "could not afford nature."[13] Since it appeared that the Mississippi was due to change its main course and follow the Atchafalaya, the Corps of Engineers intervened and built what John McPhee calls a "great fortress" to keep the Mississippi in its channel.

As enormous as these efforts have been, the great Midwestern flood of 1993 provided dramatic evidence that the river cannot and should not be fully controlled. Yet, as a result of ongoing control efforts, the Mississippi delta is rapidly disappearing. Saltwater intrusion from the Gulf of Mexico and the erosion accelerated by more than ten thousand miles of canals are decimating the delta. The Louisiana wetlands, which constitute nearly forty percent of all the coastal wetlands in the United States, are vanishing at the rate of fifty square miles a year.

In the West the Colorado River rises high in the Rocky Mountains and flows southwestward in its fifteen-hundred-mile journey to the Gulf of California. This great river is oversubscribed and suffers from dangerously high levels of salinity. It is restrained by the Glen Canyon and Hoover dams, which create the huge

reservoirs known as Lake Powell and Lake Mead. While the Colorado River is neither the largest nor the longest river in the United States, it drops nearly thirteen thousand feet, has unparalleled rapids, and carries an enormous volume of silt. Its remote canyons and wildness have sparked the American imagination, yet its modern notoriety derives from the fact that the Colorado River is likely the most legislated, debated, and litigated river in the world. It has become a symbol of the hope, conflict, and dilemma of water management in the American West and in Mexico.

Completely harnessed, the Colorado River is diverted through long siphons into the water supply reservoirs of

FIGURE 19: A dredge is used to channelize the Kissimmee River, resulting in the loss of nearly 43,000 acres of river floodplain wetlands and a dramatic ninety percent reduction in waterfowl populations throughout the river valley. At the same time, the intensification of agriculture in the river floodplain contributed to increased nutrient run-off into Lake Okeechobee. Photographs in figures 18 and 19 courtesy South Florida Water Management District.

FIGURES 20, 21, 22, 23: Lake Powell, on the border of Utah and Arizona and a part of the Glen Canyon National Recreation Area, was created in 1963 when the Glen Canyon Dam impounded the Colorado River near Page, Arizona, a growing retirement community.

This massive 200-mile reservoir has 1,960 miles of shoreline, and its side canyons, coves, and straits are extremely popular with pleasure boaters, anglers, scuba divers, and water skiers. Floyd Dominy, who was Reclamation Commissioner for the Bureau of Reclamation from 1959 to 1969 and is the author of *Lake Powell: Jewel of the Colorado* (1965), writes that "multitudes hunger for a lake in the sun." To Mr. Dominy, Lake Powell is evidence of how nature has been improved.

Phoenix, Las Vegas, San Diego, and Los Angeles, and into the irrigation canals of the Valley of the Dead, renamed the Imperial Valley. (The Salton Sea, a vast desert lake, was formed through a failed diversion of the Colorado River in 1904.) Decisions about the flow and volume of this once-wild river are made according to the peaks and valleys of urban hydroelectric power demands, while entitlements are challenged through the justice system. The Grand Canyon was once one of the most inaccessible wilderness areas in the United States; now, whitewater enthusiasts and hikers seeking its wild places must plan around water-release schedules in their departure times and camping locations.

The hubris of human management even extends to the atmosphere. We commonly have perceived the weather to be the province of "mother nature," yet in July of 1946 scientists announced they could control the weather by seeding clouds with a few grams of heat-vaporized iodide. They boasted that large, vigorously growing cumulus clouds could be induced to generate a fairly extensive local rainstorm. Armed with this information, meteorological science groups planned enormous "cloud-modification" activities. By 1951 more than one-third of all land west of the Mississippi River was under contract for cloud-seeding activities with commercial meteorological cloud-seeding companies.[14] Although these efforts to make rain failed to live up to most expectations, in 1977 the Federal Weather Modification Advisory Board compounded earlier claims by reporting that within twenty years and with proper funding the United States could control rainfall in the Midwest, the amount of snowfall in the Rockies, the velocity of the wind in the Plains, and make the science and practice of weather modification a "natural reality."[15]

Beaches, forests, mountains, plains, rivers, valleys, and even rainfall are manipulated and managed—albeit by degrees—by people and our institutions. But human influence over any habitat or biotic community does not end with the landscape: insects and wildlife are also dramatically affected by human ingenuity. Historically, people have stimulated the production and reproduction of organisms through animal husbandry and agriculture. Besides our basic role of influencing insect and wildlife populations by manipulating the food chain, human management includes inbreeding, introducing new predators, and altering habitat, thereby requiring adaptation. Recently, environmentalists and nature managers have recommended manipulating symbiotic relationships developed between species as a means of controlling insect populations and as an alternative to pesticides. Rachel Carson, one of the earliest critics of chemical

deterrents, suggested that instead of using dangerous pesticides such as DDT and malathion, environmental managers should manipulate "natural" systems. She offered solutions ranging from developing the biological control of insects by introducing their natural enemies to synthesizing insect sex attractant to lure unwanted insects into traps. More specific examples proposed in Carson's classic work *Silent Spring* (1962) involve employing such natural predators as yellowjackets, who capture soft-bodied insects for food for their young; ladybugs who feed on aphids; dragonflies who eat mosquitoes; and other parasitic insects who use their hosts as food.[16]

Today, the practice of using introduced predators is generally accepted. On Martha's Vineyard and Nantucket Island in Massachusetts, for example, scientists are planning to release large numbers of a tiny wasp (*Hunterellus*

hookeri) to control the tick population. This type of wasp eats tick nymphs.[17] In many areas, non-native plant species, such as hydrilla, are taking over bays such as the Chesapeake, lakes such as Chapala in Mexico, and many coastal areas where the fishing industry is threatened by clogged harbors. In 1965, in an attempt to solve the hydrilla problem, Florida imported several manatees to feed on these and other aquatic plants. In California blizzards of whiteflies in clouds over four miles long threaten the 18.3-billion-dollar farm industry. (Three thousand whitefly eggs are laid per square inch of foliage.)[18] To control this invasion, local entomologists hope that a tiny Pakistani wasp, released in tandem with Florida beetles, will eat the whitefly larvae and eggs. None of these plans has provoked noticeable public argument or complaint. At the same time, numerous bird and animal species, such as Canadian geese (*Branta*

FIGURE 24: U.S. Geological Survey (USGS) stream gauge number 09404115 is located about 900 feet upstream of the mouth of Javasu Creek at Colorado River mile 157 in the Grand Canyon, Arizona. This gauge provides basic data on stream flow, sediment, and water chemistry for the Glen Canyon Environmental Studies program. The National Park Service does its best to disguise gauging stations by covering them with camo-netting and river debris. But because the equipment requires periodic monitoring, the debris makes it difficult for USGS personnel to get to the gauge. Consequently, Donald Bills, a hydrologist with the USGS, took the initiative and suggested that "fake-rocks" cover the site. With the necessary approval, he began the process of drawing up specifications and gathering collective bids. The 1991 contract price for the "rocks" was $6,267; additional expenses to cover labor, travel, and per diem costs raised the total price to about $7,700. Photograph by Donald Bills, 1991. Courtesy U.S. Geological Survey.

FIGURE 25: Technicians from the Desert Research Institute in Reno, Nevada, dismantle for the season one of twenty cloud-seeding generator sites: (left to right) Monte Stark, Greg Adams, Tom Swafford, and Steve Batie. These generators are located throughout the region: nine sites near Lake Tahoe, five sites near Bridgeport/Walker in the Sierra Nevada, and six sites near Elko in eastern Nevada. These generators release silver iodide particles into the atmosphere during storms to enhance snowfall amounts. The seeding reportedly increases snowfall by ten to fifteen percent in the target area. Cloud-seeding activities are suspended during high wind or avalanche conditions, when the snowpack has already reached levels well above normal depths, and when unusually warm storm systems might cause flooding by melting the existing snowpack. Seeding operations are also suspended during peak holiday traffic periods as a convenience to travelers. The Desert Research Institute is a nonprofit statewide environmental research division of the University and Community College System of Nevada.

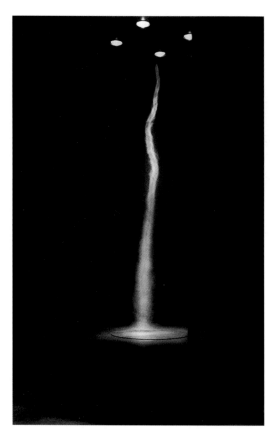

FIGURE 26: A human-made tornado at the North Carolina Museum of Life and Science in Durham, an exhibit made by Ned Kahn: "The overhead fan draws the air upward, imitating the updraft that occurs in the core of a tornado-spawning thunderstorm. Air blowing from the tubes starts the updraft spinning, creating what is called an air vortex. A fog machine injects tiny droplets of water that make the airflow visible." Although the exhibit is strictly educational, it does demonstrate our propensity and ability to mimic natural processes.

canadensis) and the raccoon (*Procyon lotor*), have developed a symbiotic relationship with human presence.

The quest to improve nature has led geneticists and biologists to manipulate the gene pools of living organisms. Biotechnologists envision a genetically altered and engineered Garden of Eden as they strive to develop more efficient animal husbandry, improve human health, and eliminate the expensive use of pesticides. Promises include producing cow's milk that will be more nutritional and more digestible for infants, creating bioengineered vaccines, and altering microbes to consume toxic wastes. In April of 1987 scientists from Advanced Genetic Sciences applied the first genetically engineered bacteria on a strawberry field in Brentwood, California. This synthetic microbe, called Frostban, is designed to prevent crop losses from frost damage. Genetically altered trees have already been planted in national forests in an attempt to influence the disease and insect resistance of the woodlands.

The most common method of genetic engineering, gene splicing, involves taking a piece of DNA (genetic material) from one species and placing it into another. Researchers have already discovered that it is possible to splice genetic material from mushrooms into pigeons, from rats into bacteria, and from cabbages into people. For example, agricultural scientists are trying to lower the saturated fat content of soybeans and of the popular oil-seed canola. They plan to redesign these plants by incorporating genes from oily fish such as mackerel and salmon.[19] The insect repelling odor

of the *Polyzonium* millipede found in American beech-hemlock forests might be transferred via genetic engineering to cereal crops.[20] In Alabama, dozens of fish modified in the laboratory—salmon, trout, walleyed pike, and goldfish— carry genes from other fish, chickens, cows, and people. Fifty thousand transgenic carp now include a growth hormone gene harvested from rainbow trout, and, according to researchers, this alteration makes them grow forty percent faster than normal.[21]

Through embryonic transfers, biotechnologists are crossbreeding animals of different species, creating strange new hybrid animals. Gary Anderson, a researcher in animal genetics, transferred a sheep embryo into a goat to create the first sheep/goat chimera called a "geep." This new creature, born in 1985, had a

FIGURE 27: Advertisement courtesy of SunBanks, Inc., © 1990.

17

long neck with a goat face and woolly hair. Subsequent experiments concentrated on splitting embryos in order to develop twice as many offspring.[22] Scientists are predicting that by the year 2000, calves will be cloned by producing embryos in the laboratory. The process, according to its proponents, would allow animal producers to replicate one embryo into eight or into as many as sixteen identical animals. In response to the economic potential of human-designed animals, the U.S. Patent and Trademark Office announced in 1987 that genetically engineered animals could be patented.

Unfortunately, prior efforts at managing insect, plant, and animal populations have often produced unpredictable results. The pesticide/fertilizer recipe for increased agricultural productivity has provided a formula that can result in unanticipated, destructive biotic relationships. One of the most ironic examples was reported, years ago, by the World Health Organization (WHO). Using DDT to eliminate malarial mosquitoes in the Malay Peninsula, WHO ecologists successfully documented a decline in reported cases of malaria. The effect was short-lived, however, since they also noticed and recorded a dramatic increase in rat populations. While the pesticide produced the desired effect, it also poisoned roaches and other insects, which poisoned the gecko lizards which fed on the insects, which poisoned the cats who fed on the lizards, reducing the predators for the rats. Now the rats carried lice, which in turn carried plague. Since killing rats merely encouraged the lice to

FIGURE 28: The black-footed ferret (*Mustela nigripes*), one of the most endangered mammals in the world, used to inhabit prairie dog burrows from Canada to Mexico. Early in the twentieth century, ranchers believed that prairie dogs competed with cattle for grass, and as a consequence the federal government promoted programs to eliminate the prairie dog, thus severely depleting the black-footed ferret population. By 1981, there was only a single known black-footed ferret colony, and those animals were decimated by canine distemper during the summer of 1985. At that point, wildlife technicians believed that captive propagation was the best hope for the species' survival.

Captive breeding has been successful under the leadership of the Wyoming Game and Fish Department in cooperation with the U.S. Fish and Wildlife Service. By February of 1990, approximately 120 ferrets survived in three different breeding locations, thus raising hopes among wildlife scientists that reintroduction into the wild

would soon be possible. Unfortunately, these vertebrates are influenced by captivity and may not possess sufficient survival skills. The animals destined for reintroduction must be able to detect and avoid predators, find and secure food, and communicate with neighboring ferrets when they establish their social system.

Consequently, the National Zoo's Conservation and Research Center in Front Royal, Virginia, has been conducting training sessions for ferrets. Originally using "robo-badger," a stuffed bionic predator posed menacingly on the chassis of a remote-controlled toy truck, and later using a stuffed great horned owl, researchers were able to investigate the effectiveness of this predator recognition and avoidance training program. This photograph shows researcher Brian Miller (left) and Dean Biggins of the U.S. Fish and Wildlife Service teaching a ferret how to survive in the wild. Photograph by Chris Wemmer, Associate Director for the Department of Conservation, National Zoo. Courtesy of the Smithsonian.

seek human hosts, WHO ecologists successfully parachuted thousands of cats over the countryside. The cats reduced the rat population, but because the DDT spraying had to be halted, the malarial mosquitoes returned.[23]

Accidents have also contributed to our biotic heritage. While kudzu was intentionally planted, fire ants were unknowingly introduced into Mobile, Alabama, at the end of World War I. By 1962 these voracious, aggressive ants occupied most sunbelt states, from Virginia to Texas.[24] They build nests more than twelve inches high and can cover a vast amount of territory in a single day. Equally menacing are the swarms of aggressive, hybrid Africanized honey bees brought from Africa to Brazil by a scientist in 1957. They escaped the scientist's laboratory, bred with native species, and migrated north. By 1991 they had begun to threaten Texas's 11-million-dollar honey industry. The Texas House of Representatives appropriated $197,000 as an emergency measure to help combat the bees. During 1995, reports indicate that these bees, nicknamed "killer bees," have moved through Nevada and into California.[25]

In 1905, Theodore Roosevelt's administration set aside portions of a few national forests as wildlife refuges and prescribed the elimination of predators. One prime example of this type of management took place in the Kaibab National Forest on the northern Arizona plateau designated as the Grand Canyon National Game Preserve. Beginning in 1906, 4,889 coyotes, 781 mountain lions, 554 bobcats,

FIGURE 29: Appalachian Mountains, western North Carolina.

FIGURE 30: In 1995, there were very few wild quail in Texas. Near Campbellton, Texas, hunters purchased quail from Georgia with hopes of raising them to flush and fly like wild birds. Practitioners of "liberated bird shooting," these hunters are experimenting with different varieties of birds and different training techniques so they can "make it as close to the real thing as possible." Photo by Mike Leggett. Courtesy of the *Austin American-Statesman*.

FIGURE 31: In 1951 six thousand people from the towns of Ellenton, Dunbarton, and four other small farming communities nestled along the Savannah River in South Carolina had their land condemned by the U.S. government. The communities were sacrificed to construct the Savannah River [Nuclear] Site, which now includes five nuclear reactors.

At the same time, the Atomic Energy Commission (AEC) began to transform the condemned agricultural land adjoining these communities into a human-made forest system encompassing nearly three hundred square miles. By 1953, more than 200 million pine trees had been planted in this area, and the Savannah River Plant, as it was then called, had become the largest mechanized tree planting project in the United States. The forest now contains more than 3,000 white-tailed deer, of which nearly 900 are harvested annually by hunters. This aerial view shows the town of Ellenton before it was condemned.

FIGURE 32: This is the school in Ellenton before it was razed to make way for the forest. Photographs in figures 31 and 32 courtesy U.S. Department of Energy.

and 30 wolves were officially eliminated by poisoning. As a consequence, the deer population exploded from 4,000 in 1906 to 100,000 in 1924. This population explosion meant that by 1925 thousands of deer died from malnutrition, and by 1939 the herd was down to 10,000.[26] Instead of reestablishing natural predators to maintain a healthy deer population, game management policy dictated poisoning predators and substituting human hunters to keep the deer population in check. This policy continues, and today hunters have nearly replaced natural predators for many game animals.

The power of the social desire for hunting continues to have a significant impact on wildlife management. Today, the states' fish and wildlife programs are primarily funded by taxes on hunters and anglers, and those programs are designed to maintain a balance between supply

FIGURE 33: The front steps of the school are still visible under the growth.

and demand. Hunters have invested more than six billion dollars in wildlife conservation programs during the years between 1923 and the mid-1970s, mostly through fees and taxes on sporting goods, and many of these programs involve the preservation and restoration of habitats.[27] Indeed, to the surprise of many environmentalists, legendary naturalists such as John James Audubon, Jay N. "Ding" Darling (founder of the National Wildlife Federation), George Bird Grinnel (founder of the National Audubon Society), and Aldo Leopold (co-founder of the Wilderness Society) were avid hunters.

Not all species restoration efforts, however, are aimed at satisfying the hunter. In 1975 the U.S. Park Service initiated a program to reintroduce the red wolf (*Canis rufus gregoryi*) into the Great Smoky Mountains National Park. At that time,

managers trapped 400 red wolves from other locations and then discovered that only 17 had not bred with other species, such as coyotes, and were genetically "pure." These 17 animals were bred, and they produced more than 165 wolves, raising expectations that the red wolf population could exceed 500 within a few years. The long-term management plan designated that 325 of these animals would be housed in institutions for breeding purposes and the remaining 225 would be released in the "wild." These 225 wolves would wear radio/dart collars so they could be easily tracked. In addition, the collars would be fitted with two darts that could be discharged by radio command enabling the controller to tranquilize any animal that wandered beyond the park's boundaries.[28] Park managers are also considering reintroducing bison and elk, but biologists are

concerned that the elk are vulnerable to a parasitic brain worm carried by the white-tailed deer in the area.

The idea of wild nature, of wilderness, has always offered Americans a destination, another opportunity after a failed crop, or, especially in modern times, a break from the oppressive burden of urban life, congested landscapes, and from the pressure and stress of daily responsibility. John Muir spoke for many Americans when he wrote that "thousands of tired, nerve-shaken, over-civilized people are beginning to find out that going to the mountain is going home; that wildness is a necessity; and that mountain parks and reservations are useful not only as fountains of timber and irrigating rivers, but as fountains of life."[29] The more I learn about how a landscape is made and transformed, the more I recognize that the

FIGURE 34: This photograph by Gilbert Leebrick documents a "photography and nature" workshop conducted by the Appalachian Environmental Arts Center, part of the Highlands Biological Station, University of North Carolina. Historically, photography has been an important means by which we interpret and celebrate nature.

Earth *is* now a human artifact, with precious little wilderness to find. Clearly, those places represented on the map as wilderness have become self-contained parks managed for multiple use.

Most Americans still dream that nature is unchanged from what they *think* seventeenth- through nineteenth-century explorers saw in the New World during the era of westward expansion. But we know this is not the case. The air we breathe is an industrial composite. Rainfall is a human product. Rivers and lakes are elements within a water-management system. Forests are manufactured and harvested like soybeans and corn. Animals are controlled, bred, and genetically designed. Insects are raised in massive numbers, then irradiated and released. Rocks are made "natural" by spraying cement onto wire forms and adding the right colors. Plants and trees are made from plastic.

Beaches are reconstructed. Everywhere I look, nature is an illusion.

Today, nature is literally under siege as people shape every last inch of the global habitat; wilderness is now more a cultural idea than a physical reality. From creating savanna through fire to contaminating regional watersheds with industrial pollutants and radioactivity, from domesticating the land and its creatures to engineering new and radically different plants and animals, the forest primeval is now a human product. The very definition of "nature" is a human construct, and it reveals more about human culture than about the web of life, as Neil Evernden and other writers on the environment have so eloquently revealed.

The *idea* of wilderness is part of the paradigm of Nature that has evolved and is sustained in order to realize cultural, economic, and spiritual goals. In our attempt to manipulate biotic communities for human purposes, we have forgotten to account for *humanature*. We must not lose sight of the fundamental interconnectedness of life. The righteousness that contextualizes the "appropriate" management of any biotic community becomes a form of human arrogance, especially considering that the population dynamics and management ecology of nearly *all* species of animals are still largely unknown.[30] Creating "nature" only perpetuates the myth that biotic communities exist separate from people, and that human influence is, supposedly, without consequence. While biodiversity and the preservation of habitat are noble goals, only when we comprehend and respect *humanature* will we evolve constructively as a species and begin to live again in harmony with the planet we so rightly call *home*.

NOTES

1. Bill McKibben, *The End of Nature* (New York: Random House, 1989), p. 16.

2. Jared Diamond, "Playing Dice with Megadeath: The Odds Are Good That We Will Exterminate Half the World's Species within the Next Century," *Discover* Vol. 11 (April 1990): p. 56.

3. Roger Vick, "Artificial Nature: The Synthetic Landscape of the Future," *The Futurist* (July–August 1989): pp. 29–32.

4. Alfred W. Crosby, *Ecological Imperialism: The Biological Expansion of Europe 900–1900* (New York: Cambridge University Press, 1986), p. 164; *see also* pp. 94–95, 154, 175, 184, 198.

5. C. Ritchie Bell and Charles Reagan Wilson, "Kudzu," in *Encyclopedia of Southern Culture* (Chapel Hill: University of North Carolina Press, 1989), pp. 383–384.

6. As quoted in Roderick Nash, *Wilderness and the American Mind* (New Haven: Yale University Press, 1967), p. 137.

7. As quoted in René Dubos, *The Wooing of Earth: New Perspectives on Man's Use of Nature* (New York: Scribners, 1980), p. 80.

8. As quoted in Timothy O'Riordan, *Environmentalism* (London: Pion Limited, 1981), p. 37.

9. Wallace Kaufman and Orrin H. Pilkey, Jr., *The Beaches Are Moving* (Durham: Duke University Press, 1983), p. 182.

10. Ibid., p. 189.

11. John J. Berger, ed., *Environmental Restoration: Science and Strategies for Restoring the Earth* (Washington, D.C.: Island Press, 1990), p. 157.

12. As quoted in V. S. Naipaul, *A Turn in the South* (New York: Vintage Books, 1989), pp. 216–217.

13. John McPhee, *The Control of Nature* (New York: Farrar, Straus, and Giroux, 1989), p. 6.

14. W. L. Thomas, *Man's Role in Changing the Face of the Earth* (Chicago: University of Chicago Press, 1956), p. 613.

15. Kirkpatrick Sale, *Human Scale* (New York: Coward, McCann & Geoghegan, 1980), p. 153.

16. Rachel Carson, *Silent Spring* (Boston: Houghton Mifflin, 1962), p. 250.

17. John Skow, "Life in the Age of Lyme," *Time* Vol. 137, No. 25 (24 June 1991): p. 45.

18. S. Lynne Walker, "The Fly That's Eating California," *Business Week* (20 January 1992): p. 22.

19. Deborah Erickson, "Putting Down Roots," *Scientific American* Vol. 262, No. 5 (May 1990): p. 84.

20. Noel Grove, "Quietly Conserving Nature," *National Geographic* (December 1988): p. 828.

21. Mike Toner, "Cultivating 'Designer' Fish: Lab-engineered Carp to Be Tested at Alabama Hatchery," *Atlanta Journal* (21 May 1991): p 6.

22. Kathleen Longcore, "Animal Genetics Moves Farm Boy to Center of Controversy," *Grand Rapids Press* (28 February 1988): p. 1D.

23. Sale, *Human Scale*, p. 145.

24. Carson, *Silent Spring*, p. 161.

25. "Thousands of Miles Colonized by Killer Bees," *Reno Gazette-Journal* (18 October 1995): p. 3A. In another case, the mongoose was introduced in Hawaii to prey on shipborne rats, but the mongoose sought birds instead, eliminating seventy species.

26. Donald Worster, *Nature's Economy: The Roots of Ecology* (San Francisco: Sierra Club Books, 1977): p. 271.

27. Ibid.

28. Lawrence S. Earley, "Return of the Natives," *Wildlife in North Carolina* Vol. 55, No. 8 (August 1991): p. 17. For another account of the reintroduction of wolves in the northern Rockies, see Rick Bass, *The Ninemile Wolves* (Livingston, Montana: Clark City Press, 1992).

29. As quoted in O'Riordan, *Environmentalism*, p. 4.

30. David Ehrenfeld, *The Arrogance of Humanism* (New York: Oxford University Press, 1978), p. 197.

T R E E S

A drain in a human-made swamp near
Asheboro, North Carolina.

Numbered trees in the Duke Forest,
Durham, North Carolina. The trees were
thinned by the crown method in 1933,
1940, 1945, and 1950.

Fabric/bark tree (center) in a human-made national forest along the Horsepasture River in western North Carolina.

A measuring gauge for flood control on a tributary to the Chattooga River, which borders Georgia, North Carolina, and South Carolina. The Chattooga River was the site of the film *Deliverance* (1972), based on the book by James Dickey and featuring Ned Beatty, Ronny Cox, James Dickey, Burt Reynolds, and Jon Voight.

Moss on a felled tree near the Horsepasture River.

The Joyce Kilmer Memorial Forest, located in Nantahala National Forest in the Appalachian Mountains near the Tennessee–North Carolina border.

CAUTION!
Be Alert to Falling Limbs or Trees.
AVOID
This Trail During High Winds and Storms.

This trail provides hikers a unique opportunity to observe an aging virgin forest, however, it does pass near dead or dying trees that may fall or drop limbs. Natural processes, such as trees dying, are allowed to operate freely within Wilderness.

Since 1968 government policy and practice has been to set controlled fires in an attempt to mimic natural processes, such as lightning strikes. These four views record an active burn conducted by Nature Conservancy personnel at its Peachtree Rock Preserve in South Carolina, a three-hundred-acre tract it purchased in 1980.

This xeric sandhill scrub community is primarily inhabited by longleaf pine, with an understory of Highbrush blueberry and Turkey oaks. Most of these oaks are between six and fifteen feet tall. The objective of the burn was to reduce the scrub oak canopy by fifty percent and to reduce ground litter (leaves, grasses, pine needles) by ten percent.

The northeast corner was a successful test fire, followed by a blackline of the north and northeast boundary. After the northern and northeastern lines became secure, spots and strips were used to widen the blackline starting at the northeastern corner and working toward the south and southwest. Where the fuel load was heavy, more spot fires were started than strip-head fires.

The last sections to be burned were the western and southwestern corners. Members of the fire team were in radio contact with one another, and a South Carolina Forestry Commission crew was on standby with a 150-gallon pump truck and fire plow. The objectives of the burn were exceeded.

Duke Forest, Durham, North Carolina.

THE ZOO

At the North Carolina Zoological Park near Asheboro, zoo officials have adopted a "Creating the North American Landscape" program in which major physiographical regions and representative species are displayed in the park. Here, Glenn Edward Kellis, welder, works inside the armature for the construction of artificial rocks at the black bear exhibit. "Creating the North American Landscape" is a phrase first used by the Center for American Places in its book series. The phrase has since taken hold not only at this zoo, but also in college courses nationwide.

Cement is sprayed onto wire-form structures, and workers deftly carve and scrape cracks, fissures, and eroded shapes in order to create a natural look at the black bear exhibit.

Bob McCandless and workers "shoot" cement onto rock forms in the Sonoran Desert area.

Juan Angel Gomez (left) and Lenny Olivaros plant a good-size water oak (*Quercus nigra*) in the waterfowl area next to a human-made swamp. Robert Evans (not pictured), project foreman, directs this activity.

Steve Runnfeldt, assistant design technician, mixes paint for the human-made rocks in the Sonoran Desert area. Most of the design staff at the zoo were trained as painters or sculptors at leading art schools. A few of the landscape technicians traveled to the renowned Arizona Sonoran Desert Museum near Tucson where they took photographs of rocks over a three-day period. Most of the technicians had never been west of the Mississippi. Using these photographs, these experts were able to develop a palette of colors that heighten the sense of reality in this zoological desert landscape in North Carolina.

Human-made rocks under construction and
nearly completed at the "wolf landscape."

Ellen Greer (left), supervisor in the design department, with three colleagues: Paula Smith, Diana Thompson (with shovel), and Christa Cagle (right).

Plastic orange fences mark "nature areas" that are to remain undisturbed during construction.

Using modern construction techniques to create a peregrine falcon nest, a two-person crew drills into the steep rock face at the Lake Jocassee reservoir in western South Carolina. The sheer cliff was created when this mountain was quarried to supply stone for the reservoir's dam.

During the 1950s and 1960s the peregrine falcon's food supply became contaminated with the pesticide DDT, threatening the falcon with extinction. By the mid-1960s only three hundred pairs of peregrine falcons were known to exist in the eastern United States. None remained by 1970,

when the peregrine falcon was placed on the federal Endangered Species List. Dr. Tom J. Cade, now professor emeritus from Cornell University, initiated the restoration program of the peregrine falcon after DDT was banned. Some populations have been restored, principally in the western United States. As of this writing the federal government is beginning the process of removing the peregrine falcon from the Endangered Species List, and wildlife ecologists consider this a restoration success story. The nest, roughly three feet square, is cut in the rock about eighty feet above lake level.

Large sandbags, sand-colored to blend into the terrain, act as a seabreak to help save the lighthouse at Cape Hatteras, North Carolina, a national historic landmark. The lighthouse remains threatened and may have to be moved inland.

A stone wall perpendicular to the ocean-front south of Wrightsville Beach, North Carolina, a popular summer destination for tourists. This wall forms part of a groin system designed to reach out into the longshore currents to capture sand. The beach builds up behind the groins but erodes downdrift from them. Stabilization of the beaches along the Atlantic seaboard and Gulf Coast is the key to protecting coastal economic interests: no beach, no tourists.

Topsail Beach, North Carolina, a popular
resort community.

A public beach access structure under construction north of Surf City, North Carolina, on the Outer Banks.

Workers construct the parking area for Public Beach Access #4 north of Surf City: (left to right) Dale Sharpless, James D. Hatchell, William Burton, and Robert Ambrose.

An abandoned pier building north of Surf City reflects the natural damage caused by the Atlantic Ocean.

Discarded Christmas trees, temporarily stored here in the parking lot of the picnic area at Ft. Macon, North Carolina, are used to establish new sand dunes. The trees catch blowing sand allowing for the formation of new dunes. Ft. Macon was built by the U.S. Army Corps of Engineers between 1826 and 1834. The Corps, responsible for engineering works such as major dams, reservoirs, levees, and harbors, was founded in 1824.

In order to maintain the tourist economy of Virginia Beach, every year the city must spend hundreds of thousands of dollars restoring the beach. Here dredging and bulldozing commence near 7th Street along the boardwalk. A sand-and-water slurry is pumped onto the beach north of Rudee Inlet. The sand particles settle out, while the sea water drains back to the ocean. After a sufficient amount of sand builds up in the discharge area, new sections of pipe are added, extending the restoration effort further and further along the beach. (See figure 13.)

This view to the north is at the Atlantic and 35th Street access. Sand is hydraulically dredged from the Lynnhaven Inlet, stored at a nearby stockpile, and then loaded on 10-cubic-yard dump trucks and hauled to the oceanfront where it is placed on the beach. A bulldozer and scraper then grade the sand, establishing the desired beach elevations. Approximately 100,000 cubic yards of material were placed here during the 1992 spring project.

Beach erosion is a serious environmental occurrence along the Atlantic seaboard. People and businesses want to locate as close as possible to the water, but because beaches continually move, natural hazards are an inevitable consequence of such residential and commercial development.

A rephotograph of Virginia Beach during Memorial Day weekend documents successful beach restoration completed six weeks earlier. Emergency appropriations are often needed following a big nor'easter, which can erode the beach more severely than a hurricane.

The Pacific Ocean at Cabrillo National
Monument, San Diego, California.

AREA CLOSED
FOR PLANT
REHABILITATION

T H E   M I N E

A tailings plateau near Miami, Arizona. Tailings are refuse material resulting from the washing, concentration, or treatment of ground ore.

A tailings basin at the same mine site.

The tailings area of the big copper mine
near Miami, Arizona.

The Clifton-Morenci Pit, one of the largest open-pit copper mines in North America. Clifton is part of a deep, isolated canyon system in southeastern Arizona carved by the San Francisco River and its tributary, Chase Creek. Chase Creek was channelized with slag after 1906 to control floods, making the area easier to develop.

Pipes at Pinal Creek at Globe, Arizona.

This company-owned residential district, known as the Stargo Townsite, was carved into the hillsides at the upper end of Apache Gulch in the Clifton-Morenci area. Construction of the town began in 1937, and old-timers say it was abandoned about twenty years later. The mine is still active.

An abandoned mill and smelter area at the Clifton-Morenci mine.

RECLAIMED LAND

A cement truck at North Potato Creek Falls, Ducktown, Tennessee, travels through a landscape that has been completely altered by human industry.

The Tennessee Chemical Company's mining tower offers a grand view of the landscape near Copperhill, Tennessee. This region, infamous for its strip-mined appearance, is now being reclaimed not as a diverse forest, but principally with fast-growing southern pine, the preferred species for the region's many lumber and paper mills.

This photograph, made "in Natural Color" in 1955 by Walker Cline, appeared as a popular postcard with the following caption: "U.S. 64 Through the Copper Basin near Ducktown and Copperhill, Tennessee. The Copper Basin is an area that looks like the desert regions of our West. The trees and vegetation were killed a number of years ago by fumes from the copper smelters and due to erosion reforestation has been prevented." This postcard is still available for sale. Courtesy of Mrs. Cline and the W. M. Cline Company, Chattanooga, Tennessee.

A 1992 rephotograph of the Walker Cline postcard of the Copper Basin.

By 1889 at Ducktown and Copperhill, Tennessee, the open roasting of copper ore was conducted twenty-four hours a day, every day of the year. Extensive logging and the ensuing poisonous fumes from the smelting operations severely wounded this landscape. Although reforestation efforts began in the late 1930s, only after the smelter operations were halted in the mid-1980s were the restoration efforts of the Tennessee Valley Authority and the Soil Conservation Service more successful.

Kudzu (*Pueraria lobata*) is a member of a bean family indigenous to Asia. Burnt kudzu vines near Copperhill, Tennessee, already show spurts of new growth in late winter/early spring.

Although kudzu vines are killed by frost, the deep roots easily survive the relatively mild winters of the South. This dormant kudzu is at Copperhill, Tennessee.

Kudzu thrives along North Carolina Highway 421 west of Winston-Salem. This non-native, pervasive vine helps define the South as a region, just as the tumbleweed (e.g., *Salsola kali tenuifolia*), introduced from Russia, symbolizes much of the American West and the eucalyptus tree (e.g., *Eucalyptus dalryurpleana*), introduced from Australia, is a major element in many Californian and Mexican landscapes.

Vines of all stripes overwhelm the black leopard cage at the Carnivore Preservation Trust, Pittsboro, North Carolina.

THE RIVER

Flooding, long considered a natural consequence of any river system, is now governed via dams, catchment basins, levees, stream channels, and diversionary canals. South Florida's water management is extensive and includes approximately 1,350 miles of canals and levees and 143 water control structures. One of the most important management projects in Florida has been the Kissimmee Canal. Until 1960 this river ran through a series of switchbacks for more than 103 miles and connected the Kissimmee upper chain of lakes south of Orlando with Lake Okeechobee, creating the headwaters for the entire Everglades ecosystem.

The river teemed with largemouth bass and the mile-wide floodplain was a major stopping point for migratory birds on the Atlantic flyway. Ring-necked ducks, American widgeon, northern pintail, and blue-winged teal wintered along the Kissimmee. White and glossy ibis, herons, and egrets were common in the grassy wet prairies and flooded lowlands of the Lower Kissimmee Basin. Groves of cypress, oaks, and other hardwoods provided nesting habitats for other birds.

During periodic flooding, the Kissimmee resembled a large lake. Extensive flooding in 1945 and 1947, however, and a major hurricane in 1953 threatened the post–World War II sprawl of urban areas located in the Kissimmee floodplain. Consequently, between 1961 and 1971 the U.S. Army Corps of Engineers transformed the Kissimmee River into a straight, fifty-six-mile, thirty-foot-deep ditch for flood control.

Kissimmee, stemming from the Calusa Indian term for "long water," was renamed C-38, an unintended yet symbolic reference of the transformation from the lyrical to the mundane.

Today, the C-38 channel is a series of relatively stagnant reservoirs, pools A, B, C, D, and E, connected by a central canal. Denied the filtering role of miles of floodplain wetlands, this water highway has become polluted with agricultural pesticides and has lost ninety percent of its waterfowl inhabitants and six species of fish. By channelizing the river, more than 43,000 acres of marshland dried up. Cattle now graze where water birds once stalked fish, and perilously low levels of dissolved oxygen disrupt the food chain.

Since 1984 the Kissimmee River has been the focus of an intensive restoration program. Engineers and ecologists from several Florida state agencies, the South Florida Water Management District, the University of California at Berkeley, and the U.S. Army Corps of Engineers have developed a plan not only to restore a functioning river-floodplain ecosystem, but also to re-create as much of the Kissimmee River's historic ecological integrity as possible. These participants' goal is to maintain flood control while restoring sections of the Kissimmee River back to "nature."

Backfilling nearly twelve miles of the Corps-induced canal will result in about twenty-two miles of the new "natural" river, once again featuring kinks, curves, and oxbows. The plans also provide for the creation (as opposed to the restoration) of nearly eleven miles of the bending river that were destroyed in the original canal project. This is the first nationwide attempt to restore a river of this size and ecological importance. Proponents believe that this pilot project will have dramatic implications for the management of river systems throughout the United States; opponents worry about the restoration of the floodplain.

To evaluate the effectiveness of the Kissimmee River demonstration (i.e., restoration) project, the South Florida Water Management District commissioned a three-year physical and mathematical modeling study by the University of California at Berkeley. This sixty-by-eighty-foot physical model represents more than four hundred acres in Pool B, and it allows Berkeley's engineers and ecologists to simulate various components of the restoration plan. The principal investigator is Professor H. W. Shen. The project began in November of 1989 and the model was built in 1990. Here, Roger Manley, renowned artist and curator from North Carolina, poses to indicate the scale of the model.

Weir 2, in front of the U.S. Air Force Avon Park Bombing Range adjoining the west bank of the Kissimmee. (A weir is a dam in a stream that raises the water level or diverts its flow; "C" stands for the Charlie Bombing Range.) This weir was designed to divert the flow of water into a section of newly created bends and oxbows adjacent to Pool B. It is scheduled to be replaced by more permanent backfill in the restoration project for the Kissimmee River system.

This ramp and rain gauge are located at the flow-through marsh on the east side of Pool B, Kissimmee River. More than twenty thousand acres of shoreline property are scheduled to be acquired to accommodate the impact of floods from the restoration project.

Workers from the Los Angeles Conservation Corps use a water-blaster to clean graffiti off rocks along a tributary to the west fork of the San Gabriel River in the Angeles National Forest. "Taggers," or graffiti artists, have marked rocks and trees in this area for more than a decade. In response to the increasing amount of graffiti in the national forest, rangers from the Mt. Baldy Ranger District initiated a program in which inner-city youths participate in "Eco-teams" to educate some of the 32 million annual visitors about the value of preserving nature.

The Nantahala River in southwestern North Carolina is a major recreational waterway. Thought to be a wild river by kayakers, canoeists, inner tube floaters, and rubber raft enthusiasts, in reality the water level is controlled by release schedules at the Nantahala Dam, which was completed in 1941. Although quiet just after sunset in late fall, the river is defined by these racing markers. Parts of the river become quite congested during the peak summer months; a common scene is to witness inner-tubers and rafters pile up where the river narrows in class 1 and 2 rapids.

The U.S. Forest Service, South Carolina Wildlife and Marine Resources Department, and the U.S. Fish and Wildlife Service collaborate in stocking one-year-old rainbow trout into the Chattooga River of South Carolina. All fish are marked by cutting their adipose fin.

Because the Chattooga River is so remote, a helicopter must be leased—at a cost of more than $400 per hour—to drop approximately 2,500 trout from a Bambi bucket at twelve sites along the river each year.

Albino rainbow trout in the Walhalla National Fish Hatchery, U.S. Fish and Wildlife Service, near the border of North and South Carolina. The white trout are said to be easier to see by anglers.

D A M S

Dam and waterline, Sawmill Lake,
Sierra Nevada, California.

Low water at Arrowrock Reservoir, Boise
National Forest, Idaho.

Watering the sand at Palm Desert,
California.

Low water at Anderson Ranch Reservoir,
Boise National Forest, Idaho.

The golf course at the Marriott Hotel, Desert Springs Resort, Palm Desert, California. Most palm trees are exotic to the United States.

A television news crew inspects the low water at Rye Patch Reservoir near Lovelock in central Nevada.

Fish kill due to low water at Rye Patch
Reservoir.

A boy in red fishes in the stagnant water on the other side of the Rye Patch Dam after the final 800 acre-feet of water was drained for irrigation.

WILDLIFE

Sergeant Tony Robinson, a North Carolina wildlife enforcement agent for Burke and Caldwell counties, personally designed and built these radio-controlled decoy deer in his effort to reduce the ubiquitous poaching in the Piedmont region of the Appalachian Mountains. Called "artificial," "fake," "phony," or "dummy" deer by the public, the decoys directly led to nearly four hundred poaching citations during the 1990–1991 and the 1991–1992 hunting seasons. Most of the fines that are charged to convicted offenders go to the North Carolina public school system, but the court has awarded more than $11,000 for the Enforcement Decoy Fund.

To date, Sergeant Robinson has built
six radio-controlled decoys, including
a nighttime version.

Wild turkey, largemouth bass, wood duck, and white-tailed deer wait for final painting and customer pick-up, McKinsey Wildlife Taxidermy, Anderson, South Carolina. The owner of the shop, Mike McKinsey, specializes in "bringing wildlife back to life."

The National Wild Turkey Federation began a program during the 1970s to facilitate the transfer of turkeys between states. It developed special-fund accounts for each state and established a $500 charge per turkey to the receiving state. These funds are then spent on habitat acquisition, management, research, education, and restoration. In 1989, fifteen turkeys (ten hens and five adult males) were introduced into this area of South Carolina; by the end of 1991, the turkey population exceeded one hundred. After South Carolina's stocking quotas are met, extra turkeys are transported to other states to assist in their restoration efforts.

On this day, Matt Knox, assistant regional wildlife biologist, caught two turkeys. Although cracked corn was used as bait to lure turkeys to this site, it took nine hours for the intelligent, always cautious wild turkeys to show up. Once caught, the turkeys are put into cardboard boxes and transported safely. Usually hunting season is suspended for at least three years after turkeys are introduced into an area, and it may be as long as seven years before hunters are allowed to "harvest," or reduce, the population.

Virginia and the Carolinas lead the nation in raising "butterball" turkeys. The meaty breasts craved by consumers have left these white-feathered turkeys too heavy to fly or have sex. By preserving the sperm of vanishing breeds of wild turkeys such as the Crimson Dawn, Silver Auburn, and Buff (fewer than one hundred remain in the United States) these species' genetic strength will be insured, it is hoped.

The Eld's deer, native to Southeast Asia, is an endangered species. There are fewer than three thousand Eld's deer worldwide and only 150 in North America, including three main herds at the Bronx, National, and San Diego zoos. (The Bronx Zoo is a subsidiary of The International Wildlife Conservation, which recently changed their name from the New York Zoological Society.) A male Eld's deer named David poses in an outdoor yard with Linwood Williamson, wildlife technician at the National Zoo Conservation and Research Center in Front Royal, Virginia.

In 1991 the National Zoo's reproductive physiologists used preserved Eld's deer sperm from carefully protected vaults to inseminate seven different female deer. According to zoo officials, this was the first time that frozen-thawed sperm had been used on a large scale for any endangered species. In this photograph wildlife techni-cian Linwood Williamson (center), assisted by Dennis Hosack, takes a blood sample from an artificially inseminated Eld's deer named Vanessa. The newborn deer were eventually named Calypso, Geneva, Levi, Smitty, Trooper, Venus, and Noah, an acronym for New Opportunities in Animal Health Sciences.

The Carnivore Preservation Trust, Pittsboro, North Carolina, was founded in 1981 as a breeding center for rare and endangered rainforest carnivores. By locating, targeting, and breeding threatened species, the Trust aims to provide a genetic sanctuary by creating a "living time capsule." Members of CPT select animals for collection and breeding based upon the species' need for protection in their native habitats, on the lack of adequate breeding programs at other institutions, and on the importance of the animal to its rainforest habitat.

Dr. Michael Bleyman, founder of the Carnivore Preservation Trust, plays with Romeo, a male tiger whose story had been a sad one. Romeo was bred in a Missouri zoo from surplus parents and brought to North Carolina in violation of the Endangered Species Act and the Lacy Act, enacted to prevent illegal taking, capturing, and transporting of animals. Romeo's great-great-great-great tiger grandparents were the last of his ancestors to run free in the wild. Romeo ended up in a pet store in Wake Forest, North Carolina, where he was purchased by an uninformed young man. Wake County humane society officials soon confiscated Romeo, and he was officially transferred to the care of the Trust.

Nancy Schonwalter is a member of the core staff at the Carnivore Preservation Trust. This jaguar, named Bruce, was found locked in an abandoned basement where he received infrequent care for nearly six years. As a result, the animal suffered terrible physical and psychological distress, and the basement's gravel subfloor contributed to the profound deformity of his skeleton. Although Bruce has been under the care and supervision of the Trust since 1985, he still exhibits "non-purposeful" behavior. Researchers have discovered that he was born in a private zoo in Johnston County, North Carolina. The zoo was closed by the federal government due to substandard conditions and repeated violations of the Animal Welfare Act.

Jan Nichols (left) and Debbie Miller feed fruit to tayra (*Galera barbara*) at the Carnivore Preservation Trust. The tayra, often referred to as a tree otter, is closely related to the ferret/weasel group and is almost extinct as a species.

Eating binturong (*Arctictis binturong*), according to Asian folklore, insures youth, vigor, good complexion, and enhances male reproduction. Here, young binturongs at the Carnivore Preservation Trust eat Granny Smith apples. Binturong, native to Southeast Asia, resemble a small black bear. They have a prehensile tail and a long, shaggy coat and are important seed animals because their digestive processes facilitate germination through seed dispersal. Their average weight is thirty to forty pounds and their average length is five and a half feet from the nose to the tip of the tail.

All golden hamsters (*Mesocricetus auratus*) found in laboratories and pet stores are the descendants of one female and her twelve offspring discovered in a nest in Syria in 1930.

Human-made flies evoke the fear and promise of genetic engineering.

ACKNOWLEDGMENTS

Humanature depended upon the kind, generous, and thoughtful assistance of the following individuals and institutions:

Dennis Albrecht, Marian Allen, The Appalachian Environmental Arts Center, David Baumann, Jerry Best, Donald Bills, Michael Bleyman, Hubert Burnett, Cabrillo National Monument, Carnivore Preservation Trust, The Center for Documentary Studies at Duke University, Norman Christensen, City Engineer's Office at Virginia Beach, Michael Cloninger, David C. Crass, Steve Davis, Desert Research Institute at the University of Nevada, Reno, Duke Power Company, Judson Edeburn, John Eylers, James Flechtner, John Garton, Chelsea Miller Goin, Kari and Dana Goin, Ellen Greer, Peter Haff, Alex Harris, Susan Henry, Iris Tillman Hill, Dick Iverson, Terry Johnson, Matt Knox, Thomas Krakauer, Mark Leach, Gilbert W. Leebrick, Michael McFee, Michael McKinsey, Roger Manley, Thomas Maybin, Carol Mayes, Grant and Leslie Miller, James H. Miller, The Nathan Cummings Foundation, National Zoo Conservation and Research Center, Danny Nesbitt, F. Allen Nicholson, The North Carolina Museum of Life and Science, North Carolina Nature Conservancy, North Carolina Wildlife Commission, North Carolina Zoological Park, Eric Paddock, Orrin Pilkey, Peter and Nancy Pool, Sgt. Russ Reed, Tony Robinson, Theodore Rosengarten, Dena Roy, Patricia Sculley, Michael Seamster, Joan Shigekawa, Lori Simmons, Lee Smith, Dale Soblo, South Carolina Nature Conservancy, South Carolina Wildlife Commission, South Florida Water Management District, Monte Stark, Ann Thomas, University of Nevada, Reno, U.S. Army Corps of Engineers, U.S. Department of Energy, U.S. Fish and Wildlife Service, U.S. Forest Service, U.S. Geological Survey, U.S. Soil Conservation Service, Walhalla National Fish Hatchery, Chris Wemmer, Westinghouse Savannah River Company, and Linwood Williamson.

I would like to extend special thanks to George F. Thompson, President of the Center for American Places, Harrisonburg, Virginia. His determination and consistency of vision were very important to the development and completion of *Humanature*.

Humanature was funded in part by the Nathan Cummings Foundation and by a National Endowment for the Arts Fellowship, and by the University of Nevada, Reno.

All uncredited photographs are by the author.

Administrative Law

BY MICHAEL R. ASIMOW
University of California, Los Angeles

Thirteenth Edition

THE
barbri®
GROUP

A THOMSON COMPANY

EDITORIAL OFFICES: 111 W. Jackson Blvd., 7th Floor, Chicago, IL 60604
REGIONAL OFFICES: Chicago, Dallas, Los Angeles, New York, Washington, D.C.

PROJECT EDITOR
Louisa J. Nuckolls, B.A., J.D.
Attorney At Law

SERIES EDITOR
Elizabeth L. Snyder, B.A., J.D.
Attorney At Law

QUALITY CONTROL EDITOR
Sanetta M. Hister

Summary of Contents

ADMINISTRATIVE LAW CAPSULE SUMMARY   I

ADMINISTRATIVE LAW TEXT CORRELATION CHART   i

APPROACH TO EXAMS   (i)

I. SEPARATION OF POWERS AND CONTROLS OVER AGENCIES

Chapter Approach   1

A.   Separation of Powers   2

B.   Delegation of Legislative Power   2

C.   Delegation of Adjudicative Power   12

D.   Other Legislative Controls Over Administrative Action   16

E.   Executive Controls Over Administrative Action   17

II. THE CONSTITUTIONAL RIGHT TO A HEARING

Chapter Approach   23

A.   Interests Protected by Due Process—Liberty and Property   23

B.   Timing of the Hearing   31

C.   Elements of the Hearing   34

CHART: **Summary of Elements of Constitutional Protection**   **38**

D.   Issues Requiring a Hearing—The Rulemaking-Adjudication Distinction   39

III. FORMAL AND INFORMAL ADJUDICATION UNDER THE ADMINISTRATIVE PROCEDURE ACT

Chapter Approach   43

A.   Statutory Hearing Rights to Formal Adjudication   43

     CHART: **When Is a Trial-Type Hearing Required?**   **44**

B.   Adjudication Procedure in Informal Adjudication   49

CHART: **Formal Adjudication vs. Informal Adjudication—A Summary**   **51**

C.   Declaratory Orders   51

D.   The Choice Between Adjudication and Rulemaking   52

IV. THE PROCESS OF FORMAL ADJUDICATION

Chapter Approach   57

A.   The Prehearing Process   57

B.   The Process of Proof at the Hearing   60

C.   Requirement of Findings and Reasons   69

CHART: **Summary of Issues At Each Stage of Formal Adjudication**   **71**

V.   ADJUDICATORY DECISIONMAKERS

Chapter Approach   73

A.   Structure of Adjudicatory Decisions   73

     CHART: **Summary of Types of Adjudicatory Decisions**   **74**

B.   Improper Influences on Decisionmaker   76

C.   Basis for Decisionmaking   86

D.   Binding Effect on Decisionmakers   89

VI.   RULEMAKING PROCEDURES

Chapter Approach   95

A.   Introduction   96

     CHART: **Rulemaking vs. Adjudication—A Summary**   **98**

B.   Controls on Rulemaking   99

C.   Legal Effect of Rules   100

D.   The Informal Rulemaking Process   101

     CHART: **Timeline of Typical APA Informal Rulemaking Procedure**   **102**

E.   Exceptions to Informal Rulemaking Requirements   110

     CHART: **Exception to APA Rulemaking Requirements**   **115**

F.   Impartiality of Rulemakers   116

G.   The Rulemaking Record   118

VII. OBTAINING INFORMATION AND ATTORNEY'S FEES

Chapter Approach   121

A.   Agency Acquisition of Information   122

     CHART: **Subpoena Power in Nonadjudicatory Settings**   **123**

B.   Constitutional Protection from Agency Information Gathering   129

C.   Freedom of Information Act   134

D.   Government in the Sunshine Act   145

E.   Attorney's Fees   146

VIII. SCOPE OF JUDICIAL REVIEW

Chapter Approach   149

A.   Introduction   149

B.   Scope of Review of Questions of Basic Fact   150

C.   Scope of Review of Agency's Legal Interpretations   157

D.   Scope of Review of Application of Law to Fact   164

E.   Scope of Review of Agency Exercises of Discretion   168

     CHART: **Scope of Judicial Review—A Summary**   **173**

IX.   REVIEWABILITY OF AGENCY DECISIONS—REMEDIES AND PRECLUSION

Chapter Approach   175

A.   Means of Obtaining Judicial Review   175

B.   Sovereign Immunity   180

C.   Tort Liability of Government   184

D.   Tort Liability of Government Officials   187

E.   Statutory Preclusion of Judicial Review   194

F.   Commitment to Agency Discretion   198

X.   STANDING TO SEEK JUDICIAL REVIEW

Chapter Approach   201

CHART: Requirements for Judicial Review—An Approach   **202**

A.   Standing to Seek Judicial Review   203

B.   The Timing of Judicial Review   215

     CHART: Checklist of Exceptions to the Exhaustion Rule   **229**

REVIEW QUESTIONS AND ANSWERS   **237**

EXAM QUESTIONS AND ANSWERS   **281**

TABLE OF CASES   **311**

TABLE OF CITATIONS TO THE ADMINISTRATIVE PROCEDURE ACT   **319**

INDEX   **321**

Text Correlation Chart

Gilbert Law Summary ADMINISTRATIVE LAW	Asimow, Bonfield, Levin *State and Federal Administrative Law* 1998 (2d ed.)	Breyer, Stewart *Administrative Law and Regulatory Policy* 1992 (3d ed.)	Robinson, Gellhorn, Braff *The Administrative Process* 1993 (4th ed.)	Schwartz *Administrative Law* 1994 (4th ed.)	Strauss, Rakoff, Schotland, Farina *Gellhorn and Byse's Administrative Law* 1995 (9th ed.)
I. SEPARATION OF POWERS AND CONTROLS OVER AGENCIES					
A. Separation of Powers	Page 396-397	Page 19-20, 33-35, 140-141	Page 2-10, 34-37, 40-45	Page 26-42, 78-80	Page 138-141, 169-171
B. Delegation of Legislative Power	397-428	35-41, 66-99, 124-137, 320-351, 396-410	56-85	76-119	52-116
C. Delegation of Adjudicative Power	428-439	41-66, 89-90, 127-131, 399	117, 149-164	7-15, 87-96, 120-175	52-67, 116-138, 185-190
D. Other Legislative Controls Over Administrative Action	461-464	91-105	85-109	96-100, 360-373	160-171, 195-207
E. Executive Controls Over Administrative Action	464-506	105-137	109-138	26-55	61-62, 138-159, 171-191, 207-225
II. THE CONSTITUTIONAL RIGHT TO A HEARING					
A. Interests Protected by Due Process—Liberty and Property	30-31, 33-51	708-725, 729-765	624-687, 691-694, 703-721	375-377, 410-442	704-705, 708-718, 722-766, 790-811
B. Timing of the Hearing	22-32, 51-64, 215-216	725-729, 769-774, 776-777, 784-799	667-673, 687-710	397-407, 442-458	705-710, 722-731, 766-792, 798-809, 822-835
C. Elements of the Hearing	22-32, 64-73, 91	434-461, 730-739, 766-806	667-721	458-490, 502-530	726-729, 766-782, 811-822
D. Issues Requiring a Hearing—The Rule-making-Adjudication Distinction	73-82, 100-109	524-534, 806-813	407-418	327-332, 377-397	226-238, 453-456, 705
III. FORMAL AND INFORMAL ADJUDICATION UNDER THE ADMINISTRATIVE PROCEDURE ACT					
A. Statutory Hearing Rights to Formal Adjudication	8, 83-100, 223-229, 250-253	534-538, 547-559, 607-609, 621-622, 828-830	37-38, 44-45, 164-165, 270-280, 416	245-254, 573-581, 669-674	241-242, 256-257, 361-375
B. Adjudication Procedure in Informal Adjudication	85-89, 90-91, 99, 150, 199	351-361, 538, 612-621, 729, 808-810	39, 44-45, 164-165, 357		253-255, 376-384, 471, 571
C. Declaratory Orders	216		45-46	307-308, 799	
D. The Choice Between Adjudication and Rulemaking	218-223, 229-230, 352-378	11-13, 396-429, 538-547, 621-633	71-72, 415-418	259-265, 339-360	233-236, 417-453
IV. THE PROCESS OF FORMAL ADJUDICATION					
A. The Prehearing Process	163-182	12, 537-538, 806-813, 925-928, 1054-1056	37-38, 280-295, 402-403, 577-585	215-224, 491-516	263-264, 400-417, 464-477, 892-897
B. The Process of Proof at the Hearing	90, 109-110, 116-117, 182-195	224-235, 537-538, 649-660, 820-830, 860-865, 919-925	276-280, 585-595	582-662	257-286, 541-542, 958-959, 978-982
C. Requirement of Findings and Reasons	196-202	411-429, 536-538, 547, 559	316-322	677-690	286-291, 379-384

Gilbert Law Summary ADMINISTRATIVE LAW	Asimow, Bonfield, Levin *State and Federal Administrative Law* 1998 (2d ed.)	Breyer, Stewart *Administrative Law and Regulatory Policy* 1992 (3d ed.)	Robinson, Gellhorn, Braff *The Administrative Process* 1993 (4th ed.)	Schwartz *Administrative Law* 1994 (4th ed.)	Strauss, Rakoff, Schotland, Farina *Gellhorn and Byse's Administrative Law* 1995 (9th ed.)
V. ADJUDICATORY DECISIONMAKERS					
A. Structure of Adjudicatory Decisions	8, 84-93, 149-162, 566-567	24, 222-224, 301-302, 536-537, 815-855	35-38, 274-276, 301-302	530-544, 663-680	46-50, 256-264, 958-972, 978-979, 989-995, 1014-1024
B. Improper Influences on Decisionmaker	117-149, 178-179	660-667, 815-865	295-311, 379-384, 393-402	330-339, 544-581, 617-620	959-966, 972-978, 995, 998-1016, 1024-1048
C. Basis for Decisionmaking	110-117, 154-158	612-616, 860-874	366-370	639-694	286-291, 379-384, 571-584, 979-995
D. Binding Effect on Decisionmakers	202-217	506-522	384-393	293-308	652-687
VI. RULEMAKING PROCEDURES					
A. Introduction	6, 218-235, 247-262	35-41, 291-319, 500-506, 523-524, 534-547, 579-582, 592, 621-633	38-39, 404-415, 417-418, 463-476, 496-499	245-265, 273-279, 330-333	43-46, 215-225, 234-242, 329-330, 339-361, 425-426, 436-445
B. Controls on Rulemaking	304-314, 439-440	91-116, 178-181, 194-196	164-169, 420-439, 456-472, 541-543	279-293, 360-373	17-18, 45-46, 203-207, 215-225, 306-309, 434-435
C. Legal Effect of Rules	219, 336-338	474-494, 500-506, 592-606	418-420	266-279	234-238, 417-418, 425-426, 657
D. The Informal Rulemaking Process	80-81, 223-226, 235-262, 286-304, 314-322, 378-386, 606-607, 644-645	363-367, 534-537, 559-592, 606-611, 616-619, 1044	38-39, 357-375, 440, 499-528	293-297, 309-339, 391-397, 841	241-256, 286-339, 376-384, 400-417, 486-509, 584-591
E. Exceptions to Informal Rulemaking Requirements	323-358	592-606, 874-904	490-499	251-254, 312-313	339, 384-400, 564-569, 634-636
F. Impartiality of Rulemakers	264-286	667-685, 828-854	440-466, 480-490, 548-567	333-339, 547, 581, 618-620	1048-1093
G. The Rulemaking Record	110-117, 589-592	612-620	358-373	313-314, 830-831, 840-842	250, 253-255, 324-329, 578-590, 1056, 1062-1069
VII. OBTAINING INFORMATION AND ATTORNEY'S FEES					
A. Agency Acquisition of Information	8, 170-180	905-925	577-595	178-224	836-877, 892-908
B. Constitutional Protection from Agency Information Gathering	51, 170-180	905-908	584-585	180-186, 523, 605-610	376, 877-892, 895-897, 903-904
C. Freedom of Information Act	507-525	926-958	39-40, 595-615, 616-623	228-240	909-948
D. Government in the Sunshine Act	525-529	959-966	615-616	240-244	948-957
E. Attorney's Fees	627-632		293-295, 710-716	523-529	811-822
VIII. SCOPE OF JUDICIAL REVIEW					
A. In General	9, 534-535	4, 230-232, 1014-1015, 1054-1056, 1115, 1133-1135	40-49, 320-322, 357, 507-508	695-699	510-520
B. Scope of Review of Questions of Basic Fact	279-286, 428-435, 535-557	41-62, 198-276, 633-649	149-153, 275, 303-306, 311-322	830-858, 864-872, 879-890, 912	277, 520-542, 549-554, 569-570
C. Scope of Review of Agency's Legal Interpretations	557-570	276-319	316-319, 417, 529-541, 657-661, 666-667	841-842, 890-913	385-396, 521, 554-569, 570-571, 614-636

Gilbert Law Summary ADMINISTRATIVE LAW	Asimow, Bonfield, Levin *State and Federal Administrative Law* 1998 (2d ed.)	Breyer, Stewart *Administrative Law and Regulatory Policy* 1992 (3d ed.)	Robinson, Gellhorn, Braff *The Administrative Process* 1993 (4th ed.)	Schwartz *Administrative Law* 1994 (4th ed.)	Strauss, Rakoff, Schotland, Farina *Gellhorn and Byse's Administrative Law* 1995 (9th ed.)
D. Scope of Review of Application of Law to Fact	571-578	280-291	311-322, 543-576	831-834, 842-843, 872-879	555-564, 634-636
E. Scope of Review of Agency Exercises of Discretion	578-610	231, 319-393, 559-562, 572, 616-620, 649-652, 1014-1019, 1029-1047	232, 233, 251-269, 311-345, 357-373, 516-528	831, 840-841, 844, 851-864	251-255, 542-549, 571-584, 591-614, 687-698
IX. REVIEWABILITY OF AGENCY DECISIONS—REMEDIES AND PRECLUSION					
A. Means of Obtaining Judicial Review	9, 434-435, 611-621	14, 62-66, 967-980, 1000-1008, 1131-1132	40-52, 158-164, 229-232, 235-238	695-704, 795-814	127-128, 666-668, 687-689, 1106-1120, 1185-1195, 1250-1252
B. Sovereign Immunity	615, 621-624	748, 967-975, 978-984	47-48, 722-729, 739-740	822-830	1106-1107, 1113, 1260, 1287-1301
C. Tort Liability of Government	615, 622-624	976-977, 983-991, 1013-1021	722-740	822-830	1114-1115, 1280-1305
D. Tort Liability of Government Officials	624-627	981-984, 991-1021	740-760	815-822	657, 1115-1117, 1130-1131, 1261-1280
E. Statutory Preclusion of Judicial Review	632-638, 643-644, 673	1014-1054, 1098-1105	232-251	705-714	1185-1225
F. Commitment to Agency Discretion	638-646	319-393, 1029-1054	251-269	708-721	392-393, 483-488, 573-574, 687-689, 1094, 1209-1220
X. STANDING TO SEEK JUDICIAL REVIEW AND THE TIMING OF JUDICIAL REVIEW					
A. Standing to Seek Judicial Review	647-667	1054-1092	192-232	721-745	1121-1184
B. The Timing of Judicial Review	667-706	1092-1156	170-192	509-510, 745-795, 813-814, 858-864	1119-1120, 1225-1260

Capsule Summary

I. SEPARATION OF POWERS AND CONTROLS OVER AGENCIES

A. SEPARATION OF POWERS   §1
Administrative agencies are units of government created by statute to carry out specific tasks in implementing the statute. Most administrative agencies fall in the executive branch, but some important agencies are independent.

B. DELEGATION OF LEGISLATIVE POWER   §4
Theoretically, legislative power cannot be delegated, but practically, through the granting of broad rulemaking powers to administrative agencies, legislatures do so delegate. The delegation doctrine requires that: (i) the legislature at least decide the fundamental underlying policies; and (ii) the agency action fall *within the scope of the delegated power*.

1. Limits on Delegation   §5
Despite the delegation doctrine, Congress may delegate very broad rulemaking powers to federal agencies. State agencies apply the delegation doctrine more strictly.

a. Background   §6
The early cases upheld delegation of power to agencies by employing various formulas limiting agency discretion, but the NIRA cases struck down broad delegations of powers to the President under New Deal legislation, finding that there were no standards to guide the President. *Post-NIRA* cases have uniformly *upheld* broad delegations of power based on vague standards or even no standards at all.

b. Delegation doctrine today   §19
Although still a minority view, there is some current support on the Supreme Court for requiring Congress to make fundamental policy choices rather than passing them on to the agencies. However, many states, under state constitutions, invalidate broad delegations of power.

c. Substitutes for delegation doctrine   §21
Some decisions allow procedural safeguards to substitute for discretion-limiting standards. Other cases call on the *courts to construe statutes delegating power narrowly*, especially if the delegation is in an area that is constitutionally suspect.

d.   Line Item Veto Act   §25
This statute allowing the President to veto a single appropriation of a
large appropriation bill was invalidated by the Court because it gave
the President power to amend without going through the legislative
process.

e.   Delegation to federal judges   §26
Congress may delegate rulemaking power to federal judges where it
is relevant to judicial functions and where there is no danger of undermining judicial integrity or enlarging judicial power.

f.   Delegation to private parties   §27
State courts often invalidate such delegations; federal courts are
more permissive, but require safeguards.

2.   Actions Outside the Scope of Delegated Power   §30
Courts have power to set aside particular rules or other agency action under the ultra vires doctrine if the action is outside the scope of the delegated power.

a.   Judicial technique   §31
Courts may avoid *potential* delegation problems by invalidating particular rules instead of the entire statute. Alternatively, a court may
avoid *substantive constitutional issues* by narrowly construing the
scope of a delegated power, especially in the area of civil liberties.

C.   DELEGATION OF ADJUDICATIVE POWER   §34
Judicial power *can be delegated* to administrative agencies, but the standards to
be applied in agency adjudications may not be *unconstitutionally vague*. Developing case law bars agencies from imposing criminal or civil sanctions on private parties under regulations that fail to give fair warning of the conduct prohibited.

1.   Adjudication of Public and Private Rights   §38
Congress can assign the adjudication of *public rights* (e.g., claims between
private parties and the government) to non-Article III courts, such as administrative agencies, even where there would be a right to a jury trial if
the right were adjudicated in court. However, the adjudication of *private
claims* (i.e., claims between individuals) generally must be assigned to an
Article III court, except for claims involving a *new statutory right* or certain
ancillary claims.

a.   State courts   §44
State courts permit agency adjudication of private rights where necessary to implement the regulatory scheme.

2.   Appointment of Judges to Nonjudicial Duties   §45
The Court upheld the appointment of judges to the Sentencing Commission that establishes sentencing guidelines since the agency is in the judicial branch and its nonjudicial function does not undermine judicial integrity.

3. Penalties

Agencies may enact regulations providing for *criminal sanctions,* but an agency may ***not prosecute*** or imprison for violation of those regulations. Agencies may, however, impose and assess *civil penalties* without the protections afforded under the criminal law, but several decisions deny agencies the power to impose punitive damages.

D. OTHER LEGISLATIVE CONTROLS OVER ADMINISTRATIVE ACTION

1. Controls

Congress has various controls over agency action:

a. *Federal standing committees* keep abreast of agency activities;

b. *Investigations conducted by congressional committees* and special "watch-dog" committees publicize controversial administrative action;

c. *By its appropriations* Congress can limit agency spending; and

d. *The Senate must consent* to some presidential appointments.

2. Congressional Review Act

Under this statute, all rules of general applicability must be submitted to Congress and to the General Accounting Office before they take effect. Congress can veto a rule by passing a joint resolution of disapproval that must be signed by the President or passed by a two-thirds majority over a presidential veto. A disapproved rule may not be reissued by an agency absent congressional legislation authorizing reissuance.

a. Legislative veto compared

The Review Act was passed after congressional veto of administrative rules was invalidated by the Supreme Court (*Chadha* case). The Act seeks to give Congress some constitutionally valid control over agency action. Most state decisions follow the ban on legislative vetos.

E. EXECUTIVE CONTROLS OVER ADMINISTRATIVE ACTION

1. Appointment Power

Presidential appointment of agency heads requires Senate approval.

a. Congressional appointments

Congress cannot appoint the members of agencies engaged in rulemaking or adjudication or personnel who execute the law.

b. Appointment of inferior officers

Congress may vest the appointment of inferior officers in the President alone, in courts of law, or in department heads. An inferior officer is generally one who has a "superior."

c. Judicial appointments

Congress may vest appointments of inferior officers in the courts of law (*e.g.,* courts may appoint special prosecutors).

2. **Removal Power**

    a. **President** §72

    The President has power to remove executive officers whom the President has appointed unless Congress restricts the President's power to do so.

    b. **Good cause limitation** §73

    A statute can prevent removal of an executive officer by the President if the restriction ***does not impede his ability to perform constitutional duties*** (*e.g.,* independent counsel can be removed only for good cause).

    c. **Congressional participation** §77

    Congress may not remove (or share in the process of removing) officials engaged in executive functions.

3. **Fiscal Power** §78

    The President recommends budgetary allocations and changes in legislation.

4. **Organizational Power** §79

    The President has extensive power over the creation, reorganization, and abolition of executive agencies.

5. **Rulemaking** §80

    By executive order, the President has imposed substantial controls over major federal rulemaking.

6. **Inspectors General** §81

    Inspectors general are posted throughout the federal government to audit agencies and departments for fraud, waste, or abuse.

7. **Gubernatorial Veto** §83

    Some states permit the governor to veto agency rules.

II. THE CONSTITUTIONAL RIGHT TO A HEARING

A. INTERESTS PROTECTED BY DUE PROCESS—LIBERTY AND PROPERTY §84

Federal and state governments must provide ***notice and a hearing*** before taking action that deprives an individual of "liberty" or "property" (both of which are broadly defined).

1. **"Liberty"** §85

    Liberty entails those things that permit one to enjoy the qualities of life recognized as essential to the pursuit of happiness (*e.g.,* right to work, marry, etc.).

    a. **Imposition of stigma** §86

    Government action that imposes a stigma against a person such that, *e.g.,* would make it difficult for the person to be employed in the future, is a deprivation of liberty. Note that the imposition of stigma must be accompanied by some other action (***"stigma-plus"***), such as discharge from employment, and must be ***both public and allegedly false***.

b. Deprivation of constitutional rights §89

Violation of a person's *substantive* constitutional rights is a deprivation of liberty. However, in some cases, agencies need *not* provide a prior hearing; the interests can be vindicated in an action for damages under the Civil Rights Act or under state tort or contract law.

c. Deportation of aliens §90

Deportation triggers a right to a hearing, but there is *no* right to a hearing if the government seeks to *exclude* an alien attempting to enter the country.

d. Deprivation of physical liberty §93

Imprisonment, properly imposed, generally extinguishes a prisoner's liberty interests. Generally, decisions by prison authorities having an adverse effect on prisoners (*e.g.*, solitary confinement) are *not* deprivations of liberty *unless those decisions lengthen* the term of confinement. Certain exceptions may apply (*e.g.*, transfer to mental hospital, involuntary administration of psychotropic drugs).

(1) Parole or probation §97

Absent statutory directive, the *granting* of parole or probation is discretionary and thus *no hearing* is required before it is denied. However, *revocation* of parole or probation requires a *probable cause hearing before* and a *full hearing after* revocation.

e. Expulsion or suspension from school §99

If the student is dismissed from a public college or school for *disciplinary reasons,* some procedural safeguards are required; however, there is no such requirement when the dismissal is due to *academic deficiencies. High school suspensions* lasting 10 days or less require only a conference at which the student has an opportunity to state her side.

2. "Property" §103

Property includes not only tangibles such as real estate or money, but also certain intangibles such as entitlements to government benefits or licenses.

a. Welfare §104

A person properly receiving welfare benefits has an interest in continuing to receive them and is entitled to *notice and a hearing before* termination of the benefits. Similarly, eviction from *public housing* requires notice and a hearing.

b. Government employment §107

Appropriate procedures are required to discharge an employee from a protected job (*e.g.,* tenured position or job protected by statute, contract, etc.). Such employees are entitled to a *pretermination* oral or written notice, explanation of charges, and an opportunity to respond, *followed by a full hearing* after discharge.

c. Licenses §111

A license generally is a protected property interest. A hearing is usually required **before** suspension of a license. Clear standards are required to **deny** a license or a renewal of a license.

3. **Deprivation** §117
Due process applies if the state has **directly deprived** a person of liberty or property.

B. TIMING OF THE HEARING

1. **General Rule** §118
A hearing generally must occur **before** a deprivation of liberty or property. Exceptions exist for emergency situations.

2. **Balancing Test** §120
To determine whether a state must hold a hearing before acting, the Court balances: (i) the **nature of the affected private interest**; (ii) the **risk to that interest** and consideration of alternative procedures; and (iii) the **burden on government** from imposing a different procedure.

   a. **Welfare and disability benefits** §122
Because of the probability of irreparable harm being caused by the cessation of **welfare** benefits, a **trial-type hearing** is required before **benefits** are stopped. However, because different interests are involved, **disability** payments may be stopped before a hearing is provided.

   b. **Employment discharge** §125
A government or tenured employee may be suspended **without a prior hearing** if there is an **adequate predischarge procedure** to determine that there is probable cause for discharge. A prompt **post-deprivation hearing** must be held. Suspension **without pay or any pretermination procedure** is permitted in **emergency** situations.

   c. **Licenses** §128
Generally, a **prior hearing** is required for suspension or revocation of a driver's license, but certain exceptions permit suspension first and a hearing later (*e.g.,* unsafe driver, refusal to take breathalyzer test). Suspension of **professional licenses** must be followed by a prompt hearing.

   d. **Creditor's remedies** §131
Whether a creditor can seize a debtor's property before judicial determination of the debt is resolved by careful application of the balancing test: there must be probable cause that the debt is owed and that the creditor's legitimate interest requires summary action.

C. ELEMENTS OF THE HEARING §135
The same balancing test that is used for the timing of the hearing is used to determine what elements the hearing must contain to comply with due process. The following elements must be present:

1. **Timely and adequate notice** of the proposed action;

2. **Fair warning** that particular conduct is violative of the regulation;

3. *Opportunity to confront adverse witnesses*, although cross-examination may be limited;

4. *Right to impartial decisionmaker;*

5. *Decisionmaker must state the reasons* for the determination, and the decisions must be based solely on legal rules and evidence *presented at the hearing;*

6. *Right to counsel* is usually afforded in *adversary* proceedings, but the state is usually not required to provide counsel; and

7. *Right to a comparative hearing* where there are several parties competing for the same interest.

D. ISSUES REQUIRING A HEARING—THE RULEMAKING-ADJUDICATION DISTINCTION

1. No Hearing Required for Rulemaking §146
Due process requires a hearing only in certain adjudication cases; no hearing is required in rulemaking.

2. Adjudication §147
Adjudication cases involving only law or policy issues do *not require* a hearing, nor is a hearing required for a determination of generalized facts (facts applicable to a large group of persons or businesses—sometimes referred to as "legislative facts").

a. Individualized facts §148
Such facts are sometimes called "adjudicative facts." Facts about an individual private party *usually require* a trial-type hearing.

3. Rules of General Application §155
Even where the Constitution or a statute entitles a person to a trial-type hearing, the issues involved may already have been settled by a validly adopted agency rule. In these cases, the agency has preempted an area of adjudication by *legislatively determining the factual questions* and no hearing is required.

4. Administrative "Summary Judgment" §156
Private parties may be required to demonstrate that individualized facts are at issue; if they are unable to do so, the agency may use a "summary judgment" procedure.

III. FORMAL AND INFORMAL ADJUDICATION UNDER THE ADMINISTRATIVE PROCEDURE ACT

A. STATUTORY HEARING RIGHTS TO FORMAL ADJUDICATION

1. Statutory vs. Constitutional Rights §157
Often statutes provide more protection for rights to notice and an adjudicatory hearing than does due process. Sometimes, agency regulations may require a formal hearing when neither due process nor a statute calls for one.

2. Federal APA—When Applicable §158

The federal APA is applicable only when the action is *adjudication* (as that term is defined in the APA) *and* when *another statute or the Constitution* requires a *hearing on the record*.

a. Adjudication §159

Under the federal APA, adjudication is the *agency process to formulate an order*. An *order* is, in whole or in part, a final agency disposition in a *matter other than rulemaking* but including licensing.

(1) Rule §160

A rule is an agency statement of general or particular applicability and future effect. If the agency action has *particular* applicability, it is generally treated as adjudication despite the APA's definition.

(2) Construction of statute §162

In determining whether the requisite "other statute" mandates an *on-the-record hearing*, the words "on-the-record" are interpreted to mean that a record is kept (written or taped) and the decisionmaker is *confined to that record* in making factual determinations. There is a split in authority as to the meaning of statutes that require a "hearing" without using the words "on the record."

(3) Hearing required by Constitution §165

According to some cases, even absent a statute, a trial-type hearing using full APA procedures for adjudication is required if a hearing would be required by *procedural due process* in cases of deprivation of liberty or property.

(4) State APA §166

The 1981 Model State APA generally requires an appropriate *adjudication* procedure in *every* case of adjudication, even when no other statute requires it.

B. ADJUDICATION PROCEDURE IN INFORMAL ADJUDICATION

1. Gap in Coverage §167

The APA contains only a few provisions applicable to informal adjudication: a *right to appear* and be represented by counsel; enforcement of legal *subpoenas; prompt notice and explanation* by the agency of the denial of any request; and a prior warning and opportunity to correct problems in license revocations or suspensions.

a. Model State APA §173

An appropriate hearing process is required in *all cases* of adjudication. However, to avoid full formal hearings for simple disputes, states may employ *emergency procedures, conference adjudicative hearings* (which dispense with some formalities), and *summary adjudicative procedures*.

2. Judicial Innovation Under Federal APA §177

An agency can provide whatever procedures it wishes in conducting informal adjudication without court interference because the APA leaves such decisions to agency discretion. Courts, however, have sometimes interpreted "hearing" to mean a hearing "on the record" requiring formal adjudication or, in some cases, have remanded a matter for an agency explanation of an informal action.

C. DECLARATORY ORDERS §180

The APA provides that wherever an agency could have conducted a formal hearing, it may instead enter a declaratory order. Often such orders are requested by persons seeking guidance as to agency interpretation of a law. Declaratory orders *are reviewable* by the courts.

D. THE CHOICE BETWEEN ADJUDICATION AND RULEMAKING

1. Choice Is Discretionary §186

Agencies generally have broad discretion as to how to implement a statutory scheme and have traditionally made law and policy through case-by-case adjudication (which is retroactive as to the parties). Agencies are usually also empowered to determine law and policy through rulemaking, which normally has *only prospective* application.

2. Abuse of Discretion §187

Where *serious adverse consequences* occur because of the retroactivity of adjudication, the court may find that the agency abused its discretion.

a. NLRB cases §188

The NLRB has frequently been criticized for its failure to make rules of general application and its formulation of policy on a case-by-case basis. In determining whether a new rule is unfairly retroactive, a court balances at least five factors:

(i) Whether the case is one of *first impression;*

(ii) Whether the new rule represents an *abrupt departure* from well-established practice;

(iii) The extent of a party's *reliance on prior law;*

(iv) The *burden imposed* by the retroactive order; and

(v) The *statutory interest* in applying the new rule to the pending case.

(1) A new approach §189

Responding to criticism, the NLRB adopted a rule limiting the agency's discretion in determining hospital bargaining units on a case-by-case basis. This rule was emphatically upheld by the Supreme Court.

b. Proper subjects for adjudication §190

These include problems that *could not reasonably be foreseen* by the agency, areas over which the agency has *little experience*, and problems requiring *specialized solutions*.

c. Required rulemaking   §191
Some federal decisions indicate that agencies must limit their power by **adopting standards**, either by rulemaking or case-by-case adjudication. Some states are more aggressive in requiring that agency policy be made by rulemaking rather than adjudication. The 1981 Model State APA strongly favors required rulemaking.

d. Prospective adjudication   §196
The Supreme Court has **prohibited** the adoption of new policy in an adjudication that is prospective but not retroactive.

IV. THE PROCESS OF FORMAL ADJUDICATION

A. THE PREHEARING PROCESS

1. Notice   §197
All APAs require adequate notice.

2. Parties and Intervention   §198
Agencies generally permit the intervention of interested persons where it will **not unduly complicate proceedings.** Such intervention may be conditional (*e.g.*, limited as to issues or discovery). Some cases require a proposed intervenor to meet the same standards as those required for **standing** to seek judicial review.

3. Discovery   §204
There is **no** federal requirement to discovery and, in most states, parties to administrative proceedings have **no rights to discovery**. However, all parties normally have **subpoena power** and may also gather information under the **Freedom of Information Act**.

4. Settlement and Alternate Dispute Resolution   §207
A 1990 APA amendment requires agencies to use alternate dispute resolution techniques in all agency functions, although regulated parties **cannot** be forced to use them.

B. THE PROCESS OF PROOF AT THE HEARING

1. Burden of Proof   §211
Generally, the proponent of a rule or order has the burden of proving its case by a **preponderance of the evidence**. Courts sometimes manipulate the burden of proof to prevent unjust agency action.

2. Evidence in Administrative Proceedings   §215
Any relevant evidence is admissible; general rules of evidence (such as the ban on hearsay evidence) are **not** applicable.

a. Reliance on hearsay alone

(1) State courts   §219
Some states require that an agency decision must be based on a **"residuum"** of nonhearsay evidence. The 1981 Model State APA rejects the residuum rule.

(2)	**Federal rule**	**§222**

Federal courts appear to reject the residuum rule, although a decision based on ***unreliable*** hearsay may be set aside as lacking support in substantial evidence.

(3) Constitutional problem §224

Occasionally, reliance on hearsay alone may violate the due process right to confront witnesses where credibility is an issue.

3. Exclusive Record Principle §225

An agency decision must be based ***on the record*** (the transcript of testimony and exhibits). This rule has many exceptions, such as reliance on physical inspections or tests, and in some situations, assistance from staff members who have not been involved in the case.

a. Official notice §230

Another outside-the-record exception allows administrative decisionmakers to take official notice of factual material, including technical and scientific matters within the agency's area of expertise. Opponents must be allowed to rebut such evidence.

b. Agency expertise §235

An agency may rely on its own expertise in making a determination and disregard expert testimony as to matters such as causation and prediction. However, an agency cannot engage in conjecture and its decision will be sharply scrutinized when expert testimony is disregarded ***without stated reasons***.

C. REQUIREMENT OF FINDINGS AND REASONS

1. APA Provisions §239

The federal APA and Model State APA both require a statement of ***findings of fact and conclusions of law*** for all decisions issued to ensure that the fact finder evaluates the evidence.

2. Informal Adjudication §241

An agency must also state its grounds for informal action and is ***constitutionally required*** to give a statement of findings and conclusions in trial-type hearings.

3. Sufficiency of Findings §244

The agency must, in addition to a statement of ***ultimate facts***, state the ***basic underlying facts***. Courts will not imply findings that are not a part of the record to uphold the agency's action.

4. Findings at Agency Head Level §246

Frequently agency heads summarily affirm an agency's decision and no separate findings need be stated. However, lack of an explicit affirmance may cause a reviewing court to vacate the agency head's action.

5. Proposed Findings §247

Parties must have an opportunity to submit their own proposed findings and conclusions either ***before*** a decision is made or before agency review of the fact finder's decision.

V. ADJUDICATORY DECISIONMAKERS

A. STRUCTURE OF ADJUDICATORY DECISIONS

1. Decisionmaker—ALJ or Agency Head §248

Most administrative hearings, state and federal, are conducted by administrative judges (*i.e.,* staff members whose only task is to hear and decide cases) whose decisions are then reviewed by agency heads. Many but not all administrative judges are called ***administrative law judges*** ("ALJs") who have special statutory protections. In hearings under the APA, the hearing officer must be an ALJ.

2. Types of Decisions §249

ALJs may issue the following types of decisions under the federal APA:

a. Initial decisions §250

Where there is a hearing on the record, the ALJ renders an "initial decision," which becomes final unless appealed to the agency.

b. Recommended decisions §251

Where the agency requires that the record be certified ***to it*** for decision, the ALJ makes a "recommended decision."

c. Tentative decisions §252

In licensing or formal rulemaking proceedings, where a hearing on the record is required, the ALJ can make a "tentative decision."

3. Independence of ALJs

a. In-house ALJs §253

Federal, and most state, ALJs work for the agency for which they decide cases, but are organizationally independent and cannot be supervised by prosecuting personnel. In approximately 12 states, ALJs operate in a ***central panel*** from which they are assigned to the various agencies.

b. APA provisions §254

The APA enhanced the position of ALJs and provided that cases be assigned by rotation; judges cannot perform duties inconsistent with the ALJ position; judges can be removed only for good cause; and compensation paid to them is determined by the Civil Service Commission; ALJs cannot consult agency staff members about a "fact in issue."

c. Non-APA cases §255

Even in cases where the federal APA does not apply, the initial decision is made by an administrative judge. That judge, however, does not have the protections provided by the APA for ALJs.

4. Splitting Agencies §256

To further independence, in some cases Congress has split the adjudicatory function from the law enforcement function.

B. IMPROPER INFLUENCES ON DECISIONMAKER

1. **Combination of Functions** §258
   There is *no violation of due process* where *agency heads* who render the decision were involved in the investigative and/or prosecutorial stages of the proceeding, but mixing functions of *lower level staff may violate* due process. Generally, the *APA requires separation* of functions where the proceeding is a formal adjudication (meaning that staff members engaged in prosecution or investigation cannot take part in judging or advising judges). However, this provision is inapplicable to initial license applications, public utility or carrier proceedings, or to the agency heads.

2. **Bias or Prejudice** §270
   The APA provides that a decisionmaker should step aside upon a *timely* complaint of bias.

   a. **Prejudgment** §273
      A decisionmaker *must* step aside if she has a fixed opinion as to *facts of the case.* However, a decisionmaker who has made a pre-judgment regarding *legislative facts, law, or policy* is *not* disqualified. Similarly, *prior contacts with facts* of the dispute by a decisionmaker do not provide a basis for disqualification.

   b. **Economic bias** §277
      A decisionmaker's financial or personal interest in a case results in disqualification. Bias is also established when the *adjudicating agency would benefit* significantly from a decision against a party. However, a non-adjudicatory *prosecuting agency* is not disqualified even if it retains collected penalties.

   c. **Animus toward a party** §280
      Personal hostility to a party or a group to which a party belongs re-quires disqualification. However, an adjudicator's *conduct at a hear-ing* generally does not establish animus or prejudgment of facts.

   d. **"Rule of necessity"** §282
      Where the tribunal is the *only* one with the power to hear and decide the case, it may do so even though biased; judicial review will be stringent. The Model State APA permits the appointment of a substi-tute ALJ.

3. **Influence or Pressure on Fact Finder**

   a. **Congressional interference** §283
      Excessive congressional interference in a pending adjudication may require reversal of the agency action. However, courts are quite cau-tious in invalidating agency decisions on this basis because of Congress's function as overseer of agencies and because of the possi-bility of impairing the flexibility needed in the relationship between Congress and agencies. Congressional interference *prior* to the hear-ing stage of a case is less likely to require reversal than interference *after* the hearing has commenced.

   b. **Ex parte communications by interested outsiders** §286
      The APA prohibits communications *relevant to the merits* to an ALJ

or any agency employee who is, or may be, involved in the decisional process. This provision applies to **formal rulemaking** and **formal adjudication**, but not to informal proceedings.

(1) White House staff   §288
   The ban on ex parte communications is applicable to the President and White House staff. They can, however, participate ex parte in **informal rulemaking** proceedings unless barred by statute.

(2) Agency employees   §293
   Ex parte communications relevant to the merits **by** agency employees to interested outsiders is also prohibited.

C. BASIS FOR DECISIONMAKING

1. Obligation of Decisionmaker   §294
   Under *Morgan I*, the decisionmaker **must be familiar with the record**.

   a. Delegation of decisionmaking   §295
      There may be no delegation of decisionmaking authority to lower level personnel unless a **statute** or the **agency regulations** so provide.

   b. Intermediate review boards   §296
      These review decisions of the hearing examiners and satisfy requirements of *Morgan I*.

   c. Failure to hear oral argument   §297
      If the decisionmaker **is** familiar with the record, the failure to hear oral argument does **not** require reversal.

   d. Unavailability of the examiner   §300
      If an ALJ becomes unavailable, a substitute may recommend a decision **unless** issues of credibility are involved.

2. Proving a Violation of *Morgan I*   §302
   It is difficult to prove a violation of *Morgan I* because *Morgan IV* holds that it is **improper to question the decisionmaker** as to the factors considered or how the decision was made. Thus, *Morgan IV* in effect undercuts *Morgan I* since questioning the decisionmaker may be the only way to find out whether the decisionmaker became familiar with the matter.

   a. Exception   §304
      A decisionmaker may be questioned if she has failed to make findings and conclusions or after a party makes a strong showing of bad faith or improper behavior, based on external facts.

3. Requirement of Intermediate Decision   §306
   Under certain circumstances, an ALJ must provide a proposed decision so that the parties can focus their arguments (*Morgan II*). However, the Court has since retreated from *Morgan II*, holding that no report of proposed findings is necessary where the parties are aware of the agency's complaint and are heard on the issues.

a.	**Application under state law**	**§308**

Under state law, failure to disclose an ALJ's report may violate due process; under federal law, the report must be made a part of the record.

D. BINDING EFFECT ON DECISIONMAKERS §309

Agency decisions may be limited by doctrines of res judicata, equitable estoppel, or stare decisis. Also, agencies must follow their own procedural rules where those rules were intended to give procedural benefits to outside parties.

1. Res Judicata §310

Where parties have had an *opportunity to litigate* an issue, the decision precludes further agency and court decisions; this rule also *precludes the government* from relitigating the same issue against the same party in another jurisdiction or by another agency.

a. Nonmutual collateral estoppel §313

A losing party is precluded from relitigating the same issues in another case against a different party. This does *not* apply against the United States.

2. Duty of Consistency §320

Agencies may change positions taken in prior cases, but must explain when and why they have done so.

3. Equitable Estoppel §321

Sometimes an agency furnishes informal advice to the public or issues formal guidance through guidelines or bulletins. When the agency wishes to change its decision and make it retroactive, it is unclear whether estoppel or apparent authority applies against the government.

a. State law §323

Many states permit estoppel of the government if the party receiving the advice can establish reasonable and detrimental reliance.

b. Federal law §325

Traditionally, the government is immune from estoppel and apparent authority unless a *statute prevents* a governmental change of mind. The Supreme Court decisions are equivocal: estoppel *cannot* be used to obtain a money judgment against the government; the government *can* be estopped if it is guilty of *affirmative misconduct* in immigration and criminal cases.

(1) Civil or criminal sanctions §328

Mistaken government advice may negate a mental state required for a criminal conviction. Similarly, a party acting in compliance with a reasonable interpretation of an agency regulation cannot be assessed civil penalties when the agency pronounces an unexpected interpretation.

VI. RULEMAKING PROCEDURES

A. INTRODUCTION

1. Types of Rules

 a. ***Legislative rules*** are made pursuant to legislative delegation of rulemaking power and, if properly adopted and consistent with the statutory delegation, are ***as binding as a statute***. §330

 b. ***Nonlegislative rules*** are rules that do ***not*** have binding legislative effect and include interpretive rules and policy statements. §331

2. Rulemaking Procedure §332
Procedural due process is inapplicable. However, under the APA, a process of notice and public comment is required for most legislative agency rules and is referred to as ***informal rulemaking***.

 a. Formal rulemaking §334
 Occasionally, statutes require a ***hearing on the record*** for adopting rules and adjudicatory procedures must be used.

 b. Hybrid rulemaking §335
 Hybrid rulemaking results from specific procedures for specific agencies mandated by Congress but not required by the APA informal rulemaking provisions, *e.g.*, cross-examination.

3. As Technique for Policymaking §336
Rulemaking has many advantages over adjudication for formulating law and policy: rules are prospective and evenly applied to all rather than applied on a case-by-case basis; the public, rather than only the parties to a case, has an opportunity to comment; rulemaking is subject to fewer restrictions; and publication of proposed and final rules makes them more accessible.

4. Retroactive Rules §338
Legislative rules are usually prospective while interpretive rules are often retroactive. Retroactive legislative rules are prohibited ***absent an express grant*** of congressional authority.

5. Broad Construction of Statutes §340
Because of the advantages of rulemaking, courts broadly interpret agency powers to make rules to authorize agencies ***to adopt binding legislative rules***.

B. CONTROLS ON RULEMAKING

1. Judicial Controls §342
Courts review rules to assure they are not ultra vires and that their adoption was procedurally correct.

2. Legislative Controls §343
Legislatures retain significant oversight and budgetary powers, although they can no longer veto rules.

3. Executive Controls §344

The executive branch often participates in the rulemaking process and, in many states, has veto power. Examples of executive controls include the requirement that agencies develop regulatory assessments, environmental impact statements, and analyses of a rule's effect on small businesses.

C. LEGAL EFFECT OF RULES §348

Generally, agencies must follow their own rules, that can usually only be changed prospectively.

1. Procedural Rules §349

An agency is bound by a procedural rule, even if it was not required to adopt it, until it is changed. The agency is *not* required to follow a regulation intended *primarily for the agency's convenience* rather than for the benefit of outsiders.

2. Legislative Rules §351

An agency is also bound by legislative rules until it changes them.

3. Nonlegislative Rules §352

It is not settled whether an agency can depart from its interpretive rules or policy statements whenever it wishes.

D. THE INFORMAL RULEMAKING PROCESS

1. Application of APA Rulemaking Provisions §353

These provisions are applicable only to matters defined by the APA as a *rule*, which is an agency statement of *general or particular applicability* and *future effect* regarding *law or policy*. ("Regulation" is synonymous with "rule.")

a. Single company affected §359

As long as a rule is *stated in general terms* and is not disguised adjudication, APA rulemaking procedures are applicable even though only a single company is affected.

2. Notice of Proposed Rulemaking §360

Prior to adoption of a rule, the agency must *publish in the Federal Register* notice that includes the *time, place, and nature* of the proceeding, the *legal authority* therefor, and the *terms or substance of the proposed rule*. Publication is *not* necessary if the persons subject to the rule are *personally served or have actual notice*.

3. Disclosure of Basic Data §361

The agency must also publish or make available critical data underlying the rule.

4. Public Participation §364

After notice, interested parties must be given an opportunity to participate through submission of written data, views, or arguments. Oral argument is usually not required but is usually allowed.

a. Timing §365

The public must be allowed a *reasonable time to comment* on a proposed rule.

5. Revisions to Rule—Logical Outgrowth   §369

A final rule may differ considerably from the initially published proposed rule, but new notice and procedures are not required if the final rule is a *logical outgrowth of the proposed rule*. Note, however, that the mere fact that the changes were noted in comments filed by the public does not mean that the final rule is a logical outgrowth of the proposed rule. (The Model State APA prohibits a *substantially different* final rule.)

6. Statement of Basis and Purpose   §372

The agency must make a statement of the basis and purpose of the rule, which statement must include the factors considered and responses to significant, material public comments.

7. Publication   §377

Both legislative and nonlegislative rules must be published in the Federal Register upon adoption.

8. Delayed Effective Date   §378

Absent an exception, final substantive, not procedural, rules must be published in the Federal Register not less than 30 days before the effective date.

9. Right to Petition   §380

Interested persons must be given the right to petition for the issuance, amendment, or repeal of a rule.

10. Judicial Remedies   §381

If a court finds that a rule was *invalidly adopted*, it has discretion to either vacate it, causing the agency to start over, or it may *remand* the rule, thus permitting the agency to remedy the problem and reissue the rule. An agency's refusal to *institute a rulemaking procedure* after a person petitions for one is judicially reviewable.

11. Additional Procedures   §384

Courts cannot impose additional procedures (*e.g.*, oral argument) on agencies (*Vermont Yankee* case).

12. Negotiated Rulemaking   §385

As a means of alternative dispute resolution, an agency head can propose a negotiated rulemaking, in which all affected interests meet with the agency to attempt to reach a consensus. The agreed-upon rule is then subject to the ordinary notice and comment procedures.

    a. Procedure   §388

A *notice must be published* in the Federal Register announcing the intent to use negotiated rulemaking and listing the proposed participants, agenda, timetable, etc. Additional persons can apply to participate, and the public has *30 days to file comments* on the proposed procedure.

    b. Judicial review   §390

Review of the procedure relating to establishing or terminating a negotiated rulemaking committee is *not* allowed, although the final rule may be reviewed.

E. **EXCEPTIONS TO INFORMAL RULEMAKING REQUIREMENTS** §392

The federal APA and Model State APA contain many exceptions to the notice and comment requirements.

1. **Categorical Exceptions** §393

The Act does not apply to *military or foreign affairs* functions of the United States, to matters relating to *agency management or personnel,* or to *public property, grants, loans, benefits, or contracts*.

2. **Procedure Exception** §394

Agency procedural rules are exempted from notice and comment requirements and from the delayed effective date provision, but *not* from the right to petition requirement.

3. **Good Cause Exception** §395

Notice and comment is excused when an agency, for good cause, finds that the procedure is *impracticable, unnecessary, or contrary to the public interest*. Federal agencies may also dispense with the 30-day pre-effective provision for good cause. This exception is *narrowly construed* by courts.

4. **Interpretive Rules** §400

The notice and comment and delayed effective date provisions do not apply. In distinguishing legislative rules (which require notice and hearing) from interpretive rules, different courts focus on different elements such as *agency intent*, whether the rule *actually interprets*, and whether a rule results in *new law*.

a. **Inconsistent interpretive rules** §405

An interpretative rule contrary to a prior interpretive rule is considered an amendment of the legislative rule the agency is interpreting and is thus invalid unless adopted with notice and comment.

5. **Policy Statements** §408

An agency statement concerning discretion is exempt as a policy statement if it is *tentative* although the Supreme Court has suggested an exception may exist for rules regarding discretionary functions. (The Model Act exceptions are more limited.)

F. **IMPARTIALITY OF RULEMAKERS** §412

Generally, the protections to ensure fair adjudication (no ex parte contacts, separation of functions, etc.) do *not* apply to rulemaking.

1. **Ex Parte Contacts** §413

The public is permitted to submit comments on the record regarding a proposed rule but ex parte contacts are not prohibited in a rulemaking situation. However, in a rulemaking proceeding that is more like an adjudication, ex parte contacts are improper.

2. **Legislative or Executive Interference** §419

As a general rule, legislative or executive attempts to influence rulemakers through ex parte communications are *not prohibited*.

3. **Bias** §420

Impartial adjudicator rules do not apply in rulemaking since rulemaking is intended to be a political process. Disqualification may be had after a showing of clear and convincing evidence that the rulemaker has an unalterably closed mind on critical matters.

4. Separation of Functions §421

Separation of adversary staff members from the decisionmaking function is *not* required.

G. THE RULEMAKING RECORD

1. General Rule §423

A reviewing court will consider *only material that was before the agency at the time it made the decision*.

2. Exceptions §424

The exclusive record requirement is inapplicable in a case involving a *lack of or inadequate administrative findings* (*Overton Park*). However, the correct procedure in such cases would be remand to the agency for an explanation. Some cases allow *new evidence* arising *after* close of the rulemaking record as a supplement to the record. Other cases permit *expert testimony* to assist the court to understand technical matters in the record.

3. State Law §429

The Model State APA and many states *reject* the record exclusivity principle.

VII. OBTAINING INFORMATION AND ATTORNEY'S FEES

A. AGENCY ACQUISITION OF INFORMATION

1. Methods of Obtaining Information §430

Information is usually disclosed voluntarily, but if it is not, the agency can compel disclosure by *subpoena, required reports, physical inspections,* and *hearings*.

2. Subpoena Power §431

If the agency's demand for information is resisted, the agency may seek judicial enforcement, which if ignored, may result in a finding of contempt.

a. Scope of power §432

Although the early cases limited the subpoena power, the modern view recognizes a much broader power.

(1) Limitation §436

The agency must be engaged in a *lawful inquiry,* must *state its purpose,* and must comply with the *Fourth Amendment "reasonableness" requirements* (the subpoena must be specific, the subject matter must be relevant, and the inquiry must be authorized).

b. Burdensomeness of subpoena §443

Generally, the fact that compliance with the subpoena will be expensive and burdensome is *not* a defense.

c. **Adjudicative subpoenas**   §444
Where subpoenas are issued as part of the agency's discovery process in the course of an **adjudication,** greater constraints are placed on the agency than in the case of subpoenas issued in the course of agency **investigations**. Where both an investigation and an adjudication occur simultaneously, the agency should comply with any discovery rules applicable to the adjudication.

3. **Physical Inspections**

    a. **Home inspections**   §447
    Warrants are generally required but are easily obtained.

    b. **Business inspections**   §450
    Generally, a warrant is required for inspection of a business, but there are exceptions involving "pervasively" regulated businesses (*e.g.,* gun and liquor dealer searches, mine inspections, and auto junkyards).

    c. **Physical tests**   §455
    Because of special risks to the public, federal regulations subjecting railway employees after an accident or customs employees to blood, breath, or urine tests without a warrant are permissible.

B. **CONSTITUTIONAL PROTECTION FROM AGENCY INFORMATION GATHERING**

1. **Introduction**   §458
Some constitutional safeguards available in a criminal prosecution are also applicable to administrative investigations.

2. **Privilege to Refuse to Furnish Information**   §459
Witnesses called to testify may assert the Fifth Amendment privilege against self-incrimination unless the agency has conferred immunity in exchange for the testimony.

    a. **Scope of privilege**   §462
    The privilege protects **natural persons** and includes private papers **if** compelled production would involve testimonial self-incrimination. However, it does **not** protect: persons not in **possession** of protected papers; records required to be kept (the extent of protection afforded to records necessary for tax preparation is unresolved); custodian of **corporate records** (**no** privilege); **production of a child** by custodial parent; or seizures under a search warrant.

    b. **Attorney-client privilege**   §472
    This privilege also applies.

3. **Rights to Procedural Due Process**   §473
Right to notice and a hearing is generally **unavailable** in **investigatory proceedings**.

4. **Right to Counsel**   §477
A witness required to appear before an investigatory hearing is entitled to the representation of counsel, but this right is **limited** (*i.e.,* no right to

cross-examination, no right to object to questions, and no right to a private hearing).

5. Use of Information from Unlawful Searches §482

Such information is admissible in a federal administrative proceeding despite its inadmissibility in a criminal trial. However, some cases have excluded such evidence if it was obtained in a manner constituting egregious violations of the Fourth Amendment or other liberties.

C. FREEDOM OF INFORMATION ACT

1. In General §483

The Freedom of Information Act is contained in APA section 552 and provides for the rights of *private parties* to obtain information in the possession of the government.

2. APA Provisions §484

Each agency must publish its *procedures* and general *rules* and *interpretations* and make available its opinions in cases. It must make available any other *identifiable records* on request.

a. Note §490

Federal district courts may compel production of any requested record that the agency refuses to produce.

3. Exceptions to the Act §497

The court may examine requested documents in camera to determine whether they fall into one of the following exceptions to the Act.

a. *National security* matters;

b. Matters relating to an *agency's internal practices;*

c. Matters *exempted by statute;*

d. *Commercial secrets;*

e. *Inter- or intra-agency memoranda* (documents "normally" privileged in civil litigation, such as predecisional memoranda);

f. Matters involving *personal privacy* (*e.g.,* personnel files);

g. *Investigatory files* compiled for *law enforcement purposes* (includes records compiled for other purposes but now used for law enforcement);

h. *Bank regulations;* and

i. *Natural resources* information.

D. GOVERNMENT IN THE SUNSHINE ACT §525

This Act requires agency meetings to be open to the public. Exceptions to the Act are basically the same as the exceptions to the Freedom of Information Act.

E. ATTORNEY'S FEES

1. General Rule §530

All parties bear their own attorney's fees.

2. No Agency Authorization §531
Absent clear statutory authorization, an agency has no authority to pay the attorney's fees or costs of private parties incurred in connection with agency adjudication or rulemaking even if those parties were helpful to the agency.

3. Specific Statutory Provisions §532
Statutes may provide for an award of attorney's fees to private parties (*e.g.,* civil rights laws and Freedom of Information Act).

4. General Authorization §536
The Equal Access to Justice Act allows a prevailing party to recover attorney's fees incurred in an adjudication unless the agency's position was "substantially justified" or "special circumstances makes an award unjust." There is a limit, however, on the amount of fees allowed.

5. Amount §541
Where a statute calls for the award of fees, the court sets the attorney's fees by multiplying the hours spent by a reasonable hourly rate. The result is called the "lodestar." The lodestar can be adjusted upward or downward in unusual cases, but may not be adjusted upward merely because the attorney was working on a contingency fee basis.

VIII. SCOPE OF JUDICIAL REVIEW

A. IN GENERAL §542
The extent of a reviewing court's power to set aside agency decisions depends on whether the challenged issue is one of basic fact, a question of law, application of law to facts, or a question of discretion.

B. SCOPE OF REVIEW OF QUESTIONS OF BASIC FACT

1. In General §543
The scope of review of agency findings of basic fact varies depending on the situation and jurisdiction. The prevailing test is a *substantial evidence* standard. Some statutes require agency decisions to be reversed if a finding of fact is *clearly erroneous*. A *preponderance of the evidence* standard is used in rare cases.

2. "Substantial Evidence" Test §550
State and federal courts will uphold the agency's decision where the evidence *reasonably supports* the agency's *conclusion*. Note that a *court cannot substitute its judgment* if an agency's findings of facts are reasonable.

 a. Note §553
 The court must look at the *"whole record"* to determine whether the agency's findings are supported by substantial evidence, meaning that the court considers both evidence supporting *and* evidence opposing the agency's findings.

 b. Disagreements between the agency and ALJ §556
 The court may consider such disagreements. Disagreements on credibility *detract* from the substantiality of the evidence supporting the

agency's findings (*Universal Camera* case). The agency **cannot totally ignore** the ALJ's findings and conclusions.

	c.	**Application of the test**	§560

Normally the Supreme Court will not review applications of the substantial evidence test by lower courts. However, it did review a decision in which the lower court purported to apply one standard but actually applied a different one.

3. Constitutional Facts §561

Under the *Ben Avon* rule, the court can exercise **independent judgment** when reviewing an agency finding of "constitutional facts."

a. **But note—rule restricted in application** §563

Such broad review (under *Ben Avon*) has now been restricted and the rule has little more than historical interest today.

4. Jurisdictional Facts §564

Broader scope of review also is invoked where the facts found by the agency were essential to its jurisdiction (*e.g.*, citizenship in a deportation case).

a. **Note** §567

The present status of the constitutional and jurisdictional fact doctrines is uncertain, although they have never been definitively overruled.

C. SCOPE OF REVIEW OF AGENCY'S LEGAL INTERPRETATIONS

1. Agency Decisions of Law §568

Agencies frequently make decisions of law (*e.g.*, interpretation of rules and statutes, scope of agency's power). **Traditionally,** a court could **substitute its own judgment** for the agency's legal interpretation after giving **weak deference** to the agency's view. Current developments, however, have weakened the federal court's power; the traditional view is still followed by a majority of states.

a. **Factors related to weak deference** §571

In considering how much deference to give to an agency interpretation, courts may consider the following factors:

(1) **Consistency** of agency interpretation with previous agency interpretations;

(2) **Contemporaneousness** with enactment of statute;

(3) **Thoroughness of consideration** by agency;

(4) **Reenactment of statute** after agency's interpretation of it;

(5) **Agency expertise** reflected in interpretation; and

(6) **Public participation** in process producing the interpretation.

2. Modern View—Strong Deference §579

If Congress expressly or implicitly delegated law-interpretive power to an agency, courts must follow *any reasonable agency interpretation* of an *ambiguous* statute (*Chevron* case).

a. **Chevron analysis**   §580

Chevron analysis calls for two steps:

(1) **Step 1:** If the court determines that the statute's meaning is unambiguous, that meaning is determinative. The court determines this question independently. Some judges consult legislative history in deciding the Step 1 issue, but others do not.

(2) **Step 2:** If the statute's meaning was ambiguous, the court must uphold any reasonable agency statutory interpretation.

b. **Unanswered questions**   §583

Unresolved issues after *Chevron* include: (i) whether every agency interpretation is entitled to *strong deference* (legislative rules and formal and informal adjudication interpretations are entitled to deference; interpretive rules and policy statements are not); (ii) whether *Chevron* applies to *constitutional issues*; and (iii) whether an agency can *reinterpret a statute* previously clarified by the Court (probably not).

3. **Strong Deference—Agency's Own Regulations**   §593

Even before *Chevron*, courts gave strong deference to an agency interpretation of its own legislative rules unless an alternative interpretation was compelled by the regulation's plain language or other indications of contrary agency intent.

D. SCOPE OF REVIEW OF APPLICATION OF LAW TO FACT

1. **Overview**   §594

An agency must make an *ultimate finding,* *i.e.,* a decision that the facts as found either do or do not satisfy a legal standard. There is *conflicting authority* as to the scope of the court's power to review the agency's determination of the ultimate question.

2. **Reasonableness Test**   §595

If resolution of the issue falls within the agency's *area of expertise* and it is apparent that the *legislature intended* the agency to resolve such issues, the court will usually follow any reasonable agency decision.

3. **Substitution of Judgment on Application Questions**   §599

In federal cases, *Chevron* is applied so that a court must defer to any reasonable agency determination of ultimate facts. Where *Chevron* does not apply (as in most state courts), a court may independently divide application questions, especially where the issue depends more on *statutory interpretation* than on a sifting of complex facts, and also where the agency appears to have *no particular expertise* on the matter.

E. SCOPE OF REVIEW OF AGENCY EXERCISES OF DISCRETION

1. **Overview**   §602

Decisions *committed* to discretion are *not reviewable*. (Other discretionary decisions are reviewable; however this exception rarely applies and is discussed below.)

2. APA Standard §603

If reviewable (*i.e.,* not "committed" to agency discretion), discretionary decisions shall be set aside if they are arbitrary, capricious, or an abuse of discretion.

3. Meaning of the Arbitrary-Capricious Test §605

Although a discretionary decision is entitled to a presumption of regularity, a reviewing court must make a substantial inquiry into the exercise of discretion by considering the following:

a. Was the action *within the area of discretion delegated* to the agency?

b. Did the agency *consider all of the relevant factors* and not rely on irrelevant factors?

c. Was the *decision unreasonable—a clear error of judgment?*

d. Were *all procedural requirements met?*

4. Review of Policy Determinations in Legislative Rules §610

Policy or discretionary decisions made in the adoption, modification, or revocation of legislative rules are reviewable under the arbitrary-capricious standard. There must exist a rational connection between the facts found and the choice made.

5. Review of Facts Underlying Rules §612

Today, courts usually *scrutinize the factual conclusions* underlying an agency's policy determinations in legislative rules. In other words, an agency must have a supportable factual basis for its rule (if such review is especially rigorous, it is called "hard look" review).

6. Record for Review §617

Generally, a reviewing court is limited to the findings and reasons stated by the agency at the time of the decision. If the findings and reasons are insufficient for review, the court usually remands to the agency for a sufficient statement (*supra*).

7. Limited Review of Administrative Remedy §618

The court has a *very narrow scope of review* as to the remedy granted by the agency; the court may *not* substitute its own judgment for that of the agency.

IX. REVIEWABILITY OF AGENCY DECISIONS—REMEDIES AND PRECLUSION

A. MEANS OF OBTAINING JUDICIAL REVIEW

1. Statutory Procedures §621

Most statutes that create agencies indicate the procedure for obtaining review of agency decisions.

2. **Nonstatutory Procedures** §623
    Where there is no statutory provision for review, *common law writs* may be used.

    a. *Injunctions and declaratory judgments* are used to declare the action illegal and to enjoin occurrence (if jurisdictional requirements are met). §624

    b. *Mandamus* is available to compel the agency to perform a ministerial duty owed to plaintiff. §630

    c. *Certiorari* is available to review quasi-judicial administration decisions in *state* courts. §633

    d. *Habeas corpus* is used to review restriction on individual freedom. §634

    e. *Other methods* include review by means of a tort claim against the government under the Federal Tort Claims Act or in the Court of Claims. §635

3. **Review During Enforcement Actions** §636
    Courts will also review administrative decisions when asked to enforce such decisions, and defendant has a *right to a jury trial* in judicial enforcement proceedings.

B. **SOVEREIGN IMMUNITY**

1. **In General** §640
    Judicial review of administrative actions may also be precluded by the doctrine of sovereign immunity—*i.e.*, unless the government has *consented* to be sued, the governmental action is not subject to judicial review by individual suit.

2. **Eleventh Amendment** §642
    The Eleventh Amendment bars federal jurisdiction over suits against a state by citizens of a different state and also has been extended to deprive federal courts of jurisdiction over actions by citizens against their own state where the damages would be *paid by the state*; suit is allowed if the action is for an *injunction against individual defendants* or *based on statute* implementing the *Fourteenth Amendment*.

3. **Federal Waiver of Sovereign Immunity** §651
    The federal government has waived its sovereign immunity where the relief sought is *other than money damages*.

    a. **Exception** §654
        Under the Federal Tort Claims Act, tort damages are allowed in certain cases. The federal government has also consented to suit in contracts cases.

4. **Proper Venue in Cases Against the Government** §655
    Liberalized venue provisions now allow actions against the government to be brought in any of several locations.

C. TORT LIABILITY OF GOVERNMENT

1. In General §656
An action in tort may provide an effective form of review if the government has waived its immunity or the activity involved was outside the area protected by sovereign immunity.

2. Liability of State Government §657
Traditionally, the state was not liable for the torts of its agents except where the agent was engaged in a *proprietary*, rather than a governmental function.

a. Modern trend §659
Today, immunity has been *abolished* by many states. Local government entities are liable if officials deny federal constitutional rights in accordance with local law or policy.

3. Liability of Federal Government—Federal Tort Claims Act

a. Negligent torts §661
Under the Tort Claims Act, the United States is liable for the negligent acts of government employees *acting within the scope of their employment*.

b. Strict liability torts §662
The Act has *not* been applied to strict liability torts.

c. Intentional torts §663
The Act *includes* certain intentional torts committed by federal investigative or law enforcement officers (*e.g.,* assault, false arrest), but *exempts* other intentional torts such as defamation.

d. "Discretionary" functions §666
The government is *immune* from damages caused by the exercise of a "discretionary" function. High-level policy decisions are discretionary; low-level decisions taken in the course of carrying out a regulatory program may not be discretionary if the action is not permissible under the statute or regulation.

e. No indemnity against government employees §669
Where the government is liable under the Act, it has no right of indemnity against the tortfeasor-employee.

4. Other Bases of Federal Liability §670
Where the Tort Claims Act is inapplicable, the government may still be liable for *"taking property"* without just compensation, and under *private bills* passed by Congress. Also, many federal agencies have *statutory power to settle small claims*.

D. TORT LIABILITY OF GOVERNMENT OFFICIALS

1. In General §673
Federal officials are *immune* from common law tort claims based on discretionary actions within the scope of their authority.

2. Immunities for Officials

    a. Absolute immunities   §675

       Certain officials are absolutely immune from damage liability, even though their conduct is tortious or unconstitutional. These include the **President, presidential aides** performing sensitive functions, and **judges, legislators, and prosecutors** while performing their duties.

    b. Absolute immunity for authorized acts   §685

       Federal employees are absolutely immune from personal damage liability based on negligent or wrongful conduct while **acting within the scope of employment**. Such claims must be brought against the government pursuant to **statutory authority** (*e.g.,* Federal Tort Claims Act, *supra*). However, immunity does **not** apply to suits based on constitutional violations.

    c. Qualified immunity   §688

       Excepting those who have absolute immunity, officials can be sued for conduct that **violates statutory or constitutional limits** on their authority—limits of which a **reasonable person** should have been aware.

3. Legal Basis for Damage Actions

    a. Federal officials   §693

       One who is **not** performing duties within the scope of authority can be sued in tort under state law. Federal officials are also liable for constitutional violations.

    b. State officials   §694

       State officials are liable under federal civil rights legislation for damages for **intentional deprivation of civil rights** under the Constitution.

      (1) Local governments have no immunity   §700

          Local government entities have no immunity from suit under the Civil Rights Act.

E. STATUTORY PRECLUSION OF JUDICIAL REVIEW

1. In General   §704

    The APA provides that agency decisions are reviewable except to the extent that statutes **preclude** judicial review.

2. Presumption of Reviewability   §705

    Case law holds that a decision is reviewable unless there is **persuasive reason** to believe that **Congress intended to preclude review**.

3. Decisions of the President   §706

    The President is not an agency under the APA and, therefore, his decisions are not reviewable for abuse of discretion.

4. Interpretation to Avoid Preclusion   §707

    Courts often interpret apparent preclusive statutes to afford at least limited review.

5. Absolute Preclusion of Review §713

Courts will honor a statute that absolutely precludes review although it is likely (though not settled) that Congress *cannot* preclude review of *constitutional claims* and *enforcement actions*.

6. Implied Preclusion §718

Courts have occasionally inferred a statutory preclusion of review where the implication was supported by *legislative history* or where time was of the essence.

F. COMMITMENT TO AGENCY DISCRETION

1. In General §721

Under a narrow exception, discretionary acts of an agency are not reviewable if "committed to agency discretion" by law.

2. No Law to Apply §722

Action is committed to agency discretion in the rare instance where there is no law to apply; *i.e.,* statute has provided no judicially manageable standards to detect abuse. These standards can derive from legislative regulations as well as by statutes.

3. What Is "Committed to Agency Discretion"? §724

The following are exempt from review because they are entirely within an agency's discretion:

a. *Prosecution and enforcement decisions;*

b. *Intelligence officer discharge;*

c. *Admission of aliens;*

d. *Agency's refusal to reconsider its decision;*

e. *Determination of credit worthiness of applicant for rural home loan;* and

f. *Agency's decision on how to spend an unallocated Congressional appropriation.*

X. STANDING TO SEEK JUDICIAL REVIEW AND THE TIMING OF JUDICIAL REVIEW

A. STANDING TO SEEK JUDICIAL REVIEW

1. Introduction §731

To seek judicial review, a person must have standing. In federal courts, standing involves both constitutional and prudential limitations. A court must first determine constitutional standing issues before reaching the merits.

2. Constitutional Limitations §733

The "case or controversy" requirement means that a plaintiff must have a *personal stake in the outcome* of the case in order to have standing. Under modern rules, a plaintiff must (i) suffer an *injury in fact*; (ii) prove *causation*; and (iii) show that the injury will be *remedied* if she succeeds.

a. **Injury in fact**

   (1) **Background** §734

The injury in fact rule represents a liberalization of the previous *"legal rights"* test that required a common law cause of action against the government for standing. Later this rule was undermined by the concept of *"statutory standing,"* under which Congress had the power to expand the class of persons with standing to challenge agency actions. Modern cases have further expanded the class to include private attorneys general asserting public rights.

   (2) **Modern requirements** §739

Modern case law has reformulated the concepts derived from the "legal wrong" and "statutory standing" cases so that injury in fact requires a *concrete* (rather than abstract) and *particularized* (rather than generalized) injury. An injury can be *economic* (*e.g.*, competitive or consumer injury), or *noneconomic* (*e.g.*, aesthetic, environmental, or deprivation of information by an agency).

b. **Causation and remediability** §744

In addition, the injury must be *fairly traceable to the administrative action,* and *likely to be remedied by a judicial decision* in the plaintiff's favor.

3. **Prudential Limitations** §745

In addition to the above constitutional requirements, the Supreme Court has imposed prudential limitations on standing that can be eliminated by Congressional statute.

a. **"Zone of interest"** §746

A plaintiff seeking standing under the APA must show that she arguably falls within the "zone of interests" intended to be protected or regulated by the applicable statute. This is a prudential rule, not a constitutional rule.

b. **Jus tertii** §750

A person cannot sue to redress an injury to another; the injured party must bring the suit herself. This limit on third-party standing is called *jus tertii,* and it is a prudential, rather than constitutional, rule. Exceptions to the rule exist for persons if the third party would have difficulty asserting her rights and the *plaintiff himself has suffered an injury* that *adversely affects his relationship* with the third party.

c. **Associational standing** §752

Associations may sue for injuries to their members if (i) one or more members would have standing in their own right; (ii) the asserted interests are germane to the association's purposes; and (iii) neither the claim nor requested relief requires participation of individual members in the case.

4.   Role of APA   §754

The APA confers standing under both the legal rights and statutory stand-ing approaches of prior law. In practice, a person must satisfy the constitu-tional requirements of injury in fact, causation, and remediability and also the prudential "zone of interests" requirement.

5.   Specificity   §755

The plaintiff bears the burden of proof on each element of standing. If standing is attacked by a summary judgment motion, the plaintiff must make specific allegations as to the injury in fact and to the other standing requirements and support them through affidavits.

6.   Standing in Particular Circumstances

   a.   Standing as a citizen or a taxpayer

      (1)   State law   §756

Under state law, *taxpayers* have standing to seek review of state expenditures.

      (2)   Federal law   §757

In federal court, status as a *citizen* is *insufficient* for standing; a *taxpayer* has standing only to challenge a federal spending statute that violates the *Establishment Clause* of the First Amend-ment but apparently in no other cases.

   b.   Legislative standing   §762

Congressional members lack standing to challenge the constitutional-ity of legislation that diminishes their power vis-a-vis the President because the injury is neither personal to them or sufficiently con-crete. Note also that Congress *cannot grant statutory standing* to persons lacking a concrete injury in fact.

B.   THE TIMING OF JUDICIAL REVIEW

1.   In General   §764

To be reviewed, an action must be *final*, the case must be *ripe*, and the plaintiff must have *exhausted administrative remedies i.e.,* matter con-cluded at agency level.

2.   Final Order Rule   §765

A court will usually review only final orders.

   a.   Exceptions   §769

Courts will review agency actions before a final determination when *irreparable injury* will occur or when the agency *unreasonably delays* making a decision.

3.   Ripeness   §776

Agency action is not reviewable unless it is ripe. This doctrine is designed to prevent litigation prior to actual application of the administrative policy to plaintiff.

a. **Test for ripeness** §779
Courts must balance *"fitness of the issues"* for immediate review against *"hardship to the parties"* if review is withheld.

b. **Review of informal administrative action** §783
Although the early cases suggested that informal action or advisory opinions would never be ripe for review, the present trend states that *degree of formality* is only one factor to be considered, along with fitness of issues and possibility of hardship from delay in determining ripeness.

c. **Statutory time limits for review** §787
Generally, statutory time limits for seeking review of an agency decision are strictly interpreted. Review beyond the limit may be had if a party can clearly show that the rule would have been held unripe. Note that Congress can *preclude pre-enforcement review* by statute.

4. **Exhaustion of Administrative Remedies** §790
Generally, judicial review is not available until all administrative remedies have been exhausted. This rule is designed to protect agency autonomy and to promote judicial efficiency.

a. **Effect of rule—review may be precluded** §791
Normally, the rule *delays* judicial review, but where a plaintiff fails to exercise the right of appeal within the agency or fails to raise the issue in dispute before the agency, review may be totally *precluded*.

b. **Exhaustion under the APA** §792
An important exception to the exhaustion of remedies doctrine is provided by the APA: agency action is reviewable without appeal to a higher agency authority *unless* an agency rule provides otherwise.

c. **Exceptions to exhaustion rule** §796
The rule is usually a matter of judicial discretion absent a statutory directive that remedies *must* be exhausted. Exhaustion may be excused when:

(1) Plaintiff's injury is *severe and irreparable;*

(2) Administrative appeal would be *futile;*

(3) Administrative *remedies are inadequate;*

(4) Agency procedure is **unauthorized or unconstitutional;**

(5) *Constitutionality* of statutory requirements is *questioned;* or

(6) The case is a *civil rights action* based on constitutional grounds.

d. **State law** §806
State courts have been even less rigorous than the federal courts in applying the exhaustion rule.

5. **Primary Jurisdiction** §807
When both an agency and a court have jurisdiction to hear a case, the doctrine of primary jurisdiction requires that a plaintiff first seek relief

through the agency. The agency's decision is then subject to judicial review. This doctrine is to prevent inconsistent results from different courts deciding similar issues and to utilize agency expertise.

a. Factors militating against primary agency jurisdiction §809
The doctrine is usually **not** applied when the judicial forum is more appropriate:

(1) Where the issue presents a **question of law;**

(2) Where the issue seems **traditionally judicial or nontechnical;** or

(3) Where the plaintiff is **unable to use the administrative process** or cannot secure the desired remedy from the agency.

b. Judicial disposition of matters subject to primary jurisdiction §812
Where primary agency jurisdiction is found, the court still retains the matter on its docket **if the agency cannot resolve all issues**; otherwise the court will dismiss the case.

c. Specific applications §814
Primary jurisdiction has had particular impact on **antitrust regulation** where the agency may have become protective of the regulated industry, and on **labor practice regulation** where the NLRB has exclusive jurisdiction.

6. Stays Pending Judicial Review §821
Once a court has determined that an administrative decision is reviewable, it may grant a stay to postpone agency action pending outcome of the review.

a. APA provisions §822
The APA recognizes the court's power to grant a stay pending judicial review.

b. Factors considered in granting stay §823
The court considers:

(1) **Likelihood of plaintiff's prevailing** on the merits;

(2) **Irreparable injury** to plaintiff if no stay granted;

(3) **Effect of stay on the other parties;** and

(4) **Effect of stay on the public interest.**

Approach to Exams

A. GENERAL CONSIDERATIONS

1. Nature of Administrative Law

Administrative law is basically *procedural* law. Each administrative agency is responsible for a particular body of substantive law (*e.g.*, the National Labor Relations Board administers federal labor statutes), but certain procedural principles apply to all agencies.

2. Function of Agencies

Administrative agencies are entities formed by the legislature to implement desired changes in policy. The legislature creates an agency if it determines that certain functions—investigation, law enforcement, rulemaking, or adjudication—are best performed by a separate body. The impact of such rulemaking and adjudication on the general public is vast, far exceeding the impact of the judicial process.

3. Organization of Summary

This Summary, like leading casebooks and treatises, deals with the following matters:

a. The *position of the agency* in government, including the *legislative* and *executive* controls over the agency.

b. The *administrative process—i.e.*, the complexities of government activity that include the formulation of rules (other than by the legislature) and the investigation and adjudication of cases (other than by the courts). The statutory and constitutional requirements for *rulemaking* and for *adjudication* are discussed.

c. *Judicial review* of agency decisions.

4. Statutes and Due Process

In analyzing a particular administrative law problem (or exam question), you must always consider:

a. **The statute creating the particular agency**

That statute sets forth the *law* the agency is expected to implement and often contains the *procedural requirements* for the agency to follow in its investigation, rulemaking, and adjudication. Often the statute will contain specific provisions about how to seek judicial review.

b. **Agency regulations**

In many cases, the agency promulgates regulations that provide procedures that may go beyond what the statute or the Constitution would require. Your client is entitled to the benefit of the protections set forth in the regulations.

c. Administrative Procedure Act

In addition to analyzing the agency's own statute and regulations, it is always necessary to apply the federal or state Administrative Procedure Act ("APA") to the agency function in question. The APA's provisions for rulemaking and adjudication usually provide the applicable ground rules.

d. Constitution

Finally, constitutional due process requirements often provide greater protection than any applicable statute or regulation; thus, constitutional law should always be considered.

5. Judicial Review

Administrative law questions usually focus on whether a court will judicially review a particular agency action and, if so, what the court will decide. Almost all agency action is reviewable (it is seldom precluded by statute or by commitment to agency discretion), but there are severe limitations: The plaintiff must have *standing* and seek review *at the appropriate time.* In addition, the court's power to substitute its judgment for that of the agency is usually quite limited.

B. APPROACH

Administrative law exam questions generally focus on the legality and procedural validity of agency action and on various doctrines that limit the judicial review that courts will provide. For a general approach to exam questions, consider the following; for more detailed approaches, review the chapter approaches found at the beginning of each chapter as well as the exam tips and charts found throughout each chapter.

1. Delegation of Authority

Many exam questions focus on the delegation of legislative or judicial authority to an agency. While it is *unlikely that a delegation will be struck down* by a modern court, the *issue must still be addressed.* Recall that even if the delegation is valid, the agency's action may be beyond its delegated powers (*ultra vires*). Also, there are numerous executive and legislative controls over agency action that frequently come into play in administrative law exams.

2. Procedural Validity

Many issues relating to agency procedure ask whether a *hearing is required* by due process, the agency statute, the APA, or agency regulations.

a. If a hearing is required, *consider what type of hearing*—trial-type or legislative—must be provided. Also, *when* must it be provided?

b.   Note that it is critical to observe the *distinction between rulemaking and adjudication* since the entire subject is based on that distinction. Wholly different procedures are required for the two modes of agency action.

c.   In many cases, an agency can *choose* one mode of action over the other. A series of issues arise when the agency so chooses—*e.g.*, can rulemaking resolve a broad issue so that no future adjudications are needed? Can an agency choose to make policy through adjudication rather than rulemaking even though adjudication has a retroactive effect?

d.   Remember that a series of doctrines *constrain agency choices in adjudication*: equitable estoppel, res judicata, the duty of consistency, and the duty to follow procedural regulations.

e.   A series of doctrines help to assure the *impartiality of agency decisionmakers* both at the trial level (usually trials are conducted by administrative law judges ("ALJs")) and at the agency head level. Pay attention to facts showing bias, ex parte contact, separation of functions, command influence, and *Morgan I*. In addition, watch for rules relating to evidence (including the residuum rule) and official notice and rules requiring explanation and findings.

3.   Judicial Review

Analyze a judicial review question as follows:

a.   *Is the action reviewable?* Consider the doctrines of *preclusion of review* and *commitment to agency discretion.* If the plaintiff seeks a tort-type recovery, you must consider the obstacles to recovery of damages both from individual wrongdoers and from government.

b.   *What is the scope of review?* Here you must decide what type of *issue* is under challenge (basic facts, law, application of law to facts, discretion, procedure) and then apply the applicable rules concerning scope of review. In most cases, a court must *uphold a reasonable decision* by the agency even though the court might prefer a different outcome.

c.   *Is plaintiff limited by the doctrines of standing or timing?* For standing, check both the constitutional and prudential limits; as for timing, look for facts indicating applicability of the final order rule, ripeness, exhaustion of remedies, and primary jurisdiction doctrines.

Chapter One: Separation of Powers and Controls Over Agencies

CONTENTS

Chapter Approach

A.   Separation of Powers   §1

B.   Delegation of Legislative Power   §4

C.   Delegation of Adjudicative Power   §34

D.   Other Legislative Controls Over Administrative Action   §54

E.   Executive Controls Over Administrative Action   §63

Chapter

This chapter discusses l...
The most important issu...
validly delegated legislat...
ers doctrine. To answer...

1. If an agency *rule* is...
    legislative power. W...
    issue must still be...
    trine seriously. Fac...

    a. Does the stat...
        tion? If so, th...

    b. Are there *saf*...
        ticipate and j...
        will be uphel...

    c. Does the sta...
        vate parties?

    d. If the rule is...
        it *beyond th*... ...
        stitutional issues, courts may construe the delegated power narrowly so as to
        invalidate the rule on ultra vires rather than constitutional grounds.

    c. Gives the *legislature a role in remov*...
        implementing the law.

    4. Finally, keep in mind that even if...
        powers, there are numerous oth...
        that may effectively check *ille*...

    [§§1-4]

A. Separa...

1. **In Genera**
    The U...
    the...

2. If an agency *adjudicatory order* is challenged, consider whether the statute *invalidly delegates judicial power* to the agency. In general, a statute can delegate adjudicatory power that is necessary to implement a particular statutory scheme—even the power to assess civil penalties without a jury trial. However, if a statute delegates the power to decide questions of *private* rather than public right, it is of questionable validity since questions of private rights under common law (*e.g.,* breach of contract) are usually decided by courts. Also watch for issues of *vagueness of standards*, particularly in cases with constitutional overtones.

3. Also consider whether the statute *violates other provisions relating to the separation of powers doctrine or the checks and balances system.* A statute might be invalid if it:

    a. Calls for *legislative appointment* of the persons who will engage in *rulemaking or adjudication*.

    b. Contains a *legislative veto* whereby the legislature can adopt laws without giving the executive a chance to veto them.

of the persons who will engage in

agency action does not violate separation of
...er legislative and executive controls over agencies
...gal, *mistaken, or impolitic agency action.*

...ation of Powers

... [§1]
...ited States Constitution and state constitutions separate government into
...legislative, executive, and judicial branches. Administrative agencies are units
...f government created by statute to carry out specific tasks in implementing the
statute. Usually, the agencies fall within the executive branch of government; however, some important agencies are independent of the executive branch. (*See infra,*
§75, for discussion of the constitutionality of independent agencies.)

2. Judicial Enforcement of Separation of Powers [§2]
The courts are often called upon to decide whether particular statutes involving
administrative agencies violate the constitutional doctrine mandating separation of
powers. For purposes of an administrative law course, the most important separation of powers doctrine prohibits the legislature from delegating legislative powers
to agencies—but this doctrine is virtually never enforced by the federal courts. (*See
infra,* §§4 et seq.)

3. Checks and Balances [§3]
The Constitution contains numerous checks and balances so that each branch has
the means to defend itself and control the other branches (*e.g.,* the executive
branch can block legislation by vetoing it). The courts also protect the checks and
balances system. For example, a statute that invalidly attempts to permit legislation without giving the President the power to veto it (a "legislative veto") will
most likely be struck down by the courts. (*See infra,* §§60-61.)

B. Delegation of Legislative Power

1. Introduction [§4]
In theory, a legislature *cannot delegate* its *legislative* power. In practice, legislatures do so constantly by enacting statutes that confer broad rulemaking powers
on administrative agencies. The doctrine has two related parts: (i) in delegating
power to agencies, the legislature must at least make the fundamental policy
choices, leaving to the agency only the detailed implementation of the statute (the

"delegation doctrine"); and (ii) a particular agency action is invalid if it falls outside the scope of the delegated power (the *"ultra vires" doctrine*).

2. Limits on Delegation of Legislative Power [§5]

Despite the implications of two cases decided in the 1930s (*see infra,* §§11-12), the courts allow Congress to delegate extremely broad rulemaking powers to federal agencies. However, state agencies tend to apply the delegation doctrine more strictly (*see infra,* §20), and both federal and state courts are suspicious of statutes that delegate to private parties the power to regulate other private parties (*see infra,* §27). To understand the modern cases on delegation, it is helpful to chart the historical development of the doctrine.

a. Early cases—formulas to legitimate delegation [§6]

From the earliest times, Congress delegated to agencies the power to make law by adopting regulations. The Supreme Court upheld such delegations by employing various formulas of judicial review which allowed the agencies to exercise more and more power.

(1) "Ascertainment of facts" [§7]

An agency could exercise legislative power if such power was limited to ascertaining whether a "fact" had occurred.

> **e.g. Example:** Congress gave the President power to raise tariff schedules if a foreign country imposed a duty on American products which the President considered "reciprocally unequal and unreasonable." The Court upheld this delegation of power on the theory that the President was not exercising any lawmaking function, but was simply authorized to *ascertain a "fact"* (*i.e.,* the existence of unreasonable foreign duties) that would suspend a congressional statute allowing free imports. [**Field v. Clark,** 143 U.S. 649 (1892)] *Note:* Obviously, the President's decisions would turn on international economic and political issues and would be based on judgment rather than mere ascertainment of "fact."

(2) "Filling in details" [§8]

Under another formula, a delegation of legislative power to make rules to implement a vague statute was upheld on grounds that the agency was merely "filling in the details."

> **e.g. Example:** Congress gave the Secretary of Agriculture the power to make rules and regulations protecting the national forests. The Court held that no legislative power had been delegated—only the power to *fill in details.* [**United States v. Grimaud,** 220 U.S. 506 (1911)]

(3) Fixing a principle or a standard [§9]

Modern cases typically uphold legislative delegations by finding that Congress has set an "intelligible principle" or a "primary standard" for the agency to follow. When Congress establishes such a principle or standard, at least it has made the fundamental policy decisions that the agency only needs to implement. [**J.W. Hampton & Co. v. United States,** 276 U.S. 394 (1928)—President has power to impose tariffs to "equalize" differences in production costs] In fact, however, the principle or standard usually furnishes very little actual guidance to the agency.

---

e.g. **Example—lower court approach:** A statute instructs the Environmental Protection Agency ("EPA") to adopt ambient air quality standards "which in the judgment of the Administrator . . . and allowing an adequate margin of safety, are requisite to protect the public health." The EPA set a strict standard for emissions of particulate matter from diesel engines. This statute obviously gives the EPA little guidance on where to set the standard; it does not indicate how much pollution is too much. The lower court held that the statute violated the nondelegation doctrine, but it would have allowed the EPA to provide the missing intelligible principle itself. [**American Trucking Associations v. EPA,** 175 F.3d 1027 (D.C. Cir. 1999)]

---

cf. **Compare—Supreme Court holding:** The Supreme Court rejected this approach, stating that if a statute violated the nondelegation doctrine, the problem could not be repaired by having the agency adopt a narrowing standard. The Court also held that the statute *did* provide a sufficiently intelligible principle. That principle arose from the word "requisite," meaning not higher or lower than necessary to protect the public health with an adequate margin of safety, without considering any other factors (such as the cost of the regulations). As a result, the statute did not unlawfully delegate legislative power to the EPA. [**Whitman v. American Trucking Associations,** 531 U.S. 457 (2001)]

(a) Rationale

The court stated: "[Congress] must provide substantial guidance on setting air standards that affect the entire national economy. But even in sweeping regulatory schemes we have never demanded, as the court of appeals did here, that statutes provide a 'determinate criterion' for saying 'how much of the regulated harm is too much.' . . . It is therefore not conclusive for delegation purposes that . . . [particulates] inflict a continuum of adverse health effects at any airborne concentration greater than zero, and hence require the EPA to make judgments of degree. 'A certain degree of discretion, and thus of lawmaking, inheres in most executive or judicial action.' "

b. **The NIRA cases**

(1) **Background [§10]**

In early cases, the Supreme Court legitimated every congressional delegation of legislative power to an agency. However, in the 1930s, the Court twice invalidated such delegations.

(a) **Comment**

This retreat arose as a result of the far-reaching New Deal statutes passed by Congress to counter the effects of the Depression. In particular, the National Industrial Recovery Act ("NIRA"), passed in 1933, gave unusually broad powers to the President. The Supreme Court was extremely hostile to this sort of aggressive interference with the free market and with state regulation.

(2) **The "hot oil" case [§11]**

The first of these cases involved an NIRA provision that allowed the President to ban the shipment in interstate commerce of oil produced in violation of state regulations ("hot oil"). The Supreme Court held that this power was an *unconstitutional delegation* on the ground that there were *no standards* in the Act to guide the President's exercise of discretion. Although there were various declarations of policy in section 1 of the Act, the Court found them unduly vague and conflicting. [**Panama Refining Co. v. Ryan,** 293 U.S. 388 (1935)]

(a) **Dissenting argument**

Justice Cardozo dissented, pointing out that the President's delegated power (to ban the shipment of hot oil) was clearly defined—his only discretion being whether to do so. Cardozo argued that section 1 of the Act provided ample guidance since it stated that the purposes of the Act were to conserve natural resources, prevent unfair competitive practices, and utilize the productive capacity of industry. Since Congress could not, at a given moment, predict whether these purposes would be served by banning the shipment of hot oil, it had left this decision to the President.

(3) **The *Schechter Poultry* case [§12]**

The second case concerned an NIRA delegation that gave the President power to adopt codes of fair competition in cooperation with members of an industry. These codes were to set forth schedules of wages and prices, and other rules that would be binding upon entire industries. This delegation was vastly broader than the narrow provision in the *Panama Refining* case and was also held invalid. [**Schechter Poultry Corp. v. United States,** 295 U.S. 495 (1935)]

(a) Rationale

Again, the Supreme Court found an absence of standards to guide the President in deciding what regulations to impose upon the various industries. The Court was also heavily influenced by the lack of hearings or other procedures (even publication) in adopting the codes, and was concerned by the role of private industry in regulating itself—*i.e.,* that large companies might succeed in having rules adopted that would harm their competitors.

c. Post-NIRA cases [§13]

All subsequent Supreme Court cases involving the delegation issue have uniformly *upheld* broad delegations of rulemaking power to agencies—even those with vague (or sometimes no) standards. (However, no delegations of power since the 1930s have been as broad as those under the NIRA.)

(1) Public interest [§14]

Thus, the Court has upheld delegations based on meaningless standards such as the power to act "as public convenience, interest or necessity requires." [**Federal Radio Commission v. Nelson Brothers,** 289 U.S. 266 (1933)]

(2) Fair prices [§15]

During World War II, Congress authorized the Price Administrator to fix maximum prices, which "in his judgment shall be generally fair and equitable and will effectuate the purposes of this Act," namely to prevent wartime inflation and prevent profiteering. The Court upheld the delegation, since Congress obviously could not set prices itself. "Congress is not confined to that method of executing its policy which involves the least possible delegation of discretion . . . Only if we could say that there is an absence of standards for the guidance of the Administrator's action, so that it would be impossible in a proper proceeding to ascertain whether the will of Congress has been obeyed, would we be justified in overriding its choice of means . . . ." [**Yakus v. United States,** 321 U.S. 414 (1944)]

(3) No standards [§16]

Indeed, delegations have been upheld even though Congress provided *no* standards at all.

---

e.g. **Example:** The Court sustained a delegation to the Secretary of the Interior to apportion Colorado River water in times of shortage, even though there were no standards as to how this was to be done. (Three dissenters questioned the constitutionality of such a delegation.) [**Arizona v. California,** 373 U.S. 546 (1963)]

---

e.g. Example: The Court also upheld a statute that provided that a government agency could recover "excess profits" from defense contractors, but contained no definition of excess profits. The Supreme Court approved the delegation, noting that "a constitutional power implies a power of delegation of authority under it *sufficient to effect its purpose.*" [**Lichter v. United States,** 334 U.S. 742 (1948)] (This of course implies that *any* delegation is valid as long as the underlying statute is constitutionally valid.)

EXAM TIP	gilbert

Remember that even though the Court has **upheld broad delegations** of legislative power to agencies, the courts often give **lip service** to the delegation doctrine and usually look for some standards. Thus you should do so as well when you analyze an exam question that raises the issue of delegation.

---

(4) Economic stabilization [§17]

In the 1970s, Congress again enacted several vague statutes giving the President broad economic powers, again in response to inflation. Although the *Schechter* and *Panama* cases posed potential problems for these statutes, the post-1930s cases (upholding broad delegations), especially **Yakus v. United States,** *supra,* suggested that Congress essentially had a free hand.

(a) The *Meat Cutters* case [§18]

Although the Supreme Court did not consider the anti-inflation statutes, an important lower court decision upheld the Economic Stabilization Act of 1970. This Act authorized the President to stabilize wages and prices at levels not lower than those on May 15, 1970, with such adjustments as might be necessary to prevent "gross inequities." [**Amalgamated Meat Cutters v. Connally,** 337 F. Supp. 737 (D.D.C. 1971) (three-judge court)]

1) The court held that the statute—under which the President had imposed a wage-price freeze—*sufficiently "marked out" the field* in which the President was to act by setting a base date and providing for adjustment of inequities. Legislative history and previous wage-price control statutes were held to indicate the congressional intent.

2) The court also found it relevant that Congress had provided a relatively *short life span* for executive authority (so that frequently Congress would have to reexamine the President's actions) and that judicial review was available.

3) Significantly, the court in *Meat Cutters* warned the agency to set some *administrative standards* by promulgating regulations. It implied that if the agency failed to narrow the statute by enacting regulations, the whole scheme might later be held unconstitutional.

d. Status of delegation doctrine today [§19]

Although the delegation doctrine appears to be a dormant issue, there is some support on the Supreme Court for reviving it. Some concurring and dissenting opinions call for Congress to make the difficult and fundamental policy choices, rather than passing them on to the agencies. If these views become the majority on the Supreme Court, it is quite possible that the delegation doctrine will be revived. [*See, e.g.,* **Whitman v. American Trucking Associations**, *supra,* §9—Thomas dissent would reject the "intelligible principle" rule; **Mistretta v. United States**, 488 U.S. 361 (1989)—Scalia dissent held delegation of rulemaking power without other responsibilities is invalid; **Industrial Union Department v. American Petroleum Institute**, 448 U.S. 607 (1980)—Rehnquist concurrence; **American Textile Manufacturers Institute v. Donovan**, 452 U.S. 490 (1981)—Rehnquist and Burger dissent]

(1) State law [§20]

While the delegation doctrine has been largely dormant on the federal level, many states take the doctrine more seriously and invalidate under state constitutions statutes containing excessive and unnecessarily broad delegations. [*See* **Thygesen v. Callahan**, 385 N.E.2d 699 (Ill. 1979)—statute must identify persons and activities to be regulated, harm sought to be prevented, and means available to agency to prevent the harm]

e. Substitutes for delegation doctrine

(1) Duty to adopt regulations [§21]

Some decisions indicate that agencies exercising adjudicatory powers must first limit the scope of a broad delegated power by adopting their own standards, either by rulemaking or case-by-case adjudication. [*See* **Morton v. Ruiz**, 415 U.S. 199 (1974); **White v. Roughton**, 530 F.2d 750 (7th Cir. 1976); **Holmes v. New York City Housing Authority**, 398 F.2d 262 (2d Cir. 1968)] *Note:* These cases all involve benefit programs (some rely on due process, while others rely on interpretation of the statute); this principle has not often been applied outside of the welfare context.

(a) State law [§22]

Some states have been far more aggressive than the federal courts in requiring agencies to adopt regulations to limit their discretion. [**Megdal v. Oregon State Board of Dental Examiners**, 605 P.2d 273 (Or. 1980)—agency must adopt rules defining "unprofessional conduct"; *and see infra,* §192]

(b) Model Act [§23]

The 1981 Model State Administrative Procedure Act contains explicit requirements that agencies adopt rules, as soon as feasible and to the extent practicable, embodying appropriate standards, principles, and procedural safeguards that the agency will apply to the law it administers. [Model State Administrative Procedure Act of 1981 ("1981 Model State APA") §2-104(3)]

(2) Narrow construction of statute [§24]

Some decisions construe a statute narrowly so as to invalidate particular rules. This approach can avoid the problems of excessive delegation. It can also help the Court to avoid declaring the rule unconstitutional where the rule might violate other constitutional provisions such as the First Amendment. (*See infra,* §§30-33.) This technique requires Congress to take another look at the problem and clarify that it really intended the agency to have the power in question.

f. Delegation to the President—the Line Item Veto Act [§25]

The Line Item Veto Act gave the President power to veto a single appropriation out of a large appropriation bill without having to veto the entire bill. Similarly, the President could veto a single tax benefit without vetoing the entire tax bill. The Supreme Court struck down the Line Item Veto Act because it allowed the President to amend a law without going through the legislative process. It refused to find an analogy to the case law upholding delegation of rulemaking power, since the rulemaking delegation cases do not allow the President to actually change the text of laws enacted by Congress. Rulemaking delegations are intended to carry out a congressional purpose, but the Line Item Veto Act allows the President to act contrary to congressional purpose. [**Clinton v. City of New York,** 524 U.S. 417 (1998)]

g. Delegation to federal judges [§26]

Congress may delegate rulemaking powers to federal judges where the issue has an appropriate relationship to the judicial function and the delegation entails no danger of undermining the integrity of the judicial branch or expanding its powers beyond constitutional bounds. [**Mistretta v. United States,** *supra,* §19—upholding constitutionality of sentencing guidelines promulgated by commission that includes federal judges as members]

h. Delegation to private parties [§27]

Where a legislature delegates rulemaking powers to private parties, those parties may use the powers to gain a private advantage over their competitors.

(1) State cases [§28]

Numerous cases at the state level invalidate such delegations. [**Allen v. Board of Barber Examiners,** 25 Cal. App. 3d 1014 (1972)—delegation to board controlled by barbers to set minimum prices for haircutting invalid]

(2) Federal cases [§29]

At the federal level, one case in the 1930s invalidated a delegation of power to coal companies and unions to make contracts that would bind other coal companies. [**Carter v. Carter Coal Co.,** 298 U.S. 238 (1936)] Since that time, however, the federal courts have *upheld* such delegations, but in each case there were some *safeguards* against private abuse of power. [*See* **United States v. Rock Royal Cooperative,** 307 U.S. 533 (1939)—private companies could veto rules but not initiate them; **Todd & Co. v. SEC,** 557 F.2d 1008 (3d Cir. 1977)—trade association could make rules but SEC could review and veto them]

3. Actions Outside the Scope of Delegated Power [§30]

Even if a broad delegation of rulemaking authority is valid under the delegation doctrine, courts have the power to *set aside particular rules* under the "ultra vires" doctrine—*i.e.,* the court finds that the agency has adopted a rule outside the scope of its delegated power. To fix the boundaries of delegated power, the court must construe the statute to ascertain how much power the legislature intended to delegate. (*See infra,* §§568-592, for a discussion of the scope of judicial review of agency interpretations of statutes.)

a. Judicial technique [§31]

In many cases, a court's decision that a rule is ultra vires reflects judicial concern with deeper issues; *see* below.

(1) Avoiding potential delegation problems [§32]

For example, the court might believe that the statute delegated too much power, yet might be reluctant to invalidate the entire statute; a less intrusive technique is to construe the statute narrowly, thus invalidating particular rules.

(a) Illustration—OSHA rules

The Occupational Health and Safety Administration ("OSHA"), the agency that sets standards for factory safety, adopted an extremely burdensome regulation that set benzene concentrations at one part per million. This was the lowest level that was economically feasible for the chemical industry and below any level scientifically proved to be dangerous. The Court expressed severe doubts about the breadth of the delegation to OSHA, which left unclear whether the agency was to balance costs and benefits. It also expressed reservations about regulations that set standards without reference to the cost of satisfying them. As a result, the Court narrowly construed the statute, finding that OSHA first had to show that a significant health risk existed at the concentration level shown. Since OSHA had made no such finding, its rule was invalid. [**Industrial Union Department v. American Petroleum Institute,** *supra,* §19]

1) Sequel

In a subsequent case, when OSHA made the required finding that a significant health risk existed, a majority of the Court upheld a rule setting permissible concentrations of cotton dust at the lowest feasible level. It held that the statute should be construed not to permit OSHA to conduct a cost-benefit analysis of the rule. Two justices dissented, arguing that the statute was an invalid delegation of legislative power. [**American Textile Manufacturers Institute v. Donovan,** *supra*, §19]

(b) State case

A state statute allowed the agency to "deal with any matters affecting the public health." The agency adopted elaborate anti-smoking rules, such as banning smoking in various public places and requiring smoke-free work areas. The court held the rules were ultra vires, in part because the relatively standardless delegation of power left it to the agency to balance health concerns against cost and privacy interests. Moreover, the legislature itself had tried and failed to adopt anti-smoking legislation, which suggests that the agency should not have tried to fill the gap on its own. [**Boreali v. Axelrod,** 71 N.Y.2d 1 (1987)]

(2) Avoiding substantive constitutional issues [§33]

The court might believe the statute or the rule violates a constitutional right or important civil liberty; however, to avoid a difficult constitutional question, the court can construe the statute narrowly and invalidate the particular rule on ultra vires rather than substantive constitutional grounds.

---

e.g. Example—denial of passports: The Secretary of State adopted a rule denying passports to Communists, acting under a statute providing that the Secretary "may grant and issue passports . . . under such rules as the President shall designate." The Court construed the statute narrowly, holding that it did not confer authority to deny passports for political activity, thus invalidating the regulation. The Court thereby avoided having to deal with difficult constitutional issues concerning the right to travel. [**Kent v. Dulles,** 357 U.S. 116 (1958)] *Note:* In a later case, the Court upheld a regulation prohibiting the issuance of passports for travel to Cuba. Here the court found that Congress had intended the Secretary to impose area restrictions; thus, this regulation was within the delegated power. [**Zemel v. Rusk,** 381 U.S. 1 (1965)]

---

cf. Compare: In one important case, the Court refused to construe a statute narrowly so as to invalidate regulations that raised serious constitutional questions about free speech and the right to abortion. It construed the statute broadly so as to uphold the regulation and also squarely upheld the constitutional validity of the challenged regulation. The opinion suggests that the Court was anxious to reach and decide the substantive constitutional issues. [**Rust v. Sullivan,** 500 U.S. 173 (1991)— upholding a regulation prohibiting personnel in federally funded family planning centers from discussing abortion with patients]

C. Delegation of Adjudicative Power

1. Introduction [§34]

As a general rule, *judicial power can be delegated* to administrative agencies. [*See* **Freytag v. Commissioner,** 501 U.S. 868 (1991)—upholding transfer of power to the United States Tax Court, a tribunal set up by Congress outside the judicial branch to decide tax cases]

2. Vagueness Doctrine [§35]

Statutes and regulations must give fair warning of prohibited conduct. Therefore, agency decisions imposing sanctions are sometimes challenged on vagueness grounds.

a. Vagueness argument rejected [§36]

Most Supreme Court cases reject vagueness arguments.

Example: A high school rule provided that conduct that "materially and substantially interferes with the educational process is prohibited, including the use of obscene, profane language or gestures." This rule gave sufficient notice to a student who was suspended for two days following a political speech in which he relied on a sexual metaphor. However, more notice might have been required if the penalty had been more severe. [**Bethel School District v. Fraser,** 478 U.S. 675 (1986)]

Example: The Hatch Act [7 U.S.C. §§361a *et seq.*] forbids federal employees from taking an "active part in political management or political campaigns." Despite the serious civil liberties connotations of this vague statute, the Court upheld it, in part because regulations had made it more specific and because the Civil Service Commission undertook to advise employees about a proposed course of action. [**Civil Service Commission v. National Association of Letter Carriers,** 413 U.S. 548 (1973)]

b. Vagueness of regulations [§37]

An emerging body of case law holds that agencies cannot impose criminal or civil sanctions on private parties under regulations that fail to give fair warning of the conduct that is prohibited. [*See* **General Electric Co. v. EPA,** 53 F.3d 1324 (D.C. Cir. 1995)—civil money penalty for violating regulation concerning disposal of toxic chemical; **United States v. Chrysler Corp.,** 158 F.3d 1350 (D.C. Cir. 1998)—requirement that cars be recalled because of violation of auto safety standards; *and see* discussion of these cases *infra*, §138]

EXAM TIP   **gilbert**

Even though the vagueness doctrine does *not often invalidate* agency adjudicatory standards, it is worth considering when faced with an exam question regarding delegation of adjudicatory power to an agency. This is especially true if the facts of the question involve a *constitutional issue*.

---

3. **Adjudication of Public and Private Rights**

    a. **Public rights [§38]**

    Congress can assign to non-Article III courts (such as administrative agencies) the power to adjudicate claims of "public rights." It can do so even if there would be a right to a jury trial under the Seventh Amendment if the case were tried in federal court. [**Atlas Roofing Co. v. Occupational Safety & Health Review Commission,** 430 U.S. 442 (1977); **Austin v. Shalala,** 994 F.2d 1170 (5th Cir. 1993)—Congress can assign the adjudication of government's claim for overpayment of Social Security benefits to agency; *and see infra*, §50] In general, "public rights" are those involving claims between private parties and the government.

    b. **Private rights [§39]**

    The adjudication of claims involving "private rights" (*i.e.*, claims between individuals) generally *cannot* be assigned to a non-Article III court. Moreover, Congress cannot dispense with a jury trial in cases of private rights that are actions at law of the sort that generally would require jury trials. Several cases have involved attempted transfers of the right to decide such issues to bankruptcy judges who are not appointed under Article III. [**Granfinanciera, S.A. v. Nordberg,** 492 U.S. 33 (1989)—right to jury trial in fraudulent conveyance case means that case cannot be assigned to bankruptcy judge; **Northern Pipeline Co. v. Marathon Pipe Line Co.,** 458 U.S. 50 (1982)—decision in breach of contract case cannot be assigned to bankruptcy judge]

    (1) **State courts [§40]**

    Some state court cases also invalidate transfers to agencies of the power to decide private disputes. [**Wright v. Central DuPage Hospital Association,** 347 N.E.2d 736 (Ill. 1976)—transfer of right to decide medical malpractice disputes]

    (2) **Exceptions [§41]**

    The Court has made exceptions to the principle that decisions in cases involving private rights must be assigned to Article III courts:

(a) New statutory rights [§42]

Congress can create new statutory rights between private individuals and assign the adjudication of these rights to agencies (with sufficient judicial review). [*See* **Crowell v. Benson**, 285 U.S. 22 (1932)—involving workers' compensation claims; *and see infra*, §566]

(b) Ancillary claims [§43]

Congress may assign to agencies the adjudication of certain cases involving private rights that arise out of federal statutes where such delegation is viewed as necessary to make the statute operate properly and adequate judicial review is provided. [**Thomas v. Union Carbide Agricultural Products, Inc.**, 473 U.S. 568 (1985)—arbitrator can set license fees where claim arose under federal public health statute; **Commodity Futures Trading Commission v. Schor**, 478 U.S. 833 (1986)—agency with power to hear claim can decide counterclaim for breach of contract]

1) State cases [§44]

State courts agree that a statute can delegate decisions involving private rights to an agency where necessary to implement the regulatory scheme with which the agency is charged. For example, a court upheld a scheme whereby a rent control board could award tenants compensatory and restitutionary damages for charging illegal rents. This adjudicatory power was reasonably necessary to carry out a rent control scheme. However, it was considered essential that adequate judicial review be provided before the landlord was compelled to make payment. [**McHugh v. Santa Monica Rent Control Board**, 49 Cal. 3d 348 (1989)]

4. Appointment of Judges to Nonjudicial Duties [§45]

By statute, the Sentencing Commission is located in the judicial branch of government and consists in part of federal judges. The Commission adopts rules that set the range of permissible punishment for violation of federal criminal laws. The Court upheld the statute creating the Commission, finding that the Commission's function is appropriately placed in the judicial branch and that federal judges can serve on it. There is nothing in the Constitution that prevents the voluntary assignment of judges for nonjudicial service if it does not undermine the integrity of the judicial branch. [**Mistretta v. United States**, *supra*, §26]

5. Penalties [§46]

An agency's authority to impose penalties for the violation of a regulation or statute generally depends on whether the penalty is a criminal sanction or a civil penalty.

a. **Criminal sanctions [§47]**

The legislature may authorize an agency to *enact* a regulation, the violation of which is a crime—as long as *prosecution* for the violation is left to the courts. [**United States v. Grimaud,** *supra,* §8; *but see* **Lincoln Dairy Co. v. Finigan,** 104 N.W.2d 227 (Neb. 1960)—contra]

(1) Agency may not imprison [§48]

Imprisonment for violating a regulation can be imposed only by the courts, and not by an agency. [**Wong Wing v. United States,** 163 U.S. 228 (1896)]

(a) Exceptions

Temporary confinement of aliens by administrative order, when incidental to exclusion or expulsion, is accepted. Similarly, preventive *quarantine* of persons with infectious diseases is permitted.

b. **Civil penalties [§49]**

Many state and federal statutes allow agencies to *impose civil penalties* for violation of statutes or regulations.

(1) Test [§50]

Generally, if the penalty is labeled "civil" rather than "criminal," it can be assessed by an agency (instead of a court) without the protections afforded under criminal law. [**Waukegan v. Pollution Control Board,** 311 N.E.2d 146 (Ill. 1974); *and see* **Helvering v. Mitchell,** 303 U.S. 391 (1938)—agency can adjudicate the amount of tax owed by a taxpayer and can assess a penalty for fraud]

(a) Double jeopardy [§51]

Double jeopardy protects a defendant only against multiple criminal punishments. Normally, the imposition of civil penalties plus criminal penalties is not a violation of double jeopardy. Only in rare circumstances will a penalty that the legislature has described as civil be deemed by the court as criminal so as to trigger double jeopardy protection. [**Hudson v. United States,** 522 U.S. 93 (1997)]

(b) Jury trial [§52]

Moreover, a penalty can be imposed *without* a jury trial—despite the Seventh Amendment—if a "public right" created by statute is being enforced. [**Atlas Roofing Co. v. Occupational Safety & Health Review Commission,** *supra,* §38—penalties up to $1,000 for serious violations, up to $10,000 for willful or repeated violations]

(2) Punitive damages [§53]

Although agencies can be empowered to award both damages and penalties, they cannot be empowered to award punitive damages one private litigant in favor of another. This invades the judicial province. [**McHugh v. Santa Monica Rent Control Board,** *supra,* §44]

D. Other Legislative Controls Over Administrative Action

1. Federal Standing Committees [§54]

Standing committees of the United States House and Senate keep abreast of agency activities in particular areas and sponsor legislation to make necessary changes.

2. Investigations [§55]

Other congressional committees concerned with general government operations may investigate the conduct of particular agencies. Occasionally, Congress appoints "watchdog" committees to examine the operations of particular agencies and to publicize controversial administrative actions.

3. Appropriations [§56]

In making appropriations, Congress may likewise impose limitations on spending by the agencies.

4. Review Committees [§57]

Numerous states have administrative rules review committees ("ARRCs") that routinely review the legality and desirability of agency rules. In some of those states, if an ARRC disapproves a rule, the agency has the burden of proof of validity of the rule on judicial review. [1981 Model State APA §3-204(d)]

5. Appointments [§58]

The Senate must consent to presidential appointments of high-level administrative and executive positions.

6. Congressional Review Act [§59]

~~~~~~~~nal Review Act [5 U.S.C. §§801-808] requires that all rules of gen-
be submitted to Congress and to the General Accounting Office
~~fect. In the case of a "major rule," the rule cannot take effect for
~ days after it is submitted to Congress. In the case of non-major
take effect whenever the agency determines. (The definition of
ie same as that of "significant regulatory actions" defined in Ex-
866, *see infra,* §345.) In the case of either major or non-major
in veto the rule by enacting a joint resolution of disapproval. A
disapproval is like a statute; it must be approved by both houses
President (or passed by a two-thirds majority over the President's
provides for a fast-track for congressional consideration of pro-
ule goes into effect and then is disapproved by Congress, the rule is

treated as if it had never taken effect. In addition, if a rule is disapproved, the agency may not re-issue the rule in substantially the same form unless Congress enacts legislation allowing it to do so.

a. Distinguish—legislative veto [§60]

Congress cannot retain a "legislative veto" of administrative adjudication or rulemaking. [**INS v. Chadha,** 462 U.S. 919 (1983)] The legislative veto allowed Congress to retain the power to veto the rules after they were adopted (sometimes by resolution of both houses, sometimes by resolution of only one house, and *without* the President's signature). The *Chadha* decision invalidated all legislative vetoes (including two-house veto provisions) on the bases of: (i) bicameralism, which requires that legislative action be taken only by agreement of both houses and (ii) the lack of a presidential signature (or repassage of the bill by each house by a two-thirds vote). *Chadha* therefore stripped Congress of a valuable tool for controlling agency action. The Congressional Review Act seeks to reinstate that tool while passing constitutional muster.

b. State decisions [§61]

Most state decisions agree with *Chadha*. [*See, e.g.,* **Missouri Coalition for the Environment v. Joint Committee on Administrative Rules,** 948 S.W.2d 125 (Mo. 1997)] However, one state upheld a legislative veto statute. [**Mead v. Arnell,** 791 P.2d 410 (Idaho 1990)]

7. Miscellaneous Controls [§62]

Other controls by the legislature include *ombudsmen*. These are officials who investigate and correct public complaints about specific administrative action. Ombudsmen are used in a number of states and in some federal agencies. Also, *legislators* may sometimes attempt to intercede in administrative matters involving their constituents. However, this raises serious ethical questions and creates problems for the administrators (*see infra,* §§283 *et seq.*).

E. Executive Controls Over Administrative Action

1. Appointment Power [§63]

One of the most important executive controls over administrative action is the power of the President (or a governor) to appoint agency heads. Such appointments must be approved by the Senate. [U.S. Const. art. II, §2]

a. No congressional appointments [§64]

Congress cannot appoint the members of agencies engaged in rulemaking or adjudication. [**Buckley v. Valeo,** 424 U.S. 1 (1976)—agency consisted of six members, two appointed by the Senate, two by the House, and two by the President] Nor can Congress appoint the personnel to engage in executing the laws. [**Metropolitan Washington Airports Authority v. Citizens for the Abatement of Aircraft Noise, Inc.,** 501 U.S. 252 (1991)—commission to run two airports in the District of Columbia consisted of nine members of Congress]

b. Appointment of inferior officers [§65]

Congress may, by law, vest the appointment of inferior officers (as opposed to superior officers such as agency heads) in the President alone, in the courts of law, or in the heads of departments. [U.S. Const. art. II, §2] It is necessary to distinguish "inferior officers" from other appointees, but the standards for doing so are not clear. Generally, an "inferior officer" is one who has a "superior."

(1) Court martial judges [§66]

The Court upheld the appointment by the Secretary of Transportation of judges of the Coast Guard Court of Criminal Appeals because the judges are inferior officers. They are subordinate to the Judge Advocate General, who exercises administrative control over them, and to the Court of Appeals for the Armed Forces, which reviews their decisions. [**Edmonds v. United States,** 520 U.S. 651 (1997)]

(2) Special prosecutors [§67]

Special prosecutors (sometimes called independent counsel) are appointed to investigate and prosecute executive branch officials. Special prosecutors are inferior officers, and therefore need not be appointed by the President, because they can be removed (for cause) by the Attorney General, their duties are limited to the investigation of certain crimes, and their position is temporary. [**Morrison v. Olson,** 487 U.S. 654 (1988)]

(3) Mere employees [§68]

Administrative Law Judges ("ALJs") who do *not make final agency decisions* are government employees, *not inferior officers*. Thus they do not need to be appointed by the President, the heads of departments, or courts of law. [**Landry v. FDIC,** 204 F.3d 1125 (D.C. Cir. 2000)] Typically, ALJs do not make the final agency decision; the agency heads (or some other review body) have the power to make the final agency decision (even if such power is seldom exercised). *But note:* If an ALJ has the power to make the final agency decision, the ALJ would be considered an inferior officer and would have to be appointed by the head of a department or by a court of law. [**Freytag v. Commissioner,** *supra* §34—special Tax Court judges have power to make final decisions and thus are inferior officers]

c. **Appointments by the judiciary [§69]**

The Constitution allows Congress to vest appointments of inferior officers in the courts of law. Such appointments have been upheld where the particular appointment power seemed appropriate for judges.

(1) Special prosecutors [§70]

By statute, special prosecutors are appointed by federal judges. The Court found this appropriate, pointing to the long history of the appointment of prosecutors by judges. The Court also observed that in light of the fact that special prosecutors investigate members of the executive branch, the President might have a conflict of interest if he were responsible for choosing special prosecutors. [**Morrison v. Olson,** *supra*]

(2) Special Tax Court judges [§71]

A statute provided that the chief judge of the Tax Court could appoint special trial judges. The Supreme Court held that the Tax Court was a court of law for this purpose and upheld the appointments provision. [**Freytag v. Commissioner,** *supra*]

2. Removal Power

a. **Limitation—removal for good cause [§72]**

A statute can prevent the President from removing an executive branch officer without good cause if the removal restrictions do not impede the President's ability to perform his constitutional duty. [**Morrison v. Olson,** *supra*]

(1) Early view [§73]

The Supreme Court originally held that the President has a broad power of removal over executive officers in order to assure that his policies could be carried out by persons in whom he had confidence. Congress could not limit this power. [**Myers v. United States,** 272 U.S. 52 (1926)] However, later cases have sharply limited this doctrine. The *Myers* rule probably applies only to high ranking officials such as Cabinet officers who are directly involved in carrying out the President's policies at the highest level, because a removal restriction at this level would impede the President's ability to perform his constitutional duties. [**Morrison v. Olson,** *supra*]

(2) Independent counsel [§74]

By statute, an "independent counsel" is appointed to investigate and prosecute executive branch officials. The statute provides that the independent counsel can be removed by the Attorney General only for "good cause." The Court upheld the statute because the independent counsel has a relatively brief tenure, limited powers, lacks policymaking power and therefore is not "so central to the functioning of the Executive Branch" as to require that the counsel be terminable at will by the President.

[**Morrison v. Olson,** *supra*] Moreover, the Court indicated that a further provision, which made a for-cause dismissal of the counsel subject to judicial review, was also valid.

(3) Independent agencies [§75]

Many important federal agencies are independent agencies. The concept of the "independent agency" was derived from **Humphrey's Executor v. United States,** 295 U.S. 602 (1935). In that case, a statute provided that the members of the Federal Trade Commission ("FTC") could be removed only for certain stated causes. Congress deprived the President of removal power so that the agency could engage in law enforcement, rulemaking, and adjudication activity free of presidential control. This statute was upheld and a member who had been removed without cause was held to be entitled to his salary.

(4) Legislative courts [§76]

Even without a statute limiting the President's removal power, the Court held that the President could not remove a member of the War Claims Commission without cause. The Commission had a judicial function (adjudicating claims of persons suffering damage from the enemy during World War II), which made removal without cause inappropriate. [**Weiner v. United States,** 357 U.S. 349 (1958)]

b. No Congressional participation [§77]

Congress may not retain the power to remove (or share in the process of removing) officials engaged in executive functions. [**Morrison v. Olson,** *supra*]

---

e.g. **Example:** A statute required the Comptroller General to determine whether the annual federal budget deficit would exceed targets in the statute, a matter involving considerable expertise and judgment. If the deficit exceeded the targets, mandatory budget cuts followed. The Comptroller General could be removed only by Congress—not by the President. The statute was held unconstitutional because the Comptroller General would be engaged in executive action, but Congress retained the power to control him through its removal power. [**Bowsher v. Synar,** 478 U.S. 714 (1986)]

---

e.g. **Example:** By statute, a postmaster could be removed by the President only with the advice and consent of the Senate. Because Congress shared in the process of removal of the officer, the statute was invalid. [**Myers v. United States,** *supra*] Prior to *Morrison, supra,* the *Myers* case had been understood to stand for the proposition that the President was entitled to absolute power to remove executive branch officials such as postmasters. However, *Morrison* limits *Myers* to its facts (*i.e.,* **congressional sharing** in removal is invalid).

---

3. Fiscal Power [§78]

The President (through the Office of Management and Budget ("OMB"), a White House-staff agency) can control administrative requests to Congress for appropriations or changes in legislation.

4. Organizational Power [§79]

The President has extensive statutory powers to create, abolish, and reorganize agencies within the executive branch.

5. Rulemaking [§80]

By executive order, the President has imposed substantial controls over major federal rulemaking. [Executive Order 12,866—*see infra*, §345] The executive order requires the preparation of regulatory impact statements that assess the costs and benefits of proposed "major" rules. It is enforced by the OMB.

6. Inspectors General [§81]

Inspectors general are posted throughout the federal government to audit federal agencies and departments for fraud, waste, or abuse. [Inspector General Act of 1978, 5 U.S.C. app. 3] However, inspectors general are not generally empowered to audit private companies to detect noncompliance with the law; that is the job of regular agency staff. [**Burlington Northern Railroad v. Office of Inspector General**, 983 F.2d 631 (5th Cir. 1993)]

7. Ombudsman [§82]

Ombudsmen investigate and correct public complaints about specific administrative action. An ombudsman has no formal powers, but agencies normally follow the advice of an ombudsman who has decided that an agency has acted illegally or improperly. Many state and federal agencies employ ombudsmen.

8. Gubernatorial Veto [§83]

Governors in some states have the power to veto rules. [*See* 1981 Model State APA §3-202] In California, a state executive agency is authorized to veto any newly adopted administrative rule for legality, lack of clarity, or lack of necessity based on the rulemaking record. [Cal. Gov't Code §11349.1]

Chapter Two:
The Constitutional
Right to a Hearing

CONTENTS

Chapter Approach

A.   Interests Protected by Due Process—Liberty and Property   §84

B.   Timing of the Hearing   §118

C.   Elements of the Hearing   §135

D.   Issues Requiring a Hearing—The Rulemaking-Adjudication Distinction   §146

that federal and state governmer̲ nt some additional action
tion that deprives an individua̲l t be tortious (thus giving
maker must also be provided (s̲ not involve a deprivation
administrative law, the right to ṟ a hearing under due pro-
arbitrary government action. It
and helps to insure that decisic̲
hearing. It helps to instill a fee̲l ned from his government
promotes participation and dia̲ a highly unfavorable letter
process. [**Marshall v. Jerrico Inc**̲ch accordingly refused to
d no deprivation of liberty
d resigned from his job.

2. **"Liberty" [§85]**

The "liberty" interest protecte̲ equirement because it was
fined. It includes the right to c̲ discharging Plaintiff from
tablish a home, bring up childre̲ plus requirement was met
short, the right to enjoy the qua̲ 26 (1991)]
happiness. [**Board of Regents**
deprivation of liberty follow.

a. **Imposition of stigma [§86]**

If a government action aga̲
ample, make it difficult for
is a deprivation of liberty.
pose of clearing his name.
cision by a university not
additional facts, does not i̲ **substantive constitutional**

scharging an employee for
rst Amendment; the action

(1) **Public and false infor**̲
Stigmatic informatio̲r er, the Court has held that
erty interests were n̲ cases; the person's interests
not made public [**Bish**̲deral court under the Civil
rogatory information̲**ann,** 408 U.S. 593 (1972)]
nterests (such as issuance of

(2) **Stigma plus [§88]**̲ oks) require the state to pro-
In addition, governm̲l Law Summary.)
some other action ("
employment.

ggers a right to a hearing.

e.g. **Example—stigm**̲)]
drunkard, and t̲
combination of the s̲
hol met the stigma-p̲n with **exclusion** of an alien
U.S. 433 (1971)]̲ e the alien asserts a right to
nessy, 338 U.S. 537 (1950)]

cf. **Compare—no s̲**n seeking admission to the
describing Plain̲**Boyd,** 351 U.S. 345 (1956)]

gilbert

rts of libel or slander. While
the imposition of a stigma

(2) Temporary absence [§92]

However, a resident alien who left the country for a short visit and wants to return is entitled to due process when the government seeks to exclude her. [**Landon v. Plasencia,** 454 U.S. 1140 (1982)] Dictum in the *Landon* case suggests that the court might be inclined to overrule the cases that draw such a sharp distinction between deportation and exclusion and grant due process rights to aliens who claim they are entitled to admission to the country.

d. Deprivation of physical liberty [§93]

Imprisonment for a crime is the ultimate deprivation of liberty. Criminal procedure provides the process due in such cases, and, for most purposes, it extinguishes the liberty interest during incarceration. As a general rule, decisions by prison authorities having adverse effects on prisoners are *not* treated as deprivations of liberty and thus do not trigger due process rights, *unless those decisions lengthen* the prisoner's term of confinement. [**Sandin v. Conner,** 515 U.S. 472 (1995)]

(1) Prior law [§94]

Sandin overruled a series of cases that held that prisoners are deprived of liberty interests: (i) when they are subjected to disciplinary sanctions or (ii) when they are subjected to nondisciplinary sanctions under prison rules containing nondiscretionary decisional standards. [*See, e.g.,* **Hewitt v. Helms,** 459 U.S. 460 (1983)—prison regulation imposed nondiscretionary standards on decision to place prisoner in segregation for his own protection; such transfer deprived prisoner of liberty interest]

(2) Current law—*Sandin* case [§95]

Prisoner, who was serving a term of 30 years to life, was sentenced to 30 days in disciplinary segregation (*i.e.,* solitary confinement) because he resisted a strip search. Prisoner was not provided with a hearing that met due process standards. Because the prison decision did not inevitably prolong his period of confinement, Prisoner was not entitled to a hearing because he was not deprived of liberty. The fact that the decision was disciplinary in nature and was made under nondiscretionary standards (which past cases had held deprived a prisoner of a liberty interest) did not change the result. [**Sandin v. Conner,** *supra*]

(3) Exceptions [§96]

Even after *Sandin,* some decisions concerning prisoners do deprive them of liberty and thus trigger due process protections. For example:

(a) *Transfer from prison to mental hospital.* [**Vitek v. Jones,** 445 U.S. 480 (1980)]

(b) *Involuntary administration of psychotropic drugs to prisoners.* [**Washington v. Harper,** 494 U.S. 210 (1990)]

(c) *Decisions inevitably lengthening prisoner's term of confinement,* for example by canceling "good time credits." [**Wolff v. McDonnell,** 418 U.S. 539 (1974)]

(4) Parole or probation

(a) Revocation of parole or probation [§97]

The state must provide due process when it revokes parole or probation. [**Morrisey v. Brewer,** 408 U.S. 471 (1972); **Gagnon v. Scarpelli,** 411 U.S. 778 (1973)] Indeed, such decisions require a probable cause hearing before revocation and a full hearing after revocation at which the individual is entitled to show that no violation of the terms of parole or probation occurred. The state must appoint and pay for counsel if the issues are complex. [**Gagnon v. Scarpelli,** *supra*]

(b) Granting parole [§98]

Since parole is usually discretionary and is based on guesswork about a prisoner's prospects for success, the general rule is that the state is not required to provide a hearing before denying it. [**Greenholtz v. Inmates of Nebraska Complex,** 442 U.S. 1 (1979)] However, if the statute or regulations contain mandatory and explicit standards for deciding whether parole should be granted, a hearing is required before it is denied. [**Greenholtz v. Inmates of Nebraska Complex,** *supra*; **Kentucky Department of Corrections v. Thompson,** 490 U.S. 454 (1989)] The required procedure in such cases is meager: an opportunity for the prisoner to provide letters and statements. The Board is not required to explain its reasons for denying parole.

e. Expulsion or suspension from school [§99]

Expulsion or suspension from public school or college is a deprivation of liberty and triggers appropriate due process protection. [**Goss v. Lopez,** 419 U.S. 565 (1975)]

(1) Expulsion from college [§100]

Due process requires that expulsion from a public college *for disciplinary reasons* be accompanied by adequate procedural safeguards. [**Papish v. University of Missouri,** 410 U.S. 667 (1973)] While the student is clearly entitled to an oral hearing and to bring in witnesses, it is not settled whether there is a right to confront and cross-examine accusers, to examine confidential faculty files, or to have the assistance of counsel. [*See* **Dixon v. Alabama State Board of Education,** 294 F.2d 150 (5th Cir. 1961)]

(2) Academic dismissals [§101]

There is *no right* to a hearing in connection with a dismissal for academic deficiencies. The only requirement is that the school inform the student of academic problems in time for her to try to correct them and that the decision be carefully and deliberately made. [**University of Missouri v. Horowitz,** 435 U.S. 78 (1978)] *Rationale:* Subjective academic judgments are not susceptible to review by trial-type proceedings and it would be disruptive to project the courts into this arena.

(3) High school suspensions [§102]

A suspension from high school is an invasion of liberty. In the case of a suspension lasting 10 days or less, the required procedure is merely a conference with the disciplinarian and an opportunity for the student to state her side. No greater formality is required. [**Goss v. Lopez,** *supra*] In a case of a suspension lasting more than 10 days, a more formal hearing may be required.

EXAM TIP   **gilbert**

Don't be fooled by an exam question that deals with a student's expulsion from a private school. Remember that due process is triggered *only by government action*. However, expulsion from private schools does trigger a right to a hearing under the laws of some states. In addition, such a hearing might be available under a theory of express or implied contract.

---

3. "Property" [§103]

The word "property" includes far more than land or chattels. It includes "entitlements," such as welfare or legally protected employment relationships or licenses. Under prior law, such entitlements were considered "privileges" rather than rights, and thus revocable by the government without providing any procedure, but the right-privilege distinction has been abolished. [**Memphis Light, Gas & Water Division v. Craft,** 436 U.S. 1 (1978)—receipt of municipal utility service is a "property" right which cannot be cut off without a hearing if there is a factual dispute such as whether the recipient made payments]

a. Welfare [§104]

A person receiving welfare benefits under statutory and administrative standards defining eligibility has an interest in continued receipt of the benefits. If the state wants to terminate the benefits, it must provide notice and a hearing before doing so. [**Goldberg v. Kelly,** 397 U.S. 254 (1970)] *Goldberg* is the leading modern case holding that due process protects "entitlements." Welfare cannot be terminated on the theory that its receipt was a mere privilege; instead, it is a form of "new property."

(1) Public housing [§105]

Similarly, eviction from public housing requires notice and a hearing, assuming state law protects the tenants from eviction without cause. [**Escalera v. New York Housing Authority,** 425 F.2d 853 (2d Cir. 1970)]

(2) No standards [§106]

Some cases indicate that a state violates due process if it allocates public housing or other benefits to poor people without any standards. [**Holmes v. New York City Housing Authority,** 398 F.2d 262 (2d Cir. 1970); **White v. Roughton,** 530 F.2d 750 (7th Cir. 1976)]

b. Government employment [§107]

A government job is property where the jobholder is protected by law from discharge without cause. For example, a tenured teaching job or a civil service job is a form of property and the jobholder cannot be fired without appropriate procedure. If the holder of a government job can be fired at the discretion of the employer (*i.e.,* an untenured teacher), the job is not property and thus is not protected by due process. [**Board of Regents v. Roth,** *supra,* §86] However, if the holder of an unprotected job is fired for reasons that impose a stigma, the discharge is an invasion of liberty and entitles the victim to a name-clearing hearing (*see supra,* §§86-88).

(1) De facto tenure [§108]

Even if a state law provides that teachers or professors have no tenure and can be discharged without cause at the end of a school year, a discharged professor may be able to prove that the state has "de facto" tenure. This is a right arising out of implied contract that protects professors against discharge without good cause. If de facto tenure exists, a professor is entitled to a hearing to establish grounds for nonretention. [**Perry v. Sindermann,** *supra,* §89]

(2) State law [§109]

The issue of whether state statutory or contract law actually provides job protection is a matter of state law. [**Bishop v. Wood,** 426 U.S. 341 (1976)—affirming questionable construction of state law by federal district judge]

(3) Power of state to prescribe procedure [§110]

Once a state creates a tenured job, it cannot define procedural protections for that job that fall below the minimal protections of due process. [**Cleveland Board of Education v. Loudermill,** 470 U.S. 532 (1985)—disapproving contrary holding in plurality opinion in **Arnett v. Kennedy,** 416 U.S. 134 (1974)]

(a) Note

The *Arnett* plurality thought that an employee had to take the bitter with the sweet, meaning that the state could both define the job protection and the procedure for protecting it. But *Loudermill* holds that due process, not state law, provides the procedure for protecting the job, once the state has surrounded the job with protection against discharge for good cause. This means notice, an explanation of charges, and an oral or written opportunity to respond. A full-fledged oral hearing, including confrontation, can be delayed until after the discharge. [**Cleveland Board of Education v. Loudermill**, *supra*]

c. Licenses [§111]

Professional licenses are a form of "property" protected by due process. Thus, the government must provide notice and a hearing before invoking sanctions against a licensee such as suspension or revocation. The idea that a license to do business is a mere privilege, which can be granted or rescinded at pleasure, has now been rejected.

(1) Timing [§112]

While hearings must ordinarily be provided before the state acts, the state is entitled to suspend a license before granting a hearing when necessary for the protection of the public interest. [**Barry v. Barchi**, 443 U.S. 55 (1979); *and see* discussion of timing, *infra*, §§118 *et seq.*]

(2) Granting licenses [§113]

If a person is entitled to a license upon satisfaction of statutory criteria, the state must provide a hearing before denial of the license. [**Willner v. Committee on Character & Fitness**, 373 U.S. 96 (1963)—admission to the Bar]

(a) Lack of standards [§114]

Some cases indicate that a state violates due process when it denies a license if its system of granting licenses contains no standards. Such a system invites corruption or political favoritism. [**Hornsby v. Allen**, 326 F.2d 605 (5th Cir. 1964)]

(3) Renewing licenses [§115]

By the time a license comes up for renewal, the applicant is probably entitled to a hearing if the state proposes to deny renewal—even if the original grant of the license was wholly discretionary. [**Bankers' Life & Casualty Co. v. Cravey**, 69 S.E.2d 87 (Ga. 1952)]

(4) State and federal protection [§116]

State and federal administrative procedure acts define licensing as adjudication and contain specific protections for licensees (*see infra*, §172).

4. Deprivation [§117]

Due process applies if the state has *"directly" deprived* a person of liberty or property. Thus, if the state has taken action against one person, A, which results in a loss to another person, B, the injured person (B) may not have any due process rights because her deprivation was merely "indirect." [**O'Bannon v. Town Court Nursing Center**, 447 U.S. 773 (1980)]

> **Example:** Patients in a licensed nursing home have no right to a hearing before the government terminates the home's license. The home, of course, would have a right to a hearing (*see supra,* §§111-113), and the patients would have a right to a hearing if their government benefits were cut off (*see supra,* §§104-105), but they have no right to a hearing relating to disqualification of the home because the harm to them is indirect. [**O'Bannon v. Town Court Nursing Center,** *supra*]

B. Timing of the Hearing

1. General Rule [§118]

The general rule is that a hearing must occur *before* the deprivation of liberty or property occurs. The timing of the hearing is frequently of great importance, because if the state acts first and holds a hearing later, the damage to the person from even a temporary loss of liberty or property may be irreparable. [**Goldberg v. Kelly,** *supra,* §104]

2. Emergency Exception [§119]

There has always been an exception for emergency action: To protect the public health or safety, the government sometimes must act without providing any procedure at all—even though post-deprivation procedures may not be effective protection. [**North American Cold Storage Co. v. Chicago,** 211 U.S. 306 (1908)—destruction of rotting food held in cold storage; **Fahey v. Mallonee,** 332 U.S. 245 (1947)—bank is failing and jeopardizing depositors' interests]

3. Balancing Test [§120]

Under current law, the timing issue is analyzed by a balancing test. This test has led the Court to decide in numerous cases that a state is entitled to act first and hold a hearing later (or provide only abbreviated procedures first and a full hearing later). [**Mathews v. Eldridge,** 424 U.S. 319 (1976)]

a. Factors [§121]

The court considers:

   (i) *The nature of the private interest* affected;

   (ii) *The risk to that interest* posed by a challenged procedure and the likelihood that a different procedure would better protect that interest; and

   (iii) *The burden on government* from imposing the different procedure.

   [**Mathews v. Eldridge,** *supra*]

4. Application of the Balancing Test

a. Welfare and disability benefits [§122]

Welfare benefits are provided only to very poor people; if they are erroneously cut off, the damage done to the recipient may be irreparable. Therefore, a trial-type hearing must be provided to the recipient *before welfare benefits* are cut off. [**Goldberg v. Kelly**, *supra*] However, the Supreme Court distinguished *Goldberg* and allowed federal *disability* benefits to be cut off before a hearing was provided. [**Mathews v. Eldridge**, *supra*]

(1) Balancing instead of absolute rule [§123]

In **Mathews v. Eldridge**, the Court for the first time set forth its balancing test and used it to distinguish disability payments from welfare payments. Disability was found to be different from welfare in several critical respects:

(a) Private interest

Recipients of disability benefits need not be poor. Therefore, in many cases, the recipients will not be placed in "brutal need" if their benefits are erroneously cut off. Also, recipients can fall back on welfare during that period.

(b) Risk of error

Unlike welfare cases that often turn on credibility disputes, disability cases are usually decided based on written medical reports. Therefore, the risk of error in delaying a hearing is less.

(c) Government interest

In both welfare and disability cases, the government has a strong interest in cutting off benefits before a hearing. Otherwise, people who are not entitled to benefits can stall the termination decision while waiting for a hearing and it is practically impossible for the government to recoup the benefits later.

b. Employment discharge [§124]

Under the *Mathews* balancing test, the government can suspend an employee from a tenured or civil service job *without providing a full hearing* in advance. However, there must be an adequate *predischarge procedure* to establish that there is probable cause for discharge. [**Cleveland Board of Education v. Loudermill**, *supra*, §110]

(1) Probable cause procedure [§125]

Thus, a civil service employee is entitled to notice, an explanation of the employer's evidence against him, and an opportunity to present his side of the story orally or in writing. In addition, he is entitled to a *full hearing after the discharge* within a reasonable time. [**Cleveland Board of Education v. Loudermill**, *supra*]

(2) Suspension without pay in emergency [§126]

In emergency situations, the employer can suspend an employee without any pretermination procedure and without pay, provided that a reasonably prompt post-suspension hearing is provided. [**Gilbert v. Homar,** 519 U.S. 1052 (1997)—suspension of campus police officer for drug offense; **FDIC v. Mallen,** 486 U.S. 230 (1988)—suspension of bank officer indicted for crime]

(3) Reinstatement [§127]

Due process also protects an *employer* when the government orders that a discharged *employee* be reinstated under a statute protecting "whistle-blowers." However, the employer's interest is adequately protected by a pre-reinstatement procedure that includes: (i) receiving adequate notice of the employee's allegations, (ii) notice of the substance of supporting evidence, (iii) an opportunity to submit a written response, (iv) an opportunity to meet with the agency's investigator, and (v) an opportunity to present statements from rebuttal witnesses. A full-fledged oral hearing must be expeditiously provided after reinstatement and there must be an expeditious agency final decision. [**Brock v. Roadway Express, Inc.,** 481 U.S. 252 (1987)]

c. Licenses [§128]

The general rule is that a hearing is required *before suspension or revocation* of a license. [**Bell v. Burton,** 402 U.S. 535 (1971)—suspension of license of uninsured motorist involved in auto accident] However, in various circumstances the state has been allowed to *suspend first* and provide a hearing later.

(1) Unsafe driver [§129]

Where a driver has a series of traffic tickets and there is little room for the decisionmaker to exercise discretion, the state is allowed to suspend the license before granting a hearing. [**Dixon v. Love,** 431 U.S. 105 (1977)] Similarly, it may summarily suspend the driver's license of a person who refuses to take a breath test after being arrested for drunken driving. [**Mackey v. Montrym,** 443 U.S. 1 (1979)]

(2) Professional license [§130]

The state was entitled to suspend a horse trainer for 15 days after testing disclosed the presence of drugs in horses. The test provided the requisite probable cause. However, a prompt post-suspension hearing must be provided. [**Barry v. Barchi,** *supra,* §112]

d. Creditors' remedies [§131]

Whether a creditor can seize a debtor's property before judicial determination that a debt is actually owed is unclear. The issue requires careful *Mathews* balancing.

(1) Absolute rule [§132]

Early cases followed *Goldberg* and held that a creditor could *not* seize a debtor's property prior to a judicial determination of probable cause. [**Sniadach v. Family Finance Corp.,** 395 U.S. 337 (1969); **Fuentes v. Shevin,** 407 U.S. 67 (1972)—replevin statute]

(2) Judicial determination [§133]

Later cases discarded this absolute rule. They *upheld* such seizures if there was an adequate determination by a judge (rather than a court clerk) of probable cause to believe that the debtor really owed the debt and the creditor's legitimate interests required summary action. [**Mitchell v. W.T. Grant Co.,** 416 U.S. 600 (1974)—judicial authorization of the seizure]

(3) Exigent circumstances [§134]

Summary seizure of a debtor's property is not permissible, even upon approval by a judge, where the creditor shows no legitimate need for this drastic procedure (such as a preexisting interest in the property or concern that the debtor would conceal the property). [**Connecticut v. Doehr,** 501 U.S. 1 (1991)]

EXAM TIP   **gilbert**

It is helpful to remember that government deprivation of a constitutional right (e.g., liberty or property) generally requires **at least** a procedure **to determine whether probable cause exists before the deprivation** occurs. The major exceptions include situations where public safety is threatened or the affected individual has been accused of a crime, especially if that crime affects the public interest. A full hearing is usually always required before permanent deprivation of a right is allowed.

C. Elements of the Hearing

1. Same Balancing Test [§135]

In early due process cases, the Supreme Court prescribed fixed lists of the elements that a due process hearing must contain. [**Goldberg v. Kelly,** *supra,* §122] In more recent cases, however, the Court has employed the *Mathews* balancing test *to decide what elements* the hearing must contain. (*See supra,* §121.) Thus, the same balancing analysis is used both for timing and for establishment of the precise ingredients of the notice and hearing process.

2. Elements of Due Process [§136]

Due process hearings generally require:

(i)   Fair *notice*;

(ii) *Confrontation* of adverse witnesses;

(iii) An *impartial decisionmaker*; and

(iv) A *statement of reasons*.

However, the exact circumstances are critical, and *Mathews* balancing may require more formality or less formality than these four elements.

a. **Notice [§137]**

The right to a hearing entails timely and adequate notice of what the government intends to do and of the procedure by which the individual can present objections. [**Memphis Light, Gas & Water Division v. Craft,** *supra*, §103]

(1) Fair warning [§138]

If a person is subject to sanctions for violating the requirements of an agency regulation, the regulation must give fair warning that a particular conduct is in violation of the regulation. In some cases, a person has reasonably interpreted a regulation so that her conduct complied with the regulation, but the agency interpreted the same regulation in a way that caused the conduct in question to be a violation. In such situations, it is a violation of due process to sanction the person for violating the regulation. The agency might avoid this problem by publishing an interpretive rule that furnishes fair warning of the agency's interpretation. (*See infra*, §§400 *et seq.* for discussion of interpretive rules.) [**Trinity Broadcasting Co. v. FCC,** 211 F.3d 618 (D.C. Cir. 2000)—FCC's interpretation of regulation was valid but failed to give fair notice so that applicant for renewal of license could not be penalized for violating regulation; **General Electric Co. v. EPA,** 53 F.3d 1324 (D.C. Cir. 1995)—civil money penalty for violating regulation concerning disposal of toxic chemical; **United States v. Chrysler Corp.,** 158 F.3d 1350 (D.C. Cir. 1998)—requirement that cars be recalled because of violation of auto safety standards]

b. **Confrontation of witnesses [§139]**

The person affected by an agency action ordinarily must be afforded an opportunity to *confront* any adverse witnesses and present her own arguments and evidence orally. Written submissions are *not* considered a substitute for actual confrontation of adverse witnesses, particularly where credibility is at issue. Nevertheless, the requirements of due process are flexible and increasingly the Court has dispensed with cross-examination when it seemed unnecessary or counterproductive. Cross-examination is not necessary in connection with:

(1) *The commitment of children to mental institutions* [**Parham v. J.R.,** 442 U.S. 584 (1979)];

(2) *Short-term suspensions from school* [**Goss v. Lopez,** *supra*, §102]; or

(3) *The transfer of prisoners to mental institutions* [**Vitek v. Jones,** *supra*, §96].

c. Impartial decisionmaker [§140]

An impartial decisionmaker is essential to due process. This means a decision-maker who is not biased, has no conflict of interest, and is not reviewing a decision that he has previously made. [**Goldberg v. Kelly,** *supra*, §135] (Impartiality of decisionmakers is discussed in detail *infra*, §§257-292.)

d. Basis for decision [§141]

Due process also requires that the decisionmaker *state the reasons* for the determination, and indicate the evidence relied on. The conclusions must be based solely on the legal rules and evidence presented *at the hearing*. [**Goldberg v. Kelly,** *supra*]

e. Right to counsel [§142]

An affected person normally has a right to the assistance of counsel in *adversary* administrative proceedings, but not in nonadversary proceedings. [**Walters v. National Association of Radiation Survivors,** 473 U.S. 305 (1985); **Goldberg v. Kelly,** *supra*]

---

e.g. **Example—nonadversary proceedings:** A statute covering veteran's benefits claims limits the amount a claimant can pay an attorney to $10. This means that attorneys are barred from Veteran's Administration claims procedures (except for pro bono attorneys). However, free assistance is available to claimants from nonlawyer representatives employed by veterans' groups. The Court upheld the statute under the *Mathews* factors (*see supra*, §121). The most important reasons were the strong congressional policy against diversion of any portion of a recovery to attorneys, the availability of nonlawyer representatives, and the fact that Veteran's Administration proceedings are informal and nonadversarial. Although the services of an attorney would be helpful in complex cases (like those for radiation damages or involving Agent Orange), these cases are too rare to invalidate a statute that applies to 800,000 claims every year. [**Walters v. National Association of Radiation Survivors,** *supra*—three justices dissented; two more indicated that they might invalidate the statute with respect to complex claims]

---

(1) Appointed counsel [§143]

Even though a party has a right to counsel, the Supreme Court has indicated that the state is *usually not required* to provide counsel. [**Goldberg v. Kelly,** *supra*]

---

e.g. **Example:** A prisoner who resists a petition by the state that would strip her of all parental rights is not automatically entitled to the appointment of counsel. The Court held that appointment of counsel might in some circumstances be required; this would be resolved by the court considering such petitions on a case-by-case basis, using the *Mathews* factors (*supra*, §121). [**Lassiter v. Department of Social Services,** 452 U.S. 18 (1981)]

(a) But note

Counsel must be appointed for at least some probation revocation hearings and in all cases of transfers of prisoners to mental institutions. [**Gagnon v. Scarpelli,** *supra,* §97; **Vitek v. Jones,** *supra,* §139]

f. State law remedies for deprivation of liberty or property [§144]

In several situations, the judicial remedies provided by state tort or contract actions provide the necessary due process to remedy a deprivation of liberty or property.

---

e.g. **Example—liberty:** Paddling a high school student is a deprivation of liberty, but a state law tort action for damages against the teacher for excessive punishment provides all the process that the student is due. The Court decided that the burden on the school of holding a prior administrative hearing on whether to paddle a student outweighed any possible benefit to the student. [**Ingraham v. Wright,** 430 U.S. 651 (1977)] The same rule applies to random acts such as negligent or intentional destruction by prison guards of a prisoner's property. No prior hearing is practical in such cases—a state law tort action provides all the process that is due. [**Parratt v. Taylor,** 451 U.S. 527 (1981)—negligent destruction; **Hudson v. Palmer,** 468 U.S. 517 (1984)—intentional destruction]

---

e.g. **Example—property:** Where the property claimed is a right to be paid under a contract, a state law contract action provides all the process that is due. [**Lujan v. G & G Fire Sprinklers,** 121 S. Ct. 1446 (2001)] In *Lujan,* state law provided that if a subcontractor failed to pay minimum wages on a state job, the state should withhold payment from the prime contractor. The prime contractor, in turn, withheld the same amount from the subcontractor. No prior hearing was provided. Thus the subcontractor was deprived of money owed to it without any hearing on whether the withholding was justified. The Court held that no administrative hearing was required because the subcontractor could sue the state for breach of contract in state court and all factual issues would be determined in the state court action.

---

g. Comparative hearings [§145]

Normally an agency may hold hearings against several parties at once or hold separate hearings in cases involving numerous parties. However, if granting a license to one person means that a license must be denied to another, due process requires that the agency hold a "comparative hearing" involving both people so that neither will be harmed because the other had the first hearing. [**Ashbacker Radio Corp. v. FCC,** 326 U.S. 327 (1945)]

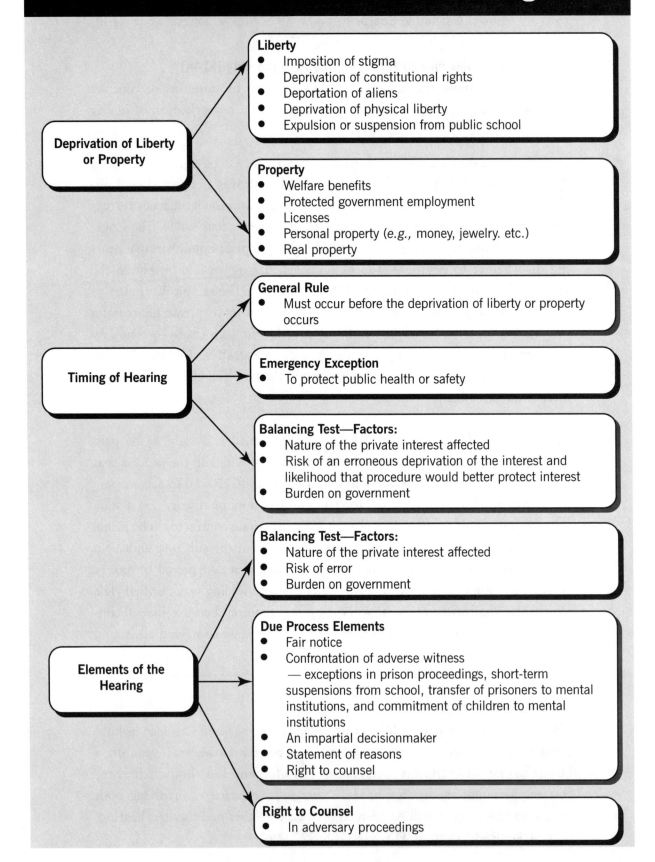

Deprivation of Liberty or Property

Liberty
- Imposition of stigma
- Deprivation of constitutional rights
- Deportation of aliens
- Deprivation of physical liberty
- Expulsion or suspension from public school

Property
- Welfare benefits
- Protected government employment
- Licenses
- Personal property (*e.g.,* money, jewelry. etc.)
- Real property

Timing of Hearing

General Rule
- Must occur before the deprivation of liberty or property occurs

Emergency Exception
- To protect public health or safety

Balancing Test—Factors:
- Nature of the private interest affected
- Risk of an erroneous deprivation of the interest and likelihood that procedure would better protect interest
- Burden on government

Elements of the Hearing

Balancing Test—Factors:
- Nature of the private interest affected
- Risk of error
- Burden on government

Due Process Elements
- Fair notice
- Confrontation of adverse witness
  — exceptions in prison proceedings, short-term suspensions from school, transfer of prisoners to mental institutions, and commitment of children to mental institutions
- An impartial decisionmaker
- Statement of reasons
- Right to counsel

Right to Counsel
- In adversary proceedings

D. Issues Requiring a Hearing— the Rulemaking-Adjudication Distinction

1. No Hearing Required for Rulemaking [§146]

Not all agency actions require a trial-type hearing. Such a hearing is required by due process only in cases of adjudication—not in rulemaking.

2. Hearing May Be Required for Adjudication [§147]

Even in cases of adjudication, a hearing is not always required. There need be no hearing on issues of *law or policy*. Also, no hearing is required for the determination of *"generalized" facts*—only for a determination of *"individualized" facts*.

a. Individualized facts [§148]

"Individualized" or "adjudicative" facts are facts about an *individual private party*. They often, but not always, require a determination of credibility or state of mind and are thus suitable for trial-type hearings.

b. Generalized facts [§149]

"Generalized" or "legislative" facts are facts of general application, *common to large groups* of people or businesses. They often arise in the course of rulemaking proceedings. Since generalized facts can usually be determined through documentary or statistical evidence, trial-type hearings may be inappropriate to determine such facts.

3. Application of Rulemaking—Adjudication Distinction

a. Traditional leading cases [§150]

The rulemaking-adjudication distinction was first drawn in two early cases involving taxation.

(1) Adjudication [§151]

A city ordinance levied assessments on property owners for street improvements. The decision to pave the streets and the determination of the total paving cost did not require a trial-type hearing. However, the division of costs between particular owners did require a hearing because there was a question of how much each piece of property had benefited. [**Londoner v. Denver,** 210 U.S. 373 (1908)]

(2) Rulemaking [§152]

A state board increased the valuation of all property in Denver by 40%. A Denver taxpayer had no right to a hearing on the reevaluation. [**Bi-Metallic Investment Co. v. State Board of Equalization,** 239 U.S. 441 (1915)]

(a) Rationale

"Where a rule of conduct applies to more than a few people, it is impracticable that everyone should have a direct voice in its adoption . . . . Their rights are protected in the only way [possible] in a complex society, by their power, immediate or remote, over those who make the rule." [**Bi-Metallic Investment Co. v. State Board of Equalization,** *supra*]

(b) Comment

The *Bi-Metallic* case involves generalized or legislative facts—facts concerning all the property owners in Denver. Thus it is more like rulemaking than adjudication. The *Londoner* case, on the other hand, involved "a relatively small number of persons . . . who were exceptionally affected in each case on individual grounds." Thus *Londoner* involved individualized facts about specific properties.

b. Modern application [§153]

The Court has often drawn on *Londoner* and *Bi-Metallic* in evaluating due process.

> **Example—railroad rates:** Due process does not apply to an order raising the rates charged by all railroads. The facts are not individualized but apply to all railroads. However, an order changing the rates of an individual railroad would require a trial-type hearing. [**United States v. Florida East Coast Railway,** 410 U.S. 224 (1973)]

> **Example—food stamp reductions:** Nor does due process apply to a legislative amendment to the formula for computing food stamp benefits that has the effect of lowering benefits for many persons. Similarly, there is no right to advance notice or to a hearing with respect to the automatic recalculation required by this amendment. However, if an individual claims that because of facts specific to her the calculation was erroneous, she has a right to a hearing with respect to determination of such facts. [**Atkins v. Parker,** 472 U.S. 115 (1985)]

(1) Oral proceedings unnecessary [§154]

Due process does not require trial-type oral proceedings if no useful purpose would be served thereby. If all issues of fact are resolved by written documents (and oral testimony would be redundant), the agency can dispense with oral proceedings. [**FDIC v. Mallen,** *supra*, §126]

4. Rules of General Application [§155]

In many situations, a person would be entitled, either under the Constitution or a statute, to a trial-type hearing. However, the issue involved has already been settled by a validly adopted agency rule. In effect, the rule has preempted an area of adjudication by *legislatively determining the factual questions* in issue. In that situation, the agency can deny a hearing. However, the agency should ordinarily permit the person to petition for a variance from the rule on the theory that the person's individualized circumstances are unusual and not contemplated by the rule. [**United States v. Storer Broadcasting Co.,** 351 U.S. 192 (1956)]

Example: The National Labor Relations Board ("NLRB") must decide on the appropriate bargaining unit for organization of employees. An NLRB rule established that there should be eight such units in hospitals. The Court upheld this rule, holding that the statute gave the NLRB power to resolve bargaining unit issues either by adjudication or rulemaking. If the eight-unit test proves unsuitable for certain hospitals, the NLRB retains the power to make exceptions in extraordinary circumstances. [**American Hospital Association v. NLRB,** 499 U.S. 606 (1991)]

Example: A statute granted disability benefits only if an individual could not engage in any gainful activity by reason of the disability. The agency by rule adopted a "grid" system that indicated whether a disabled person with particular qualifications could obtain a job. The Court held that the applicant was not entitled to a hearing (under the Constitution or the statute) on the issues settled by the rule. [**Heckler v. Campbell,** 461 U.S. 458 (1983)]

Example: The same principle applied to a Civil Aeronautics Board ("CAB") regulation which allowed certain pricing provisions to be used by all-freight (but not passenger-freight) carriers. The regulation changed the existing licenses of the passenger-freight carriers, who claimed statutory and constitutional rights to a hearing. The court of appeals found that no hearing was necessary because the policy questions involved had already been settled by the regulation which applied to *all carriers alike.* Resolving such questions by rulemaking was found to be far more efficient than resolution through adjudication. [**American Airlines v. CAB,** 359 F.2d 624 (D.C. Cir. 1966)]

---

5. **Administrative "Summary Judgment" [§156]**

Sometimes even though a hearing would ordinarily b

quire private parties to make a preliminary showing

issue. If the party is unable to do so, it would be a

hold a hearing. Thus, the agency is permitted to use

mary judgment procedure. [**Weinberger v. Hynson, W

U.S. 609 (1973)]

Chapter Three: Formal and Informal Adjudication Under the Administrative Procedure Act

---

CONTENTS

Chapter Approach

A.	Statutory Hearing Rights to Formal Adjudication	§157
B.	Adjudication Procedure in Informal Adjudication	§167
C.	Declaratory Orders	§180
D.	The Choice Between Adjudication and Rulemaking	§186

Chapter Approach

The previous chapter considered whether the due process guarantees of the United States Constitution required a trial-type hearing and what the elements of that hearing are. In addition to the Constitution, statutes often provide for adjudicatory hearings. Therefore, you should always analyze *both statutory and constitutional rights* to procedural protection. Some key points to remember are:

1. **Federal APA**

   The federal Administrative Procedure Act ("APA") provides for formal adjudication *only if some other statute provides for a hearing on the record*. Therefore, it is necessary to analyze other statutes to see if an on-the-record hearing is provided for. Note that under the *Wong Yang Sung* case, where due process requires a hearing, it can be argued that the procedures of the federal APA must be employed.

2. **State Law and Agency Regulations**

   Where no external source requires a hearing, the agency is free to provide whatever protection it wishes. However, if its regulations provide for a hearing, it must abide by them. The 1981 Model State APA requires the agency to provide for a hearing whether or not an external source calls for one.

3. **Agency Policy**

   Agencies have discretion to make policy either through rulemaking or case-by-case adjudication, unless this choice has unfair retroactive effects. Under *Wyman-Gordon*, an agency should not engage in prospective-only adjudication.

A. Statutory Hearing Rights to Formal Adjudication

1. **Statutory vs. Constitutional Rights [§157]**

   Chapter II considered constitutional rights to fair notice and a hearing where the government deprived a person of liberty or property. In addition to analyzing constitutional issues, it is essential to examine the rights to notice and an adjudicatory hearing provided by *statutes*. In many cases, statutory rights furnish far more protection than constitutional due process—either because due process is inapplicable to the dispute in question or because the statute provides for more protective procedures than the Constitution. Sometimes, when neither the Constitution nor a statute calls for a formal hearing, *agency regulations*, or even agency practice, may provide some protections.

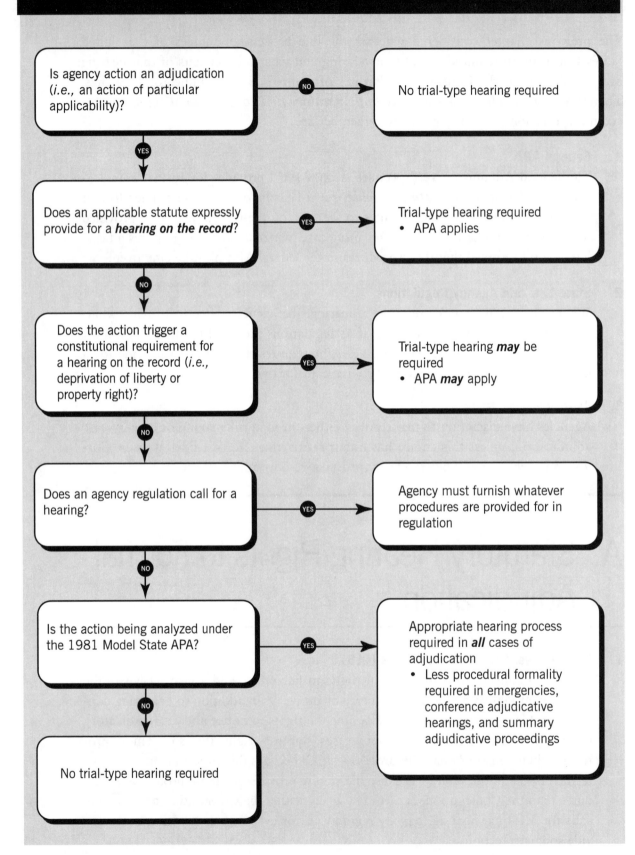

Is agency action an adjudication (*i.e.,* an action of particular applicability)?

NO → No trial-type hearing required

YES ↓

Does an applicable statute expressly provide for a ***hearing on the record***?

YES → Trial-type hearing required
- APA applies

NO ↓

Does the action trigger a constitutional requirement for a hearing on the record (*i.e.,* deprivation of liberty or property right)?

YES → Trial-type hearing ***may*** be required
- APA ***may*** apply

NO ↓

Does an agency regulation call for a hearing?

YES → Agency must furnish whatever procedures are provided for in regulation

NO ↓

Is the action being analyzed under the 1981 Model State APA?

YES → Appropriate hearing process required in ***all*** cases of adjudication
- Less procedural formality required in emergencies, conference adjudicative hearings, and summary adjudicative proceedings

NO ↓

No trial-type hearing required

2. Federal APA—When Applicable [§158]

The federal APA contains detailed provisions for "formal adjudication." [5 U.S.C. §§554, 556, 557—the federal APA will be cited *infra* without the prefatory 5 U.S.C.] However, the APA is *not* applicable in every case of adjudication conducted by federal agencies. Thus, to ascertain whether the APA applies, it is essential to analyze (i) whether the action is *adjudication* and (ii) whether *another statute or the Constitution* requires a hearing on the record. Both elements must be satisfied before the adjudication provisions of the federal APA are applicable.

a. "Adjudication" [§159]

The APA defines "adjudication" as the *"agency process to formulate an order."* [APA §551(7)] However, to understand this definition, it is necessary to examine other key definitions in section 551:

(i) A *"rule"* is "the whole or a part of any agency statement of general or particular applicability and future effect. . . . ," including prescription on wages or prices. [APA §551(4)]

(ii) *"Rulemaking"* is the "agency process for formulating, amending, or repealing a rule." [APA §551(5)]

(iii) An *"order"* is the "whole or a part of a final disposition . . . of an agency *in a matter other than rulemaking but including licensing . . . ."* [APA §551(6)]

(1) Application

Thus, if the agency output falls within the definition of a *"rule,"* it is to be resolved *through "rulemaking,"* not "adjudication." Only if the output is an *"order"* is it resolved *through "adjudication."*

 Example: An "order" includes "licensing"; therefore, any licensing dispute is resolved by adjudication.

---

(2) General vs. particular applicability [§160]

Although the term "rule" is defined to cover "an agency statement of general or particular applicability," most authorities treat this definition as defective. If the agency action has *particular* rather than general applicability, it is adjudication, not rulemaking (unless it consists of prescription of wages or prices).

 Example: Agency orders A to desist from false advertising. Under the APA, this disposition might be considered a rule since it is of "particular applicability" and "future effect." Yet invariably this is treated as "adjudication," and the APA adjudication procedures will be applicable, not its rulemaking procedures.

EXAM TIP

EXAM TIP　　　　　　　　　　　　　　　　　　　　　　　**gilbert**

Be careful not to "skip steps" in addressing this issue on an exam. Before you attach an adjudication discussion to an agency's statement of particular applicability, you should explain that although the statement *may be defined as a rule* under the APA, most authorities consider the APA definition defective and *treat the matter as adjudication*.

b. External source of hearing requirement [§161]

The APA does not in itself require anything in cases of adjudication. Instead, it only applies "in every case of adjudication required by statute to be determined on the record after opportunity for agency hearing . . . ." [APA §554(a)] Thus it is critical to find *another statute* besides the APA that requires the agency to hold an *on-the-record* hearing. If there is no such statute, the APA adjudication provisions *do not apply*. Instead, the matter is described as "informal adjudication" and is not controlled by the APA.

(1) Construction of statute [§162]

In deciding whether another statute calls for an on-the-record hearing, it is often necessary to construe that other statute. Many statutes use the word "hearing" but do not make clear whether they mean a "hearing on the record." In this context, the words "on the record" mean not only that a record is kept (*i.e.*, written down or taped), but also that the decision-maker is *confined to that record in making factual determinations*. Of course, there are many legislative-type "hearings" that are designed to gather information, but they are not "on the record" because the decision-maker is not limited to the information submitted at the hearing.

(a) Rulemaking situation [§163]

Under the APA, if a statute calls for a hearing on the record in the case of rulemaking, the agency is obliged to use a process called "formal rulemaking," which is very inefficient. Thus, if the agency is making a rule rather than adjudicating, the courts will construe a statute calling for a "hearing" as *not* calling for a "hearing on the record." [**United States v. Florida East Coast Railway**, *supra*, §153—industry-wide ratemaking proceeding; the word "hearing" in the statute does not mean "hearing on the record"]

(b) Adjudication situation [§164]

Where the agency is engaged in adjudication, there is a split in authority as to whether a statute that calls for a "hearing" should be construed to mean a "hearing on the record."

1) First Circuit view

A federal statute requires a "hearing" in connection with issuance of a permit by the EPA to discharge pollutants into the water. The case involved the discharge of hot water by a nuclear power plant. This is a case of adjudication because it involves a license. [APA §551(6), (7), (8)] The statute did not state whether the hearing should be "on the record." However, the court required formal adjudication because of the great importance of the issues involved, and because the statute providing for judicial review appeared to contemplate that formal adjudication be conducted. [**Seacoast Anti-Pollution League v. Costle,** 572 F.2d 872 (1st Cir.), *cert. denied,* 439 U.S. 824 (1978)]

2) Seventh Circuit view

The Atomic Energy Act requires the Nuclear Regulatory Commission ("NRC") to conduct a hearing before approval of licenses, including licenses to build nuclear power plants and much less significant licenses (such as permission to process thorium ore). The court construed the statute to require formal adjudication for approval of a nuclear power plant but not for approval of a license to process thorium. The court was concerned with overburdening the NRC with unnecessary hearings, and it found that the issues in a thorium license case could be readily resolved by written submissions. A trial-type procedure was not necessary. [**City of West Chicago v. NRC,** 701 F.2d 632 (7th Cir. 1983)]

3) D.C. Circuit view

A statute that requires the agency to hold an adjudicatory "hearing" is ambiguous; consequently, a court is required to uphold a reasonable agency interpretation of the statute. Under this approach, the EPA's rules requiring only an informal, non-APA hearing to review corrective orders to toxic waste dumps was found to be a reasonable interpretation of the statute, and thus it was upheld. [**Chemical Waste Management, Inc. v. EPA,** 873 F.2d 1477 (D.C. Cir. 1989)—applying the judicial review rule of **Chevron, USA v. Natural Resources Defense Council,** *see infra,* §§579 *et seq.*]

EXAM TIP   **gilbert**

In determining whether a statute involving adjudication calls for a hearing on the record (so that the APA adjudication sections apply), consider the *importance of the subject* of the statute (*e.g.,* its possible impact on public policy or safety issues) *and the complexity* of the subject. The greater the impact on the public, and the greater the complexity of the subject, the more likely it is that a hearing on the record will be required.

(2) Hearing required by Constitution rather than statute [§165]

Suppose that the applicable statute does not call for formal adjudication (*i.e.,* does not demand a hearing on the record), but a trial-type hearing is required by *procedural due process* (*i.e.,* a deprivation of liberty or property has occurred and determination of individualized facts is required). In such cases, the Court has held that Congress intended that the full array of APA formal adjudication procedures would apply. [**Wong Yang Sung v. McGrath,** *supra,* §90—deportation; APA provision for separation of functions applies]

(a) But note

Congress quickly repudiated the *Wong Yang Sung* case. It explicitly provided that the APA procedures would *not* apply to deportation cases. The Supreme Court upheld the constitutionality of the revised statute. [**Marcello v. Bonds,** 349 U.S. 302 (1955)]

(b) Present status

The present status of *Wong Yang Sung* is obscure. Recall that recent Supreme Court cases have held that due process often requires much less than an elaborate trial-type hearing. (*See, e.g., supra,* §§99-102—suspensions from school.) Therefore, it is not credible to think that Congress wants to apply the elaborate APA procedures in every case in which the federal government is required by due process to provide some kind of hearing. [*See* **Clardy v. Levy,** 545 F.2d 1241 (9th Cir. 1976)—full APA hearing not required; *but see* **Collord v. Department of the Interior,** 154 F.3d 933 (9th Cir. 1998)—since due process requires trial-type hearing, APA applies and prevailing party can apply for attorneys' fees under the Equal Access to Justice Act ("EAJA"); for a discussion of the EAJA, *see infra,* §§536-540]

(3) State APA [§166]

The 1961 Model State APA followed the federal APA; no formal adjudication was required unless some other statute required a formal hearing. However, following the lead of some states (such as Wisconsin and Florida), the 1981 Model State APA takes an entirely different approach. It generally *requires an appropriate adjudication* procedure in *every* case of adjudication, whether or not some other statute requires it. An "appropriate" procedure means that the hearing procedure is as formal as the situation calls for. [1981 Model State APA §§4-101, 4-201]

---

e.g. **Example:** Under a Wisconsin statute, a person is entitled to a hearing if a *substantial interest of the person is injured* by the agency action and there is a dispute of material fact. Thus, a local agency required by a state agency to line sewer tunnels with concrete was entitled to a formal hearing. The cost of lining the tunnels was very substantial, so the local agency that wanted to avoid these costs was suffering injury to a "substantial interest." [**Milwaukee Metropolitan Sewerage District v. Wisconsin Department of Natural Resources,** 375 N.W.2d 648 (Wis. 1985)]

EXAM TIP	gilbert

Note that the federal APA would probably not have required a hearing on the record in this case because no statute outside the APA called for a hearing on the record. As a result, the question of whether the sewers must be lined with concrete was an issue that probably could have been decided on the basis of written submissions. On an exam, be sure to remember whether you are dealing with a *state* APA or the *federal* APA.

B. Adjudication Procedure in Informal Adjudication

1. Gap in Coverage [§167]

The federal APA sets forth detailed procedural rules for formal adjudication and for rulemaking. However, where no statute calls for a hearing on the record, and due process does not require a trial-type hearing (*see supra,* §§161-166), there are almost no statutory requirements. This is the area of "informal adjudication" and covers a vast range of agency decisionmaking.

a. APA provisions [§168]

The APA sets forth a few provisions applicable to informal adjudication.

(1) Right to appear [§169]

The APA provides a right to appear personally before an agency and to be represented by counsel. Also, it requires the agency to conclude matters within a reasonable time. [APA §555(b)]

(2) Enforcement of subpoenas [§170]

The APA provides that subpoenas and reports can be enforced only as authorized by law. [APA §555(c), (d)]

(3) Explanation of denial [§171]

The APA requires an agency to give prompt notice and explanation of the denial of any application, petition, or other request. [APA §555(e)]

(4) Licensing provisions [§172]

The APA requires a prior warning and opportunity to correct the problem in cases of license revocation or suspension. However, this provision does not apply in cases of willfulness or in which public health, interest, or safety requires otherwise. Also, where a licensee applies to renew a license, the former license does not expire until the application has been finally determined by the agency. [APA §558(c)]

b. Model Act [§173]

Under the 1981 Model State APA, an appropriate hearing process is required in *all cases of adjudication*—whether or not some other statute requires a hearing or due process applies. [1981 Model State APA §4-101(a)] An "appropriate" hearing means a hearing with the level of formality appropriate for the particular dispute. Consequently, there is no gap for informal adjudication. This sweeping provision could require agencies to provide far more formality than would be appropriate for relatively small and simple disputes. Therefore, the 1981 Model State APA provides for several informal hearing models.

(1) Emergencies [§174]

As discussed earlier, due process often permits agencies to dispense with formal procedures before taking emergency action. (*See supra*, §119.) The 1981 Model Act also makes provision for emergency adjudicative procedures in situations involving an immediate danger to the public health, safety, or welfare. In such cases, the agency can act first and hold the required hearing afterwards. [1981 Model State APA §4-501]

(2) Conference adjudicative hearings [§175]

A conference hearing is an agency proceeding that dispenses with some of the elements of a formal trial such as subpoenas, discovery, oral testimony by nonparties, and cross-examination. Instead, the parties may testify and present written exhibits. Conference hearings are particularly useful for cases that involve disputes of law or policy but not disputed adjudicative facts. The conference hearing must first be authorized by agency rules. The Model Act gives states a choice: They can allow conference hearings in *any* proceedings described in agency rules or only in particular types of cases that do not involve disputed issues of material fact or that involve only relatively minor stakes (such as monetary amounts of not more than $1,000 or disciplinary sanctions against a prisoner). [1981 Model State APA §§4-401 - 4-403]

(3) Summary adjudicative proceedings [§176]

A summary proceeding is merely an opportunity for a party to be informed of the agency's view and to explain the party's side of the dispute. Any person named by the agency can be the decisionmaker. The decisionmaker must state findings, conclusions, and reasons. There is ordinarily a provision for reconsideration by a higher level official. Again, summary proceedings must be authorized by rule and the Model Act gives states a choice of applying them to all cases described in agency rules or to only very minor matters. [1981 Model State APA §§4-502 - 4-506]

2. Judicial Innovation Under Federal APA [§177]

A federal agency that is not required to conduct formal adjudication can provide whatever procedures it wishes—if any—in conducting informal adjudication. The courts are precluded from requiring agencies to engage in any particular procedure, because the APA intended to leave this decision to agency discretion. [**Pension Benefit Guaranty Corp. v. LTV Corp.**, 496 U.S. 633 (1990)—applies the principles of the *Vermont Yankee* case to informal adjudication; *see infra* §384]

a. Exception [§178]

Where a statute requires an agency to conduct a "hearing," but not a "hearing on the record," the agency is not required to follow the procedures for formal adjudication under the APA. However, it is possible that despite **Pension Benefit Guaranty Corp. v. LTV Corp.** (above), a court could derive procedural requirements from the word "hearing."

b. Exception [§179]

A court can remand a case to an agency to require it to explain its decision in an informal action so that the court can review it. In unusual cases, where the agency has failed to explain its action, it is also possible to conduct a trial in which agency officials must explain their decision. [**Citizens to Preserve Overton Park v. Volpe,** 401 U.S. 402 (1971); *see infra,* §§304, 425] However, this is not the preferred approach. [**Pension Benefit Guaranty Corp. v. LTV Corp.,** *supra*]

FORMAL ADJUDICATION VS. INFORMAL ADJUDICATION—A SUMMARY **gilbert**	FORMAL ADJUDICATION	INFORMAL ADJUDICATION
REQUIREMENTS	• Must be adjudication • Statute or Constitution requires hearing on the record	• Must be adjudication • No hearing on the record required by statute or Constitution
EFFECT	APA's detailed procedural rules apply	Few APA rules apply; agency can provide whatever procedures it wishes

C. Declaratory Orders

1. Introduction [§180]

One important type of formal agency adjudication is the declaratory order. Persons subject to agency regulation often need guidance on how the agency will interpret the law. In most cases, they can obtain this guidance through seeking formal or informal advice from the agency staff, but the agency is *probably not absolutely bound* by this advice. (*See infra*, §§321 *et seq.* for discussion of estoppel.) If the person seeks *authoritative guidance*, he may seek a declaratory order from the agency. This is the administrative equivalent of a declaratory judgment in court; *i.e.*, it is an authoritative statement on how the law will be applied but without seeking any other remedy.

2. APA Provisions [§181]

The federal act provides: "The agency . . . as in the case of other orders, and in its sound discretion, may issue a declaratory order to terminate a controversy or remove uncertainty." [APA §554(e)] The Model State APA contains a more detailed provision with precise time limits. It requires the agency to issue a requested declaratory order unless agency rules preclude the issuance of declaratory orders in the particular circumstances involved. [1981 Model State APA §2-103]

3. Broad Power [§182]

In construing the language of APA section 554(e), the Supreme Court has ruled that wherever the agency could have conducted its usual trial-type hearing (*e.g.*, to revoke a license), it may enter a declaratory order instead. [**Red Lion Broadcasting Co. v. FCC,** 395 U.S. 367 (1969)]

a. Implied power [§183]

Some commentators feel that an agency also has the *implied power* to issue a declaratory order in cases *not* requiring a hearing.

4. Judicial Review [§184]

Declaratory orders are reviewable by the courts in the same manner as any other administrative order. [*See* **Red Lion Broadcasting Co. v. FCC,** *supra*]

a. Abuse of discretion [§185]

It is not clear whether agency discretion under APA section 554(e) *not* to issue a declaratory order can be abused and, if so, whether such abuse is reviewable. Some commentators argue that if the agency arbitrarily refuses to grant such an order, a reviewing court should force it to exercise its discretion.

D. The Choice Between Adjudication and Rulemaking

1. Choice Is Discretionary [§186]

An agency generally has broad discretion to choose how it will implement the statutory scheme. Traditionally, agencies have made law and policy through case-by-case adjudication, like the common law courts. Often, the result is the retroactive application of a new principle to the parties in the case. Usually agencies are also empowered to make law and policy through rulemaking rather than adjudication. One major advantage of rulemaking, as opposed to adjudication, is that a rule is normally *prospective*; therefore, the parties subject to it are on notice and cannot be surprised by a retroactive change in the law. (For discussion of other advantages of rulemaking, *see infra,* §337.) Nevertheless, the courts have been reluctant to force agencies to use the rulemaking approach rather than the adjudication approach.

2. Abuse of Discretion [§187]

As mentioned, the choice between proceeding by general rule or by case-by-case adjudication generally lies within the "informed discretion" of the agency. However, where retroactive application of a new policy would have *serious adverse consequences,* a reviewing court may find that the agency abused its discretion. [**SEC v. Chenery Corp.,** 332 U.S. 194 (1947) ("*Chenery II*"); **NLRB v. Bell Aerospace Co.,** 416 U.S. 267 (1974)]

a. Application—*Chenery II* case

During reorganization of a public utility holding company, insiders purchased securities in the company and sought to convert them under the reorganization plan. The SEC refused to permit conversion, relying on "equitable principles" announced in previous court decisions. The Supreme Court in **SEC v. Chenery Corp.,** 318 U.S. 80 (1943) ("*Chenery I*"), reversed the SEC's decision on the ground that the precedents cited did not support the SEC's result. The SEC then again refused to permit conversion, this time basing the result on its expertise in public utility reorganizations. In *Chenery II*, the Court affirmed the SEC ruling. It noted that every case of first impression has a retroactive effect, and that making policy by means of adjudication is not per se an abuse of discretion because of such effect.

(1) But note

Abuse would be present if the harm from retroactivity outweighed the harm to the public interest from allowing the problem raised by the instant case to go uncorrected.

(2) Comment

At the same time, the Court noted that *rulemaking was generally preferable* where possible, since it avoided the problems of retroactivity.

b. NLRB cases [§188]

Despite a statutory grant of rulemaking power, the NLRB has traditionally chosen to formulate policy on a case-by-case basis rather than by rulemaking. Where this choice is appropriate to the problem, and no substantial adverse consequences result, it is not an abuse of discretion. [**NLRB v. Bell Aerospace**

Co., *supra*—NLRB can determine that buyers are "managerial employees" under NLRA by means of adjudication]

(1) Frequent criticism

The NLRB has frequently been criticized for its failure to make rules of general application, and some courts have refused to enforce its adjudicative policies where they represent an abuse of discretion.

(a) Factors

A court deciding whether a new case law rule is unfairly retroactive should balance at least five factors: (i) whether the case is one of first impression, (ii) whether the new rule represents an abrupt departure from well-established practice as opposed to filling a void in an unsettled area of the law, (iii) the extent to which the party relied on prior law, (iv) the degree of burden that a retroactive order imposes, and (v) the statutory interest in applying a new rule to the case at hand. [**Clark-Cowlitz Joint Operating Agency v. FERC**, 826 F.2d 1074 (D.C. Cir. 1987), *cert. denied*, 485 U.S. 913 (1988); **Retail, Wholesale, & Department Store Clerks Union v. NLRB**, 466 F.2d 380 (D.C. Cir. 1972)]

---

e.g. Example: The NLRB held that the employer committed an unfair labor practice in refusing to rehire strikers when jobs opened up after the strike. This was a change in the law. The NLRB not only required the strikers to be rehired, it also required the employer to pay back wages. The court upheld the order to rehire the strikers but reversed the requirement of back pay. The employer relied on well-established prior law in refusing to rehire the strikers and in arguing that the requirement to pay back wages based on this retroactive change in law was an abuse of discretion. [**Retail, Wholesale, & Department Store Clerks Union v. NLRB**, *supra*]

---

(2) A new approach [§189]

Taking a new approach, the NLRB adopted a rule that constrained its discretion in determining appropriate bargaining units in hospitals. Because of the rule, it did not make case-by-case determinations of bargaining units. The Supreme Court emphatically upheld this rule. [**American Hospital Association v. NLRB**, *supra*, §155]

c. Proper subject matter for adjudication [§190]

The Court has enumerated several types of subject matter as to which policy *may* properly be formulated on a case-by-case basis:

(i) *Problems that could not reasonably have been foreseen* by the agency;

    (ii) *Problems as to which the agency has only a tentative judgment,* due to lack of experience in the particular area; and

    (iii) *Problems so specialized and varied* as to be incapable of resolution by general rule.

[**SEC v. Chenery Corp.,** *supra,* §187]

d. Required rulemaking

  (1) Duty to adopt rules—federal cases [§191]
    Some decisions indicate that agencies must limit the scope of a broad delegated power by adopting their own standards, either by rulemaking or case-by-case adjudication. [*See* **Morton v. Ruiz,** *supra,* §21; **Allison v. Block,** 723 F.2d 631 (8th Cir. 1983); **White v. Roughton,** *supra,* §106; **Holmes v. New York City Housing Authority,** *supra,* §106] These cases involve benefit programs; some rely on due process, others on interpretation of the statute. This principle has not often been applied outside of the government benefits context.

  (2) Duty to adopt rules—state cases [§192]
    Some states have been far more aggressive than the federal courts in requiring agencies to adopt regulations to limit their discretion. [**Megdal v. Oregon State Board of Dental Examiners,** *supra,* §22]

    Example: In *Megdal,* a state board revoked a dentist's license for "unprofessional conduct" because he made a false statement on his malpractice insurance application. The court held that the agency was required to adopt rules defining the meaning of this broad term before a licensee could be disciplined. This would serve the purpose of giving fair notice to licensees and confining the board's exercise of discretion. The decision was based on a finding that the legislature so intended, not on due process.

  (3) Model Act approach [§193]
    The 1981 Model State APA moves strongly in the direction of required rulemaking.

    (a) Preference for rulemaking over adjudication [§194]
      First, the Model Act requires the agency to adopt rules in preference to making policy through adjudication. The agency shall "as soon as feasible and to the extent practicable, adopt rules . . . embodying appropriate standards, principles, and procedural safeguards that the agency will apply to the law it administers . . . ." [1981 Model State APA §2-104(3)] This is a statutory embodiment of the *Megdal* case, *supra.*

(b) Replacement of adjudicatory law with rules [§195]

Second, if the agency has previously been making law and policy through case-by-case adjudication, the Act requires that the agency replace the case law with rules. Each agency shall "as soon as feasible and to the extent practicable, adopt rules to supersede principles of law or policy lawfully declared by the agency as the basis for its decisions in particular cases." [1981 Model State APA §2-104(4)]

e. Prospective adjudication [§196]

The Supreme Court prohibited the adoption of *prospective rules* by means of adjudication. [**NLRB v. Wyman-Gordon Co.,** 394 U.S. 759 (1969)]

(1) Application—*Wyman-Gordon* case

Wyman-Gordon followed an earlier case [**Excelsior Underwear,** 156 N.L.R.B. 1236 (1966)] in which the Board held that a company must furnish the union with a list of all employees for electioneering purposes. This policy was announced by the Board as *prospective* only; *i.e.,* it was not applied to the parties in the *Excelsior* case. The Supreme Court in *Wyman-Gordon* held the *Excelsior* rule invalid because a prospective order should be *adopted as a rule* under section 553, in compliance with the statutory provisions for rulemaking.

(a) Note

Ironically, the Court nonetheless enforced the Board's order in *Wyman-Gordon* because a specific and valid order had been directed to respondent to furnish the list; the adjudication stood on its own and did not depend on the invalidly adopted *Excelsior* rule.

Chapter Four:
The Process of Formal Adjudication

CONTENTS

Chapter Approach

A.   The Prehearing Process   §197

B.   The Process of Proof at the Hearing   §211

C.   Requirement of Findings and Reasons   §239

Chapter Approach

If you have decided that the formal adjudication procedures of the APA apply (as discussed in the previous chapter), then you must make sure that these procedures have actually been provided by the agency during each phase of the case. The federal and state APAs provide a detailed roadmap through the process of formal adjudication. They contain provisions for numerous procedural details: notice, discovery, proof, findings, and the like. This chapter summarizes the detailed provisions for the formal adjudication process.

In analyzing a fact situation, watch for the following requirements:

1. **Prehearing Process**

   Make sure that the party receives *proper notice* and any appropriate rights to discovery. If other persons wish to participate in the hearing, they should be allowed to intervene if their participation will not complicate the proceeding. There should be opportunity for settlement or mediation.

2. **Hearing Process**

   Recall that the *proponent has the burden of proof*, normally by a preponderance of the evidence. Generally *any relevant evidence* offered is admissible but, in many states, findings must be supported by some evidence other than hearsay. Note that the decision must be based on material in the record but official notice is permissible (given an opportunity for the opponent to rebut).

3. **Post-Hearing Process**

   Normally at this stage there must be findings of basic and ultimate fact and a statement of reasons.

A. The Prehearing Process

1. Notice [§197]

All APAs contain provisions relating to notice. The federal act provides that persons entitled to notice of an agency hearing shall be timely informed of: (i) the time, place, and nature of the hearing; (ii) the legal authority and jurisdiction under which the hearing is to be held; and (iii) the matters of fact and law asserted. [APA §554(b)] A much more detailed provision is set forth in the Model State APA. [1981 Model State APA §4-206] The details of each agency's pleading rules vary greatly; these are generally set forth in the agency's regulations.

2. Parties and Intervention

a. Purpose of intervention [§198]

In addition to the named parties, additional parties often seek to intervene in agency proceedings. They do so because their legal rights or other legal interests may be affected by the proceeding and they have a position they believe will not be adequately represented by the named parties and the agency staff. [1981 Model State APA §4-209(a)]

b. Discretion [§199]

Generally agencies permit such intervention as long as the new party or parties will **not unduly complicate the proceeding**. [APA §555(b); 1981 Model State APA §4-209(a)(3), (b)] Often, the intervention is conditional: The intervenors can participate on some issues but not all, or are limited in their use of discovery or cross-examination. [1981 Model State APA §4-209(c); **Office of Communications of the United Church of Christ v. FCC,** 359 F.2d 994 (D.C. Cir. 1966)—TV viewers have right to intervene to protest renewal of station's license, but FCC can adopt rules to limit the number of parties]

c. Relation between intervention and standing

(1) Same criteria not applied [§200]

The criteria for intervention and standing to seek judicial review are not the same, even though some earlier cases seem to equate the two situations. For example, a party that lacks standing might still be entitled to intervene if it could make a significant contribution to the administrative proceeding. [**Koniag, Inc. v. Andrus,** 580 F.2d 601 (D.C. Cir. 1978)] By the same token, a party that can meet the requirements for standing might still be denied the right to intervene if intervention would unduly complicate the proceeding or otherwise violate the agency's own rules. [**Envirocare of Utah, Inc. v. Nuclear Regulatory Commission,** 194 F.3d 72 (D.C. Cir. 1999)]

Example: The Nuclear Regulatory Commission's statute allows intervention "on the request of any person whose interest may be affected by the proceeding." Petitioner (Envirocare) has an NRC license to dispose of nuclear waste. Petitioner wishes to intervene in NRC proceedings that consider whether to give a similar license to Q. Petitioner complains that the NRC does not intend to compel Q to meet all of the high standards that Petititioner had to meet. The NRC refused to allow Petitioner to intervene in Q's case, even though Petitioner probably could meet the requirements for standing to challenge the NRC decision in court. One reason for the NRC's decision was that Petitioner's participation would unduly complicate Q's case. Under *Chevron,* discussed in §§579 *et seq., infra,* the court must defer to the NRC's reasonable construction of the ambiguous word "interest" in the statute. The NRC's construction was reasonable in light of the understanding of the word "interest" in 1954 when the statute was enacted. It was also reasonable in light of the NRC's decision that Petitioner's participation would unduly complicate Q's case. [Envirocare of Utah, Inc. v. Nuclear Regulatory Commission, *supra*]

(2) Practical distinctions [§201]

The questions of standing and intervention each have a different impact on the "manageability" of administrative proceedings. [**National Welfare Rights Organization v. Finch,** 429 F.2d 725 (D.C. Cir 1970)]

(a) Increased complexity [§202]

In *intervention,* the granting of full cross-examination rights to the intervenor necessarily increases the complexity and expense of the hearing. In contrast, granting *standing* to seek review does not complicate the case, because the matter is appealed by only one party.

(b) Limited participation [§203]

An intervenor's participation in the hearing can be *limited* (*e.g.,* by limitations on the right to cross-examine witnesses), whereas there is no way to limit an appeal once standing is granted.

3. Discovery [§204]

There is *no* federal requirement to discovery in agency proceedings. Similarly, most states *do not provide* any rights to prehearing discovery to parties to administrative proceedings. However, in some states, parties to administrative proceedings have the same rights to prehearing discovery (*e.g.,* to take depositions) as do litigants in civil cases. [1981 Model State APA §4-210(a)] In one state, the court held that, as a matter of common law, an administrative respondent in a license revocation case should have the same access to the documents and interviews in agency files as a criminal defendant would have. [**Shively v. Stewart,** 65 Cal. 2d 475 (1966)]

EXAM TIP   **gilbert**

Keep in mind that an agency hearing, even a formal adjudication, is *not a court case*. Therefore some of the rules of procedure that apply in court cases do not necessarily apply in agency hearings. Prehearing discovery is one area where the agency rules usually differ from court rules.

---

a. Subpoena power [§205]

Normally, all parties to administrative proceedings have subpoena power so that they can compel the presence of witnesses at the hearing. Similarly, by using a subpoena duces tecum, parties can compel witnesses to bring documents with them. In federal agencies, the issuance of such subpoenas is automatic on request [APA §555(d)], but in some state agencies, the issuance of subpoenas is discretionary with the presiding officer.

b. Freedom of Information Act [§206]

An individual can often receive important information in government files by making a request under the Freedom of Information Act or corresponding state statutes. (*See infra,* Chapter VII.) This information may be quite useful for purposes of pretrial discovery.

4. Settlement and Alternate Dispute Resolution [§207]

As in civil litigation, parties to administrative litigation try to settle their cases without trial. In 1990, Congress amended the APA to require agencies to explore and use alternate dispute resolution ("ADR") techniques in all agency functions, including adjudication and rulemaking. [Administrative Dispute Resolution Act, P.L. 101-552]

a. APA amendments [§208]

The ADR Act amended the APA by changing section 556(c)(6), and by adding section 556(c)(7) and (8) to encourage the use of ADR techniques to settle disputes and to permit an administrative law judge ("ALJ") to require participation in settlement conferences.

b. ADR techniques [§209]

The ADR Act amended Title 5 of the United States Code to add new sections authorizing and encouraging agencies to use the whole range of ADR techniques: settlement negotiations, conciliation, facilitation, mediation, fact finding, minitrials, and arbitration.

c. When ADR is used [§210]

Despite the statute's requirement to explore the use of ADR, *ADR procedures are voluntary*; regulated parties cannot be compelled to use them. The statute also suggests that there are situations in which ADR is not appropriate, such as when an authoritative resolution of the matter is required for precedential value.

B. The Process of Proof at the Hearing

1. Burden of Proof [§211]

The rules relating to the burden of producing evidence and the burden of persuasion in administrative hearings are roughly the same as in civil litigation.

a. Placement of burden [§212]

Under the federal APA, ". . . the proponent of a rule or order has the burden of proof . . . . A sanction may not be imposed or rule or order issued except on consideration of the whole record or those parts thereof cited by a party and supported by and in accordance with the reliable, probative and substantial evidence." [APA §556(d)]

(1) Burden of persuasion

APA section 556(d), which places the burden of proof on the proponent of a rule or order, refers to the *burden of persuasion*, not the burden of going forward with the evidence. Thus, an applicant for a benefit must prove his case by a preponderance of the evidence.

> **e.g.** **Example:** The Supreme Court overturned an agency decision that held that the applicant would win if the applicant's and the employer's evidence were evenly balanced. The agency's view (known as the "true doubt" rule) violates section 556(d) by failing to place the burden of proof on the applicant. [**Director, Office of Workers' Compensation v. Greenwich Collieries,** 512 U.S. 267 (1994)]

(2) Proving an exception

The burden of proving an exception to the applicability of a statute lies with the party asserting that exception. [**NLRB v. Kentucky River Community Care, Inc.,** 532 U.S. 706 (2001)]

> **e.g.** **Example:** By statute, employers must bargain with a union representing their employees, if the employees vote for representation, but the statute does not apply to employees who are "supervisors." Although the NLRB has the burden of proof to establish that the duty to bargain has arisen, the employer has the burden to show that particular employees are supervisors. [**NLRB v. Kentucky River Community Care, Inc.,** *supra*]

b. Standard of proof [§213]

The general rule is that a case must be proved by a *preponderance of the evidence*—not the higher standards such as clear and convincing evidence or beyond a reasonable doubt. [**Steadman v. SEC,** 450 U.S. 91 (1981)] *Note:* The *Steadman* case involved sanctions against a licensee for fraud. In a contract case, fraud must be proved by clear and convincing evidence, but this is not required in administrative proceedings.

(1) Exceptions [§214]

Courts sometimes manipulate the burden of proof to make it more difficult to impose harsh sanctions. For example, to deport an alien, the government must prove its case by "clear, unequivocal, and convincing evidence." [**Woodby v. INS,** 385 U.S. 276 (1966)] And according to some state cases, a licensing agency must prove its case by clear and convincing evidence to a reasonable degree of certainty in order to revoke a professional license. [**Ettinger v. Board of Medical Quality Assurance,** 135 Cal. App. 3d 853 (1982)]

2. Evidence in Administrative Proceedings

a. Admissibility of evidence [§215]

The general rule is that *any relevant evidence* is admissible in administrative proceedings, *regardless of the rules of evidence* applicable in civil litigation. Thus, hearsay evidence is admissible regardless of whether it falls under one of the hearsay exceptions.

(1) Federal APA [§216]

The federal APA provides: "Any oral or documentary evidence may be received, but the agency as a matter of policy shall provide for the exclusion of irrelevant, immaterial, or unduly repetitious evidence." [APA §556(d)]

(2) Model State APA [§217]

The 1981 Model Act similarly provides that the presiding officer can admit any evidence, regardless of the rules of evidence. It also provides that evidence can be received in written form if doing so will expedite the hearing without substantial prejudice to any party. [1981 Model State APA §4-212(a), (d)]

EXAM TIP   **gilbert**

An important area where agency procedure differs from court procedure concerns admissible evidence. Remember that many of the rules of evidence used by courts *do not apply in an agency formal adjudication*. However, keep in mind a very important limitation: The evidence presented *must be relevant*. However, administrative judges tend to admit much more evidence than do judges in civil cases. Also note that in some states, the decision must be supported by at least a "residuum" of nonhearsay evidence (see below).

---

b. Reliance on inadmissible evidence [§218]

While hearsay evidence is freely admissible in administrative cases, there is a split in authority whether the agency can rely on *hearsay alone* in making a finding.

(1) State courts—"residuum rule" [§219]

Many state courts follow the rule that the agency's decision must be based on at least *some* (a "residuum" of) evidence that is *not* hearsay. [**Carroll v. Knickerbocker Ice Co.,** 218 N.Y. 435 (1916)] However, the residuum rule is rejected by 1981 Model State APA section 4-215(d).

(a) Illustration

In *Carroll,* workers' compensation was awarded to the widow of a deceased employee. Before his death, the employee had stated that his injury was caused by a block of ice falling on him, although all objective evidence indicated the contrary. Reversing the agency's decision, the court held that the agency could admit hearsay evidence, but there had to be a *residuum of evidence other than hearsay* on which the decision was based.

1) Limitation

The *Carroll* rule was subsequently limited by the New York courts. A later decision held that an award could be based exclusively on hearsay evidence where *all other circumstances were consistent* with the hearsay statement. [**Altschuler v. Bressler,** 289 N.Y. 463 (1943)]

(b) Entitlements [§220]

Some states preserve the residuum rule in cases where a *substantial right* (*e.g.,* a statutory entitlement or the right to earn a livelihood) is at stake. [**Trujillo v. Employment Security Commission,** 610 P.2d 747 (N.M. 1980)]

(c) Model State APA [§221]

As mentioned, the 1981 Model Act abolished the residuum rule. "Findings must be based on the kind of evidence on which reasonably prudent persons are accustomed to rely in the conduct of their serious affairs and may be based upon such evidence even if it would be inadmissible in a civil trial." [1981 Model State APA §4-215(d)] The result is that an agency's decision may be based on hearsay evidence alone, provided that the presiding officer chooses to admit it, which is left to his discretion.

(2) Federal rule [§222]

The residuum rule does not apply in the review of the decisions of federal agencies. [**Richardson v. Perales,** 402 U.S. 389 (1971)]

(a) But note

The *Perales* case is somewhat weak authority because it was decided on alternative grounds. The issue in *Perales* was whether a claimant was permanently disabled. The reports of several doctors were introduced in opposition to the claim. The doctors were not called to testify, and the claimant did not seek to subpoena them. Under evidence law, the doctors' reports were inadmissible hearsay. The Court upheld the decision denying benefits even though the doctors' reports were the only evidence against the claimant. Thus, the Court appeared to reject the residuum rule. Among the grounds for the decision, however, was that the claimant had waived his right of cross-examination by failing to subpoena the doctors. Thus, it can be argued that the *Perales* decision might have gone the other way if the claimant had attempted unsuccessfully to subpoena the doctors.

(3) Judicial review [§223]

Even though the residuum rule has been abolished, a decision based upon **unreliable** hearsay evidence might be set aside as lacking support in substantial evidence.

---

e.g. **Example:** The Army deprived Plaintiff of security clearance on the basis of various incidents that it claimed jeopardized security. Plaintiff denied or adequately explained each of the incidents. All of the Army's evidence was based on hearsay (the statements of one Hiley), and it did not produce Hiley to testify (he was unavailable). There was great personal hostility between Plaintiff and Hiley. The court held that substantial evidence did not support the Army's decision because the hearsay evidence was not sufficiently credible. [**Hoska v. Department of Army,** 677 F.2d 131 (D.C. Cir. 1982)]

---

(4) Constitutional problem—reliance on hearsay alone [§224]

Note that hearsay evidence is evidence of a statement made by an **out-of-court** declarant and it is offered to prove the truth of the statement. Thus, the opponent of the hearsay is denied the right to confront the declarant. In an extreme case, reliance on hearsay alone could violate the due process right to confront witnesses. This might occur if the hearsay does not fall within any judicial exception to the hearsay rule, if credibility issues were critical, and especially if the declarant were available but the agency failed to produce the declarant despite a timely request to do so. [*See* **Carlton v. Department of Motor Vehicles,** 203 Cal. App. 3d 1428 (1988)—serious due process problem if the only evidence against a driver is a computer entry based on a police report that was based on the statement of another driver]

3. Exclusive Record Principle [§225]

An agency may **not rely** on evidence that is **outside the record**. Under the federal APA, "the transcript of testimony and exhibits, together with all papers and requests filed in the proceeding, constitutes the exclusive record for decision . . . ." [APA §556(e)] This is a fundamental principle of administrative law. [*See* **Seacoast Anti-Pollution League v. Costle,** *supra*, §164—reliance on scientific evidence that was not in the record] However, this basic principle has a number of limitations:

a. Physical inspections [§226]

Agency decisions can be based upon physical inspections or tests, provided that these are conducted in a way that is fair to the parties involved.

b. Assistance to adjudicators [§227]

Administrative law judges and agency heads are entitled to the assistance of law clerks and other staff members to help them understand the evidence, find testimony in the record, and write the decision. Just as a judge can have a law clerk, administrative judges are entitled to similar assistance. Of course, the assistant cannot supplement the facts in the record; she can merely help the decisionmaker to understand the record or give advice about policy. Moreover, the staff member clearly cannot have been an adversary in the case—that is prohibited by separation of functions provisions. (*See infra,* §§257 *et seq.*)

(1) Model Act [§228]

A provision in the 1981 Model State APA confirms that staff assistance is permissible. Section 4-213(b) provides: "A presiding officer may receive aid from staff assistants if the assistants do not (i) receive ex parte communications of a type that the presiding officer would be prohibited from receiving, or (ii) furnish, augment, diminish, or modify the evidence in the record."

(2) Federal rule [§229]

Whether a federal administrative law judge can receive staff assistance is unclear. APA section 554(d)(1) provides that an ALJ may not "consult a person or party on a fact in issue, unless on notice and opportunity for all parties to participate." In dictum, the Supreme Court stated that this provision applies to conferences between an ALJ and "any person or party, including other agency officials." [**Butz v. Economou**, 438 U.S. 478 (1978)] However, it is arguable that the Supreme Court did not mean to preclude conferences between an ALJ and other nonadversary staff members that are designed to assist in understanding the record, since such conferences might not be about a "fact in issue."

c. Official notice [§230]

A trier of fact is permitted to take official notice of factual material. Official notice is similar to judicial notice in that it relieves the party who has the burden of proof of producing facts to prove the matter asserted. Noticed material is treated as evidence. Official notice is a great time saver; it allows matters that are unlikely to be disputed to be treated as proved. Nevertheless, the opponent generally must have an opportunity to rebut it.

(1) What can be officially noticed? [§231]

Traditionally, official notice was no broader than judicial notice. Thus, it was largely limited to matters that were indisputable. However, the modern view is that agencies can take official notice of "technical or scientific materials within the agency's specialized knowledge," even though such items are not necessarily indisputable. [1981 Model State APA §4-212(f)]

Example: A medical panel can take official notice of community standards of medical practice. [**Franz v. Board of Medical Quality Assurance,** 31 Cal. 3d 124 (1982)]

(2) Opportunity to contradict [§232]

APA section 556(e) provides: "When an agency decision rests on official notice of a material fact not appearing in the evidence in the record, a party is entitled, on timely request, to an *opportunity to show the contrary.* (Section 4-212(f) of the 1981 Model State APA is similar.)

(a) Criteria for rebuttal [§233]

If the agency fails to afford an opportunity to contradict the noticed material, there is a substantial chance that the court will reverse the agency's decision. This is especially true if the material involves *adjudicative facts,* is subject to *dispute,* or is *critical* to the result.

Example—ratemaking: In a case involving the setting of rates for telephone service, the regulatory commission refused to disclose the source of computations it used to discover relevant price trends. The Supreme Court found that this procedure violated due process because the utility affected had no chance to examine, analyze, explain, or rebut the information used to set the rates. [**Ohio Bell Telephone Co. v. Public Utilities Commission,** 301 U.S. 292 (1937)] The Court noted an "even deeper" objection in that the agency's failure to disclose the facts made meaningful review impossible; an appellate court could not determine whether the agency's findings were supported by the evidence when the evidence was not available for consideration.

Example—immigration: An immigration judge took official notice of the following facts without furnishing an opportunity for rebuttal: (i) Violeta Chamorro had been elected president of Nicaragua; (ii) her coalition gained a majority in parliament; (iii) the Sandinistas had been ousted from power; and (iv) Plaintiff's family had nothing more to fear from the Sandinistas. The court held that the first two facts were both legislative and nondisputable, and thus, no rebuttal opportunity was required. The third fact was legislative but disputable. The fourth fact was adjudicative and disputable. The judge should have provided an opportunity for rebuttal of the third and fourth facts. [**Castillo-Villagra v. INS,** 972 F.2d 1017 (9th Cir. 1992)]

(b) When opportunity to rebut must be furnished [§234]

In many cases, the facts are noticed by the agency heads when the heads consider an ALJ's proposed decision. This creates a problem: How should the heads furnish the affected party an opportunity to rebut the noticed facts? Most cases allow the rebuttal opportunity to be furnished through a motion to reopen the case. [**Rhoa-Zamora v. INS,** 971 F.2d 26 (7th Cir. 1992)] However, one court held that the agency heads could not decide the case unless they first furnished the party an opportunity to rebut the noticed facts. [**Castillo-Villagra v. INS,** *supra*]

d. Use of expertise in evaluating evidence [§235]

Agency fact finders become experts in deciding particular types of cases. This expertise enables them to make predictions about the future without a solid evidentiary basis and allows them to disbelieve the testimony of expert witnesses and rely on their own expertise instead. Generally, use of this expertise is allowed: "The presiding officer's experience, technical competence, and specialized knowledge may be utilized in evaluating evidence." [1981 Model State APA §4-215(d)]

---

e.g. Example: An expert fact finder is not bound by expert testimony as to the cause of an injury. [**McCarthy v. Sawyer-Goodman Co.,** 215 N.W. 824 (Wis. 1927)—agency finding that hernia was not caused by industrial injury upheld]

---

(1) Matters of prediction [§236]

Likewise, precise support in the record is not required to uphold an agency's conclusion as to matters of prediction or allocation of resources.

---

e.g. Example—prediction of effect of decreased railroad rates: An agency order decreasing railroad rates—based upon its predictions as to the effect of the decrease on traffic—was upheld without supporting evidence in the record. The Court took into consideration the agency's experience with the railway and the experimental nature of the decrease. [**Market Street Railway v. Railroad Commission,** 324 U.S. 548 (1945)]

---

(2) Limitation—conjecture [§237]

However, an agency will *not* be permitted to rely upon its own expertise where the matter is *not technical* and the agency is clearly indulging in *conjecture.* [**F.A. McDonald Co. v. Industrial Commission,** 26 N.W.2d 165 (Wis. 1947)]

(3) Limitation—lack of reasons [§238]

Reliance on expertise will be sharply scrutinized when the agency, without giving warning at the hearing, disregards the testimony of an expert witness and substitutes its own conclusions. [**Davis & Randall, Inc. v. United States,** 219 F. Supp. 673 (W.D.N.Y. 1963)]

Example: In **Davis & Randall, Inc.,** the court held that the Interstate Commerce Commission ("ICC") was not *always* free to disregard the uncontested testimony of an expert:

> A rejection of unopposed testimony by a qualified and disinterested expert on a matter susceptible of reasonably precise measurement, without the agency's developing its objections at a hearing, ought to be upheld *only when the agency's uncommunicated criticisms* appear to the reviewing court to be *both so compelling and so deeply held* that the court can be fairly sure the agency would not have been affected by anything the witness could have said had he known of them; *and* [when] the Court would have been bound to affirm, despite the expert's hypothetical rebuttal, out of deference for the agency's judgment on so technical a matter.

---

(4) Note

Results in this area vary on a case-by-case basis. Much depends on the credibility of the administrator's opinion, its presentation on appeal, the susceptibility of the issue to precise proof, the agency's demonstrated expertise, whether an opportunity to contradict the evaluation was ever provided, and judicial confidence in the fairness of the agency and its procedures.

SUMMARY OF EXCLUSIVE RECORD PRINCIPLE	gilbert
RULE	The transcript of testimony and any exhibits constitute the *exclusive record* for decision; the agency cannot rely on evidence outside of that record.
LIMITATIONS	• Physical inspection or test allowed • Assistance of agency staff allowed as long as stick to record • Official notice of facts allowed but must be an opportunity to rebut • Agency expertise may be used to evaluate evidence and make predictions

C. Requirement of Findin[...]
Reasons

1. APA Provisions

a. Federal act [§239]

The APA provides: "All decisions, including i[...]
tive decisions, are a part of the record and sl[...]
findings and conclusions, and the *reasons o[...]
rial issues of fact, law, or discretion *presente*[...]
propriate rule, order, sanction, relief, or deni[...]

b. Model Act [§240]

Similarly, the Model Act requires orders to include findings of fact, conclusions of law, "and policy reasons for the decision if it is an exercise of the
agency's discretion, for all aspects of the order, including the remedy prescribed . . . . Findings of fact, if set forth in language that is no more than
mere repetition or paraphrase of the relevant provision of law, must be accompanied by a concise and explicit statement of the underlying facts of
record to support the findings." [1981 Model State APA §4-215(c)]

2. Informal Adjudication [§241]

Even when the APA formal adjudication provisions are not applicable, the agency
must state its grounds for denying any written application, petition, or other request made in connection with any agency proceeding. [APA §555(e)] In addition,
a court may imply a requirement that an agency provide an explanation from the
underlying statute [**Dunlop v. Bachowski,** 421 U.S. 560 (1975)] or derive the requirement from its need to know what an agency has done and why in order to review that action [**Citizens Committee of Georgetown v. Zoning Commission,** 477
F.2d 402 (D.C. Cir. 1973); **Ship Creek Hydraulic Syndicate v. State of Alaska,** 685
P.2d 715 (Alaska 1984)]. However, the implication of procedural requirements
that go beyond the requirements of the APA may be improper. [*See* **Pension Benefit Guaranty Corp. v. LTV Corp.,** *supra,* §179]

3. Constitutional Requirement [§242]

In addition to being required under the APA, a statement of findings and conclusions is necessary where a "trial-type" hearing is required by due process. [**Goldberg
v. Kelly,** *supra,* §143]

4. Purpose [§243]

The requirement that findings and conclusions be stated assures that the fact finder
will carefully evaluate the evidence and consider its discretionary choices. Furthermore,

quate findings and conclusions by the agency, the courts would have
of determining the basis on which the agency had acted, and the parties
not decide whether to seek review. [**Dunlop v. Bachowski,** *supra*]

Sufficiency of Findings [§244]

When findings are required, the agency must make more than a finding of *ultimate fact* couched in the statutory language; it must also state the *"basic facts"* underlying the ultimate question and explain the logical connection between basic and ultimate facts. [**United States v. Pierce Auto Lines,** 327 U.S. 515 (1946); **Topanga Association for a Scenic Community v. Los Angeles,** 11 Cal. 3d 506 (1974)]

6. **Courts Will Not Imply Findings [§245]**

Administrative decisions will be reviewed and enforced only on the basis of findings and conclusions that are a *part of the record*. Courts will not infer or imply other findings in order to uphold agency action—or accept "post hoc" rationalizations supplied in the briefs.

---

e.g. **Example:** In the first *Chenery* case [**SEC v. Chenery Corp.,** *supra*, §187], the SEC required insiders to forfeit profits they had made on trading stock, relying upon equitable doctrines for this result. However, since the SEC had *misapplied* these doctrines, the Supreme Court reversed. The Court indicated that it could not uphold the SEC order by supplying *different reasons* from those on which the agency had relied. To do so would project the Court into the administrative sphere.

---

7. **Findings at Agency Head Level [§246]**

Frequently, an administrative law judge decides a case, rendering a decision that includes findings and reasons. The agency heads summarily affirm the ALJ decision. The heads are not required to state findings and reasons; by adopting the ALJ's decision, the heads state the same findings and reasons as the ALJ. [**Guentchev v. INS,** 77 F.3d 1036 (7th Cir. 1996)] However, if the heads state that the ALJ reached a "substantially correct result," the heads have not summarily affirmed the ALJ, and the reviewing court cannot be sure precisely which of the ALJ's findings or reasons the heads have adopted. [**Armstrong v. Commodity Futures Trading Commission,** 12 F.3d 401 (3d Cir. 1993)] As a result, the agency's affirmation may be vacated.

8. **Party Must Have Opportunity to Submit Own Findings [§247]**

Before a decision is made on the findings of fact and conclusions of law—or before the agency decides to review the administrative law judge's decision—the parties must have a reasonable opportunity to submit their *own proposed findings and conclusions,* or their *exceptions to the decisions* already made. The record must show the administrative law judge's ruling as to each finding, conclusion, or exception thus presented. [APA §557(c)]

PREHEARING PROCESS

Proper Notice — check statutory requirements

Intervention — allowed if does not complicate proceeding

Discovery — generally not allowed, but check statute; subpoenas allowed

Opportunity for Settlement or Mediation

HEARING PROCESS

Burden of Proof — on proponent of rule or order, normally by a preponderance of the evidence

Admissibility of Evidence — generally any relevant evidence

Exclusive Record Principle — decision must be based on record; some limitations on this rule (*e.g.,* official notice)

POST-HEARING PROCESS

Findings and Reasons — must be stated

Chapter Five:
Adjudicatory Decisionmakers

CONTENTS

Chapter Approach

A.	Structure of Adjudicatory Decisions	§248
B.	Improper Influences on Decisionmaker	§257
C.	Basis for Decisionmaking	§294
D.	Binding Effect on Decisionmakers	§309

Chapter Approach

Once you have decided that APA formal adjudication applies, and you have ascertained that the various hearing requirements discussed in the previous chapter were provided, analyze whether the decisionmaking process meets statutory and constitutional requirements:

1. Generally, the initial decision is made by an administrative law judge ("ALJ") and appealed to the agency heads. Be sure to ascertain that the *ALJ's independence was protected* as provided in the APA.

2. Although a single agency combines functions, the APA provides significant protections against the *same person engaging in both adversary and adjudicatory responsibility*. Make sure these provisions were observed.

3. The Constitution guarantees an impartial adjudicator. Make sure that both the ALJ and agency heads were *free from bias* in the form of prejudgment of the factual issues, animus against the party, or economic conflict of interest. But remember that the *rule of necessity* may require a biased decisionmaker to serve.

4. Make sure that *no illegal ex parte communications* were made to adjudicatory decisionmakers.

5. Make sure the decisionmaker was *adequately familiar with the record* as required in *Morgan I.*

6. Finally, see whether the decision was constrained by the requirements of *res judicata, equitable estoppel, or stare decisis.*

A. Structure of Adjudicatory Decisions

1. Decisionmaker—ALJ or Agency Head [§248]
Agency heads can preside over administrative hearings, but seldom do so. Most hearings governed by the APA are conducted by administrative law judges ("ALJs") in both federal and state agencies. These professional fact finders were formerly called "hearing officers." The typical pattern is that the ALJ renders an initial decision, and the final agency decision is made by the agency heads who review the ALJ's decision (or in some cases a judicial officer who has been delegated this function).

2. Types of Decisions [§249]
APA section 557(b) describes the types of decisions made by the ALJ in various situations.

a. Initial decision [§250]

Where a hearing must be conducted "on the record," but the agency head does not preside at the taking of evidence, the ALJ hears the case and renders an *"initial decision"*—which becomes final unless appealed to the agency.

(1) Note

On review of the initial decision, the agency has all the powers it would have had in making the initial decision. [APA §557(b)]

b. Recommended decision [§251]

The agency—in specific cases or by general rule—may require the entire record developed by the ALJ to be certified to *it* for decision. In such cases, the ALJ merely makes a "recommended decision."

c. Tentative decision [§252]

In initial *license* proceedings, or in formal *rulemaking* where a hearing on the record is required, the agency itself can issue a tentative decision.

(1) Note

The recommended or tentative decision can be omitted entirely if necessary for the timely execution of agency functions.

SUMMARY OF TYPES OF ADJUDICATORY DECISIONS	gilbert
TYPE OF DECISION	
INITIAL	— ALJ hears evidence "on the record"; decision final unless appealed
RECOMMENDED	— ALJ develops record for agency so agency can decide; ALJ recommends decision
TENTATIVE	— In initial license proceedings or formal rulemaking where a hearing on the record is required, the *agency itself* may issue a tentative decision

3. Independence of ALJs

a. In-house ALJs [§253]

In the federal government and in most states, ALJs work for the agency for which they decide cases. However, they are organizationally independent; they cannot be supervised by personnel who are engaged in prosecution. [APA §554(d)(2)]

(1) Central panel

In over twenty states, ALJs operate in a "central panel." This means they do not work for the agencies but are assigned out to the various agencies when needed to conduct a hearing. The advantage of this arrangement is that the ALJs are perceived as being independent of the agency that is prosecuting the case. The disadvantage is that the ALJs are less specialized and possess less expertise than those who decide cases only for a single agency.

b. APA provisions to assure independence [§254]

The original section 11 of the APA (now codified in various provisions of Title 5 of the United States Code) was designed to enhance the position of ALJs, and to that end provided that such judges:

(1) *Be hired by a process controlled by the Office of Personnel Management* (rather than by the employing agency);

(2) *Be assigned to cases by rotation*, as far as practicable;

(3) *Not perform duties inconsistent with their duties as administrative law judges*;

(4) *Be removed only for good cause*, as determined by the Merit Systems Protection Board (and not removed by the agency that had appointed them); and

(5) *Be entitled to compensation* set by the Office of Personnel Management *independent of agency recommendations* or ratings (so their pay could not be cut by the agency if it disapproved of their decisions).

c. Non-APA cases [§255]

Even where the federal APA does not apply (*e.g.*, because no statute requires a hearing on the record or because Congress has provided that it should not apply), the initial decision usually is still made by an administrative judge. However, that judge lacks the protections provided by the APA for ALJs. For example, immigration cases are decided by immigration judges, but a statute provides that the APA does not apply to immigration cases. As a result, immigration judges are not accorded the guarantees of independence provided by section 11 of the APA. If due process applies, however, administrative judges are still required to be unbiased.

4. Splitting Agencies [§256]

To assure even more adjudicatory independence, Congress in some cases has split the adjudicatory function from the law enforcement function. For example, the Occupational Safety and Health Administration ("OSHA") *enforces* the worker safety laws and adopts regulations to implement the law. However, when OSHA seeks *sanctions* against employers who violated the rule, the case is tried by the Occupational Safety and Health Review Commission ("OSHRC"), a separate agency which employs its own ALJs and is headed by officials who exclusively adjudicate cases.

a. Judicial deference

Where OSHA and OSHRC differ on a question of law, the courts must decide which agency to defer to (*see infra*, §§568-592 for discussion of judicial deference to agency legal interpretations). The Supreme Court held that the courts should defer to OSHA's interpretations, not OSHRC's, because OSHA was likely to have greater expertise and familiarity with its own regulations. [**Martin v. Occupational Safety and Health Review Commission**, 499 U.S. 144 (1991)]

b. Lack of quorum

In one case, all of the members of OSHRC had resigned, and the President failed to name replacements. Therefore, a party was denied the right to have an unfavorable ALJ decision reviewed by OSHRC because the statute provided that if OSHRC took no action, the ALJ's decision became final. Because OSHRC could have reversed the ALJ, the respondent was denied an important procedural right, and the sanctions against it were reversed. [**Ed Taylor Construction Co. v. Occupational Safety and Health Review Commission**, 931 F.2d 1458 (5th Cir. 1991)]

B. Improper Influences on Decisionmaker

1. In General [§257]

Numerous factors may prevent an adjudicator from making an impartial decision. The adjudicator may have been: (i) involved in the investigative or prosecutorial stages of the proceeding, (ii) politically biased or have an economic interest in the outcome of the case, (iii) prejudiced against a particular party to the case, or (iv) subject to improper outside pressures.

2. Combination of Functions [§258]

Where the same persons investigate the facts of a case, institute proceedings, and ultimately adjudicate the matter, it may be difficult to maintain an absence of bias or prejudgment.

a. No violation of due process [§259]

Nonetheless, such a combination of functions *at the level of the agency heads* has been held *not* to violate the requirements of due process. [**Withrow v. Larkin,** 421 U.S. 35 (1975)]

(1) Illustration—licensing boards

In *Withrow,* a medical licensing board held an investigatory hearing against a doctor, recommended to the district attorney that the doctor be prosecuted, and then adjudicated the revocation of the doctor's license.

The Supreme Court upheld the procedure, finding that prior contact with the facts did not necessarily establish bias on the part of the fact finder.

(a) Note

The Court distinguished cases in which bias had been shown as a result of prior contacts, noting that in such cases the fact finder had been found *incapable of altering previously fixed beliefs* about the issues (*see infra, §275*).

(b) Comment

The Court considered it significant that APA section 554(d) (below) permits *agency heads* to perform more than one function.

(2) Distinguish—lower level staff

However, a mixing of functions in the same person *below the level of agency heads may be a violation of due process.* [**Goldberg v. Kelly,** *supra, §242*—in welfare decisions, an impartial decisionmaker is essential; prior involvement in some aspects of a case will not necessarily bar a welfare official from acting as a decisionmaker, but he should not have participated in making the determination under review]

b. APA provisions [§260]

APA section 554(d) places *strict limitations* on the mixing of functions in formal adjudication.

(1) Separation of functions generally required

(a) Command influence [§261]

Section 554(d) provides that the ALJ may not "be responsible to or subject to the supervision or direction of an employee or agent engaged in the performance of an *investigative or prosecuting* function for an agency."

(b) Investigative or prosecuting employee [§262]

Section 554(d) further provides: "An employee or agent engaged in the performance of investigative or prosecuting functions for an agency in a case may not, in that or a factually related case, *participate or advise in the decision*, recommended decision, or agency review . . . except as witness or counsel in public proceedings."

(2) APA separation of functions [§263]

A staff member who has functioned as a prosecutor, investigator, or advocate in a case (*i.e.,* an "adversary") cannot serve as a decisionmaker in that case or a factually related case. [APA §554(d)] Similarly, an adversary cannot furnish off-the-record advice to a decisionmaker. However, a staff member who is *not an adversary can furnish off-the-record advice to a decisionmaker* (so long as the adviser does not supplement the factual record in the case).

(a) Factually related case

Note that the separation of functions rule applies on a case-specific basis: it applies only if a staff member has been an adversary in the case under decision or a factually related case. A person who has been an adversary in a factually similar but unrelated case can serve as an adjudicator in a later case. [**Marshall v. Cuomo,** 192 F.3d 473 (4th Cir. 1999)—staff member not disqualified as adviser even though he was an adversary in a similar case brought earlier against the very same respondent]

(3) Exception [§264]

However, the restrictions above do *not* apply to:

(i) *Applications for initial licenses* [APA §554(d)(A)];

(ii) *Proceedings involving the rates, facilities, or practices of public utilities or carriers* [APA §554(d)(B)]; or

(iii) *The agency itself* or any member(s) of the body comprising the agency [APA §554(d)(C)].

EXAM TIP   **gilbert**

Remember that to help ensure fair and unbiased adjudication, the APA generally **prohibits** an employee—other than an agency head—of the investigative or prosecuting arm of an agency **to supervise or direct** an ALJ, or to participate or advise in a case that she investigated or prosecuted, except in initial license applications and in most cases involving public utilities or carriers.

(a) "Agency heads" [§265]

The last exception permits agency heads to prosecute, investigate, and subsequently adjudicate the same case. The exception also covers the personal staffs of agency heads who therefore can participate in discussions about whether to issue a complaint and can later advise the agency heads in the final decision of the case. [**Grolier, Inc. v. FTC,** 615 F.2d 1215 (9th Cir. 1980)]

1) Limitation

However, the personal adviser to the agency head cannot participate in a decision to initiate prosecution and then serve as an administrative law judge in the same case. [**Grolier, Inc. v. FTC,** *supra*]

(b) Scope of exception for agency heads [§266]

The agency heads exception applies *only if the individual was a member of the agency throughout the entire case*. It does not allow an individual to serve as a prosecutor and then adjudicate the same case after being appointed a member of the agency. [**Amos Treat & Co. v. SEC,** 306 F.2d 260 (D.C. Cir. 1962)]

(c) Advisers and agency heads [§267]

Despite the agency heads exception, persons engaged in investigation and prosecution cannot advise the agency heads when they make the final decision in the case. Agency heads may be advised only by persons who have not engaged in prosecution or investigation. [*See, e.g.,* **Greene v. Babbitt,** 943 F. Supp. 1278 (W.D. Wash. 1996)—policy and legal advice by prosecutor to agency head violated §554(d)] However, *before* the decision is made to engage in adjudication, the agency heads are permitted to discuss a case with prosecutors and investigators to decide whether to issue a complaint or designate a matter for hearing. [*See* **Environmental Defense Fund v. EPA,** 510 F.2d 1292 (D.C. Cir. 1975)]

(d) Model Act [§268]

The Model State APA provision on separation of functions contains *no* exception for agency heads. [1981 Model State APA §4-214]

(4) Deportation hearings [§269]

Where an immigration inspector hearing a deportation case was also engaged in the prosecution and investigation of similar cases, APA section 554 was violated. [**Wong Yang Sung v. McGrath,** *supra,* §165]

(a) But note

In response to this decision, Congress removed deportation hearings from APA coverage, thereby restoring the previous combination of functions. The Court upheld this procedure, finding no due process violation. However, this decision may be limited solely to deportation proceedings. [**Marcello v. Bonds,** 349 U.S. 302 (1955)]

3. Bias or Prejudice [§270]

An adjudicative decisionmaker is disqualified from deciding a case in which the decisionmaker is biased. The prohibited forms of bias include: (i) prejudgment of the facts, (ii) pecuniary bias, or (iii) personal animus against a party.

a. APA provision [§271]

APA section 556(b) provides: "On the filing in good faith of a timely and sufficient affidavit of personal bias or other disqualification of a presiding or participating employee, the agency shall determine the matter as a part of the record and decision in the case." This provision contemplates that, upon complaint of bias, an ALJ will step aside ("recuse" herself). If she fails to do so, the agency heads (and the reviewing court) will consider the ALJ's failure to recuse herself as one of the issues in the case. The same principles apply to agency heads. If an agency head is biased, she should recuse herself. Note that if an agency head refuses to recuse herself, the APA does not indicate whether the other agency heads have power to disqualify her from voting.

(1) Timing [§272]

A party must challenge a biased decisionmaker by filing the affidavit referred to in section 556(b) as soon as the party learns the pertinent facts. A failure to make an immediate disqualification motion is a waiver of the right to do so. [**Marcus v. Director, Office of Workers' Compensation Programs,** 548 F.2d 1044 (D.C. Cir. 1976)]

b. Prejudgment of the facts [§273]

Where circumstances indicate that the decisionmaker has a fixed opinion regarding the facts about the parties that are at issue in the case, the decisionmaker must be disqualified.

(1) Public statements [§274]

In most cases, prejudgment of the facts is revealed by extra-judicial statements made by the decisionmaker.

> **e.g.** **Example—congressional report:** An FTC Commissioner had previously served as counsel to a Senate subcommittee investigating the drug industry, during which time he had made statements indicating his belief that American Cyanamid had violated antitrust laws, and had helped draft a committee report critical of the company. This was held sufficient to disqualify him from FTC hearings involving the same company and issues. [**American Cyanamid Co. v. FTC,** 363 F.2d 757 (6th Cir. 1966)]

> **e.g.** **Example—public speech:** Statements in a speech that indicated an agency head had already made up his mind about the guilt of a party showed the Commissioner had prejudged the facts (even though he did not mention the party by name). [**Cinderella Career & Finishing Schools, Inc. v. FTC,** 425 F.2d 583 (D.C. Cir. 1970); *and see* **Bakalis v. Golembeski,** 35 F.3d 318 (7th Cir. 1994)—adjudicator made public statements that the college president should be dismissed before deciding the case]

(2) Prejudgment of legislative facts, law, or policy [§275]

A decisionmaker who has already made up her mind about issues of law or policy is not disqualified. Similarly, a decisionmaker who has made up her mind on issues of legislative facts (*i.e.*, facts that do not concern the individual party) is not disqualified. Otherwise, the expertise acquired by an agency would be a handicap rather than an advantage. [**FTC v. Cement Institute,** 333 U.S. 638 (1948)—prior FTC report that pricing system violated Sherman Act did not disqualify it from proceeding against cement companies using that pricing system]

(3) Contacts with facts arising while decisionmaker is in-role [§276]

A decisionmaker is not disqualified by reason of exposure to facts of a dispute while carrying out an assigned task for the agency (*i.e.*, while "in-role"), absent a strong showing that the decisionmaker has a closed mind on the issue.

> (e.g.) **Example—ALJ:** An ALJ is not disqualified simply because he has already heard and decided the same case at an earlier time. [**NLRB v. Donnelly Garment Co.,** 330 U.S. 219 (1947)]

> (e.g.) **Example—pre-decisional conference:** Agency heads are not disqualified from deciding a case in which they previously heard evidence from agency prosecutors and decided to issue a complaint. [**Withrow v. Larkin,** 421 U.S. 35 (1975)]

> (e.g.) **Example—dealing with illegal strike:** Agency heads are not disqualified from conducting hearings concerning the discharge of employees who engaged in an illegal strike simply because the agency heads previously negotiated with the strikers. [**Hortonville Joint School District v. Hortonville Educational Association,** 426 U.S. 482 (1976)]

> (e.g.) **Example—press release:** The customary issuance of press releases prior to adjudication—warning consumers there is "reason to believe" a law has been violated—does *not* unfairly bias the adjudicative proceedings. Although fact finders may be subject to pressure to vindicate the charges in the press release, such an element of "prejudgment" is inevitable where the agency has the power to both prosecute and adjudicate. [**FTC v. Cinderella Career & Finishing Schools, Inc.,** 404 F.2d 1308 (D.C. Cir. 1968)]

c. Economic bias [§277]

A decisionmaker who has a financial or other personal interest in the case to be decided should be disqualified. [**Tumey v. Ohio,** 273 U.S. 510 (1927)—a judge whose compensation depended on fines paid by persons he convicted is disqualified; **Aetna Insurance Co. v. Lavoie,** 475 U.S. 813 (1986)—a judge who is conducting personal litigation involving the same legal issue as in present case must be disqualified]

(1) Institutional interest [§278]

Bias may also be established if the adjudicating agency would benefit significantly from a decision against a party. [**Ward v. City of Monroeville,** 409 U.S. 57 (1972)—traffic court judge disqualified because he was also mayor and fines went into the city budget; **AEP Chapter Housing Association v. City of Berkeley,** 114 F.3d 840 (9th Cir. 1997)—rent control agency not disqualified even though about 5% of its budget depends on registration fees it collects from landlords found to be subject to rent]

(a) Prosecutors distinguished

A prosecuting agency that does no adjudication is not disqualified even though it retains the penalties it collects. [**Marshall v. Jerrico, Inc.,** 446 U.S. 238 (1980)] In dictum, however, the Court indicated that a prosecutorial agency might be disqualified upon a much clearer showing of financial bias.

(2) Professional interest—licenses [§279]

A recurring problem is whether a professional interest in a case should disqualify a decisionmaker. This problem arises frequently in connection with licensing boards. A board that licenses doctors is not disqualified from deciding a case that will add or subtract one more doctor from the group of doctors in a large city or state. But if the decisionmaker was the only doctor in a town, he might well be disqualified from deciding whether a second doctor should receive a license to practice in the town. [**Stivers v. Pierce,** 71 F.3d 732 (9th Cir. 1995)—dictum]

(a) Optometry cases

By statute, a majority of the agency heads of the optometry board must be independent optometrists (*i.e.*, not employees of corporations such as Wal-Mart). The agency is considering whether to revoke the licenses of all employed optometrists. The agency is not disqualified from deciding this case, absent a more focused showing that they cannot decide it fairly. [**Friedman v. Rogers,** 440 U.S. 1 (1979)] However, this case seems inconsistent with an earlier one, which held that if *all* of the agency heads had to be independent optometrists, a court could find that the agency is biased against employed optometrists. [**Gibson v. Berryhill,** 411 U.S. 564 (1973)]

d. Animus toward a party [§280]

A decisionmaker should be disqualified if it can be shown that she is personally hostile toward a party or a group to which the party belongs. This sort of personal hostility is often referred to as "animus." [**Berger v. United States,** 255 U.S. 22 (1921)—judge's statements evidenced hostility toward Germans] Some cases indicate that an adjudicator should be disqualified if she has been the subject of personal abuse or criticism from a party. [*See, e.g.,* **Mayberry v.**

Pennsylvania, 400 U.S. 455 (1971)—"no one so cruelly slandered is likely to maintain that calm detachment necessary for fair adjudication"]

(1) Conduct at hearing [§281]

Normally, an adjudicator's conduct toward a party at the hearing does not establish animus or prejudgment of the facts, even though the adjudicator speaks harshly and critically about the party, rules against the party on every issue, and disbelieves all its witnesses. [*See, e.g.,* **NLRB v. Pittsburgh S.S. Co.,** 337 U.S. 656 (1949); **McLaughlin v. Union Oil Co.,** 869 F.2d 1039 (7th Cir. 1989)] Such conduct simply reflects the opinions the decisionmaker has formed about the party based on what transpired at the hearing. Nevertheless, animus or prejudgment of the facts may be suggested by comments at the hearing together with highly irregular hearing procedures. [**Stivers v. Pierce,** *supra,* §279—harshness, harassment, and delays at the hearing combined with other evidence of pecuniary interest and personal animus]

e. The rule of necessity [§282]

If the only adjudicators with power to hear and decide a case are biased, they are still permitted to hear and decide the case under the rule of necessity. Otherwise, nobody could decide the case and wrongdoers might go unpunished. [**Brinkley v. Hassig,** 83 F.2d 351 (10th Cir. 1936)] However, judicial review is likely to be more stringent than usual. And, under the Model State APA, the problem can be avoided because the authority that appointed the biased administrator is required to appoint a substitute for the purpose of hearing the case. [1981 Model State APA §4-202(e)]

4. Influence or Pressure on Fact Finder

a. Congressional interference [§283]

Congressional pressure on agency adjudicators while a case is in the hearing stage may deprive the parties to the adjudication of due process. [*See, e.g.,* **Koniag, Inc. v. Andrus,** 580 F.2d 601 (D.C. Cir. 1978); **Pillsbury Co. v. FTC,** 354 F.2d 952 (5th Cir. 1966)]

(1) Illustration—*Pillsbury* case

In *Pillsbury Co.,* an initial FTC decision was severely criticized in a congressional subcommittee hearing. The FTC chairman was closely questioned, and other FTC members were also present. The chairman then withdrew from further proceedings in the matter, but others who were present and questioned did take part in the final decision against Pillsbury. The court found this congressional intervention unwarranted and a *violation of due process. But note:* Nevertheless, the FTC was not permanently disqualified from hearing the case because during the 13 years since the case began, there had been a sufficient change in personnel so that the matter could be remanded to the FTC for decision.

(2) Narrow application of *Pillsbury* [§284]

Courts in subsequent cases have been very cautious in their application of the *Pillsbury* rule. Thus congressional interference in a pending case *prior* to the time the case enters the hearing phase is less likely to require reversal than interference *after* it reaches the hearing phase. [*See, e.g.,* **DCP Farms v. Yeutter,** 957 F.2d 1183 (5th Cir. 1992)]

(3) Causing consideration of irrelevant factors [§285]

Congressional pressure that caused the agency to consider an irrelevant factor in making a discretionary decision would render the agency decision arbitrary and capricious. [*See* **D.C. Federation of Civic Associations v. Volpe,** 459 F.2d 1231 (D.C. Cir. 1971), *cert. denied,* 405 U.S. 1030 (1972)—agency approved construction of bridge only after Congressmen threatened to withhold funding of the D.C. subway unless bridge was built]

(a) Narrow application

Courts appear quite cautious in applying this standard to invalidate agency decisions. They are concerned that a rigid application of the standard would interfere with legitimate congressional oversight as well as impair agency flexibility in dealing with Congress. [**ATX, Inc. v. Department of Transportation,** 41 F.3d 1522 (D.C. Cir. 1994)—introduction of bills in Congress did not pressure agency; **DCP Farms v. Yeutter,** *supra*—pressure concerned relevant rather than irrelevant factor]

b. Ex parte communications by outsiders to agency adjudicators

(1) Adjudicatory proceedings [§286]

The APA prohibits any interested person *outside* the agency from making (or causing to be made) any ex parte communication relevant to the merits to a member of the agency, an ALJ, or any other employee who is or may reasonably be expected to be involved in the decisional process. [APA §557(d)(1)] This APA provision applies to *formal rulemaking* as well as to *formal adjudication, but not to informal adjudication or informal rulemaking.*

(a) "Interested person" [§287]

The term "interested person" is broadly applied. It means anyone outside the agency whose interest in the proceedings is greater than that of the general public.

 Example: Albert Shanker, prominent head of a teacher's union, is an "interested person" with respect to a case involving an illegal strike by a federal employees' union. [**Professional Air Traffic Controllers' Organization v. Federal Labor Relations Authority,** 672 F.2d 109 (D.C. Cir. 1982)]

(b) Outside the agency—White House staff [§288]

The President and members of the White House staff are considered persons outside the agency and may not engage in ex parte contact with adjudicators. [**Portland Audubon Society v. Endangered Species Committee,** 984 F.2d 1534 (9th Cir. 1993)—contacts between White House staff and "God Squad" members adjudicating whether to grant exceptions to the Endangered Species Act violated APA §557(d)]

1) Distinguish—rulemaking

The President and members of his staff may participate ex parte in *informal rulemaking* proceedings (unless this is prohibited by a specific statute). [**Sierra Club v. Costle,** 657 F.2d 298 (D.C. Cir. 1981)] However, APA section 557 does apply to *formal rulemaking*. (*See infra,* §334 for discussion of the difference between formal and informal rulemaking.)

(c) "Ex parte communication" [§289]

An ex parte communication is defined as an oral or written communication that is not on the public record with respect to which reasonable prior notice to all parties was not given. However, a request for a "status report" is not considered an ex parte communication. [APA §551(14)]

(d) Relevant to the merits [§290]

A communication is relevant to the merits if it concerns any substantive issue in the case (*i.e.,* whether it is an issue of fact, law, policy or discretion). However, communications concerning procedural issues or settlement are not considered relevant to the merits. [**Louisiana Association of Independent Producers v. Federal Energy Regulatory Commission,** 958 F.2d 1101 (D.C. Cir. 1992)] Similarly, so-called status inquiries (whether from members of Congress or from the parties) are not considered ex parte communications. [APA §551(14); **Massman Construction Co. v. TVA,** 769 F.2d 1114 (6th Cir. 1985)—request by party to find out when decision would be issued was permissible status inquiry]

(e) Effect of ex parte contact [§291]

If an ex parte contact is made in violation of the APA, the writing must be placed on the record and a memorandum of any oral contact must be prepared and placed on the record. The agency may, to the extent consistent with the interests of justice and the policy of the underlying statute, require the party who made the communication to show cause why the claim should not be dismissed, denied, disregarded, or adversely affected.

(f) Judicial review [§292]

A reviewing court has discretion whether or not to vacate a decision tainted by ex parte contacts. It should consider whether the contacts irrevocably tainted the proceeding so as to make the ultimate agency judgment unfair. The court will consider such factors as (i) whether the communication probably influenced the decision, (ii) whether the party who made the contact benefited by it, (iii) whether the opponents had adequate opportunity to respond, and (iv) whether vacating the decision would serve any useful purpose. [**Professional Air Traffic Controllers' Organization v. Federal Labor Relations Authority**, *supra*—many improper contacts, but remand would be futile; strong dissent]

(g) Reciprocal prohibition for agency employees [§293]

The APA also prohibits ex parte communications relevant to the merits *by* agency employees involved in the decisional process *to* interested persons outside the agency.

C. Basis for Decisionmaking

1. Obligation of Decisionmaker to Be Familiar with Record [§294]

Although the decisionmaker need not personally preside at the taking of evidence, his decision must be based upon the evidence and argument presented at the hearing. "The one who decides must hear"—at least in the sense of being familiar with the record. [**Morgan v. United States**, 298 U.S. 468 (1936) ("Morgan I")]

Example: In *Morgan I* (there were four *Morgan* cases), the Department of Agriculture conducted a lengthy inquiry into the reasonableness of stockyard rates. The trial examiner heard the evidence and the Secretary of Agriculture allegedly set the rate schedule without hearing or reading any of the evidence or argument presented at the hearing. The parties were never advised of the proposed rate schedule nor of the trial examiner's findings. The Court held that the parties had been denied a "full hearing": "If the one who determines the facts which underlie the order has not considered evidence or argument, it is manifest that the hearing has not been given." *Note:* The Court conceded that the evidence could be taken by an examiner and sifted and analyzed by subordinates. But the person responsible for making the final decision had to be *familiar* with the record.

a. Delegation of decisionmaking [§295]

Agencies have often attempted to meet the requirements of *Morgan I* by delegating decisionmaking authority to lower level personnel. However, such delegation must be provided for by *statute or agency regulations* or it is invalid.

---

e.g. Example: Petitions for review in labor cases were required by statute and agency regulation to be decided by the NLRB or by a three-member panel of the Board. When a decision was made by one member and the legal aides for two others, it was held invalid as a violation of the *Morgan I* rule. [**KFC National Management Corp. v. NLRB,** 497 F.2d 298 (2d Cir. 1974)]

---

b. Intermediate review boards [§296]

Another way of satisfying *Morgan I* is to have *intermediate* review boards, composed of agency subordinates who review decisions of hearing examiners, with only very limited appeal to the full commission.

c. Failure to hear oral argument [§297]

As stated above, failure to actually hear the oral argument does not require reversal *if* the decisionmaker is nonetheless familiar with the record.

(1) Rationale

Oral argument is not constitutionally required, even in a "trial-type" hearing. [*See* **FCC v. Station WJR,** 337 U.S. 265 (1949)]

(2) Reading transcript [§298]

Even where oral argument *is* required, agency members need not hear the argument but can acquire sufficient familiarity with the case by reading a transcript. [**McGraw Electric Co. v. United States,** 120 F. Supp. 354 (E.D. Mo.), *aff'd,* 348 U.S. 804 (1954)]

(3) Distinguish—credibility in issue [§299]

However, where questions of credibility are involved, the decisionmakers at the initial hearing (as opposed to the agency head review of the initial decision) *must see and hear all the witnesses.* [**Asbury Park v. Department of Civil Service,** 111 A.2d 625 (N.J. 1955)]

---

e.g. Example: In *Asbury Park,* each of the three persons responsible for a decision heard some, but none heard all, of the witnesses. Since significant questions of credibility were involved, this procedure was held to be a violation of due process; no single person had heard and weighed all the conflicting testimony.

---

d. Unavailability of examiner [§300]

APA section 554(d) requires that "the employee who presides at the reception of evidence . . . shall make the recommended decision or initial decision . . . *unless he becomes unavailable* to the agency."

(1) Exception—credibility in issue [§301]

However, if issues of credibility are involved, it is improper to have a substitute ALJ prepare the findings and conclusions and recommend a decision. Thus, APA section 554(d) does not confer *complete* discretion to substitute trial examiners. [**Gamble-Skogmo, Inc. v. FTC,** 211 F.2d 106 (8th Cir. 1954)—examiner had reached retirement age, but could have continued at discretion of the agency]

2. Proving a Violation of *Morgan I* [§302]

It is quite difficult to actually prove a violation of the *Morgan I* decision, because it is *improper to question* the decisionmaker as to his mental processes. [**United States v. Morgan,** 313 U.S. 409 (1941) ("Morgan IV")]

a. Effect of *Morgan IV* [§303]

As a practical matter, *Morgan IV* substantially undercuts the impact of *Morgan I*, since ordinarily it would be impossible to find out whether the decisionmaker had in fact "heard" the matter by becoming familiar with the record.

b. Exception—lack of findings [§304]

However, where the decision is challenged as an abuse of discretion, and the decisionmaker has failed to explain the decision or make findings and conclusions, the decisionmaker can be cross-examined at trial about the reasons for the decision—an important departure from *Morgan IV*. [**Citizens to Preserve Overton Park v. Volpe,** *supra,* §179; *and see infra,* §605]

c. Defects in decisionmaking process [§305]

Inquiry into the decisionmaker's reasoning is not allowed "absent a strong showing of bad faith or improper behavior." [**Citizens to Preserve Overton Park v. Volpe,** *supra*] However, such improper behavior must first be shown by external facts. It would be improper to take the depositions of the decisionmakers to determine whether they had the necessary familiarity with the case or were biased. Similarly, the court will not examine the transcript of a closed meeting just because a party believes that the transcript will show improper decisional behavior; a party must first establish the impropriety before the court will examine further. [**San Luis Obispo Mothers for Peace v. Nuclear Regulatory Commission,** 789 F.2d 26 (D.C. Cir. 1986)]

3. Requirement of Intermediate Decision [§306]

In some circumstances, an ALJ must provide some sort of proposed decision to the parties so that they can focus their arguments to the agency head. [**Morgan v. United States,** 304 U.S. 1 (1938) ("Morgan II")]

a. Illustration—*Morgan II*

In *Morgan II*, a hearing officer took evidence and passed it on to the agency head, but there was no intermediate decision that allowed the parties to know exactly what the agency proposed to do. The Court indicated that the parties were entitled to be advised of the proposed action before the final decision was made. In addition, there was a violation of the separation of functions principle (*see supra,* §§258 *et seq.*) in *Morgan II,* since agency prosecutors consulted with the agency head at the time of the final decision.

b. Sequel to *Morgan II*—*Mackay* [§307]

In a later decision, the Court retreated from the full implications of *Morgan II.* Where the parties are fully aware of the nature of the agency's complaint and its proposed action, and are afforded full opportunity to be heard on the issues, no report of proposed findings is necessary. [**NLRB v. Mackay Radio & Telegraph Co.,** 304 U.S. 335 (1938)]

(1) Result

Taken together, *Morgan II* and *Mackay* indicate that in broad and unfocused proceedings, the contentions of each party must be made known to the other (rather than advanced ex parte) *before* the matter is ultimately submitted. However, there is no specific time nor manner in which this focusing must be done, and advance notice will serve as well as an administrative law judge's report.

c. Application under state law [§308]

The *Morgan II* doctrine was strictly applied in a state license revocation case where the ALJ filed a report of his findings and conclusions, but *the report was not disclosed* to the licensee. Failure to disclose the report was held to violate due process, on the grounds that the report was—as a matter of constitutional law—a part of the record that must be disclosed, and that the decision must be based exclusively on matters in the record (*supra,* §225). [**Mazza v. Cavicchia,** 105 A.2d 545 (N.J. 1954)]

(1) Note

Under *federal* law, APA sections 556(e) and 557(c) *require* that the ALJ's report (if there is one) be made a part of the record and thus available to the parties.

D. Binding Effect on Decisionmakers

1. Introduction [§309]

In certain circumstances, administrative decisionmakers are not free to make whatever decision seems appropriate in the circumstances. They can be limited by the doctrines of res judicata, equitable estoppel, or stare decisis. In addition, agencies are required to follow their own procedural rules, even when they were not required to adopt those rules.

2. Res Judicata [§310]

The rules of res judicata and collateral estoppel (*i.e.,* claim preclusion and issue preclusion) apply to administrative adjudicatory decisions, although not as strictly as they apply to judicial decisions.

a. General rule [§311]

When an administrative agency acts in a judicial capacity and resolves issues of fact properly before it, which the parties have had an adequate opportunity to litigate, the decision has *preclusive effect* on future agency and court decisions. [**United States v. Utah Construction & Mining Co.,** 384 U.S. 394 (1966); Restatement (Second) of Judgments §83]

b. Preclusion against the government [§312]

The government can be precluded from relitigating issues of fact or law after losing a case. [**United States v. Stauffer Chemical Co.,** 464 U.S. 165 (1984)—government loses on legal issue in one circuit; cannot relitigate *same issue* against *same party* in another circuit; **FTC v. Texaco,** 517 F.2d 137 (D.C. Cir. 1975)—decision by one agency precludes relitigation by a second]

c. Nonmutual collateral estoppel [§313]

The Supreme Court has broadly endorsed nonmutual collateral estoppel. This means that a party who loses in one case is precluded from relitigating the same issues in another case even though in the second case he faces a different opponent. [**Parklane Hosiery Co. v. Shore,** 439 U.S. 322 (1979)]

---

e.g. **Example:** In *Parklane Hosiery Co.,* a stockholder's class action was brought against the defendant corporation and its officers and directors, claiming the corporation's proxy statement was false and misleading. Before this action came to trial, the SEC brought suit against the same defendants making a similar claim. The district court entered a declaratory judgment for the SEC. The plaintiffs in the class action then moved for summary judgment on issues relating to the proxy statement, arguing that defendants were estopped from relitigating the issues already resolved in the SEC action. The Supreme Court agreed, holding that the defendants were collaterally estopped on the issues resolved in the SEC action because they were already afforded a "full and fair" opportunity to litigate these issues.

---

(1) Exception [§314]

Nonmutual collateral estoppel does not apply against the United States. Thus, if the government loses an earlier district court decision and does not appeal, it can relitigate the *same issue* against *other parties.* [**United States v. Mendoza,** 464 U.S. 154 (1984)]

EXAM TIP   **gilbert**

It is important to remember that while the government may not relitigate the *same issue* against the *same party* after it loses a case, it may relitigate the *same issue* against a *different party* after it loses. The rationale may help you remember the distinction. The government can relitigate an issue it lost against different parties because it should not be compelled to appeal every case it loses. Moreover, the government should be able to relitigate and create a conflict between circuits so the issue can "percolate" to the Supreme Court for resolution.

(2) Intra-circuit nonacquiescence [§315]

Although the issue is not settled, it appears that the government must "acquiesce" in an unfavorable court of appeals decision. It can relitigate the issue against other parties only in other circuits. [*See* **Lopez v. Heckler,** 713 F.2d 1432 (9th Cir. 1983), *decision stayed,* 464 U.S. 879 (1984), *injunction granted,* 725 F.2d 1489 (9th Cir. 1984)]

d. Exceptions to administrative res judicata [§316]

Res judicata clearly applies less strictly in the administrative context than in the judicial. Numerous exceptions to res judicata have been recognized.

(1) Statutory policy [§317]

When the legislature indicates that a prior agency decision should not be preclusive, the issue can be relitigated later. [**University of Tennessee v. Elliott,** 478 U.S. 788 (1986)]

Example: In *University of Tennessee,* Elliott alleged that he had been fired from a state job because of racial discrimination. He lost a state administrative decision. He then sued in federal court under 42 U.S.C. section 1983 and under Title VII of the Civil Rights Act of 1964. The Court held that the prior adjudication precluded Elliott from relitigating under section 1983 but *not under Title VII.* Congress wanted to preserve a federal court remedy for antidiscrimination plaintiffs.

---

(2) Full and fair opportunity to litigate [§318]

If the loser of the first case did not have a full and fair opportunity to litigate the issue, the first decision should not be res judicata. For example, if different rules of evidence, burden of proof, cross-examination or discovery might have changed the result in the first case, the first decision should not preclude the second. [**North Carolina v. Chas. Pfizer & Co.,** 537 F.2d 67 (4th Cir.), *cert. denied,* 429 U.S. 870 (1976)—FTC findings of antitrust violation do not preclude court because of different procedural and evidentiary practices; Restatement (Second) of Judgments §83(2)]

(3) Other factors [§319]

The second tribunal has the discretion to decide whether to preclude a litigant, and many factors might cause an adjudicator to permit relitigation. [*See, e.g.,* Restatement (Second) of Judgments §83(3)—first decision not preclusive if the scheme of remedies permits assertion of second claim despite adjudication of the first]

3. Duty of Consistency [§320]

Agencies are free to change legal or policy positions taken in prior adjudicatory decisions, but they must explain when they have done so and why. They are not at liberty to ignore prior precedents without explanation. [**Atchison, Topeka & Santa Fe Railway v. Wichita Board of Trade,** 412 U.S. 800 (1973); **Shaw's Supermarkets, Inc. v. NLRB,** 884 F.2d 34 (1st Cir. 1989); **United Automobile Workers of America v. NLRB,** 802 F.2d 969 (7th Cir. 1986)] Moreover, if a party attacks an existing agency precedent as irrational, the agency must explain why it rejected this claim and adhered to existing precedent. [**Flagstaff Broadcasting Federation v. FCC,** 979 F.2d 1566 (D.C. Cir. 1992)]

4. Equitable Estoppel [§321]

An agency often furnishes oral or written advice to members of the public in need of guidance. Similarly, guidance can also be furnished more formally through agency guidelines or interpretive bulletins. However, occasionally the agency changes its mind, decides that the guidance previously given was wrong, and wishes to issue a subsequent decision that retracts it retroactively.

a. Estoppel and apparent authority [§322]

In the private sector, a person who detrimentally and reasonably relies on statements made by another can often claim that the latter is estopped to change its position. Similarly, in the private sector, a principal is bound by the actions of its agent under either actual or apparent authority. Apparent authority arises if the principal has caused third parties reasonably to believe that the agency has authority to act—even if the agent has no such authority. However, it is not clear whether the principles of estoppel and apparent authority apply against the government.

b. State law [§323]

The law of many states permits the government to be estopped very much as a private sector entity might be. [*See, e.g.,* **Foote's Dixie Dandy, Inc. v. McHenry,** 607 S.W.2d 323 (Ark. 1980)—mistaken advice to taxpayer about whether form must be filed]

c. Federal law [§324]

Traditionally, the federal government has been *immune* from estoppel and apparent authority. Unless a *statute prevents the government from changing its mind* (and there are numerous such statutes), it is free to do so despite the harm caused by detrimental reliance. However, numerous lower court cases have estopped the government in particularly compelling fact situations, especially where the government performs a proprietary function (such as making contracts). [*See, e.g.*, **Portmann v. United States,** 674 F.2d 1155 (7th Cir. 1982)—mistaken advice by post office clerk that package was insured; estoppel applies] The Supreme Court has not entirely closed the door on estoppel, but its most recent cases suggest that it is rarely, if ever, appropriate.

(1) Federal cases [§325]

The Supreme Court decisions vacillate; some suggest that estoppel is possible against the government but others suggest that it is never possible.

(a) Money judgment cases [§326]

It is clear that estoppel *cannot* be used to obtain a money judgment against the government. [**Office of Personnel Management v. Richmond,** 496 U.S. 414 (1990)]

1) *Richmond* case

P was receiving a government pension. He sought advice about whether he could take a job without decreasing the pension. Officials advised him that he could. The advice was wrong because the applicable statute had changed and the officials did not know about the change. P took the job and his pension was reduced. Because P sought a money judgment, the Court held that the government could not be estopped. Such payment would violate the applicable statute and thus violate the Appropriations Clause of the Constitution, which prohibits disbursements except pursuant to congressional appropriations. Dictum in the decision suggests that most justices would never allow an estoppel claim, even for nonmonetary benefits, but the Court did not eliminate this possibility. [**Office of Personnel Management v. Richmond,** *supra*]

2) *Community Health* case

Prior to *Richmond*, dictum in one Supreme Court decision was more favorable towards estoppel. [**Heckler v. Community Health Services,** 467 U.S. 51 (1984)] Although the Court in that case found that a hospital's reliance on erroneous oral advice was neither detrimental nor reasonable, the decision suggested that estoppel could lie under more compelling facts. Dictum in the *Richmond* case appears far more hostile to such claims.

3) *Merrill* case

Earlier cases revealed strong hostility to estoppel and apparent authority. Unlike *Richmond*, they do not rest on the Appropriations Clause. For example, a wheat farmer wrongly advised that federal crop insurance would cover his crop could not recover when the crop was destroyed. [**Federal Crop Insurance Corp. v. Merrill,** 332 U.S. 380 (1947)]

(b) Immigration cases [§327]

In immigration and naturalization cases, the Supreme Court has indicated that the government *can be estopped* if it is guilty of *"affirmative misconduct."* Note that the relief being sought (*i.e.,* United States residency or citizenship) is nonmonetary so that the Appropriations Clause problem identified in *Richmond* is not present. However, it is not clear what is required to show "affirmative misconduct."

1) *Hibi* case

At a minimum, the government's failure to act does *not* qualify as "affirmative misconduct." Where the government failed to advise certain noncitizens that they qualified for naturalization, and failed to provide any means for exercising that right, the government was not estopped. [**INS v. Hibi,** 414 U.S. 5 (1973)]

2) *Moser* case

One early Supreme Court case might be an example of "affirmative misconduct." The government mistakenly advised an alien that applying for a draft exemption would not forfeit the right to apply for citizenship. The alien was later permitted to apply for naturalization because he had reasonably relied on this advice. [**Moser v. United States,** 341 U.S. 41 (1951)]

(c) Civil or criminal sanctions [§328]

Mistaken government advice might negate the mental state required for a criminal conviction. [**United States v. Pennsylvania Industrial Chemical Co.,** 411 U.S. 655 (1973)—government estopped to prosecute chemical company that reasonably relied on regulations that appeared to permit conduct in question] Similarly, a party who engages in conduct that appears to be legal under a reasonable interpretation of regulations cannot be subject to civil penalties when the agency interprets the regulations in an unexpected manner that causes the party's conduct to be a violation of the regulations. [**General Electric Co. v. EPA,** 53 F.3d 1324 (D.C. Cir. 1995)—order imposing civil money penalty for violating regulation concerning disposal of toxic chemical remanded because EPA did not provide company with fair warning of its interpretation of regulations, which were unclear; **United States v. Chrysler Corp.,** 158 F.3d 1350 (D.C. Cir. 1998)—manufacturer not liable for recalling cars because of unexpected violation of auto safety standards]

Chapter Six:
Rulemaking Procedures

CONTENTS

Chapter Approach

A.   Introduction   §329

B.   Controls on Rulemaking   §341

C.   Legal Effect of Rules   §348

D.   The Informal Rulemaking Process   §353

E.   Exceptions to Informal Rulemaking Requirements   §392

F.   Impartiality of Rulemakers   §412

G.   The Rulemaking Record   §422

Chapter Approach

If you have decided that agency action is rulemaking rather than ad[justify], next decide whether it is *formal or informal* rulemaking. Formal rul[e] some *external statute* (*i.e.,* other than the APA) requires an on-the-reco[rd] not, the APA informal rulemaking provisions apply. Under the *Vermont Y*[ankee] courts are not free to supplement the APA procedures.

In analyzing rulemaking, consider the following:

1. **Legislative or Executive Controls**

   Do any legislative or executive controls apply, such as the requirement to provide a regulatory impact statement or an environmental impact statement?

2. **APA Procedures**

   Were the various APA procedures complied with? These include:

   a. *Notice* of proposed rulemaking (watch for excessive variance between the proposed and final rule and for agency failure to disclose critical documents or studies);

   b. *Public participation* through written comments or, in some cases, an oral legislative-type hearing;

   c. A concise *statement of basis and purpose* (which must respond to material comments);

   d. *Publication of the rule* in the Federal Register;

   e. A *30-day grace period*; and

   f. A *right to petition* the agency to adopt or revise a rule.

3. **Exceptions to APA Procedures**

   Remember, however, there are numerous exceptions to APA rulemaking procedure. Check to see if any apply:

   a. *Military or foreign affairs function;*

   b. *Agency management or personnel;*

   c. *Public property, loans, grants, benefits, or contracts;*

ty apply, although mostly they do not.

contacts;

e or legislative interference; and

1. **Types of Rules [§329]**

In addition to adjudicating specific cases, agencies adopt generally applicable rules. Note that the words "rule" and "regulation" mean the same thing and are used interchangeably. Agency rules are legislative rules or nonlegislative rules.

a. **Legislative rules [§330]**

If the rule is made pursuant to a legislative delegation of rulemaking power, it is referred to as a *legislative* rule and, if it is within the scope of delegated power, it is *as binding as a statute*. (*See supra*, §§4-34 on the delegation and ultra vires doctrines.)

b. **Nonlegislative rules [§331]**

In addition, agencies frequently adopt rules that do *not* have binding legislative effect:

(1) *Interpretive rules* set forth the agency's interpretation of statutes or prior legislative rules.

(2) *Policy statements* set forth the manner in which the agency intends to exercise discretion.

2. **Rulemaking Procedure [§332]**

Procedural due process does not apply to rulemaking, so that there is no constitutionally required procedure to make rules. (*See supra*, §§146 *et seq*.)

a.   **Informal rulemaking procedure [§333]**

Nevertheless, all administrative procedure acts mandate a process of notice and public comment, referred to as *informal rulemaking* for many, but not all, agency rules. Informal rulemaking procedure is the subject of this chapter.

b.   **Formal rulemaking [§334]**

In rare cases, statutes require a *hearing on the record* for adopting rules, in which case adjudicatory procedure must be used. [*See* APA §553(c), last sentence] This is called *formal rulemaking*. Because it is extremely inefficient, formal rulemaking is seldom used and the courts try to avoid it. [**United States v. Florida East Coast Railway,** *supra*, §163—statutory requirement of a "hearing" for adopting general rules does not mean a "hearing on the record"; thus, informal rather than formal rulemaking can be used]

c.   **Hybrid rulemaking [§335]**

In numerous rulemaking statutes applicable to specific agencies, Congress has called for specific procedures (such as cross-examination) that are not required by the APA's informal rulemaking provisions. Yet Congress has not converted these rulemaking processes into formal rulemaking. As a result, these agency-specific procedures are referred to as "hybrid rulemaking," since they fall in between formal and informal rulemaking. [*See, e.g.,* **Harry and Bryant Co. v. FTC,** 726 F.2d 993 (4th Cir.), *cert. denied,* 469 U.S. 820 (1984)—agency did not violate the requirement that it provide cross-examination in cases of disputed issues of material fact]

3.   **Rulemaking as Technique for Policy Making [§336]**

As a technique for making law and policy, rulemaking has many advantages over adjudication. As a result, courts have broadly interpreted statutes authorizing agencies to make rules.

a.   **Advantages of rulemaking [§337]**

As noted earlier, rules are ordinarily *prospective* rather than retroactive; therefore, they are less likely to disappoint well-founded reliance interests. (*See supra*, §§186 *et seq.*) Rules *apply across the board*, so no individual or company is singled out for special treatment. In addition, the informal rulemaking process is well designed to gather *broad public input*, thus improving the quality of the rules; the adjudication process, on the other hand, furnishes input only from the parties to the case. Also, rulemaking is not encumbered by various restrictions, such as separation of functions and ex parte contacts, which can inhibit communications to the decisionmakers. Proposed and final rules are also published in the Federal Register and the Code of Federal Regulations, thus making them far more accessible than adjudicatory opinions.

RULEMAKING VS. ADJUDICATION—A SUMMARY	**gilbert**

RULEMAKING	ADJUDICATION
• Usually prospective rather than retroactive	• Usually retroactive and therefore can disappoint reliance interests
• Applies across the board	• Often singles out an individual or individual company
• Conducive to broad public input	• Input only comes from parties to the case
• Not subject to restrictions regarding separation of functions and ex parte contact	• Subject to restrictions regarding separation of functions and ex parte contact
• Publication in C.F.R. and Federal Register promote accessibility	• Not readily accessible to nonparties

4. Retroactive Rules [§338]

Legislative rules are ordinarily prospective in application, although interpretive rules are frequently retroactive. Absent an *express grant of authority* from Congress, agencies are not authorized to adopt retroactive legislative rules. [**Bowen v. Georgetown University Hospital,** 488 U.S. 204 (1988)]

a. Application

In *Georgetown University Hospital*, an agency adopted a rule in 1981. A later court decision invalidated the rule because it was not adopted with the appropriate notice and comment procedure. In 1984, the agency adopted the same rule after notice and comment—but made it retroactive to 1981. The Court found no express grant of authority that permitted the agency to adopt retroactive regulations. Consequently, under the rule of construction adopted by the majority, the retroactive effective date was invalid.

(1) Note

In a concurring opinion, Justice Scalia argued that the APA by its own terms prohibits retroactive rules. Section 551(4) defines "rule" as an agency statement of "future effect." This means, he argued, that the rule must be prospective, not retroactive, unless Congress has specifically authorized retroactive rules.

b. Prior law—retroactive rule [§339]

In a case predating the APA, where a legislative rule was found invalid because it used an improper factor, the Supreme Court directed the agency to make its new rule retroactive in order to protect the class of people to whom the rule applied. [**Addison v. Holly Hill Fruit Products,** 322 U.S. 607 (1944)] However, this case might not be followed after *Georgetown University Hospital.*

EXAM TIP   **gilbert**

If you see a legislative rule applied retroactively on an exam, remember that *such rules generally cannot be retroactive in effect*. Look at your facts—first determine whether the adopted rule will affect past events. If so, then check to see if Congress has specifically authorized the adoption of retroactive rules for that matter. If there is no congressional authorization, then you should find the rule invalid.

---

5. Broad Construction of Statutes [§340]

Because of the advantages of rulemaking over adjudication, the courts frequently interpret statutes giving agencies the power to make rules to authorize agencies to adopt binding *legislative rules* rather than mere interpretive or procedural rules. [**National Petroleum Refiners Association v. FTC,** 482 F.2d 672 (D.C. Cir. 1973), *cert. denied*, 415 U.S. 951 (1974)] In the *National Petroleum* case, the court stressed the advantages of adopting generally applicable binding rules to regulate unfair trade practices rather than merely attacking them on a case-by-case basis. Thus, it interpreted the FTC's statute to authorize such rules and the decision has been confirmed by later legislation.

B. Controls on Rulemaking

1. Introduction [§341]

The three branches of government have retained significant controls over agency rulemaking.

2. Judicial Controls [§342]

The courts judicially review the rules to assure they are not ultra vires (*see supra,* §§30-33) and that they are adopted in conformity with correct procedures.

3. Legislative Controls [§343]

The legislature retains significant oversight and budgetary powers, although it is no longer able to use the legislative veto (*see supra,* §§54-61).

4. Executive Controls [§344]

The executive branch frequently participates in the rulemaking process (*see infra,* §419) and in many states holds veto powers over rules (*see supra,* §83).

a. Regulatory assessment—executive order [§345]

At the federal level, a presidential executive order requires agencies to adopt a "regulatory assessment" early in the process of adoption of a "significant regulatory action." The regulatory assessment must make a careful examination of alternative approaches and perform a cost-benefit analysis. A "significant regulatory action" means that the rule would have an annual effect on the economy of $100 million or more or adversely and materially affect the economy, a sector of the economy, jobs, the environment, or state or local government. [Executive Order 12,866, 58 Fed. Reg. 51735 (1993)] This order is enforced by the Office of Information and Regulatory Affairs ("OIRA") in the Office of Management and Budget ("OMB"). The Executive Order applies only to executive branch agencies—not to independent agencies. (*See supra*, §75 for discussion of independent agencies.) The Model Act also contains a parallel requirement that agencies adopt a "regulatory analysis" before adopting a rule if such analysis is requested by various political entities such as the governor or by 300 persons. [1981 Model State APA §3-105]

b. Environmental impact statements [§346]

The National Environmental Policy Act ("NEPA") requires agencies that recommend legislation or take any "major" federal action (including rulemaking) to make an environmental assessment of the action, including consideration of less environmentally damaging alternatives. [42 U.S.C. §4332(2)(C)]

c. Impact on small business [§347]

The Regulatory Flexibility Act ("RFA") requires that agency rules take into account their effect on small business, unless the agency certifies that the rule would not have a significant impact on small business. The notice of rulemaking must include an initial regulatory flexibility analysis that focuses on the impact of the rule on small business and highlights alternatives that might minimize the burden. The final rule must respond to comments raised by the initial analysis and explain why less burdensome alternatives were rejected. Compliance with the RFA is subject to judicial review. Courts will determine whether the agency made a reasonable, good faith effort to carry out the mandates of the RFA. [5 U.S.C. §§601-612; **Associated Fisheries of Maine, Inc. v. Daley,** 127 F.3d 104 (1st Cir. 1997)]

C. Legal Effect of Rules

1. In General [§348]

In general, agencies are obligated to follow their own rules. If they wish to change the rules, they can do so only prospectively.

2. Procedural Rules [§349]

In many cases, an agency will adopt a procedural rule that is favorable to outsiders. Although the agency was not required by any statute or constitutional provision to adopt the rule, once it did so it is bound by the rule until it is changed, even if following the rule becomes inconvenient. [**Vitarelli v. Seaton,** 359 U.S. 535 (1959)]

a. Rules of convenience [§350]

However, the agency is *not* required to follow a regulation that was intended *primarily for the convenience of the agency* rather than for the benefit of outside parties. [**American Farm Lines v. Black Ball Freight Service**, 397 U.S. 532 (1970)]

3. Legislative Rules [§351]

An agency is also bound by its legislative rules until it changes them. [*See, e.g.,* **Arizona Grocery Co. v. Santa Fe Railway,** 284 U.S. 370 (1932)—agency was bound by railroad rates it had previously adopted; the rates could not be retroactively repealed]

4. Nonlegislative Rules [§352]

Some authority indicates that an agency is not bound by its interpretive rules or policy statements and can depart from them whenever it wishes. [**Vietnam Veterans of America v. Secretary of the Navy**, 843 F.2d 528 (D.C. Cir. 1988)] However, the point is not yet settled. Such action might trigger equitable estoppel against the agency (*see supra*, §§321-328). And in some states, an agency would be required to follow nonlegislative rules because the statute requires it to follow *all rules.* [1981 Model State APA §5-116(c)(8)(ii)—requires agency to observe all of its rules]

D. The Informal Rulemaking Process

1. Application of APA Rulemaking Provisions [§353]

For the informal rulemaking provisions of APA section 553 to apply, the item in question *must be a "rule"* as defined in the APA.

a. Definitions

(1) "Rule" [§354]

A "rule" is "the whole or a part of an agency statement of *general or particular applicability* and *future effect* designed to implement, interpret, or prescribe *law or policy* or describing the organization, procedure, or practice requirements of an agency . . . ." [APA §551(4)]

(2) "Rulemaking" [§355]

"Rulemaking" is the "agency process for formulating, amending, or repealing a rule." [APA §551(5)]

(3) "Regulation" [§356]

The term "regulation" is synonymous with "rule," and the terms are used interchangeably.

TIMELINE OF TYPICAL APA INFORMAL RULEMAKING PROCEDURE

Publish notice of rule in Federal Register, including:

- Time, place, and nature of proceedings

- Legal authority under which rule is proposed

- Terms or substance of rule or a description of subjects involved

→

Publish or make available critical data, such as scientific methodology

→

Receive public comments on proposed rule through submission of written data, views, or arguments (oral presentation generally not required)

→

Change rule based on comments as agency deems appropriate; provide additional notice and comment period if the rule as modified is not a logical outgrowth of the proposed rule

→

Write a statement of basis and purpose identifying the main issues raised by the public comments and explaining why the suggestions were not followed or how problems were resolved

→

Publish the final rule in the Federal Register, along with the Statement of Basis and Purpose, not less than 30 days before the rule's effective date, unless an exception applies

→

Give interested persons the right to petition for the issuance, amendment, or repeal of the rule

b. Characteristics of a "rule" [§357]

Thus, an administrative "rule" (as opposed t
to describe the results of adjudication) is:

(i) *Addressed to future* situations;

(ii) *Usually addressed to a class* of persons
provides for "particular applicability" a
and

(iii) *Often needs to be made specific* by sub
particular parties.

(1) Distinguish—definition of rule in Model A
In the Model State APA, rule is limited to
cability." Thus, it avoids the ambiguity o
rules as statements of "general or particul~ ~pp..~~~...y." [1981 Model
State APA §1-102(10)] Under the Model State APA, for example, the
setting of rates for a single railroad would be adjudication, while under
the federal APA, this would be treated as rulemaking.

c. Single company affected [§359]

As long as a rule is *stated in general terms*, APA rulemaking procedures are
applicable even though only a single company is affected by the rule. Of
course, the courts must be alert for situations in which the proceeding in
question is really adjudication (*i.e.*, involving the determination of *individualized, adjudicative facts about a single company*) rather than rulemaking. If
in substance the agency was engaged in adjudication rather than rulemaking,
adjudicatory procedure would apply and, if a deprivation of liberty or property were involved, due process would apply as well. [*See* **Anaconda Co. v.
Ruckelshaus**, 482 F.2d 1301 (10th Cir. 1973)]

Example: In *Anaconda*, the agency proposed a rule about pollution from
a particular smelting process in a single county. Only one company actually engaged in that process in that county. However, the rule was stated in
general terms and thus was considered a rule, as defined in the APA, not an
adjudication. Moreover, even if due process did apply, the court thought that
the notice and comment rulemaking procedures would satisfy due process
since the facts at issue could be fairly and efficiently determined through the
rulemaking process.

2. Notice of Proposed Rulemaking [§360]

Prior to adopting a rule, an agency must *publish in the Federal Register* (a daily
publication of the federal government) a notice of proposed rulemaking, unless
persons subject to the rule are named and either are *personally served or otherwise
have actual notice.* The notice must include:

ent of the *time, place, and nature* of public rulemaking proceedings;

erence to the *legal authority* under which the rule is proposed; and

Either the *terms or substance of the proposed rule* or a *description of the subjects and issues* involved.

[APA §553(b)]

3. Disclosure of Data [§361]

The agency is required to publish or make available critical data, such as scientific methodology, so that persons commenting on the rule can make meaningful submissions and criticisms. [**Portland Cement Association v. Ruckelshaus,** 486 F.2d 375 (D.C. Cir. 1973), *cert. denied,* 417 U.S. 921 (1974); **National Black Media Coalition v. FCC,** 791 F.2d 1016 (2d Cir. 1986)]

a. Limitation [§362]

Only basic data must be supplied, not every bit of background information in the agency file. [**B.F. Goodrich Co. v. DOT,** 541 F.2d 1178 (6th Cir. 1976)]

b. Impact of *Vermont Yankee* case [§363]

As discussed *infra,* §384, **Vermont Yankee Nuclear Power Corp. v. National Resources Defense Council,** 435 U.S. 519 (1978), prohibits courts from adding procedural requirements to the APA rulemaking provisions. It has yet to be decided whether the disclosure principle is consistent with *Vermont Yankee.* Arguably, the disclosure principle is consistent with the APA because disclosure can be construed to be part of the APA's notice provisions. Alternatively, the disclosure principle may be consistent with the APA because nondisclosure prevented outsiders from commenting on pertinent issues so that the agency failed to consider relevant factors, thus rendering the rule arbitrary and capricious. [**United States v. Nova Scotia Food Products,** 568 F.2d 240 (2d Cir. 1977); *see infra,* §607 for discussion of agency's obligation to consider all relevant factors]

4. Public Participation [§364]

The APA provides that "after notice required by this section, the agency shall give interested persons an opportunity to participate in the rulemaking through submission of written data, views, or arguments with or without opportunity for oral presentation." [APA §553(c)]

a. Timing [§365]

The APA does not make clear how long a period must be allowed for the public to submit comments on a proposed rule. Probably a reasonable time under the circumstances must be provided. [**Florida Power & Light Co. v. United States,** 846 F.2d 765 (D.C. Cir. 1988)—15 day period not unreasonable where agency already received a substantial number of comments which affected the contents of the final rule]

(1) Caution

Do not confuse the question of how much time must be allowed for the public to comment on a proposed rule with the different issue of the *effective date of the final rule.* Unless an exception applies, the agency must allow 30 days *after* publishing a final rule before the rule becomes effective. [APA §553(d)]

(2) Model Act [§366]

The 1981 Model State APA requires at least 30 days for the public to submit comments. Also it requires an explanation of the purpose of the proposed rule. [1981 Model State APA §3-103]

b. Oral presentation [§367]

Thus, the APA does not require oral argument, a much less trial-type procedure. However, some statutes do superimpose additional procedural requirements on top of the APA, such as a requirement of oral argument or even cross-examination on disputed issues of material fact. Rulemaking that is modified by the addition of ad hoc procedural requirements is called "hybrid rulemaking." (*See supra,* §335 for additional discussion of hybrid rulemaking.)

c. Model Act [§368]

The Model Act calls for oral proceedings on a proposed rule if requested by various governmental agencies or by 25 persons. [1981 Model State APA §3-104(b)]

5. Revisions to Rule—Logical Outgrowth [§369]

As finally adopted, the rule may be quite different from the version initially published in the Federal Register. This may occur because public comments caused the agency to make changes in the rule. However, the agency is *not* required to provide a new notice and start the procedure all over again, as long as the final rule is a *"logical outgrowth" of the proposed rule.* The rationale is that the public received adequate opportunity to comment if the final rule is logically connected to the proposed rule. [**American Medical Association v. United States,** 887 F.2d 760 (7th Cir. 1989); **Chocolate Manufacturers Association v. Block,** 755 F.2d 1098 (4th Cir. 1985)] However, if the proposed rule did not even place interested parties on notice that an issue in which they were interested was "on the table," the rule fails the logical outgrowth test and should be set aside. [**National Black Media Coalition v. FCC,** 791 F.2d 1016 (2d Cir. 1986)—proposed rule gave no clue that agency was considering abandonment of its minority preference policy]

a. Public comments do not serve as proper notice [§370]

A rule failed the logical outgrowth test even though the provisions in the final rule that differed from the proposed rule were noted in various comments filed by the public. The *agency* must give adequate notice of the significant changes in the rule, not the comments. Moreover, a challenger to the rule need not show that he would have made different arguments to the agency if there had been proper notice; there is no requirement of showing prejudice from improper notice. [**Shell Oil Co. v. EPA,** 950 F.2d 741 (D.C. Cir. 1991)]

b. Model Act [§371]

The Model Act prohibits adoption of a rule that is *"substantially different"* from the proposed rule. [1981 Model State APA §3-107] This is probably a more demanding standard than the federal "logical outgrowth" test, since a final rule might be logically connected to the proposed rule yet contain "substantially different" requirements (*i.e.*, more severe limitations or narrower exceptions).

EXAM TIP **gilbert**

Where the final version of the adopted rule is different from the original proposed rule published in the Federal Register, the federal rule for resolving this issue is probably more lenient than the Model State APA rule. Under the federal rule, the "differing" rule may still be adopted as long as the public had adequate opportunity to comment on the proposed rule and as long as the final rule is a *logical outgrowth* of the proposed rule. The Model Act, however, prohibits adoption of a rule that is *substantially different* from the proposed rule.

---

6. Statement of Basis and Purpose [§372]

The APA provides: "After consideration of the relevant matter presented [by the comment process], the agency shall incorporate in the rules adopted a concise general statement of their basis and purpose." [APA §553(c)] This provision therefore requires that the agency: (i) actually *consider the comments* it has received and (ii) *prepare a statement of reasons* for the rule.

a. "Concise and general" [§373]

The courts have interpreted this provision to require a statement of findings and reasons as part of the final rule. This statement enables a reviewing court "to see what major issues of policy were ventilated by the informal proceedings and why the agency reacted to them as it did." As a result, the statements cannot really be either "concise" or "general." [**United States v. Nova Scotia Food Products Corp.,** *supra* §363; **Automotive Parts & Accessories Association v. Boyd,** 407 F.2d 330 (D.C. Cir. 1968)]

Example: An agency adopted rules allowing subsidized ships used in foreign commerce to shift to the domestic market after repaying the subsidy. It failed to explain in its statement of basis and purpose how this action furthered the statutory purpose of maintaining sufficient capacity in foreign commerce. Instead, the agency relied on arguments of economic efficiency, though these are not mentioned as relevant factors in the statute; it failed to explain how efficiency was consistent with the statute. In short, the adequacy of the statement of basis and purpose is linked with the court's obligation to ascertain whether the rule is arbitrary and capricious; the statement needs to ventilate the major issues involved so that the court can determine whether the rule is arbitrary. [**Independent U.S. Tanker Owners Committee v. Dole,** 809 F.2d 847 (D.C. Cir.), *cert. denied,* 484 U.S. 819 (1987)]

---

b. **Response requirement [§374]**

The statement of basis and purpose must contain a response to significant and material comments made by the public, explaining why those suggestions were not followed or how problems raised by the public were resolved. [**United States v. Nova Scotia Food Products Corp.,** *supra*; **Rodway v. USDA,** 514 F.2d 809 (D.C. Cir. 1975)]

(1) Adding material to the record [§375]

In responding to comments, the agency can place supporting documentation into the rulemaking record after the comment period closes. [**Rybachek v. EPA,** 904 F.2d 1276 (9th Cir. 1990)—permissible to place 6,000 pages in response to comments] However, if the material added by the agency was critical to its conclusions, providing the only scientific support for the rule, its action would prevent adequate public comment and requires the rule to be set aside. [**Idaho Farm Bureau Federation v. Babbitt,** 58 F.3d 1392 (9th Cir. 1995)]

c. **Post hoc rationalizations [§376]**

In supporting the rule on judicial review, the agency is *limited to the reasons articulated* in the statement of basis and purpose. The agency may not concoct additional explanations at the time of judicial review. [**Motor Vehicle Manufacturers Association v. State Farm Mutual Auto Insurance Co.,** 463 U.S. 29 (1983); 1981 Model State APA §3-110(b)]

7. **Publication [§377]**

After it completes consideration of the rule, the agency must publish the rule in the Federal Register. The requirement of publication in the Federal Register covers not only legislative rules but also generally applicable interpretive rules and policy statements, as well as procedural rules. [APA §552(a)(1)] Legislative rules are then codified in the Code of Federal Regulations ("CFR"), which is broken down by agencies and indexed. (*See infra,* §484.)

8. **Delayed Effective Date [§378]**

Unless an exception applies, the publication of a final rule in the Federal Register is to be made not less than 30 days before the effective date of a rule. [APA §553(d)] This provision applies only to substantive, not to procedural rules, and is intended to provide time for regulated persons to accommodate themselves to a new rule.

a. **Exceptions [§379]**

The grace period requirement does not apply:

(1) To a substantive rule that grants or recognizes an exemption or relieves a restriction;

(2) To interpretive rules and statements of policy (*see infra*, §§400-411); or

(3) For good cause found and published with the rule (this exception is discussed *infra*, §§395-399).

9. Right to Petition [§380]

An agency must give an interested person the right to petition for the "issuance, amendment, or repeal of a rule." [APA §553(e); 1981 Model State APA §3-117] While the federal APA does not impose a time limit for action on such petitions nor require the agency to state reasons when it rejects a petition, another provision requires "prompt notice" of the denial of a petition and a "brief statement of the grounds for denial." [APA §555(e)] The Model Act requires action on petitions within 60 days and a statement of the reasons for denial of the petition.

10. Judicial Remedies

a. In general [§381]

If a court finds that a rule was invalidly adopted (either because the APA requirements were not followed or because the rule is found to be substantively invalid), the court has two choices: (i) it can vacate the rule, which invalidates the rule and requires the agency to start over, or (ii) it can remand the case to the agency for further consideration which allows the agency to keep the rule in effect, remedy the problem, and readopt the rule. Which approach to take is a matter for the discretion of the reviewing court, which should consider, among other factors, the damage to the public interest that would occur if the rule is set aside. [**Checkosky v. SEC**, 23 F.3d 452 (D.C. Cir. 1994)] However, the dissenting judge in *Checkosky* argued that remanding without vacating is contrary to the APA. Section 706(2)(A) of the APA provides that a reviewing court faced with an agency action that it has found substantively or procedurally invalid "*shall*" (not "may") "hold unlawful and set aside" such agency action.

b. For refusal of petition—judicial review [§382]

An agency's refusal to institute a rulemaking proceeding after a member of the public petitions for one is judicially reviewable. [**Auer v. Robbins**, 519 U.S. 452 (1997)] *Auer* holds that a party who believes that an existing agency rule should be updated must first petition the agency to institute a rulemaking proceeding. The party is not permitted to seek judicial review—on the theory that the existing rule that was once reasonable has become unreasonable—without first petitioning the agency to amend the rule.

(1) Scope of review [§383]

The scope of review of an agency's decision to refuse to institute a rulemaking proceeding after the public petitions for one is quite narrow. The court is likely to defer to the agency's decision not to allocate resources to the particular project requested by the public. [**WWHT, Inc. v. FCC,** 656 F.2d 807 (D.C. Cir. 1981)]

11. Imposition of Additional Procedures [§384]

Courts are not free to require the agencies to follow additional rulemaking procedures not prescribed in the APA, such as oral argument or cross-examination. [**Vermont Yankee Nuclear Power Corp. v. National Resources Defense Council,** *supra,* §363]

a. Rationale

If courts could impose additional procedures, the hearing requirements would be so uncertain as to cause agencies to hold full trial-type hearings in all cases, which would impair the administrative process.

b. Note

In *Vermont Yankee, supra,* the Court acknowledged that additional procedures **could be required** in rulemaking proceedings where a very small number of persons would be "exceptionally affected" by a proposed rule, each upon individual grounds. In such cases, individualized facts might be at issue and thus due process could apply. [**Londoner v. Denver,** *supra,* §151] *Vermont Yankee* also noted that an agency might be required to employ trial-type procedures if it had historically done so, but had departed from its own prior practice.

12. Negotiated Rulemaking [§385]

Numerous agencies have experimented with negotiated rulemaking, in which all affected interests are called together by the agency to try to reach a consensus. The agreed-upon rule is then the subject of ordinary notice and comment procedure.

a. Negotiated Rulemaking Act [§386]

In 1990, Congress enacted several pieces of legislation to encourage alternate dispute resolution ("ADR") techniques in administrative law, including the Negotiated Rulemaking Act ("NRA"). [5 U.S.C. §§581 *et seq.*] Congress found that "negotiated rulemaking can increase the acceptability and improve the substance of rules, making it less likely that the affected parties will resist enforcement or challenge such rules in court. It may also shorten the amount of time needed to issue final rules."

(1) When negotiated rulemaking used [§387]

The NRA provides that an agency head can propose negotiated rulemaking if it would be in the public interest to do so. In making this determination, the agency head should consider whether there are a *limited number of identifiable interests* that will be significantly affected by the rule and a reasonable likelihood that a committee can be convened with a balanced representation of *persons who can represent those interests* and are willing to negotiate in good faith to reach a consensus on the proposed rule.

(2) **Procedure [§388]**

The agency must publish a *notice in the Federal Register* announcing its use of negotiated rulemaking, together with a list of proposed committee members, a proposed agenda, a timetable, and other information. Additional persons can apply for membership on the committee. The public has 30 days to *file comments* on this announcement. After considering comments, if the agency wishes to proceed, it establishes a negotiated rulemaking committee (generally of fewer than 25 persons) and provides appropriate administrative support to the committee.

(3) **Agency participation [§389]**

An agency representative participates in the committee deliberations. The committee can appoint a facilitator to chair the meetings and assist the members in negotiating.

(4) **Judicial review [§390]**

The NRA provides that agency action relating to establishing, assisting, or terminating a negotiated rulemaking committee shall *not* be subject to judicial review. If the negotiated rulemaking procedure produces a rule, the rule may be judicially reviewed, and if so it may not be accorded any greater deference by a court than a normal rule.

(a) **Agency commitment to adopt a negotiated rule [§391]**

Suppose an agency participates in a negotiated rulemaking, agrees to a particular rule, then changes its mind and proposes a different rule. *Held:* The agency is permitted to do this. It cannot bind itself to adopt whatever rule the negotiated rulemaking committee came up with. [**USA Group Services, Inc. v. Riley**, 82 F.2d 708 (7th Cir. 1996)]

E. Exceptions to Informal Rulemaking Requirements

1. **Introduction [§392]**

The federal APA and the Model Act contain numerous exceptions to the informal rulemaking requirements.

2. **Categorical Exceptions [§393]**

The provisions of the federal act do not apply to a *military or foreign affairs* function of the United States or a matter relating to *agency management or personnel* or to *public property, loans, grants, benefits, or contracts*. [APA §553(a); **Humana of South Carolina v. Califano**, 590 F.2d 1070 (D.C. Cir. 1978)—a regulation limiting amount hospital can charge Medicare patients relates to "benefits" and thus is exempt from APA rulemaking requirements] These very broad exceptions are construed narrowly by the courts on the theory that Congress wanted informal rulemaking procedure to apply whenever possible. There are no comparable exceptions to the Model State APA.

3. Procedure Exception [§394]

"Rules of agency organization, procedure, or practice" are exempted from both *notice and comment* requirements and from the *delayed effective date* provision, but *not* from the right to petition requirement. [APA §553(b)(A)] There is no comparable exception to the Model State APA. To distinguish "procedural" rules from "substantive" rules, the courts consider whether a nominally procedural rule modifies substantive legal rights. [**United States Department of Labor v. Kast Metals Corp.,** 744 F.2d 1145 (5th Cir. 1984)—agency's plan for selecting enforcement targets is procedural because it does not modify target's substantive legal rights]

> **e.g.** **Example—agency organization:** In dictum, the Supreme Court indicated that an agency's decision to discontinue a particular health service might be a rule of agency "organization." [**Lincoln v. Vigil,** 508 U.S. 182 (1993)]

4. Good Cause Exception [§395]

The APA's good cause exception applies both to the notice and comment requirements and also to the delayed effective date provision.

a. APA provisions [§396]

Notice and comment is excused "when the agency for good cause finds (and incorporates the finding and a brief statement of reasons therefor in the rules issued) that notice and public procedure thereon are *impracticable, unnecessary, or contrary to the public interest.*" [APA §553(b)(B); 1981 Model State APA §3-108] To dispense with the 30-day delayed effective date provision, a federal agency must find good cause to do so [APA §553(d)(3)], and under the Model Act, the agency can do so only when there is "imminent peril to the public health, safety, or welfare" [1981 Model State APA §3-115(b)(2)(iv)].

b. Unnecessary exception [§397]

A rule falls under the "unnecessary" prong of the good cause rule if it is totally noncontroversial. Very minor, technical amendments of rules are often adopted without prior notice and comment under the "unnecessary" prong. A common federal practice that relies on the "unnecessary" exception is often referred to as "direct final rules." Under this approach, an agency publishes notice that it proposes to adopt a rule without public participation because the agency believes it would not be necessary. If within a short period (often 30 days), a single member of the public submits an adverse comment, the rule is withdrawn and resubmitted as a proposed rule as to which public comments are invited. If no adverse comments are received, the agency adopts the rule at the end of the 30-day period without further procedures.

c. Impracticable or contrary to the public interest [§398]

"Impracticable" means a situation in which the execution of agency functions would be prevented by prior notice and comment. "Contrary to the public interest" means that the interests of the public would be defeated by advance notice. [Attorney General's Memorandum on the APA 30-31 (1947)] The courts are quite strict in requiring that a real emergency situation be present before an agency is allowed to dispense with prior notice and comment. Typically, agencies are able to sustain good cause claims in the case of a public health or safety emergency or an environmental crisis. [**Northern Arapahoe Tribe v. Hodel,** 808 F.2d 741 (10th Cir. 1987)—urgent need for hunting regulations where the season had already begun and herds could dwindle to extinction] In other situations, prior announcement of a proposed rule would have negative economic effects. For example, prior announcement of a price freeze might cause prices to shoot up before the rule could become effective. [**DeRieux v. Five Smiths, Inc.,** 499 F.2d 1321 (Temp. Emer. Ct. App. 1974)] Still another situation where good cause can be claimed occurs if the rules must be adopted by a statutory deadline and it is not possible to conduct notice and comment proceedings before the deadline. [**Sepulveda v. Block,** 782 F.2d 363 (2d Cir. 1986)]

d. Interim-final rules [§399]

Federal agencies that adopt rules under the "impracticable" or "contrary to the public interest" prongs of the good cause exception often do so in the form of so-called "interim-final" rules: a rule is adopted without prior notice and comment under the good cause exception, but the public is invited to submit comments on the rule after it becomes effective. The agency commits itself to consider those comments, then to modify the rule before making it final. Thus the interim-final rule serves not only as an immediately effective rule, but also as a proposed rule: it gives notice to the public that the agency is considering a final rule and invites public comment on that rule. Some decisions hold that the agency's open-minded consideration of these post-effective comments is a relevant factor in determining whether the agency had good cause for adopting the interim-final rule in the first place. [**Mid-Tex Electric Cooperative v. Federal Energy Regulatory Commission,** 822 F.2d 1123 (D.C. Cir. 1987)]

5. Interpretive Rules [§400]

The notice and comment and delayed effective date provisions do not apply to "interpretive" (or "interpretative"—both words are in common use) rules. [APA §553(b)(A)] These are rules intended to explain the meaning of particular terms in a statute or a previous rule. The courts have found it quite difficult to distinguish interpretive rules from legislative rules.

a. Definition of interpretive rules [§401]

Courts focus on several different approaches in defining "interpretive rules."

(1) Agency intent [§402]

Some courts focus on the agency's intention. A rule is legislative if the agency had power to make legislative rules and intended to use it. A rule is interpretive if the agency lacked delegated legislative power or (even if it had such power) did not intend to use it. [**General Motors Corp. v. Ruckelshaus,** 742 F.2d 1561 (D.C. Cir. 1984)] Since this test turns on the agency's intention, the label chosen by the agency when it adopted the rule will usually determine the status of the rule. [*See, e.g.,* **Shalala v. Guernsey Memorial Hospital,** 514 U.S. 87 (1995)—guideline explaining accounting rule is interpretive because it explains legislative regulation] However, a reviewing court can disregard the agency's label and find that a rule that was labeled interpretive really has legislative effect because it compels behavior independent of any legislative rule. [**Chamber of Commerce v. OSHA,** 636 F.2d 464 (D.C. Cir. 1980)]

(2) Whether rule interprets [§403]

Other courts focus on whether the rule actually interprets language in the statute or a prior legislative regulation. A rule cannot be "interpretive" unless it explains the meaning of language. [**Hoctor v. United States Department of Agriculture,** 82 F.3d 165 (7th Cir. 1996)] In *Hoctor*, a legislative rule required that dangerous animals be confined in facilities appropriate for the animals involved. A second rule, adopted without notice and comment, stated that dangerous animals must be confined by a perimeter fence eight feet high. Since the second rule did not interpret any language in the first one, it was not an interpretive rule and therefore was not properly adopted.

(3) Whether rule results in new law [§404]

Another group of cases asks whether a rule "creates rights, assigns duties, or imposes obligations, *the basic tenor of which is not already outlined in the law itself.*" Thus if the purported interpretive rule seems to effect a substantive change in a legislative regulation, the new rule is itself legislative. [**La Casa del Convaleciente v. Sullivan,** 965 F.2d 1175 (1st Cir. 1992)]

b. Inconsistent interpretive rules [§405]

Another recurring problem involves inconsistent interpretive rules that interpret a legislative rule. The D.C. Circuit has held that if a second interpretive rule is contrary to an earlier interpretive rule, the second interpretive rule is treated as an amendment of the legislative rule and is thus invalid unless adopted with notice and comment. [*See, e.g.,* **Alaska Professional Hunters Association v. FAA,** 177 F.3d 1030 (D.C. Cir. 1999)] However, there is contrary authority. [*See, e.g.,* **Chief Probation Officers v. Shalala,** 118 F.3d 1327 (9th Cir. 1997)—later rule would have to be inconsistent with a legislative rule, not an earlier interpretive rule]

c. Rule binding on agency personnel [§406]

An interpretive rule does not become legislative even though it is intended to be binding on agency personnel, including ALJs. [**Warder v. Shalala,** 149 F.3d 73 (1st Cir. 1998)]

d. Model Act approach [§407]

The Model Act does not contain a broad exception for interpretive rules. Instead, it allows the agency to dispense with notice and comment in adopting an interpretive rule only if the agency did not have delegated power to adopt a legislative rule. If the agency could have adopted a legislative rule, it must use notice and comment in adopting an interpretive rule instead. In addition, where the agency does dispense with public participation when adopting an interpretive rule, the reviewing court must review the interpretation de novo (instead of giving it the deference usually accorded to agency interpretations—*see infra*, §§568-591). [1981 Model State APA §3-109]

6. Policy Statements [§408]

The notice and comment and delayed effective date provisions do not apply to "general statements of policy." [APA §553(b)(A)] There is no corresponding exception under the Model State APA, although there is an exception for rules relating to law enforcement or disputes with the public where disclosure of the rule would enable law breakers to avoid detection or give an improper advantage to persons adverse to the state. [1981 Model State APA §3-116(2)]

a. Definition of policy statement [§409]

A policy statement indicates the manner in which an agency intends to exercise a discretionary function, such as future prosecutions, investigations, or adjudications.

b. Test [§410]

An agency pronouncement will be treated as a policy statement if it is *tentative*; i.e., it informs the public and the agency staff of the manner in which the agency intends to exercise discretion, but it cannot be definitive. If the rule definitively establishes how the staff will exercise discretion, it will be treated as a legislative rule. Thus, the courts must draw a difficult line between tentative rules (which are policy statements) and binding rules (which are legislative). [**Pacific Gas & Electric Co. v. FPC,** 506 F.2d 33 (D.C. Cir. 1974); **Guardian Federal Savings & Loan Association v. FSLIC,** 589 F.2d 658 (D.C. Cir. 1978)] Again, while the courts are likely to defer to the label that the agency has chosen, they are not required to do so. [**American Bus Association v. United States,** 627 F.2d 525 (D.C. Cir. 1980)]

(1) Supreme Court undercuts the tentativeness rule [§411]

A Supreme Court opinion apparently undercuts the rule that a policy statement must be tentative rather than definitive. It suggests that a rule concerning a discretionary function is a policy statement even though it was quite definitive. [**Lincoln v. Vigil,** *supra,* §394]

	FEDERAL APA	MODEL STATE APA
CATEGORICAL EXCEPTIONS	Provisions do not apply to: • Military or foreign affairs functions of the United States • Agency management or personnel matters • Public property, loans, grants, benefits, or contracts	• No comparable exceptions
PROCEDURE EXCEPTION	• Rules of agency organization, procedure, or practice are exempted from notice and comment requirements and from delayed effective date provision, but *not* from the right to petition requirement	• No comparable exception
GOOD CAUSE EXCEPTION	• Notice and comment requirements excused where agency for good cause finds them impracticable, unnecessary, or contrary to the public interest • 30-day delayed effective date provision may be excused for good cause	• Same standard for notice and comment requirements • 30-day delayed effective date provision excused only where there is imminent peril to the public health, safety, or welfare
INTERPRETIVE RULES	• Notice and comment requirements and delayed effective date provisions do not apply	• Notice and comment requirements excused only where agency did not have delegated power to adopt a legislative rule • No comparable exception to delayed effective date provision
POLICY STATEMENTS	• Notice and comment requirements and delayed effective date provisions do not apply to general statements of policy	• No comparable exception

(a) *Lincoln* case

In **Lincoln v. Vigil**, an agency discontinued a particular program of health services to Indian children; it decided to use the money for different purposes. The Court indicated that notice and comment procedure was not required even if this decision was a "rule," an issue it did not decide, because it was a general statement of policy. The Court apparently believed that because the decision to discontinue the program was discretionary, the agency's decision exercising this discretion was a policy statement. The Court failed to discuss the fact that the agency's decision was definitive and final, not at all tentative.

F. Impartiality of Rulemakers

1. Introduction [§412]

The previous chapter considered various rules designed to assure fair adjudication, such as separation of functions, a ban on ex parte contacts and congressional interference, and assurance that the decisionmaker would not be biased. Generally, these requirements do *not apply* in rulemaking, because rulemaking is analogized to the legislative process (where virtually anything goes) rather than to adjudication.

2. Ex Parte Contacts [§413]

Generally, the public submits comments on proposed rules, and the comments are part of a public file. However, persons who are very concerned about a proposed rule may sometimes wish to make ex parte contacts with the decisionmakers in addition to (or instead of) putting comments on the public record. There is uncertainty about whether a rule can be invalidated because of ex parte contacts with the decisionmakers.

a. *Sangamon* rule [§414]

In some situations, a proceeding that is nominally rulemaking is really more like adjudication in the sense that it decides a dispute between several outside parties. In this situation, ex parte contact from one of the disputants is improper and will result in setting aside the agency rule. [**Sangamon Valley Television Corp. v. United States**, 269 F.2d 211 (D.C. Cir. 1959)]

b. *Home Box Office* rule [§415]

In one important case, the court invalidated a generally applicable rule that appeared to be the result of an ex parte deal between the cable television and over-the-air television industries. The court felt that this was fundamentally unfair to members of the public who were cut out of the backroom dealing. Moreover, the court could not review a rule that resulted from ex parte contact rather than from the record that was made by public comments. [**Home**

Box Office, Inc. v. FCC, 567 F.2d 9 (D.C. Cir.), *cert. denied,* 434 U.S. 829 (1977)]

(1) But note

The rule in *Home Box Office* might be contrary to the rule in *Vermont Yankee* (*supra,* §384), which precludes courts from adding procedural requirements to those set forth in the APA.

c. Subsequent developments [§416]

Later cases have seriously undercut *Home Box Office.* The general consensus now is that ex parte contacts in rulemaking **are permissible,** unless the *Sangamon* rule applies or unless some statute other than the APA prohibits such contacts or requires them to be disclosed on the record. [**Action for Children's Television v. FCC,** 564 F.2d 458 (D.C. Cir. 1977); **Sierra Club v. Costle,** *supra,* §288]

EXAM TIP	gilbert

If confronted with an exam question involving ex parte communications, be sure to note whether you are dealing with an adjudication situation or a rulemaking situation, because the rules are very different: Ex parte communications are **prohibited** in adjudication. If an ex parte communication does occur, it must be made part of the record, the party making the contact may be penalized, and a decision that may have been "tainted" by ex parte contact **may** be vacated by the court. In contrast, ex parte communications are **generally permitted** in rulemaking unless a statute or regulation prohibits ex parte contact or unless the situation is only nominally rulemaking and is actually more like adjudication. In such a case, ex parte contact is improper.

---

d. Agency rules [§417]

Influenced by *Home Box Office,* some agencies, including the FCC, require disclosure of written and oral ex parte contacts with decisionmakers during the rulemaking process.

e. Model Act [§418]

The Model Act requires written materials received by the agency during rulemaking to be included in the record but makes no such requirement for oral ex parte communications. [1981 Model State APA §3-112(b)(3)]

3. Legislative or Executive Interference [§419]

Generally there is **no prohibition** against either legislative or executive attempts to influence rulemakers through ex parte communications. [**Sierra Club v. Costle,** *supra*]

Example—presidential communications: *Sierra Club* involved meetings between the agency head and the White House staff. The court thought these were wholly appropriate since the President is constitutionally responsible for all executive branch decisions.

Compare: In an earlier case a Congressman threatened to hold up appropriations for a subway system until the agency approved plans for a bridge.

The court set aside the decision to build the bridge because of this pressure. [**D.C. Federation of Civic Associations v. Volpe,** *supra,* §285] The court in *Sierra Club* did not disapprove the *D.C. Federation* case, but distinguished it because the pressure there was based on an irrelevant factor (as opposed to genuine support or opposition to the decision under consideration).

4. Bias [§420]

The rules guaranteeing an impartial adjudicator do ***not apply*** in rulemaking since rulemaking is intended to be a political process. A rulemaker is disqualified only upon a "clear and convincing showing that he has an unalterably closed mind on matters critical to the disposition of the rulemaking." [**Association of National Advertisers v. FTC,** 627 F.2d 1151 (D.C. Cir. 1979), *cert. denied,* 447 U.S. 921 (1980); **C & W Fish Co. v. Fox,** 931 F.2d 1556 (D.C. Cir. 1991)]

Example: In the *National Advertisers* case, the FTC was considering rules restricting advertising on children's television. The chairman had given several speeches indicating his intense antagonism to advertising directed toward children. The court found that these speeches did not establish the "closed mind" that would disqualify the chairman.

5. Separation of Functions [§421]

The rules requiring separation of adversary staff members from the decisionmaking function do not apply in rulemaking. [**United Steelworkers of America v. Marshall,** 647 F.2d 1189 (D.C. Cir. 1980), *cert. denied,* 453 U.S. 913 (1981)—outside consultants and advocates for worker protection rule permitted to advise Assistant Secretary of Labor]

G. The Rulemaking Record

1. Introduction [§422]

Frequently, agency rules are challenged before the courts. An important issue that arises on review is the nature of the record before the court. Clearly, that record includes such matters as the notice of proposed rulemaking, the public comments, transcript of a public hearing (if any), and the agency's statement of basis and purpose. However, it is not clear whether that is the *exclusive* record. In many circumstances, the agency wishes to submit additional materials to establish the reasonableness of its rule. Similarly, the challengers wish to submit materials to show the unreasonableness of the rule.

2. General Rule [§423]

The general rule is that the record is exclusive. The court will consider only *material that was before the agency at the time it made the decision.* [**Camp v. Pitts,** 411 U.S. 138 (1973)] Similarly, as pointed out *supra,* the agency cannot advance new rationalizations for the rule on judicial review; it is limited to those articulated in its statement of basis and purpose. (*See supra,* §376.)

3. Exceptions [§424]

The courts have carved out numerous exceptions to the exclusive record principle. [*See* Stark & Wald, "Setting No Records: The Failed Attempts to Limit the Record in Review of Administrative Action," 36 Admin. L. Rev. 333 (1984)]

a. Lack of administrative findings [§425]

In a case involving inadequately explained informal adjudication rather than rulemaking, the Supreme Court remanded to the district court to conduct a trial on the agency's decisionmaking process. [**Citizens to Preserve Overton Park v. Volpe,** *supra,* §304] However, this part of the *Overton Park* decision is seldom followed. If adequate explanation is lacking, the correct course of action is to remand the case *to the agency* to prepare the explanation. [**Camp v. Pitts,** *supra*] The *Overton Park* approach is probably faulty because the mental processes of judges and agency decisionmakers should not be the subject of trials. [**United States v. Morgan,** *supra,* §302) (*Morgan IV* decision)]

b. New evidence [§426]

Some cases allow evidence arising *after the rulemaking record closed* to be admitted at the time of judicial review. Since the agency could not have considered this evidence, it does not violate the exclusive record rule and is helpful to the court in evaluating the reasonableness of the rule. [**Amoco Oil Co. v. EPA,** 501 F.2d 722 (D.C. Cir. 1974)]

c. Expert testimony [§427]

If the court requires assistance in understanding technical material in the record, some cases allow the introduction of expert testimony for this purpose. [**Bunker Hill Co. v. EPA,** 572 F.2d 1286 (9th Cir. 1977)]

4. Model Act [§428]

The Model Act does not accept the record exclusivity principle. It provides that the rulemaking record need not constitute the exclusive record for agency action or for judicial review [1981 Model State APA §§3-112(c), 5-114(a)(3)], although all written materials considered by the agency must be in the record [1981 Model State APA §3-112(b)(3)]. Thus, additional factual evidence can be received but the agency cannot advance any new reasons for the rule. [1981 Model State APA §3-110(b)]

5. State Law [§429]

Numerous state decisions reject the concept of exclusive record and allow introduction of factual materials on judicial review. [*See* **Liberty Homes v. Department of Industry,** 401 N.W.2d 805 (Wis. 1987)]

Chapter Seven: Obtaining Information and Attorney's Fees

CONTENTS

Chapter Approach

A.	Agency Acquisition of Information	§430
B.	Constitutional Protection from Agency Information Gathering	§458
C.	Freedom of Information Act	§483
D.	Government in the Sunshine Act	§525
E.	Attorney's Fees	§530

Chapter Approach

An agency must be able to acquire information as a basis for both adjudicative and rule-making proceedings. This chapter considers the agency's power to obtain information, and the corresponding rights of the public to obtain and refrain from giving information. It also considers the agency's obligation to hold public meetings and the circumstances in which the agency can or must pay the attorney's fees of private parties.

Exam questions in these areas are likely to focus on the following topics:

1. **Agency Seeks Information from the Private Sector**
    When the agency tries to get information from a private party, it will:

    a. **Subpoena information**
        In such cases, consider whether the subpoena is *"reasonable"*—*i.e.*, for a proper purpose and not excessively burdensome. Also think about any applicable *constitutional privileges* (*e.g.*, self-incrimination, unlawful search or seizure) or any *common law privileges* (*e.g.*, attorney-client privilege) that are violated by the subpoena.

    b. **Conduct a physical search**
        Ask yourself if the search requires a *warrant* (*i.e.*, the industry is not pervasively regulated), and if a warrant is required, has it been obtained?

2. **Private Party Seeks Information from an Agency**
    When someone in your fact pattern is trying to get information from the agency, consider the following:

    a. **Freedom of Information Act**
        First, check whether the information is *required to be published or made generally available* under the Freedom of Information Act ("FOIA"). If the agency is not required to make such information available, specific documents can still be *requested* unless they fall under an exception to the Act. (Watch especially for the inter- or intra-agency memorandum exception for predecisional, nonfactual documents.)

    b. **Sunshine Act**
        Remember that many agency meetings must be open to the public.

3. **Attorney's Fees**
    The general rule is that private parties *cannot recover* attorney's fees from the government. However, there are *exceptions* to this rule that you should consider: are there *specific statutory provisions* providing for the award of attorney's fees (*e.g.*, in civil rights cases or under the FOIA); or is there *general authorization* for such an award as under the Equal Access to Justice Act?

A. Agency Acquisition of Information

1. Methods of Obtaining Information [§430]

Most information acquired by agencies is obtained voluntarily. However, an agency may also be entitled to compel information through (i) *subpoena* power; (ii) required *reports*; (iii) physical *inspections*; or (iv) *hearings*.

a. APA provisions on gathering of information

(1) *Section 555(c) provides:* "Process, requirement of a report, inspection, or other investigative act or demand may not be issued, made, or enforced, except as authorized by law. A person compelled to submit data or evidence is entitled to retain or, on payment of lawfully prescribed costs, procure a copy or transcript thereof, except that in a nonpublic investigatory proceeding the witness may for good cause be limited to inspection of the official transcript of his testimony."

(2) *Section 555(d) provides:* "Agency subpoenas authorized by law shall be issued to a party on request and, when required by rules of procedure, on a statement or showing of general relevance and reasonable scope of the evidence sought. On contest, the court shall sustain the subpoena or similar process or demand to the extent that it is found to be in accordance with law. In a proceeding for enforcement, the court shall issue an order requiring the appearance of the witness or the production of the evidence or data within a reasonable time under penalty of punishment for contempt in case of contumacious failure to comply."

2. Agency Power to Subpoena [§431]

If the agency's demand for information is resisted, it may ordinarily seek judicial enforcement of its request. If the judicial order is ignored, the court may hold the resisting party in contempt.

a. Early view—subpoena power restricted [§432]

In its earlier decisions, the Supreme Court narrowly limited the subpoena power of agencies.

(1) Power to enforce subpoenas [§433]

The Court suggested in an early case that an agency did not have contempt power to enforce its own subpoenas. [**ICC v. Brimson,** 154 U.S. 447 (1894)] Whether this dictum would be followed today is unclear. However, agencies generally do not have contempt power.

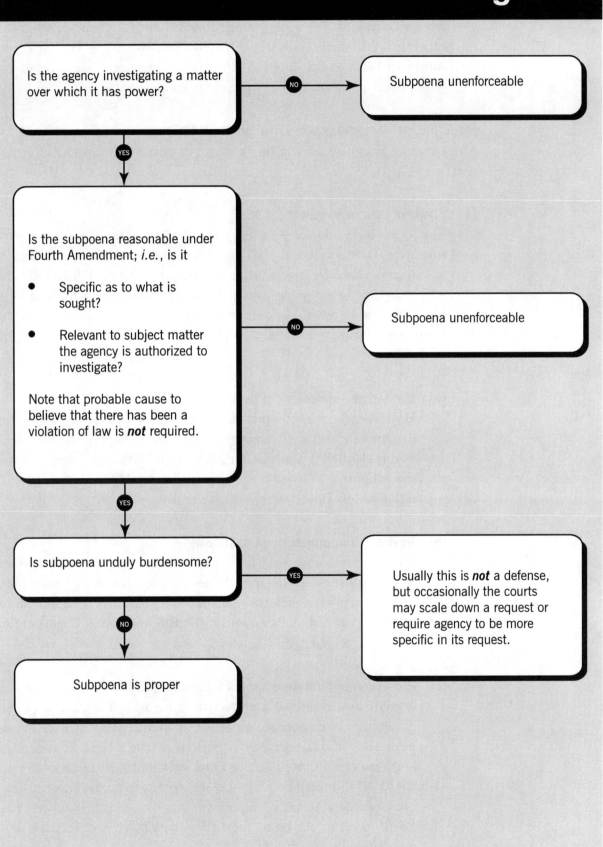

Is the agency investigating a matter over which it has power?

NO → Subpoena unenforceable

YES ↓

Is the subpoena reasonable under Fourth Amendment; *i.e.*, is it

- Specific as to what is sought?

- Relevant to subject matter the agency is authorized to investigate?

Note that probable cause to believe that there has been a violation of law is *not* required.

NO → Subpoena unenforceable

YES ↓

Is subpoena unduly burdensome?

YES → Usually this is *not* a defense, but occasionally the courts may scale down a request or require agency to be more specific in its request.

NO ↓

Subpoena is proper

(2) "Fishing expeditions" prohibited [§434]

The Court also declared that, absent specific congressional language, an agency was not empowered to demand vast amounts of written material from a defendant. The agency must show grounds for believing that the requested documents will actually prove violations of law. [**FTC v. American Tobacco Co.,** 264 U.S. 298 (1924)—agency request for all letters between company and its jobbers for entire year denied]

b. Modern view—broader power to subpoena [§435]

Modern cases recognize a much broader agency power to subpoena information.

(1) Scope of subpoena power [§436]

The courts have allowed an agency to subpoena information from *persons* over whom the agency has no jurisdiction as long as the agency is investigating a *matter* over which it has power. [**Link v. NLRB,** 330 F.2d 437 (4th Cir. 1964)—union officials, being "shadowed" by detective, filed unfair labor practice charge against employer; detective held in contempt for refusing to disclose to NLRB who hired him to "shadow" the officials]

(a) Limitation—statement of purpose [§437]

However, the agency *must state its purpose* so that the court can determine whether it is engaged in a lawful inquiry. If the investigation is clearly for a purpose unauthorized by the governing statute, the subpoena will not be enforced. [**FTC v. Miller,** 549 F.2d 452 (7th Cir. 1977)]

(b) Review for improper purpose [§438]

A court that is requested to enforce a subpoena may consider whether the agency's request is actually designed to *harass or intimidate,* rather than to obtain information. However, a difficult burden of proof must be met to show harassment. [**Shasta Minerals & Chemical Co. v. SEC,** 328 F.2d 285 (10th Cir. 1964)]

(c) Protection of First Amendment interests [§439]

A court should impose a protective order against disclosure by the government of subpoenaed material that would harm the First Amendment associational interests of persons whose affairs are described in the material. [**Dole v. Service Employees Union,** 950 F.2d 1456 (9th Cir. 1991)—union members' refusal to attend future meetings because of federal officials' subpoena of union meeting minutes was sufficient to make out prima facie case showing impact on members' associational rights]

(2) Fourth Amendment limitations [§440]

Although the agency need not show probable cause for the investigation, it must comply with the "reasonableness" requirements of the Fourth Amendment.

Example—probable cause unnecessary: The Walsh-Healy Act required government contractors to comply with prevailing wage rates. The Secretary of Labor issued a subpoena for wage information concerning a factory that processed raw materials for ultimate purchase by the government. Even though there was no probable cause to suspect that wages were too low, or even that the factory was subject to the Act, the Court held that the district court must enforce the subpoena. [**Endicott Johnson Corp. v. Perkins,** 317 U.S. 501 (1943)]

(a) Subpoena must be "reasonable" [§441]

An agency subpoena must be "reasonable" within the meaning of the Fourth Amendment. That is, the subpoena must be *specific* as to what is sought, and the object of the subpoena must be *relevant* to subject matter that the agency is *authorized* to investigate. [**Oklahoma Press Publishing Co. v. Walling,** 327 U.S. 186 (1946)—subpoena for corporate records upheld as reasonable]

1) Test of relevance [§442]

During the investigation phase, the standard of relevance is very relaxed. The agency need merely show that the information might possibly be useful to its investigation. However, at least some theory of relevance must be spelled out. [**CAB v. United Airlines, Inc.,** 542 F.2d 394 (7th Cir. 1976); **FTC v. Texaco, Inc.,** 555 F.2d 862 (D.C. Cir.), *cert. denied,* 431 U.S. 974 (1977)]

Example—disclosures held "reasonable": A regulation requiring banks to report all depositor transactions involving more than $10,000 in currency was upheld against a Fourth Amendment attack. Such disclosures were held "reasonable" in light of the connection between many such transactions and criminal behavior, the fact that banks traditionally maintain records of this kind, and the fact that corporations may enjoy less Fourth Amendment protection than individuals. [**California Bankers Association v. Shultz,** 416 U.S. 21 (1974)]

---

c. Burdensomeness of subpoena [§443]

Generally the fact that compliance with a subpoena will be expensive and burdensome is not a defense. [*See **In re** FTC Line of Business Report Litigation,*

595 F.2d 685 (D.C. Cir.), *cert. denied,* 439 U.S. 958 (1978)] Occasionally, however, a court will scale down a request that is deemed unduly burdensome or require the agency to be more specific in its requests. [*See* **Hunt Foods & Industries, Inc. v. FTC,** 286 F.2d 803 (9th Cir. 1960)] A trial court has substantial discretion to limit the burden of a subpoena (for example, by requiring the agency to inspect documents at the subpoenaed party's place of business).

d. Adjudicative subpoenas [§444]

When subpoenas are issued as part of the agency's discovery process in the course of *adjudication,* statutes or rules frequently impose somewhat greater constraints on the agency. For example, an administrative law judge might have to pass on whether the subpoenaed information meets relevance standards. However, subpoenas issued in the course of agency *investigations* generally have no such constraints. When both an adjudication and an investigation are conducted simultaneously, the agency should take care that information subpoenaed in the investigation is not passed "through the back door" to personnel who are conducting the adjudication without compliance with the discovery rules applicable to adjudication. [**FTC v. Atlantic Richfield Co.,** 567 F.2d 96 (D.C. Cir. 1977)]

e. Third party subpoenas [§445]

Frequently, an agency will conduct an investigation of someone (the "target") and will subpoena information from someone else about the target. Absent some statutory limitation, the target is not entitled to notice of the third-party subpoena, even though the third party may voluntarily comply with the subpoena before the target can intervene and raise objections that the subpoena seeks irrelevant or privileged information. [**SEC v. Jerry T. O'Brien, Inc.,** 467 U.S. 735 (1984)]

3. Agency Power to Make Physical Inspections [§446]

Enforcement of health, safety, and welfare laws often requires government officials physically to inspect homes and businesses or conduct physical tests of employees. Although such searches fall within the Fourth Amendment prohibition on unreasonable searches and seizure, the requirements for obtaining a warrant are lenient, and in many situations no warrant is required at all.

a. Home inspections [§447]

For administrative inspections of homes, warrants are required.

Example: A building inspector must obtain a warrant before inspecting a dwelling for housing code violations unless a householder's consent is first obtained. [**Camara v. Municipal Court,** 387 U.S. 523 (1967)—tenant jailed for refusing entry to city inspectors attempting to inspect his residence without a warrant]

(1) Probable cause [§448]

It is not necessary to cite specific reasons to obtain a warrant. Probable cause is satisfied if information as to the neighborhood indicated the likelihood of violations. In the case of a health or public safety emergency (*e.g.,* extreme structural decay, rodent feces), no warrant would be required. [**Camara v. Municipal Court,** *supra*]

(2) Exception—welfare [§449]

The Court upheld a state statute requiring welfare recipients to submit to unannounced, warrantless inspections. The Court upheld this procedure, distinguishing *Camara,* because it held the inspection was not a "search" and the penalty for refusing entry was "merely" loss of benefits rather than criminal prosecution. [**Wyman v. James,** 400 U.S. 309 (1971)]

b. Warrants required for some business inspections [§450]

Whether a warrant will be required for an administrative business inspection is much less certain.

(1) General rule [§451]

Earlier cases simply applied *Camara* to the business inspection situation. [**See v. Seattle,** 387 U.S. 541 (1967)—inspection of locked warehouse by fire inspector requires warrant]

(2) OSHA inspection [§452]

Similarly, a warrant must be obtained to inspect business premises for compliance with employee safety rules, despite the danger that the employer might conceal defects while the inspector gets a warrant. [**Marshall v. Barlow's Inc.,** 436 U.S. 307 (1978)] Furthermore, *Barlow's* held that to obtain a warrant, the inspector must establish that his choice of this particular employer was based on reasonable standards, such as statistical sampling techniques.

c. Exceptions [§453]

A statute can validly authorize *warrantless* inspections of "pervasively" regulated businesses.

(1) Requirements for warrantless inspection [§454]

The business must be subject to close and detailed regulation, and the statute must meet Fourth Amendment reasonableness standards. This requires that:

(a) There be a *substantial government interest* in the regulatory scheme;

(b) Warrantless inspections are *necessary* to further that scheme; and

(c) The statute must *perform the functions of a warrant* by advising the owner of the business that *periodic searches will be made* and the statute must *limit the time, place, and scope* of the inspections.

(2) Application

(a) Auto junkyards

A New York statute validly permits warrantless inspection of auto junkyards. The state has a substantial interest in preventing auto theft; unannounced searches of junkyards are necessary to further that scheme (because stolen property disappears quickly); the statute provides for frequent and regular inspections of licensed premises; they are limited in time, place, and scope. The fact that such searches are used primarily to turn up evidence of crime is irrelevant in light of their regulatory nature. [**New York v. Burger,** 482 U.S. 693 (1987)] *But note:* New York refused to follow this case and required a warrant for the junkyard search under the state constitution. [**People v. Scott,** 79 N.Y.2d 474 (1992)]

(b) Gun and liquor dealers

On similar reasoning, warrantless inspection of liquor and gun dealers has been upheld. [**United States v. Biswell,** 406 U.S. 311 (1972)—guns; **Colonnade Catering Corp. v. United States,** 397 U.S. 72 (1970)—liquor]

(c) Mines

Underground mines must be inspected four times each year. The regularity and consistency of such inspections make them distinguishable from the OSHA inspections involved in **Marshall v. Barlow's Inc.** (*supra,* §452). Virtually every business in the nation is subject to an OSHA search and the inspectors have a great deal of discretion about which ones to inspect. [**Donovan v. Dewey,** 452 U.S. 594 (1981)]

d. Physical tests [§455]

Government employers increasingly subject their employees to blood, breath, or urine tests to detect the use of drugs or alcohol. Persuasive governmental interests can override privacy interests and permit testing of persons for drug use without a warrant or even without any basis for individualized suspicion of drug or alcohol use.

(1) Railway accidents [§456]

Federal regulations requiring alcohol and drug tests of railway employees following railroad accidents were upheld. The regulations provided for no warrant and applied regardless of whether there was any basis to suspect drug use (other than the happening of an accident). While the testing is a search under the Fourth Amendment, it is a reasonable search. There is no need for a warrant because the regulations require tests in all railway accident situations (rather than leaving anything to the discretion of law enforcement officers). And the strong government interest in assuring safety, investigating crashes, and deterring drug use outweighs the employees' privacy interests in avoiding urine testing. [**Skinner v. Railway Labor Executives' Association,** 489 U.S. 602 (1989)]

(2) Customs employees [§457]

Federal regulations requiring drug tests of customs employees also were upheld. Urine testing of front-line customs employees (whose responsibility includes interdiction of drug smuggling) and of those who carry firearms is reasonable, even without any individualized basis of suspicion and even though there is no drug problem among customs employees (only five of 3,600 tests were positive). However, the Court remanded for further proceedings with respect to drug testing for those who handle classified material. The Court was unsure whether the same persuasive governmental interests applied to all of those who might come into contact with classified material. [**National Treasury Employees Union v. Von Raab,** 489 U.S. 656 (1989)]

B. Constitutional Protection from Agency Information Gathering

1. Introduction [§458]

While administrative investigations are not criminal proceedings, they often will result in the imposition of criminal penalties. Therefore, some—but certainly not all—of the constitutional safeguards that protect a defendant in criminal proceedings have been held applicable to administrative investigations and hearings.

2. Privilege to Refuse to Furnish Information [§459]

Witnesses called to testify in an agency investigation may assert the *Fifth Amendment privilege* against self-incrimination in refusing to answer specific questions.

a. When privilege arises [§460]

If the information requested could supply a link in a chain leading to criminal conviction, the witness may claim the privilege.

(1) Immunity [§461]

However, since an immunity statute frequently applies in these situations, an agency *can* compel testimony by granting the witness immunity from use of the evidence against him in a subsequent prosecution. [*See* **Kastigar v. United States,** 406 U.S. 441 (1972)]

(2) Privilege limited to natural persons [§462]

In addition, the privilege against self-incrimination is *not* available to a corporation, a union, or a partnership. [**Bellis v. United States,** 417 U.S. 85 (1974)]

Example: The custodian of records for a corporation, union, or partnership may not refuse to produce *documents*. However, the custodian may have a personal privilege and thus may refuse to answer specific *questions* the answer to which could incriminate the custodian.

---

b. Scope of Fifth Amendment privilege

(1) Private papers [§463]

The Fifth Amendment does not protect a witness's private papers or business records from disclosure even if the content of those documents is incriminating. [**United States v. Doe,** 465 U.S. 605 (1984)] However, the Fifth Amendment does apply to compelled production of the documents if the act of producing them would be incriminating. Thus production of papers might be, in effect, incriminating testimony that the papers actually existed or that they were in the witness's possession or were authentic. [**Fisher v. United States,** 425 U.S. 391 (1976)]

Example: In *Fisher,* the Court held that compelling a taxpayer to produce his accountant's workpapers would *not* involve testimonial self-incrimination. *Rationale:* The papers were prepared by the accountant, not by the taxpayer. Thus, their production would not incriminate the taxpayer, since the accountant would testify as to their correctness.

(a) Only possessor can assert privilege [§464]

Only the person in possession of documents can assert the Fifth Amendment privilege not to produce them. [**Couch v. United States,** 409 U.S. 322 (1973)—taxpayer cannot assert privilege as to records in possession of his accountant]

(b) Corporate papers [§465]

The custodian of the records of an entity (such as a corporation or partnership) *cannot* claim any Fifth Amendment privilege for such papers, even if the act of producing them might be incriminatory, since the custodian holds such papers in a representative capacity. [**Braswell v. United States,** 487 U.S. 99 (1988)]

(c) Search warrant [§466]

Private papers can be seized pursuant to the authority of a valid search warrant. The Fifth Amendment does not apply, since the person from whom the documents are seized has not been compelled to admit anything about the documents. [**Andresen v. Maryland,** 427 U.S. 463 (1976)]

(2) Required records [§467]

The Fifth Amendment privilege does *not* extend to records that are *required to be kept.* [**Shapiro v. United States,** 335 U.S. 1 (1948)]

Example: In *Shapiro,* persons subject to maximum price regulations were required to preserve all records of sales and produce them for examination. The Court held that there was no Fifth Amendment protection as to records required to be kept by statute, as long as the records were relevant to an activity that Congress could regulate.

(a) Application of *Shapiro*

1) Production of child [§468]

Shapiro applies to an order to a mother to produce her child because the mother had custody pursuant to an earlier order of the juvenile court that conditioned custody on a variety of protective provisions which the mother had ignored. Because the order arose out of a regulatory, noncriminal process, the mother could not resist the order on the basis of the Fifth Amendment privilege. [**Baltimore Department of Social Services v. Bouknight,** 493 U.S. 549 (1990)—dictum: mother might have used immunity for any incriminating evidence arising out of the compelled production of the child]

2) Distinguish—tax records [§469]

Taxpayers are required to maintain all business records necessary to compute their income tax. It appears that the Fifth Amendment protects these records from compelled production, where such production would constitute testimonial incrimination. Fifth Amendment protection exists if the documents were prepared by the taxpayer (or perhaps the taxpayer's employees) and are in the possession of the taxpayer or the taxpayer's attorney. [*See* **Couch v. United States,** *supra*; **Fisher v. United States,** *supra*] Logically *Shapiro* would seem to remove Fifth Amendment protection from these records. However, the manner in which the *Shapiro* rule applies to tax records is unresolved.

3) Distinguish—records of criminal activity [§470]

The potential scope of *Shapiro* has also been *limited* in cases involving statutory requirements that persons engaged in criminal activity retain records that would prove their criminality. [**Marchetti v. United States,** 390 U.S. 39 (1968)]

---

e.g. **Example:** *Marchetti* involved a prosecution for failure to register and provide detailed information concerning payment of a gambling tax. The Court held that the statute required a gambler to incriminate himself.

---

a) Note

The *Marchetti* case distinguished *Shapiro* on three grounds: (i) Marchetti was obligated to keep records that were *not* those customarily kept by those in business; (ii) there were public aspects to the records *Shapiro* was required to keep, but not as to Marchetti's; and (iii) the record-keeping requirement in *Shapiro* arose from a noncriminal and regulatory activity, whereas the requirement in *Marchetti* was imposed on a *select group inherently suspect* of criminal activity.

(3) Simultaneous administrative and criminal cases [§471]

Suppose a party is the subject of *both* an administrative and a criminal investigation. The party might wish to defer the administrative proceedings until after the criminal case is completed, so that he could assert his Fifth Amendment privilege in the criminal case but testify in the administrative case. A court has discretion to stay the administrative proceeding in the interests of justice. [*See* **Keating v. Office of Thrift Supervision,** 45 F.3d 322 (9th Cir. 1995)—refusing to defer administrative proceeding because of the important public interest in immediate resolution]

c. Availability of other privileges [§472]

The extent to which other privileges are available in refusing to furnish required information to agencies is unclear. The *attorney-client* privilege is available. [**Fisher v. United States,** *supra*] The *accountant-client* privilege is not available. [**Couch v. United States,** *supra*] There is no privilege for accountant's workpapers analogous to the attorney work product privilege. [**United States v. Arthur Young & Co.,** 465 U.S. 805 (1984)]

3. Rights to Procedural Due Process in Investigations

a. Notice and hearing [§473]

The due process rights of notice and hearing—usually accorded in administrative adjudications (*see supra,* §§84 *et seq.*)—are generally *not* available in investigatory hearings.

(1) Illustration

The United States Civil Rights Commission conducted hearings on voting irregularities in the South and was alleged to have violated due process by failing to give notice of the charges, failing to disclose the names of informants, and failing to allow cross-examination. The Supreme Court held that these procedural protections were **not** required because the hearings were merely "investigatory." [**Hannah v. Larche,** 363 U.S. 420 (1960)] *Note:* The fact that criminal prosecutions might follow the Commission's report was held not to make the hearings part of the criminal process.

EXAM TIP   **gilbert**

Don't fall prey to an exam question that involves an investigatory hearing on a fundamental right. Remember that due process will **not** be triggered in an investigatory hearing **just because** a fundamental right is involved. For example, the Supreme Court held that due process procedural protections were not needed in hearings on voting irregularities conducted by the U.S. Civil Rights Commission because the hearings were merely "investigatory."

---

(2) Distinguish—proceedings accusatory in nature [§474]

However, where the investigatory hearings appear to be part of a *prosecutorial process,* the agency must provide the "accused with the right to call witnesses of his own and to confront witnesses called to testify against him." [**Jenkins v. McKeithen,** 395 U.S. 411 (1969)—agency was limited to uncovering and publicizing criminal activity]

b. Right to subpoena witnesses [§475]

Even where the proceeding is not accusatory, it is now quite common for federal agencies having a subpoena power to allow private parties to subpoena witnesses in their defense. And where the agency has no subpoena power (*e.g.,* student disciplinary bodies, state and local agencies), private parties may be allowed to call witnesses on their own behalf.

(1) APA provision [§476]

APA section 555(d) provides that in exercising its subpoena power upon a party's request, the agency may require a statement or showing of general *relevance* for the evidence sought. In this respect, agencies differ from the federal district courts, which issue subpoenas in blank.

4. Right to Counsel [§477]

A witness required to appear before an investigatory hearing is entitled to the representation of counsel.

a. APA provision [§478]

APA section 555(b) provides: "A person compelled to appear in person before an agency or representative thereof is entitled to be accompanied, represented and advised by counsel or, if permitted by the agency, by other qualified representative."

b. Scope of right

(1) No right to cross-examination [§479]

Representation by counsel under APA section 555(b) apparently does **not** include any right of cross-examination if the proceeding is merely investigatory. [*See* **Hannah v. Larche,** *supra*]

(2) No right to object [§480]

And counsel apparently may be precluded from **objecting to questions.** [*See* **FCC v. Schreiber,** 329 F.2d 517 (9th Cir. 1964), *rev'd on other grounds,* 381 U.S. 279 (1965)]

(3) No right to private hearing [§481]

The *Schreiber* case also indicates that the party being investigated has no right to a **private hearing**; *i.e.,* it is up to the agency whether to hold a public or private hearing.

5. Use of Information from Unlawful Searches [§482]

Even though evidence seized in an unlawful search is inadmissible in a criminal proceeding, it may be admitted in a federal administrative proceeding. [**United States v. Janis,** 428 U.S. 433 (1976)—evidence obtained pursuant to defective state search warrant admissible in federal civil tax proceeding; **INS v. Lopez-Mendoza,** 468 U.S. 1032 (1984)—civil deportation proceeding] According to some authority, however, evidence must be excluded in administrative proceedings if the manner in which it was obtained constituted egregious violations of the Fourth Amendment or other liberties. [**Gonzalez-Rivera v. INS,** 22 F.3d 1441 (9th Cir. 1994)—border patrol officer's stop of deportee based solely on his Hispanic appearance held to be an "egregious constitutional violation"]

EXAM TIP   **gilbert**

On an exam question covering use of information from unlawful searches, use the general rule that evidence seized in an unlawful search *may be admitted in a federal administrative proceeding.* However, if the question includes a search and seizure scenario that seems incredibly outrageous, discuss *both* schools of thought in your analysis, but be sure that the facts *clearly* support the position offered in *Gonzalez-Rivera* (egregious constitutional violation) if you conclude that the evidence should be excluded.

C. Freedom of Information Act

1. In General [§483]

The Freedom of Information Act ("FOIA") is contained in APA section 552. The Act provides a comprehensive statement of the rights of *private parties* to obtain information in the possession of the government. Although its primary purpose is to provide information to the general public, the Act can also be useful as a method of discovery for those litigating against the government. [**Renegotiation Board v. Bannercraft Clothing Co.,** 415 U.S. 1 (1974)]

2. APA Provisions

a. Publication of procedures and rules [§484]

Section 552(a)(1) requires that each agency publish (in the Federal Register) a description of its organization, the party from whom the public can obtain information, a statement of its *procedures,* and its general *rules* and *interpretations.* A person cannot be bound or adversely affected by any matter not so published, unless she has actual notice thereof.

Example: This provision was applied to invalidate eligibility rules for Indian welfare payments, where the Bureau of Indian Affairs failed to publish the rules in the Federal Register. [**Morton v. Ruiz,** *supra,* §191]

---

b. Opinions available for public inspection [§485]

Section 552(a)(2) requires that each agency make available for public inspection and copying: its *opinions* in decided cases, its statements of *policy and interpretations* not published in the Federal Register, and any administrative staff manuals that affect the public.

(1) Definition of terms

(a) "Opinion" vs. "memorandum" [§486]

A distinction must be drawn between "opinions," which are to be made available under section 552(a)(2), and "memoranda," which may be exempt from the Act under section 552(b)(5) (*see infra,* §506).

Example: A communication from the FTC to its staff, explaining the effect of an agency order, is an "opinion." But memoranda from staff members to the Commissioners—and from individual Commissioners to staff—are "intra-agency memoranda." [**Sterling Drug, Inc. v. FTC,** 450 F.2d 698 (D.C. Cir. 1971)]

(b) "Interpretations" [§487]

Among other things, an "interpretation" includes a private ruling by the IRS (*e.g.,* in a letter advising as to tax consequences of a particular transaction). [**Tax Analysts & Advocates v. IRS,** 505 F.2d 350 (D.C. Cir. 1974)]

(2) Quarterly index [§488]

Each agency is also obligated to publish quarterly a current index of those matters required to be made available by section 552(a)(2).

(3) Invasion of privacy [§489]

Identifying details in all required publications can be deleted to prevent unwarranted invasions of privacy.

c. Other records must be made available [§490]

Section 552(a)(3) requires that each agency, upon a request for *any other identifiable records,* make such records promptly available to *any person.* If the agency fails to disclose the requested information, the federal district courts have jurisdiction to compel production, and the burden of proof is on the agency to sustain any failure to disclose.

(1) Procedure [§491]

An agency must respond to requests for records within 10 days. And if a refusal to produce can be appealed within the agency, the appeal must be decided within 20 days.

(a) Attorney's fees

Attorney's fees incurred in seeking agency records can be awarded if the request is denied by the agency but the requesting party substantially prevails in court.

(b) But note

The district court may *deny* attorney's fees, even if the plaintiff has substantially prevailed, in its sound discretion. It may consider such factors as the benefit to the public, whether the defendant's refusal to disclose had a plausible basis in law, and whether the award of attorney's fees was really needed as an incentive to bring the suit. Where the plaintiff has ample commercial incentive to seek the information, there is no need to award attorney's fees as additional incentive to sue. [**Chamberlain v. Kurtz,** 589 F.2d 827 (5th Cir. 1979)]

(2) Agencies and records covered [§492]

The Act covers all agencies, including all executive and military departments, government-controlled corporations, and the executive office of the President. [APA §552(e)] However, the Act does not require disclosure from the President nor from his immediate staff or assistants (*e.g.,* the National Security Adviser). [**Kissinger v. Reporters Committee for Freedom of the Press,** 445 U.S. 136 (1980)] Nor does it cover a private research organization—even though it is funded and supervised by a federal agency and the agency could have (but did not) obtain the documents in question. [**Forsham v. Harris,** 445 U.S. 169 (1980)]

(a) Limitation

An agency only need disclose records that actually were *in its possession* at the time they were requested—even records that had been wrongfully removed from its custody are not covered by the Act. [**Kissinger v. Reporters Committee for Freedom of the Press,** *supra*]

(b) "Records" [§493]

The term "record" is broadly construed. For example, it covers a film. [**Save the Dolphins v. Department of Commerce**, 404 F. Supp. 407 (N.D. Cal. 1975)] An "agency record" includes documents used in agency functions but not personal papers of agency employees. [**Bureau of National Affairs v. Department of Justice**, 742 F.2d 1484 (D.C. Cir. 1984)—daily agendas of agency head must be disclosed but not his personal appointment book]

(3) Judicial enforcement [§494]

There is considerable disagreement concerning the precise nature of judicial power to enforce this provision of the Act.

(a) Equitable power to enjoin [§495]

The Supreme Court has stated that the equity powers of the courts go *beyond* mere enforcement of the remedy provided by statute (*i.e.*, an injunction ordering disclosure). For example, a court might have the power to enjoin all agency proceedings against a private party until the agency has furnished the requested document.

Example: During renegotiation proceedings with the government, three defense contractors were denied production of certain documents by the Renegotiation Board. The contractors brought suit under the Freedom of Information Act, seeking an injunction against the Board's withholding of the documents. The Court held that the Act did *not* limit the equitable powers of the court merely to enforcement of the statutory remedy. [*See* **Renegotiation Board v. Bannercraft Clothing Co.**, *supra*, §483] Note, however, that the Court found that the nature of the renegotiation process demanded that the contractors first pursue their administrative remedy. Once the renegotiation process was finished, the contractors could institute a de novo proceeding in the Court of Claims, where the usual rights of discovery would be available.

(b) Discretion to refuse [§496]

A court has no equitable discretion to *refuse* to order disclosure in the absence of a pertinent exception (*see* below). [**Federal Open Market Committee v. Merrill**, 443 U.S. 340 (1979)]

3. Exceptions to the Act [§497]

APA section 552(b) sets out exceptions to the Freedom of Information Act. The court is allowed privately to examine the requested documents ("in camera") to determine whether any of these exceptions apply. However, the agency must make a detailed and indexed statement of its claim for an exemption, identifying the reasons why a particular exemption is relevant, to aid the court in its examination of the disputed material. [**Mead Data Central, Inc. v. United States Department of** the Air Force, 566 F.2d 242 (D.C. Cir. 1977); **Vaughn v. Rosen,** 484 F.2d 820 (D.C. Cir. 1973), *cert. denied,* 415 U.S. 977 (1974)]

a. National security [§498]

Materials specifically authorized by an executive order to be kept secret in the interest of *national defense or foreign policy* need not be disclosed. [APA §552(b)(1)]

(1) But note

The court may review such classified materials in camera and order them disclosed if it finds they have not been properly classified.

b. Internal matters [§499]

Materials related solely to *internal personnel rules and practices* of an agency are also exempt from disclosure. [APA §552(b)(2)]

(1) Note

This exception makes relatively trivial agency rules (*e.g.,* sick leave policies) immune from disclosure. However, important internal rules in which the public has an interest must be disclosed, unless disclosure would pose a danger that the rules would be circumvented. [**Department of the Air Force v. Rose,** 425 U.S. 352 (1976)]

c. Statutory exemptions [§500]

Materials specifically exempted from disclosure by statute need not be produced. [APA §552(b)(3)] However, the statute must either *require* that the matters be withheld from the public (without giving the agency any discretion) or spell out *particular criteria* for withholding the documents. The provision that states that the agency does not have any discretion overrules a prior case that exempted material from disclosure because the agency had discretion to withhold the document. [**FAA v. Robertson,** 422 U.S. 225 (1975)]

Example: By statute, the IRS need not disclose information if disclosure would seriously impair tax administration. This is a narrowly drawn statute with sufficiently defined standards and satisfies section 552(b)(3). [**Chamberlain v. Kurtz,** *supra,* §491]

---

d. Commercial secrets [§501]

Trade secrets and commercial or financial information that is *privileged or confidential* need not be disclosed. [APA §552(b)(4)]

(1) "Trade secrets" [§502]

This term refers to information that is secret and concerns the production process. [**Public Citizens Health Research Group v. FDA,** 704 F.2d 1280 (D.C. Cir. 1983)]

(2) "Confidential" [§503]

Whether information is "confidential" depends on whether it was furnished to the government voluntarily or under compulsion. If information that has been requested under the FOIA was previously furnished to the government *voluntarily*, it is "confidential" *if it is "of a kind that would customarily not be released* to the public by the person from whom it was obtained." If the information has been furnished to the government *under compulsion*, it is "confidential" *if disclosure would cause substantial harm* to the competitive position of the person from whom the information was obtained. [**Critical Mass Energy Project v. Nuclear Regulatory Commission,** 975 F.2d 871 (D.C. Cir. 1992)]

(3) Partly confidential [§504]

If the information is only *partly* confidential, the balance must be disclosed by the agency. [**Grumman Aircraft Corp. v. Renegotiation Board,** 425 F.2d 578 (D.C. Cir. 1970)]

(4) Scope of Act [§505]

The Freedom of Information Act does not restrict the government from disclosing confidential information if it wishes to do so. Instead, the Act protects the *agency* from disclosing information it wishes to keep secret; it does not protect the company that submitted the material from disclosure by the agency. [**Chrysler Corp. v. Brown,** 441 U.S. 281 (1979)]

(a) Distinguish—Trade Secrets Act

A different federal statute, the Trade Secrets Act, furnishes protection against disclosure. [18 U.S.C. §1905] Under the Act, it is a crime for a government employee to disclose trade secrets and similar confidential statistical, financial, or technical material unless disclosure is "authorized by law." If an agency proposes to disclose material in violation of the Act, the submitter of the material can obtain judicial review under the APA.

1) Scope

The scope of section 1905 is the same as the FOIA exemption for trade and commercial secrets. Thus, if material submitted to an agency is "confidential," and if no valid agency rule permits disclosure, the agency cannot disclose it voluntarily. But if the material does not meet the test of confidentiality, *or* if a valid agency rule allows disclosure, the agency is free to disclose the material voluntarily. [**CNA Financial Corp. v. Donovan,** 830 F.2d 1132 (D.C. Cir. 1987)]

Example: In *Chrysler Corp.*, *supra*, Chrysler sued to prevent an agency from disclosing confidential employment information that Chrysler had provided to the agency. The agency argued that disclosure was authorized by an agency rule. However, the Court ruled that the agency rule was both substantively and procedurally invalid. Therefore, the disclosure was not "authorized by law."

---

e. Inter- or intra-agency memoranda [§506]

Memoranda that would not be available *by law* to a party (other than an agency) in litigation with the agency are also exempted from disclosure. [APA §552(b)(5)]

(1) Criteria—discovery standards [§507]

The document in question must be analyzed by the usual standards of discoverability used in federal courts. In other words, if the document would "normally" be privileged in civil litigation (*i.e.,* protected from disclosure by executive privilege, attorney-client privilege, or the attorney work product rule, except in cases of compelling need), it falls within section 552(b)(5). [**FTC v. Grolier, Inc.,** 462 U.S. 19 (1983); **NLRB v. Sears, Roebuck & Co.,** 421 U.S. 132 (1975)]

(2) Predecision memoranda [§508]

Generally, predecision memoranda (*i.e.,* those involving recommendations to decisionmakers to help them decide) are protected from disclosure. The theory is that disclosure of such documents may inhibit frank discussion within the agency. However, memoranda that explain policy or decisions *already made* do not come within the exemption.

(a) Definition unclear [§509]

It may not always be clear whether a given document is a predecision memo or whether it is a *"final opinion,"* which must be disclosed under section 552(a)(2)(A).

> **Example:** Under the NLRA, a person complaining of an unfair labor practice may appeal to the General Counsel if the local director refuses to prosecute the charge. The General Counsel will recommend either that a complaint be issued or that the charge be terminated. This decision will be communicated to the local director in an "appeal memorandum." The Supreme Court held that appeal memoranda that *terminate* the charge are *"final opinions,"* and thus subject to disclosure. But memoranda that recommend issuance of a *complaint* are "predecisional," and therefore protected by the exemption. [**NLRB v. Sears, Roebuck & Co.,** *supra*]

> **Example:** Reports used by the Renegotiation Board in deciding whether profits under government contracts are "excessive" have been held to be predecisional. *Rationale:* The reports are merely *advisory* and have no final effect. [**Renegotiation Board v. Grumman Aircraft,** 421 U.S. 168 (1975)]

1) Incorporation by reference [§510]

A predecisional memorandum, otherwise protected by the

exemption, must be disclosed where it is incorporated by reference in a final opinion.

a) But note

A reference in a final opinion to "circumstances of the case" is *not* sufficient to compel disclosure of predecision documents that explain the "circumstances." Nor must documents within the "law enforcement" exception, below, be produced if referred to in a final opinion. [**NLRB v. Sears, Roebuck & Co.**, *supra*; **International Paper Co. v. Federal Power Commission**, 438 F.2d 1349 (2d Cir. 1971)]

(3) "Factual" material not exempt [§511]

Section 552(b)(5) applies only to *policymaking* material, and does not protect *factual* statements. If a given document contains *both* types of material, the courts must inspect the document in camera and release the unprivileged portions. [**EPA v. Mink**, 410 U.S. 73 (1973)]

(a) But note

If disclosure of factual information would harm the agency's deliberative process, section 552(b)(5) authorizes withholding of the factual material. [**Mead Data Central Inc. v. United States Department of the Air Force**, *supra*, §497]

(4) Executive privilege [§512]

Exemption (5) of the FOIA also includes the executive (or presidential) privilege. Executive privilege covers communications to and from the President, as well as those to or from members of the White House staff who have significant responsibility for formulating advice to be given to the President. This privilege covers both predecisional and postdecisional communications, as well as factual materials. [*In re* **Sealed Case**, 116 F.3d 550 (D.C. Cir. 1997)] However, the privilege can give way in cases in which a criminal grand jury has an important need for the information and it is unavailable from other sources. [**United States v. Nixon**, 418 U.S. 683 (1974)—executive privilege protecting documents and tapes must yield to the need to use the materials in a criminal case, especially since they were unavailable from other sources]

(5) Government commercial information [§513]

An additional discovery privilege that the government may use to avoid disclosure is the qualified privilege for a "trade secret or other confidential research, development, or commercial information." [Fed. R. Civ. P. 26(c)(7); **Federal Open Market Committee v. Merrill**, *supra*, §496]

(a) Illustration—*Federal Open Market Committee v. Merrill*

In **Federal Open Market Committee v. Merrill**, the plaintiff requested disclosure of memoranda by the Open Market Committee of the

Federal Reserve System that established its policy for the current month on buying or selling securities. These transactions are used to control the money supply and, it was alleged, immediate disclosure would have a detrimental effect on Federal Reserve operations.

1) The Court found that the memoranda might be privileged as confidential "commercial information" relating to the making of government contracts. The trial court was instructed to decide whether the privilege was in fact applicable, based upon an analysis of whether immediate disclosure would indeed place the government at a competitive disadvantage or otherwise be harmful to the government program involved.

2) The Court indicated that if the memoranda were indeed privileged, the need for the privilege disappeared after a month—when a new, current memorandum was produced. Thus, the memoranda had to be published after a new one was issued.

f.   Personal privacy [§514]

Personnel, medical, and similar files, the disclosure of which would constitute a clearly unwarranted invasion of personal privacy, are exempt. [APA §552(b)(6)] This exemption calls for balancing the public's need for information against the privacy interest involved (*i.e.*, the extent to which disclosure would be objectionable and intrusive to the individuals involved). For purposes of this balancing, it is the need of the **general public** for the information, not the specific requestor's need, that is considered. The strongest cases of public need arise in cases where the subject of the request provides information on how the government agency in question is functioning. [**United States Department of Justice v. Reporters Committee for Freedom of the Press**, 489 U.S. 749 (1989)] Also, if the government had pledged confidentiality, this is a factor (although not a determinative one) in favor of nondisclosure.

FOIA Disclosure Balance

(1) Illustration—rap sheets [§515]

A request for law enforcement records about a private citizen that provides no information about a government agency is always "unwarranted" within the meaning of Exemption 6. [**United States Department of Justice v. Reporters Committee for Freedom of the Press,** *supra*—request for FBI's arrest records of an individual who may have been involved in corruption scandal]

(2) Illustration—addresses [§516]

A union requested the home addresses of federal government employees so it could contact them. The public's interest in this information is slight, since it tells the public nothing about what the government is up to, while the privacy interest of the employees is great. [**United States Department of Defense v. Federal Labor Relations Authority,** 510 U.S. 487 (1994)]

(3) Illustration—public interest in ordering disclosure [§517]

The exemption does not apply to statements filed by consultants for the National Cancer Institute which disclosed organizations in which they had a financial interest. The court noted the great public interest in detecting possible conflicts of interest by these consultants.

(a) Rationale

Since similar financial information is required by statute of most government employees (but not consultants), the public interest in disclosure of such information is manifest. [**Washington Post Co. v. Department of Health & Human Services,** 690 F.2d 252 (D.C. Cir 1982)]

(4) Distinguish—Air Force disciplinary records [§518]

Records of Air Force Academy disciplinary proceedings, edited to delete names and other identifying details, are subject to disclosure. In this situation, the public's "need to know" outweighed the risk that some persons could be identified from the edited material. [**Department of the Air Force v. Rose,** *supra,* §499]

g. Law enforcement [§519]

Investigatory records compiled for law enforcement purposes are also exempt from disclosure. [APA §552(b)(7)] Records that were once gathered for other purposes, but have now been compiled for purposes of law enforcement, qualify for exemption from disclosure. [**John Doe Agency v. John Doe Corp.,** 493 U.S. 146 (1990)—plaintiff cannot obtain documents prepared during a 1978 audit that have now been assembled for use in grand jury criminal investigation]

(1) Exemption is limited [§520]

As in the case of predecision memoranda, the whole investigatory file is not exempt. This exemption protects *only* those items that would:

(i) *Interfere with enforcement* proceedings;

(ii) *Deprive a party of the right to a fair and impartial adjudication*;

(iii) *Constitute an unwarranted invasion of personal privacy*;

(iv) *Disclose the identity of a confidential source*;

(v) *Disclose, in criminal prosecutions or national security investigations, information* furnished by a confidential source;

(vi) *Disclose investigative techniques* or procedures or *prosecution guidelines*; or

(vii) *Endanger the physical safety* of law enforcement personnel.

---

e.g. **Example:** The NLRB need not disclose the statements of witnesses to an employer before the hearing. Such disclosure might result in the coercion of witnesses. In general, the Act is not intended primarily as a tool for discovery of facts prior to administrative litigation. [**NLRB v. Robbins Tire & Rubber Co.**, 437 U.S. 214 (1978)]

---

(2) Summaries of law enforcement information [§521]

The exemption protects summaries of law enforcement information as well as the original documents themselves. [**FBI v. Abramson**, 456 U.S. 615 (1982)—exemption covers summaries prepared for political purposes and sent by FBI to the White House]

(3) Distinguish—inactive files [§522]

Most information gathered in connection with *completed* (or abandoned) enforcement proceedings probably is discoverable.

h. Bank regulations [§523]

Examination, operating, or condition reports prepared by (or for the use of) agencies that regulate *financial institutions* are exempt from the disclosure requirements of the Act. [APA §552(b)(8)]

i. Natural resources [§524]

And finally, *geological or geophysical information* need not be disclosed. [APA §552(b)(9)]

EXCEPTIONS TO THE FREEDOM OF INFORMATION ACT gilbert

THE FOLLOWING ARE EXEMPT FROM DISCLOSURE UNDER THE FOIA:

- ☑ National security materials
- ☑ Internal matters of an agency
  - Personnel rules and practices
- ☑ Statutory exemptions
- ☑ Commercial secrets
  - Trade secrets
  - Privileged or confidential commercial or financial information
- ☑ Inter- or intra-agency memoranda
- ☑ Personal privacy files
  - Personnel, medical files
  - Rap sheets
  - Home addresses
- ☑ Law enforcement investigatory records
- ☑ Bank regulations
- ☑ Natural resources
  - Geological or geophysical information

D. Government in the Sunshine Act

1. **General Rule [§525]**

   The Government in the Sunshine Act requires that, generally, agencies hold their meetings *open to the public.* [APA §552b]

   a. **Definition of agency [§526]**

      An agency for this purpose means one headed by a collegial body of two or more members and any subdivision thereof authorized to act on behalf of the agency. [APA §552b(a)(1)]

   b. **Definition of meeting [§527]**

      A meeting for this purpose is defined as the deliberations of agency members that determine or result in the conduct or disposition of official agency business. [APA §552b(a)(2)]

   c. **Consultations [§528]**

      The Sunshine Act does not apply to an informal international conference between a committee of FCC members and counterpart European agencies. The conference concerned only an exchange of views about licensing issues, not a decision on discrete proposals on which an agency subdivision might act. [**FCC v. ITT World Communications,** 466 U.S. 463 (1984)]

2. Exceptions [§529]

The Sunshine Act sets forth many exceptions to the open meeting rule. Many of them parallel exceptions to the Freedom of Information Act (*see supra,* §§497-524). In general, where the agency can refuse to disclose documents under the Freedom of Information Act, it can close meetings to prevent disclosure of similar information. [*See* APA §552b(c)(1) - (10)] In addition, meetings can be closed when the meeting is likely to:

(i) *Involve accusing any person of a crime* or formally censuring any person;

(ii) *Significantly frustrate* implementation of a proposed agency action; or

(iii) *Concern the agency's issuance of a subpoena* or its participation in civil litigation or the initiation, conduct, or disposition of any formal agency adjudication.

[APA §552b(c)(5), (9)(B), (10)]

E. Attorney's Fees

1. General Rule [§530]

The general rule in American law is that all parties bear their own attorney's fees. [*See* **Alyeska Pipeline Service Co. v. Wilderness Society,** 421 U.S. 240 (1975)]

2. No Agency Authorization [§531]

Absent clear statutory authorization, an agency is not authorized to compel a party to pay the litigation costs of other parties even in a case of egregious bad faith conduct. [**Unbelievable, Inc. v. NLRB,** 118 F.3d 795 (D.C. Cir. 1997)] Moreover, it appears that an agency has no authority to pay the attorney's fees or costs of private parties incurred in connection with agency adjudication or rulemaking, even if the input of the private party was helpful to the agency. [**Pacific Legal Foundation v. Goyan,** 664 F.2d 1221 (4th Cir. 1981); **Greene County Planning Board v. Federal Power Commission,** 559 F.2d 1227 (2d Cir. 1977), *cert. denied,* 434 U.S. 1086 (1978); *but see* **Chamber of Commerce v. USDA,** 459 F. Supp. 216 (D.D.C. 1978)]

3. Specific Statutory Provisions [§532]

Nevertheless, there are many specific provisions of federal law that provide for the award of attorney's fees to private parties. For example, the Freedom of Information Act provides for such awards (*see supra,* §491) as does the Federal Trade Commission Act [5 U.S.C. §18(h)(i)] and various environmental and civil rights provisions [*e.g.,* 42 U.S.C. §1988].

a. Prevailing parties [§533]

These fee-shifting statutes generally provide for an award of attorney's fees only to "prevailing parties." Generally, a prevailing party is one who has secured judicial relief by prevailing on the merits of at least some of its claims through a judgment or a consent decree. [**Buckhannon Board & Care Home, Inc. v. West Virginia Department of Health and Human Resources,** 121 S. Ct. 1835 (2001)] Even an award of nominal damages might suffice if the award of fees is otherwise appropriate. [**Farrar v. Hobby,** 506 U.S. 103 (1992)]

(1) Voluntary change will not warrant fee award [§534]

However, a party is *not* entitled to a fee award simply because its lawsuit brought about the desired effect through a *voluntary change* in the defendant's conduct. For example, in *Buckhannon Board & Care Home, supra,* the plaintiff filed suit hoping to invalidate a state statute as being preempted by federal law. As a result of the lawsuit, the state legislature changed the statute and the defendant moved to dismiss the lawsuit as moot. Although the plaintiff's lawsuit was the "catalyst" for the legislative action, it was not a "prevailing party" because the change did not come about as the result of a judicial judgment or consent decree.

b. Standards for appropriateness [§535]

Such statutes frequently call for awarding attorney's fees "if appropriate." This vague standard has caused courts and agencies considerable difficulty. Under one formulation of the test, a party is entitled to receive attorney's fees under an "if appropriate" standard if the party has served the public interest by substantially contributing to the goals of the Act. [**Carson-Truckee Water Conservation District v. Secretary of the Interior,** 748 F.2d 523 (9th Cir. 1984)]

4. General Authorization [§536]

Under the Equal Access to Justice Act ("EAJA"), an agency must award attorney's and expert's fees to a "prevailing party" in a formal adjudication where the United States was represented by counsel unless the agency's position was "substantially justified" or special circumstances make an award unjust. [5 U.S.C. §504] In addition, a court must award fees against the government under the same standard in any civil action brought by or against the United States, including judicial review of agency action. [28 U.S.C. §2412(d)] Under both sections 504 and 2412(d), the agency has the burden to show that its conduct (both the conduct that gave rise to the dispute and the conduct during litigation) was "substantially justified."

a. Limitation on fees [§537]

Attorney's fees charged to agencies under the EAJA cannot exceed $125 per hour [28 U.S.C. §2412(d)(2)(A)] (unless a higher figure is justified by a special factor such as the limited availability of qualified attorneys). [*See* **Pierce v. Underwood,** 487 U.S. 552 (1988)—fees can exceed statutory amount only if some distinctive knowledge or skill is needed (*e.g.,* practice in patent law or knowledge of foreign language)]

b. Net worth limitations [§538]

To recover fees under the EAJA, an individual's net worth cannot exceed $2 million. A business must have net worth under $7 million and have less than 500 employees. A publicly supported charity can recover fees regardless of its net worth.

c. Justification [§539]

To sustain its burden of substantial justification, the agency must establish that its position was justified to a degree that could satisfy a reasonable person. [**Pierce v. Underwood,** *supra*]

d. Adjudications covered [§540]

Section 504 covers only formal adjudication to which section 554 of the APA applies. By statute, deportation cases are not subject to the APA, even though the agency provides formal adversary hearings in such cases. Because the APA does not apply, however, EAJA is also inapplicable and the prevailing party in a deportation case cannot collect attorney's fees from the agency. [**Ardestani v. Immigration & Naturalization Service,** 502 U.S. 129 (1991)] However, in a questionable decision, one court held that if a trial-type hearing is required by due process rather than statute, this renders the APA applicable; therefore, the private party can apply for fees under the EAJA. [**Collord v. Department of the Interior,** 154 F.3d 933 (1998); *and see* discussion of the *Wong Yang Sung* case *supra,* §165]

5. Amount [§541]

Where a statute calls for the award of fees, the court should set the attorney's fees by multiplying the hours spent on the matter (if reasonable) by a reasonable hourly rate (the product is called the "lodestar" and is presumed to be a reasonable fee).

a. Setting the rate

The hourly rate is based on rates charged in the market by comparably qualified attorneys for comparable services—not the amount charged to the client (if anything). [**Blum v. Stenson,** 465 U.S. 886 (1984)] The fee can vastly exceed the amount of damages recovered by the client. [**City of Riverside v. Rivera,** 477 U.S. 561 (1986)] Fees can be charged for nontraditional services such as participation in rulemaking.

b. Adjustment of lodestar

Although the "lodestar" can be adjusted upward or downward in unusual cases, it should not ordinarily be adjusted for such factors as exceptional success, novelty, complexity of the claim, or superior skill of the attorneys. No upward adjustment is permitted merely because the plaintiff's attorney is working on a contingency fee basis and would get nothing if the case were lost. [**City of Burlington v. Dague,** 502 U.S. 1071 (1992)]

Chapter Eight: Scope of Judicial Review

CONTENTS

Chapter Approach

A.	Introduction	§542
B.	Scope of Review of Questions of Basic Fact	§543
C.	Scope of Review of Agency's Legal Interpretations	§568
D.	Scope of Review of Application of Law to Fact	§594
E.	Scope of Review of Agency Exercises of Discretion	§602

1. **Scope of Review—In General** [ar]ticularly in cases in which a vested,
The most critical issue in dete Proc. Code §1094.5; **Frink v. Prod,**
administrative agencies is the e
for that of the agency. This is
Sometimes it is called the *"sta*
be determined every time a pa Service Board were upheld if sup-
scope of review will vary, depe s very limited review, since the find-
a question of *basic fact,* a qu re is *any evidence* in the record to
facts, or a question of *discretio* lled the "scintilla" rule.

B. Scope of Re[view] *e binding* upon the reviewing court,
Basic Fact wed.

rds of review may not be terribly sig-
gency finding of fact is wrong, it will

1. **In General [§543]** t purports to apply.
A question of *basic fact* means
edge of the applicable law. M[o]
case. Thus, agency findings as test is the *prevailing test* in both fed-
questions of basic fact. Ordina rally applied where the statute is not
nation of the credibility of wit[n] w. For example, a statute providing
sic fact may depend on the situ pported by "evidence" would prob-

   a. **"Substantial evidence" [§**
   The *majority rule* is that
   supported by "substantial set aside all agency fact determina-
   ample, is that the reviewi[ng] substantial evidence" on the "whole
   supported by "substantia[l]
   evidence standard is simil[ar]
   nations, and is discussed i
   is the same. [1981 Model t evidence that "a reasonable mind
   t a conclusion." [**Consolidated Edison**

   b. **Evidence "clearly erroneo[us]**] Thus, the substantial evidence test
   In some instances, a cour[t] e its judgment for that of the agency.
   of fact if it is "clearly err[o] he agency's findings, it *must affirm*
   firmly convinced that the
   standard generally used i
   judge's factual determina that the court must look at *both sides*
   sion of the Model State A merely look at the evidence that sup-
   Defries v. Association of C iversal Camera Corp. v. NLRB, 340
   iew of an agency's determination of

   c. **"Preponderance of the evi[dence]** ongress had expressed a "mood" in
   In rare cases, a court is r[e] f agency determinations of fact than
   side preponderates. In son

(3) Inferences of fact [§554]

The substantial evidence test also applies to *inferences* drawn from the basic facts. For example, the agency's determination of the *motives* of those who have acted must be sustained if the appellate court finds that the determination was reasonable. [**Radio Officers' Union v. NLRB,** 347 U.S. 17 (1954)]

(4) Preference for uniformity [§555]

The Supreme Court has held that there is an important interest in maintaining uniformity when courts review agency action. Thus, a court must use the substantial evidence test of section 706 unless some other law clearly requires application of a different standard. [**Dickinson v. Zurko,** 527 U.S. 150 (1999)—determinations of the Patent and Trademark Office must be reviewed under the substantial evidence standard rather than the clearly erroneous standard even if, historically, the clearly erroneous standard has been used]

b. Disagreement between agency and administrative law judge [§556]

Frequently, the ALJ who heard the case will decide to believe witness A and disbelieve witness B. But the agency heads, when they review the ALJ's decision, will accept the testimony of B instead of A. When the case is judicially reviewed, the reviewing court must take this disagreement into account in deciding whether substantial evidence supports the basic fact findings of the agency. The rule is that the disagreement on credibility *detracts* from the substantiality of the evidence that supports the agency's findings. [**Universal Camera Corp. v. NLRB,** *supra*]

(1) Illustration—*Universal Camera* case

In *Universal Camera,* an employee challenged his dismissal, alleging that he had been fired for testifying at an earlier NLRB proceeding, and not for reasons of discipline (as alleged by the employer). The ALJ believed the employer's witnesses, but the full Board reversed and found that the discharge was an unfair labor practice. The Supreme Court held that on issues of *credibility,* the decision of the ALJ was entitled to some weight because it was part of the record; *i.e.,* it should be considered in deciding whether substantial evidence supported the decision of the Board.

(2) Aftermath of *Universal Camera* [§557]

Following *Universal Camera,* lower courts held that the findings of an ALJ as to credibility could not be reversed by the agency without a *very substantial preponderance* of the evidence against the judge's conclusion. [**NLRB v. Thompson & Co.,** 208 F.2d 743 (2d Cir. 1953)]

(a) But note

This rule was later held to have gone too far: Since the agency is ultimately responsible for the decision, it can set aside the ALJ's findings even without a preponderance of the evidence against the conclusion. Rather, the ALJ's findings are only *one factor* in determining whether substantial evidence supports the agency's decision. [**Allentown Broadcasting Co. v. FCC,** 349 U.S. 358 (1955)]

(3) Demeanor findings [§558]

As a rule, courts will reverse an agency's finding that rests *exclusively* on testimonial evidence rejected by the ALJ because of conclusions about the witness's demeanor. Where the agency finding rests *partly on independent evidence* and partly on testimonial evidence rejected by the ALJ on demeanor grounds, the court may or may not accept the agency's finding, but the agency's finding will be critically reviewed by the court. [**Penasquitos Village, Inc. v. NLRB,** 565 F.2d 1074 (9th Cir. 1977)]

(a) Note

Where the ALJ's findings do not turn on credibility—*e.g.,* inferences drawn from undisputed testimony, or matters involving the agency's expertise—reversals of the ALJ's conclusions have even less significance.

c. Ignoring administrative law judge's decision [§559]

The agency *cannot totally ignore* the findings and conclusions of the administrative law judge; it must at least take them into account. [**Cinderella Career & Finishing Schools, Inc. v. FTC,** *supra,* §274]

(1) Application

In the *Cinderella* case, the ALJ found that certain advertisements were not misleading, after hearing detailed testimony from consumers. The FTC nevertheless held that the ads *were* misleading, ignoring the testimony relied upon by the ALJ. The court held that the agency was not free to disregard the evidence taken, and the findings made by, the law judge without an explanation—even though the issues did not turn on credibility.

d. Application of substantial evidence test [§560]

Normally, the Supreme Court will not review applications of the substantial evidence test by lower courts. However, in one recent case it did so because the NLRB was actually applying a different evidentiary standard than the one it claimed to be applying. [**Allentown Mack Sales & Service Inc. v. NLRB,** 521 U.S. 359 (1998)]

(1) Facts of *Allentown Mack*

The issue in *Allentown Mack* was whether an employer was entitled to poll its employees to ascertain whether they wanted to reject a union. The NLRB allows such polling to occur only if the employer has a "reasonable doubt based on objective considerations" that a majority of the employees no longer support the union. A number of employees told the employer that they believed the union no longer enjoyed majority support. However, the NLRB found that the employer did not have reasonable doubt based on objective considerations. The Supreme Court held that the NLRB's finding was not supported by substantial evidence.

(2) Underlying basis for decision

In *Allentown Mack*, the NLRB actually applied a different evidentiary standard than the one it purported to apply. A much higher degree of proof was required to establish "reasonable doubt based on objective considerations" than had been applied in the past. The Court held that this was an example of unreasoned decisionmaking. The NLRB could, perhaps, adopt a presumption against "reasonable doubt" and require a much higher standard of proof, but it must do so openly. It could not purport to apply one standard but actually apply a different one. Under the *Chenery* principle (*see supra*, §245), the courts could not affirm an NLRB decision on a ground different from the one that the agency stated.

3. Constitutional Facts [§561]

For many years, a broader scope of judicial review was permitted where agency findings of fact affected a claimant's constitutional rights.

a. *"Ben Avon* rule" [§562]

In 1920, the Supreme Court declared that a reviewing court had the power to make an ***independent judgment*** with respect to agency findings of "constitutional facts." [**Ohio Valley Water Co. v. Ben Avon Borough,** 253 U.S. 287 (1920)]

(1) Application

Ben Avon involved the setting of utility rates based on an estimated value of the utility's property. The utility complained that the valuation was much too low and resulted in an unreasonable return, thereby confiscating its property. The Court held that the question of confiscation was a "constitutional fact," which required an independent determination by the reviewing court.

(a) Rationale

The Court apparently thought it significant that setting rates was a "legislative" function. If the legislature itself had set the rates, the reviewing court could make a full examination of whether the rate was confiscatory. Hence, the mere delegation of rate-setting powers to the agency could not limit the scope of judicial review.

(2) Distinguish

In a later case, the Court reaffirmed *Ben Avon,* but ruled that the exercise of independent judgment did *not* require a trial de novo. In other words, the court could conduct its independent review *on the record* made by the agency. [**St. Joseph Stock Yards Co. v. United States,** 298 U.S. 38 (1936)]

(a) Note
Furthermore, the Court held that the regulated entity had the *burden of proof* in reversing agency findings, and that the burden would be strictly enforced.

b. *Ben Avon* rule restricted in application [§563]
The broad scope of review set forth in *Ben Avon* has gradually become eroded by exceptions.

> **e.g.** **Example—services:** The Supreme Court *declined* to apply the *St. Joseph Stock Yards* test to a confiscation claim involving rate setting for *services*. [**Acker v. United States,** 298 U.S. 426 (1936)]

> **e.g.** **Example—production limits:** A further decline in the "independent judgment" test occurred in a case involving a prorating of oil by a state agency which, in effect, prevented maximum oil production. The Court made it clear that independent judgment should *not* be exercised in the judicial review of such administrative orders. [**Railroad Commission v. Rowan & Nichols Oil Co.,** 311 U.S. 570 (1941)]

> **e.g.** **Example—"end result" test:** Finally, the Court held that a reviewing court need not consider the *method* of valuation used by the FPC in setting rates as long as the *end result* provided adequate compensation to the utility. [**Federal Power Commission v. Hope Natural Gas Co.,** 320 U.S. 591 (1944)] Under the *Hope* decision, valuation of the utility's property was no longer reviewable in rate-setting cases. As a result, *Ben Avon* and *St. Joseph* have little more than historical interest today.

4. Jurisdictional Facts [§564]
Similarly, courts for many years assumed a broader scope of review where the "facts" found by the agency were essential to its jurisdiction.

a. Deportation cases [§565]
In a deportation case, a key issue is whether the deportee is a citizen or an alien. If he is a citizen, of course, he is not subject to deportation. The Supreme Court has held that the issue of citizenship is a jurisdictional fact, and one that the reviewing court should decide by conducting a *trial de novo*. [**Ng Fung Ho v. White,** 259 U.S. 276 (1922)]

(1) Comment
This holding went *beyond Ben Avon* and *St. Joseph,* which simply required

broad judicial review. Here, the entire matter had to be *retried* before the reviewing court.

(2) Distinguish—exclusion

Oddly enough, the issue of citizenship does not require *any* judicial review in a case of *exclusion* from the United States (as opposed to deportation). [**United States v. Ju Toy,** 198 U.S. 253 (1905)]

b. Workers' compensation cases [§566]

The jurisdictional fact doctrine has also been applied to cases arising under the Longshoremen's and Harbor Workers' Act—a legislative scheme providing benefits to injured longshoremen. Before the Act can apply, the agency must find that the employee was injured within the course of employment and that the injury occurred in navigable waters. These issues were held to be jurisdictional and, as such, to be retried by a court on an entirely *new record*. [**Crowell v. Benson,** *supra,* §42]

(1) Basis

The decision in *Crowell* was clearly influenced by the Court's hostility to New Deal legislation. (*See* the discussion of the *Panama Refining* and *Schechter Poultry* cases *supra,* §§11-12.)

(2) Note

The *Crowell* case drew considerable adverse reaction, since jurisdiction issues, in one form or another, are present in almost every federal administrative determination. If every such issue were to be fully retried by the reviewing court, the powers of the agencies would be vastly diminished.

(3) Limited application

The *Crowell* decision *has never been applied* outside the Longshoremen's Act. And even there, modern cases hold that no judicial retrial should occur unless it would serve a "worthwhile purpose." [**Morrison-Knudson Co. v. O'Leary,** 288 F.2d 542 (9th Cir. 1961)]

c. Present status [§567]

The present status of the constitutional fact and jurisdictional fact doctrines is murky. However, they have never been squarely overruled and remain available as a technique for courts who wish to limit agency powers over sensitive matters.

---

e.g. **Example:** As held in *Ng Fung Ho,* the issue of citizenship still requires a judicial trial. Similarly, in obscenity cases, courts independently reexamine the evidence on which an agency relied. (*See* Constitutional Law Summary.)

---

(1) Note

Crowell v. Benson was discussed with approval in a 1982 decision that invalidated a system delegating adjudicatory powers to untenured bankruptcy judges. Article III judges must have independent power to decide matters involving contract disputes as well as constitutional rights. Although the Court indicated that *Crowell's* discussion of jurisdictional fact had been undermined by later cases, its general principle, which reserves certain matters for judicial determination, remains valid. [**Northern Pipeline Construction Co. v. Marathon Pipeline Co.,** *supra,* §39]

C. Scope of Review of Agency's Legal Interpretations

1. Agency Decisions of Law [§568]

Agencies frequently interpret the meaning of statutes, their own regulations, or other sources of law. Such interpretation can occur when: (i) an agency *adjudicates a case* and writes a decision; (ii) it *adopts an interpretive rule*; and (iii) it *adopts a legislative rule* (in doing so the agency must interpret the statute that delegates rulemaking power to it as well as other words in the statute). The traditional view was that a court could substitute its own judgment for the agency's legal interpretation. However, current developments greatly diminish the court's power.

2. Traditional View—Substitution of Judgment [§569]

Under the traditional view, a court has the power to ignore an agency's determination and *substitute its own view*. This was the accepted interpretation of APA section 706: ". . . the reviewing court shall decide all relevant questions of law, interpret constitutional and statutory provisions, and determine the meaning or applicability of the terms of an agency action." It is still the majority view under state law. [*See, e.g.,* **Madison v. Alaska Department of Fish & Game,** 696 P.2d 168 (Alaska 1985)]

a. Weak deference [§570]

However, even under the traditional view, courts usually give some deference to the agency's view, recognizing that the agency's expertise gave it an advantage in construing the law. This deference is known as "weak deference," meaning that the court may, but need not, treat the agency's interpretation as having more authority than that of some other litigant. [*See* **Skidmore v. Swift & Co.,** 323 U.S. 134 (1944)—"We consider that the rulings, interpretations and opinions of the Administrator under this Act, while not controlling upon the courts by reason of their authority, do constitute a body of experience and informed judgment to which courts and litigants may properly resort for guidance."]

b. Factors related to weak deference [§571]

The degree to which a court should give weak deference to an agency interpretation depends on various factors. "The weight of such a judgment in a particular case will depend upon the thoroughness evident in its consideration, the validity of its reasoning, its consistency with earlier and later pronouncements, and all those factors which give it power to persuade, if lacking power to control." [**Skidmore v. Swift & Co.**, *supra*] Courts generally consider the following:

(1) Consistency [§572]

The agency interpretation is more worthy of deference if maintained consistently. [**Morton v. Ruiz**, *supra*, §484]

(2) Contemporaneousness [§573]

The interpretation is more worthy of deference if adopted soon after the statute was passed, since the agency was probably familiar with the legislative purpose. [**Ford Motor Co. v. Milhollin**, 444 U.S. 555 (1980)]

(3) Thoroughness of consideration [§574]

An interpretation is more worthy of deference if the agency carefully considered it at a high level (as opposed to, for example, the unstudied response of a low-level staff member). [**Skidmore v. Swift & Co.**, *supra*] Similarly, the formality by which the interpretation is expressed (*e.g.*, in a published regulation or a reasoned adjudicatory opinion, rather than an informal letter) is relevant to deciding how much deference it is owed. [**United States v. Mead Corp.**, 533 U.S. 218 (2001)]

(4) Reenactment [§575]

The interpretation is more worthy of deference if the legislature reenacted the statute with knowledge of the agency's interpretation of it.

(5) Agency expertise [§576]

The interpretation is more worthy of deference if it reflects agency expertise in dealing with the issues. In contrast, courts have more expertise in applying the common law or in construing nontechnical statutes.

(6) Public participation [§577]

If the public participated in the process that produced the interpretation (*e.g.*, through notice and comment rulemaking), the rule is more worthy of deference. [**Pacific Gas & Electric Co. v. FPC**, *supra*, §410]

c. Illustration—anti-discrimination law [§578]

The Equal Employment Opportunities Commission ("EEOC") construed Title VII of the Civil Rights Act to preclude the use of standardized intelligence tests for employment because of the tests' racially discriminatory effect. Although the EEOC lacks delegated legislative rulemaking power, the Court held that its interpretation was entitled to great deference, was in accord with legislative history, and should be sustained. [**Griggs v. Duke Power Co.,** 401 U.S. 424 (1971)]

3. **Modern View—Strong Deference [§579]**

Under the decision in the *Chevron* case, if Congress expressly or implicitly delegated law-interpreting power to the agency, the Court must follow *any reasonable agency interpretation* of an ambiguous statute. [**Chevron, USA v. Natural Resources Defense Council,** 467 U.S. 867 (1984)] *Chevron* introduced the era of "strong deference": A court *must* (not may) *defer* to the agency's interpretation of law.

a. **Illustration—*Chevron* case**

In *Chevron*, the EPA adopted a legislative rule defining the statutory term "stationary source." Under the EPA's interpretation, the "stationary source" is an entire factory, not a particular polluting source in the plant. As a result, a manufacturer can install a new source of pollution in the plant if it removes another source of equal or greater pollution. This is known as the "bubble approach." The lower court held that the bubble approach was improper under the statute. The Court held that Congress had delegated to the EPA the power to construe the meaning of the statute, and the reviewing court must follow the agency's interpretation if reasonable.

b. ***Chevron* analysis [§580]**

Chevron requires two steps:

(1) **Step one—determine whether statute is clear [§581]**

"First, always, is the question whether Congress has directly spoken to the precise question at issue. If the intent of Congress is clear, that is the end of the matter; for the court, as well as the agency, must give effect to the unambiguously expressed intent of Congress."

(a) **Criteria for identifying clarity**

In determining whether the statute is clear, a court should examine all relevant criteria, including dictionary definitions of the terms of the statute. In addition, it should examine all of the provisions of the statute to place the disputed provision in context and thus achieve a harmonious construction of all the terms of the statute. It can also examine other statutes passed previously or subsequently by Congress.

(b) **Legislative history**

The Supreme Court sometimes examines the legislative history of the provision to determine whether its meaning is clear. Thus, the Court examined legislative history in *Chevron* in determining that Congress had not spoken to the precise question at issue. Some justices, however, refuse to examine legislative history. [**Green v. Bock Laundry Machine Co.,** 490 U.S. 504 (1989)—Scalia, J. concurring]

(c) Application—tobacco case

The Food and Drug Administration ("FDA") asserted it had jurisdiction to regulate tobacco products because nicotine is a "drug" and cigarettes are "drug delivery devices." Applying *Chevron's* step one, the Court held that the FDA had no authority to regulate tobacco. Among the arguments the Court accepted were that the FDA is required to ban unsafe drugs, but tobacco products can never be safe. Thus if nicotine were a drug, the FDA would be required to ban tobacco products. Yet Congress clearly did not contemplate that tobacco products would be banned entirely, given numerous statutes (such as cigarette labeling laws) that contemplate the sale of tobacco products. Moreover, the Court was guided by its own common sense—it was simply unimaginable that Congress had implicitly delegated to the FDA such an extraordinary power as the power to ban tobacco products. [**FDA v. Brown & Williamson Tobacco Corp.,** 529 U.S. 120 (2000)] *Note:* This case was a 5-4 decision; the dissenters argued that the FDA had remedial jurisdiction and could regulate tobacco products without banning them entirely.

(2) Step two—determine reasonableness of agency interpretation of ambiguous statute [§582]

In step two, the court should determine whether the agency's interpretation of an ambiguous statute was reasonable. "[I]f the statute is silent or ambiguous with respect to the specific issue, the question for the court is whether the agency's answer is based on a permissible construction of the statute." Thus, the question before the lower court in *Chevron* was not whether in its view the bubble concept was "inappropriate," but rather whether the administrator's view—that it was appropriate in the context of the particular program—is a reasonable one. [**Chevron, USA v. Natural Resources Defense Council,** *supra*] The determination of whether the agency's interpretation was "reasonable" is similar, if not identical, to the court's power to determine whether agency discretionary decisions are arbitrary and capricious. (*See supra*, §§605 *et seq.*) Under *Chevron's* step two, the court can find that an agency's interpretation of ambiguous statutory language is unreasonable if the interpretation is one that the statutory language cannot support. An agency "cannot construe the statute in a way that completely nullifies textually applicable provisions meant to limit its discretion . . . An interpretation . . . so at odds with [the statute's] structure and manifest purpose cannot be sustained." [**Whitman v. American Trucking Associations,** 531 U.S. 457 (2001); **NLRB v. Kentucky River Community Care, Inc.,** *supra,* §211]

c. Unanswered questions under *Chevron* [§583]

Chevron represented a major shift in the allocation of power between courts and agencies. Some unresolved issues remain.

(1) Is delegation automatic? [§584]

Chevron does not mean that *every* agency interpretation is backed up by a delegation of interpretive power that entitles the interpretation to strong deference. In *Chevron*, the interpretation was situated in a legislative rule and involved both highly technical and difficult environmental questions and clashing policies; this is the strongest case for finding a delegated interpretive power. However, it may be argued that agencies that lack delegated rulemaking or adjudication power might not have the power to impose their interpretations on the courts.

(2) Not every interpretation is entitled to strong deference [§585]

Chevron involved an interpretation contained in a legislative rule. However, agencies interpret statutes in many formats other than legislative rules.

(a) Interpretive rules and policy statements [§586]

An agency's legal interpretation contained in an interpretive rule or policy statement is *not* entitled to *Chevron* deference. [**Christensen v. Harris County,** 529 U.S. 576 (2000)] In *Christensen*, the Department of Labor expressed its views in an opinion letter. The interpretation was "not one arrived at after, for example, a formal adjudication or notice-and-comment rulemaking. Interpretations such as those in opinion letters—like interpretations contained in policy statements, agency manuals, and enforcement guidelines, all of which lack the force of law—do not warrant *Chevron*-style deference." Instead, the Court held that the multi-factor analysis in **Skidmore v. Swift,** *supra*, §570, applies to interpretations contained in interpretive rules or policy statements. All but one member of the Supreme Court in *Christensen* agreed with the application of *Skidmore* rather than *Chevron* in this situation.

(b) Ruling letters [§587]

Chevron deference is also inapplicable to ruling letters written by the Customs Service in which the Service states its position about which tariff classification a particular imported item should receive. These letters are binding on the Customs Service, in the sense that the importer who received the letter is entitled to rely on it. Similarly, the ruling is binding on the importer, if it is not appealed, but the importer is entitled to a de novo judicial determination of the issue. Such rulings do *not* receive *Chevron* strong deference but are entitled to *Skidmore* weak deference since they arise in a technical area and the Customs Service has considerable expertise in interpreting the law. [**United States v. Mead Corp.**, *supra*, §574—classification of imported day planners as "diaries"]

1) Application

In *Mead*, the Court stated: "We have recognized a very good indicator of delegation meriting *Chevron* treatment in express congressional authorizations to engage in the process of rulemaking or adjudication . . . [such as when Congress makes provision for a] relatively formal administrative proceeding tending to foster the fairness and deliberation that should underline a pronouncement of such force." Yet, the absence of such procedure in *Mead* was not dispositive, "for we have sometimes found reasons for *Chevron* deference even when no such administrative formality was required and none was afforded . . . " Here, however, the Court found no evidence of Congressional intention to delegate law-making power even though the written rulings bind the Customs Service and often have precedential value. Thousands of such rulings are produced by low-level personnel in 46 different Customs offices, usually furnishing only a conclusion without reasoning (although the ruling in this particular case came from headquarters and did contain explanation and legal reasoning). These facts suggest that Congress would not have wanted such rulings to be entitled to receive strong deference in court.

(c) Formal adjudication [§588]

Interpretations arising out of formal agency adjudication qualify for strong deference, at least so long as the adjudicating agency also had rulemaking power. [**Christensen v. Harris County**, *supra*—dictum; **Holly Farms Corp. v. NLRB**, 517 U.S. 392 (1996)] However, some decisions suggest that interpretations by adjudicating agencies that lack rulemaking power are not entitled to strong deference. [**Atchison, Topeka, & Santa Fe Railway v. Pena**, 44 F.3d 437 (7th Cir. 1994) (en banc), *aff'd on other grounds*, 516 U.S. 152 (1996)]

(d) Informal adjudication [§589]

The Court has applied *Chevron* to agency informal adjudications where the agency had rulemaking power. [**Nationsbank of North Carolina v. Variable Annuity Life Insurance Co.**, 513 U.S. 251 (1995)—agency head's letter approving transaction given strong deference] However, the *Mead* and *Christensen* cases might cause the Supreme Court to decide that interpretations contained in informal adjudications that lack the basic procedure protections provided in the APA are not entitled to *Chevron* deference. The dissenting opinion in *Mead* observed that this issue remains undecided.

(e) Agency litigating positions [§590]

In some cases, agency positions articulated in briefs in the course of the matter currently being litigated have been accorded strong deference if the positions taken represent the agency's "fair and considered judgment on the matter in question" (as opposed to a post hoc rationalization supplied by counsel). [**Martin v. Occupational Safety and Health Review Commission**, *supra*, §256; **Auer v. Robbins**, *supra*, §382—both cases involving agency interpretation of its own regulations—*see infra*, §593] In contrast, interpretive arguments made by agency counsel that are viewed as post hoc rationalizations for agency determinations arrived at for other reasons are entitled to no deference. [**Bowen v. Georgetown University Hospital**, *supra*, §339]

(3) Should *Chevron* apply when constitutional issues are involved? [§591]

Several decisions indicate that *Chevron* does not apply when the agency's interpretation raises serious constitutional questions. [**Solid Waste Agency of Northern Cook County v. Army Corps of Engineers**, 531 U.S. 159 (2001)—regulation defining ambiguous term "navigable waters" to include isolated pond is invalid absent clear indication that Congress intended that result because of constitutional concerns; **Miller v. Johnson**, 515 U.S. 900 (1995)—Georgia redistricting plan violated equal protection; **Edward De Bartolo Corp. v. Florida Gulf Coast Council**, 485 U.S. 568 (1988)] Yet the Supreme Court has indicated that *Chevron* applies to a reasonable agency interpretation of a statute despite the fact that the interpretation raised serious constitutional issues. [**Rust v. Sullivan**, *supra*, §33—regulation banning personnel in federally funded family planning centers from discussing abortion with clients] Thus, this application of *Chevron* remains uncertain.

(4) Can agency reinterpret statute previously clarified by the Court? [§592]

Suppose an ambiguous statute has been clarified by a previous Supreme Court opinion. Can the agency now depart from that meaning by reasonably reinterpreting the statute? The theory of *Chevron* suggests that such reinterpretation should be permissible, but the Court suggests that it is not. Once the Court has interpreted a statute, that fixes its meaning permanently. [**Lechmere, Inc. v. NLRB**, 502 U.S. 527 (1992)]

4. Strong Deference to Agency Interpretations of Its Own Regulations [§593]

Even before *Chevron*, courts accorded strong deference to an agency's interpretations of its own legislative rules, on the theory that Congress intended to delegate such interpretive power. Thus, the court must adhere to an agency interpretation of its legislative rules unless "an alternative reading is compelled by the regulation's plain language or by other indications of the [agency's] intent at the time of the regulation's promulgation." [**Thomas Jefferson University v. Shalala**, 512 U.S. 504 (1994); **Auer v. Robbins**, 519 U.S. 452 (1997)]

D. Scope of Review of Application of Law to Fact

1. Overview [§594]

In virtually every case, an agency must make an "ultimate" finding—*i.e.*, a decision that the facts as found either do or do not satisfy a legal standard.

e.g. **Example:** A statute gives benefits to an employee who quits a job for "good cause" but not to one who quits for other reasons. An employee resigns, claiming that the reason was sexual harassment. In a given case, an agency must make findings about why the employee quit. These are findings of **basic fact,** to which the substantial evidence test (discussed above) applies. The agency must also define the term "good cause" in abstract **legal terms** (*i.e.,* did the legislature intend to allow an employee who quits for noneconomic reasons to get benefits?). Under *Chevron*, the court must follow any reasonable agency interpretation if the term "good cause" is ambiguous; in most states, however, the court can substitute judgment on this question. Suppose the court determines that "good cause" can include "compelling" noneconomic reasons. Once the facts are found and the law is interpreted, the "ultimate" question is whether this particular employee quit for good cause. That is an **application** of the law to the facts. [**McPherson v. Employment Division,** 591 P.2d 1381 (Or. 1979)]

a. Conflicting cases

There is a split in authority on the court's power to review the "ultimate" question. Assume that the court substitutes judgment on legal interpretation questions (either because *Chevron* does not apply in that jurisdiction or, if *Chevron* applies, because the court finds the statute has a plain meaning). Assume further that the court applies the substantial evidence test as to findings of basic fact. Which of the two standards applies to the question of application? Is it more like a finding of fact (to which the substantial evidence test applies and the court must follow the agency's view if its decision was reasonable) or is it more like a conclusion of law (as to which the agency has power to substitute its judgment regardless of the reasonableness of the agency's decision)?

2. Reasonableness Test [§595]

Where resolution of the issue falls within the agency's *area of expertise* and apparently is an issue that the legislature *intended the agency to resolve,* the court will usually follow any reasonable agency decision rather than substitute its judgment. The reasoning is similar to that of *Chevron*: The legislature intended to delegate the application question to the agency. Therefore, courts should not substitute their judgment for that of the agency. **[McPherson v. Employment Division,** *supra*—"good cause" requires agency to complete a value judgment that legislature has only indicated; thus, court must follow reasonable agency application of law to fact]

a. Federal rule [§596]

The federal rule is that the application of broad statutory terms to the facts is treated the same as a question of basic fact—the agency must be upheld if its decision is reasonable. **[NLRB v. Hearst Publications, Inc.,** 322 U.S. 111 (1944)—whether a "newsboy" is an "employee" for purposes of federal labor law; court must uphold reasonable application by agency, not substitute its judgment]

(1) Illustration—"employee" [§597]

In the *Hearst* case, the NLRB had declined to follow common law tort rules in defining the term "employee" and, instead, defined the term in the context of policies underlying the NLRA—*i.e.,* any workers who needed the Act's protection were considered "employees" (the employees in question were newsboys). The Supreme Court held that, as a question of *law,* the common law approach would be wrong. But it left the Board to decide, as a question of *fact,* whether particular individuals were employees within the "need for protection" test.

(a) Rationale

The Court noted that where the agency must make the initial application of a broad statutory term, its interpretation should be upheld by the reviewing court "if it has 'warrant in the record' and a reasonable basis in law." The Court emphasized that Congress intended the agency to have *primary responsibility* for applying the law. Thus, Congress intended to *delegate* application issues to the NLRB.

(2) Illustration—"course of employment" [§598]

An employee of Brown-Pacific drowned while making a rescue attempt in hazardous waters surrounding an employee recreation center. The applicable statute provided compensation for injuries suffered by employees of government contractors only if sustained during the "course of employment." The agency held that the employee had died in the course of employment, and the Court treated the agency's determination as one of fact rather than law. [**O'Leary v. Brown-Pacific-Maxon, Inc.,** 340 U.S. 504 (1951)]

(a) Rationale

The Court ruled that the "course of employment" requirement was satisfied if the conditions of employment created a "zone of special danger" out of which the injury arose. In deciding whether the "zone of danger" test applied, the agency was resolving an issue of *fact*, not law.

3. Substitution of Judgment on Application Questions [§599]

In numerous cases involving judicial review of the application of law to fact, courts have substituted their judgment rather than deferring to a reasonable agency application. Logically, this could occur only where *Chevron* does not apply (since *Chevron* requires deference to reasonable agency decisions even on questions of law). Courts are more likely to substitute judgment on application questions where the issue turns more on **statutory interpretation** than on a sifting of complex facts, and where the agency appears to have **no particular expertise** in solving the particular problem.

a. Illustration—"employee" revisited [§600]

In another case involving the question of whether certain individuals were "employees," the issue was held to be one of statutory **construction** rather than **application** (as in the *Hearst* case, *supra*). Consequently, the Court treated the issue as a question of law, rather than fact. [**Packard Motor Car Co. v. NLRB,** 330 U.S. 485 (1947)]

Example: In *Packard Motor Car*, the issue was whether the foremen (as opposed to newsboys, as in *Hearst*) were "employees" under the NLRA, and the NLRB held that they were. Packard argued that under the NLRA, an "employer" was "any person acting in the interest of an employer," and since foremen acted in that manner they could not be "employees" as well. The Court found nothing in the Act to prevent a person from being *both* an employer and employee. Since the issue was one that turned on statutory construction—a process in which the courts, not the agencies, are the experts—it was appropriately treated as an issue of law.

---

4. Method for Analyzing an Application Question [§601]

A question of application of law to fact should be approached as follows:

a. Step one—find pure issues of law

Single out the pure issues of law involved—*i.e.*, those that do not involve the facts at all. On all such issues, the reviewing court may substitute its judgment (if that is appropriate under the rules relating to the scope of review of questions of law such as *Chevron* (see supra, §§568-592)).

(1) Application

The following questions of law can be answered *without reference to the facts* of the case:

(a) In the *Hearst* case, *supra*: (i) Did Congress intend to use the common law definition of "employee"? (No) and (ii) Did Congress intend the term to be defined with reference to an individual's need for statutory protection? (Yes).

(b) In the *Packard* case, *supra*: Did the statute preclude a person acting in the employer's interest from being classified as an "employee"? (No).

b. Step two—analyze basic facts against statutory standard

The basic *facts* of the case must then be analyzed against the statutory standard. For example: Are newsboys "employees" as defined in the statute? This is an application question where the cases divide—some treating the issue like a question of fact, others like a question of law. The following criteria are helpful in predicting how a court will treat the issue:

(1) *What are the comparative qualifications* of the court and the agency for determining the issue? Courts are more qualified than agencies in analyzing legislative history or the common law, and perhaps in reaching broad compromises that involve questions of policy. On the other hand, agencies may be more qualified to make judgments that are highly technical or require specialized knowledge.

(2) *How much confidence* does the court have in the independence and competence of the particular agency?

(3) *Does the agency's view seem persuasive* and well reasoned? Has the agency been consistent in holding that view, or has it vacillated?

(4) *Has there been an express or implied legislative determination* to commit this particular question to *agency discretion,* thus *delegating* primary responsibility for law application to the agency?

(5) *What is the role of the basic facts* in determining this particular question? If there is a complicated fact pattern—one that will vary greatly among different cases in which the same statutory term must be applied—the mixed question is apt to be treated as one of fact. But if the term is defined so as to make factual variations irrelevant (or at least easy to manage), the mixed question will probably be treated as one of law. *Examples:*

(a) In *Hearst,* "employees" was interpreted to mean "those in need of protection," and there could be numerous factual variations in later cases applying this term. Hence, the mixed question was correctly treated as a question of fact.

(b) Similarly, once the Court in *O'Leary* (*supra*, §598) defined "course of employment," there was a large area of potential conduct which might or might not fall within the "zone of danger." Thus, the issue was treated as one of fact.

(c) But in *Packard*, once the question of law was resolved—*i.e.*, that the same person **could** be both an employer and an employee—its future application was very simple. Consequently, no agency expertise was needed to determine that foremen were "employees," and this was treated as a question of law.

EXAM TIP　　　　　　　　　　　　　　　　　　　　　　**gilbert**

Analyzing a question dealing with application of law to fact is essentially a two-step process: First, single out the *"pure" issues of law*. Second, *analyze the basic facts* of the question *against the statutory standard*. Use the following factors to help you determine whether the court will treat the issue as one of fact or one of law: (i) the *comparative qualifications* of the court and the agency in determining the issue, (ii) the *confidence* placed in the competence and independence of the agency, (iii) how *persuasive* the agency's view is, (iv) whether there has been an *express or implied legislative determination* to leave the issue to the agency's discretion, and (v) the *role or relevance* of the basic facts of the question.

E. Scope of Review of Agency Exercises of Discretion

1. Overview [§602]

Statutes give agencies broad discretion in deciding how to implement a statute and how to apply it in individual cases. Courts are frequently called upon to review agency exercises of discretion. For example, an agency often has discretion as to whether to adopt a strong or a weak rule, whether to address a particular problem, or whether to revoke the license of a licensee who has violated the statute. The first issue in such cases is whether the decision is reviewable at all. If the decision is *"committed to agency discretion,"* it is *not reviewable*. [APA §701(a)(2)] This issue is discussed *infra*, §§721-729. In this section, assume the decision is reviewable and turn to the second issue: How broad is the court's power to *overturn the exercise of discretion*?

2. APA Standard [§603]

Under the APA, the court shall "hold unlawful and set aside agency action, findings, and conclusions found to be . . . arbitrary, capricious, an abuse of discretion or otherwise not in accordance with law . . . ." [APA §706(2)(A)] All three terms—arbitrary, capricious, abuse of discretion—mean the same thing and the test will be referred to below as the "arbitrary-capricious test."

a. Model Act [§604]

The drafters of the 1981 Model Act were uncertain whether to give courts this power to overturn agency decisions and left it up to the states to decide whether to adopt an arbitrary-capricious standard. [1981 Model State APA §5-116(c)(8)(iv)]

3. Meaning of the Arbitrary-Capricious Test [§605]

In the leading case on this question, the Supreme Court stated that the court that is called on to review an exercise of discretion must engage in a "substantial inquiry." Although the decision is entitled to a "presumption of regularity," that presumption must not prevent a "thorough, probing, in-depth review." [**Citizens to Preserve Overton Park v. Volpe,** *supra,* §425]

a. Scope of authority [§606]

First, the court must determine whether the discretionary action falls within the *area of discretion delegated to the agency* by the legislature. This is a question of statutory interpretation. Thus, if *Chevron* applies, and if the statute is ambiguous, the court must accept any reasonable interpretation of the bounds of the agency's discretion.

b. Factors [§607]

Second, the court must determine whether the decision was based on a consideration of the relevant factors. This means that the agency must consider *all of the relevant factors* and not consider irrelevant factors. Note that an agency need not consider the policies and goals of *all* federal statutes as relevant factors in making a complex economic decision. In general, the agency should consider only the policies and goals of the statute it is charged with enforcing. It lacks expertise in the other statutory areas and such a requirement would render a very large number of agency decisions of questionable validity. [**Pension Benefit Guaranty Corp. v. LTV Corp.,** *supra,* §241]

c. Reasonableness of agency action [§608]

Even if the agency exercised discretion within statutory bounds and considered all the right factors, the court should reverse if the agency's decision was unreasonable—the agency made a *"clear error of judgment."* [**Citizens to Preserve Overton Park v. Volpe,** *supra*] This is often referred to as *hard look review*. This standard requires a court to familiarize itself with the record and the agency's reasoning process in order to decide whether in fact the decision was reasonable.

d. Proper procedure [§609]

The court must also consider whether the agency *followed all appropriate procedures* when it exercised discretion. If the discretionary action was part of a rulemaking process, for example, the court should ascertain whether the requirements for rulemaking were observed.

4. Review of Policy Determinations in Legislative Rules [§610]

The arbitrary-capricious standard applies to the policy or discretionary determinations embodied in the adoption, modification, or revocation of legislative rules. [**Motor Vehicle Manufacturers Association v. State Farm Mutual Insurance Co.,** *supra,* §376]

---

e.g. **Example:** In 1977, the National Highway Traffic Safety Administration ("NHTSA") adopted a rule requiring all new cars produced after September 1982 to use air bags or automatic seat belts (*i.e.,* seat belts that restrain the occupant without buckling up). This rule was upheld by the courts. In 1981, however, NHTSA rescinded the rule, because it found that passive restraints could be easily detached and there was no reason to expect seat belt usage to increase sufficiently to justify the costs of the new equipment. The Supreme Court held that revocation of the rule was arbitrary and capricious. [**Motor Vehicle Manufacturers Association v. State Farm Mutual Insurance Co.,** *supra*]

---

a. Standard [§611]

The policy decision embodied in a legislative rule is reviewable under the arbitrary-capricious standard of APA section 706(2)(A). The same standard applies to adoption and to revocation of rules. The Supreme Court held that this standard requires a "rational connection between the facts found and the choice made." The Court added:

> Normally, an agency rule would be arbitrary and capricious if the agency has relied on factors Congress has not intended it to consider, entirely failed to consider an important aspect of the problem, offered an explanation for its decision that runs counter to the evidence before the agency, or is so implausible that it could not be ascribed to a difference in view or the product of agency expertise.

(1) Application

Under this standard, the Court invalidated the revocation of the rule.

(a) Air bags

All members of the Court agreed that the agency had failed to explain why the rule could not be modified to require the use of air bags. The explanation, if there was one, could not be supplied by the briefs. The rationale must be articulated by the agency itself.

(b) Passive restraints

By a vote of 5 to 4, the Court also held that NHTSA's decision to abandon the use of automatic seat belts was arbitrary and capricious. NHTSA decided that the available evidence did not indicate that there would be a sufficient increase in use of the equipment to justify the cost of installing it. NHTSA failed to explain why this problem could not be solved through the installation of nondetachable belts. Moreover, even as to detachable seat belts, the only evidence before the agency indicated that a substantial increase in use would occur. NHTSA rejected these studies as statistically invalid, but the court felt that NHTSA's decision to revoke the rule was arbitrary because it had failed to conduct additional tests to resolve the uncertainty.

5. Review of Facts Underlying Rules

a. Traditional rule [§612]

Traditionally, the court would *assume the existence of facts* supporting the rule. This "minimum rationality" test was the same one used to ascertain whether a statute denied substantive due process. [**Pacific States Basket & Box Co. v. White,** 296 U.S. 176 (1935)] The minimum rationality test no longer applies to the review of legislative rules. [**Motor Vehicle Manufacturers Association v. State Farm Mutual Insurance Co.,** *supra*] It is still applied in some states, however. [**Borden, Inc. v. Commissioner of Public Health,** 448 N.E.2d 367 (Mass. 1983)]

b. Modern rule [§613]

The courts today *scrutinize the factual conclusions* underlying discretionary decisions such as the policy determinations in legislative rules.

---

e.g. **Example:** In reviewing a rule phasing out lead additives in gasoline, the court took a "hard look" at the factual underpinnings of an EPA decision that lead in auto emissions "will endanger the public health or welfare." The court noted that it must immerse itself in the evidence (which was highly technical and highly disputed) to find out which evidence was relied on and which discarded, which choices were open to the agency, and which ones were actually made. All this is necessary to satisfy the court that the agency decision was rational and based on consideration of relevant factors. [**Ethel Corp. v. EPA,** 541 F.2d 1 (D.C. Cir. 1976) (en banc), *cert. denied,* 426 U.S. 941 (1976)]

---

(1) Response to criticism [§614]

The agency must respond to critical comments about the factual basis of its proposed rule, and the methodology on which it is based, if those comments step over a threshold requirement of materiality. [**Portland Cement Association v. Ruckelshaus,** *supra,* §361]

(2) Scientific frontiers [§615]

However, the Court has cautioned that reviewing courts must be unusually deferential when reviewing rules based on predictions within the agency's area of expertise that are at the frontiers of scientific knowledge. [**Baltimore Gas & Electric Co. v. Natural Resources Defense Council,** 462 U.S. 87 (1983)]

(3) Substantial evidence standard [§616]

Several statutes require reviewing courts to use the "substantial evidence" standard in assessing legislative rules. This standard may require a more detailed review than has generally been made of such rules, and it may require agencies to produce a better record of their rulemaking proceedings. [*See* **Mobil Oil v. FPC,** 483 F.2d 1238 (D.C. Cir. 1973); *but see* **Association of Data Processing Service Organizations v. Federal Reserve System,** 745 F.2d 677 (D.C. Cir. 1984)—no difference between substantial evidence and arbitrary-capricious tests]

EXAM TIP   **gilbert**

Don't be misled by terminology stating that a decision was left to the agency's discretion. When applying the arbitrary-capricious test, be sure to closely scrutinize the facts to determine whether the facts actually support the agency's decision. Be sure to determine whether the agency *considered all relevant factors*, whether the agency's *action was reasonable* or was a clear error of judgment, and whether the agency *followed all appropriate procedures* in exercising its discretion.

---

6. Record for Review [§617]

The general rule is that a reviewing court is limited to the findings and reasons stated by the agency at the time it made the decision. If the findings and reasons are not sufficient to enable the court to review the decision, it ordinarily remands to the agency to state proper findings and reasons. Similarly, the court reviews the decision based on the materials that were before the decisionmaker—not on a new record compiled for the purposes of review. (For further discussion of the record, *see supra,* §§422-429.)

7. Limited Review of Administrative Remedy [§618]

The court has a *narrow scope of review* as to the remedy granted by an agency; the court may *not* substitute its own judgment for that of the agency.

Example: The USDA issued a cease-and-desist order against a packinghouse for short-weighting cattle, and suspended its operations for 20 days. The court of appeals set aside the suspension as being more severe than previous USDA action in similar cases. The Supreme Court held that the agency's remedy must be upheld unless it was *"without warrant in law or justification in fact."* The mere fact that the remedy was unusually severe did *not* necessarily indicate that the suspension violated this standard. [**Butz v. Glover Livestock Co. of Texas,** 411 U.S.

182 (1973)] However, note that where an agency fails to explain why a particular remedy used in recent, similar cases was not employed, the matter may be remanded to the agency so that its rationale can be made clear. [**NLRB v. Food Store Employees Union,** 417 U.S. 1 (1974)]

---

a. Scope of remedy within agency discretion [§619]

The agency's decision to proceed against an entire industry, or merely to attack a problem on a company-by-company basis, is entirely within its discretion. A strong showing of abuse of discretion is required to overturn an agency's judgment on such matters. [**FTC v. Universal-Rundle Corp.,** 387 U.S. 244 (1967)]

(1) Note

Similarly, an agency's order to cease and desist illegal conduct can, if appropriate, go *beyond* the specific conduct proved in the hearing. Otherwise, the respondent might seek alternative means to circumvent the decision. [**FTC v. Mandel Brothers, Inc.,** 359 U.S. 385 (1959)]

b. Public policy [§620]

An agency's choice of remedy often reflects the agency's policy views. A court should refrain from injecting its own choice of the relevant policies. [**ABF Freight Lines, Inc. v. NLRB,** 510 U.S. 317 (1994)—board ordered employee reinstated even though he had committed perjury in the hearing—remedy upheld]

SCOPE OF JUDICIAL REVIEW—A

BASIC FACT	CONCLUSION OF LAW
Court must affirm agency's decision if finding was reasonable (*substantial evidence on the whole record* test)	Court must defe agency's *reason interpretation* if interpreted law *ambiguous*

182 (1973)] However, note that where an agency fails to explain why a particular remedy used in recent, similar cases was not employed, the matter may be remanded to the agency so that its rationale can be made clear. [**NLRB v. Food Store Employees Union,** 417 U.S. 1 (1974)]

a. Scope of remedy within agency discretion [§619]

The agency's decision to proceed against an entire industry, or merely to attack a problem on a company-by-company basis, is entirely within its discretion. A strong showing of abuse of discretion is required to overturn an agency's judgment on such matters. [**FTC v. Universal-Rundle Corp.,** 387 U.S. 244 (1967)]

(1) Note

Similarly, an agency's order to cease and desist illegal conduct can, if appropriate, go *beyond* the specific conduct proved in the hearing. Otherwise, the respondent might seek alternative means to circumvent the decision. [**FTC v. Mandel Brothers, Inc.,** 359 U.S. 385 (1959)]

b. Public policy [§620]

An agency's choice of remedy often reflects the agency's policy views. A court should refrain from injecting its own choice of the relevant policies. [**ABF Freight Lines, Inc. v. NLRB,** 510 U.S. 317 (1994)—board ordered employee reinstated even though he had committed perjury in the hearing—remedy upheld]

SCOPE OF JUDICIAL REVIEW—A SUMMARY			**gilbert**
BASIC FACT	**CONCLUSIONS OF LAW**	**APPLICATION OF LAW TO FACT**	**EXERCISE OF DISCRETION**
Court must affirm agency's decision if finding was reasonable (*substantial evidence on the whole record* test)	Court must defer to agency's *reasonable interpretation* if interpreted law is *ambiguous*	Court must accept agency's application of statute to facts if (i) it is *reasonable*, (ii) *Chevron* is applicable, or (iii) *legislature delegated* application issue to agency	Court should *scrutinize the facts* in the record to determine if they support agency's discretionary action; however court *must not* substitute its judgment (*arbitrary-capricious* test under the APA)

Chapter Nine: Reviewability of Agency Decisions—Remedies and Preclusion

CONTENTS

Chapter Approach

A.	Means of Obtaining Judicial Review	§621
B.	Sovereign Immunity	§640
C.	Tort Liability of Government	§656
D.	Tort Liability of Government Officials	§673
E.	Statutory Preclusion of Judicial Review	§704
F.	Commitment to Agency Discretion	§721

Chapter Approach

If an exam question involves judicial review, it is necessary to consider the possible remedies a court might grant and also to decide whether review is *precluded* because of sovereign immunity, by statute, or because of commitment to agency discretion. Keep in mind the following:

1. **Remedies**

   If the statute does not provide for judicial review, the most satisfactory remedies are *injunction* and *declaratory judgment*, although mandamus and certiorari will sometimes work. A court will also review an agency rule in an enforcement action.

2. **Sovereign Immunity**

   Although the federal government has *waived* sovereign immunity in an action that does *not seek money damages*, many *states* enforce the doctrine, and it is also embodied in the Eleventh Amendment.

3. **Tort Liability of Government**

   Government agencies are frequently liable in tort for actions of their officials. The federal government is liable under the *Federal Tort Claims Act*, but watch for the *discretionary function exception*. State governments are often liable under section 1983 for *civil rights violations*. Government *officials* may also be personally liable in tort, but watch for absolute and qualified immunities.

4. **Statutory Preclusion of Judicial Review**

   There is a *presumption* that agency action *is reviewable*, but it can be *precluded* by an explicit statute. However, review of constitutional issues probably *cannot* be precluded.

5. **Agency Discretion**

   Agency action is unreviewable if it is committed to agency discretion. Generally, this means that there is no law to apply. Also it is likely that agency decisions not to enforce the law are unreviewable.

A. Means of Obtaining Judicial Review

1. Statutory Procedures [§621]

Most statutes creating federal agencies indicate the procedure for obtaining judicial review of agency decisions. For large regulatory agencies, this is usually by appeal to the court of appeals (often the Court of Appeals for the District of Columbia), and sometimes by an action in federal district court.

a. State agencies [§622]

In many states, a single statute sets forth general procedures for review of decisions made by state agencies. [*See, e.g.,* 1961 Model State APA §15; 1981 Model State APA §5-101; N.Y. Civ. Prac. L., art. 78; Cal. Code of Civ. Proc. §1094.5]

2. Nonstatutory Procedures [§623]

Where there is no statutory provision for judicial review, the party seeking review must resort to one of the *common law writs*. These include:

a. Injunction and declaratory judgment [§624]

These remedies are usually sought together; *i.e.,* the court is asked to *declare* that the action taken or contemplated by the agency is illegal and to *enjoin* the agency from taking such action. Although irreparable injury is a prerequisite to obtaining an injunction, it does not apply to declaratory judgments. [**Steffel v. Thompson,** 415 U.S. 452 (1974)]

(1) Federal jurisdiction [§625]

In federal court, jurisdiction must be based upon an appropriate section of the United States Code—typically 28 U.S.C. section 1331, which gives jurisdiction to district courts in cases arising under the Constitution, laws, or treaties of the United States.

(a) "Amount in controversy" requirement eliminated [§626]

There is *no requirement* that the amount in controversy exceed a specified dollar amount in actions under section 1331.

(b) Additional provisions [§627]

Additional sections granting jurisdiction are 28 U.S.C. section 1337 (involving an act of Congress regulating commerce), section 1343 (deprivation of constitutional rights by state officials), and section 1361 (action in nature of mandamus). None of these sections has an amount in controversy requirement.

(c) APA not jurisdictional [§628]

Note that section 702 of the APA (discussed *infra,* §754) does *not* grant jurisdiction to the federal courts. [**Califano v. Sanders,** 430 U.S. 99 (1977)]

(2) Writ is discretionary [§629]

Injunctions and declaratory judgments are discretionary remedies and can be denied if the court determines that they are not appropriate. (*See* Remedies Summary.)

b. Mandamus [§630]

The common law writ of mandamus is available in most states, and in federal courts under 28 U.S.C. section 1361. Section 1361 gives district courts jurisdiction of any mandamus-type action to compel a federal officer, employee, or agency to perform a duty owed to the plaintiff.

(1) "Discretionary" duties [§631]

Mandamus *cannot* be used to require performance of a duty that is "discretionary" (as opposed to "ministerial").

(a) Distinguish—exercise of discretion

However, some cases indicate that mandamus will lie to compel a defendant to *exercise* discretion (where defendant refuses to do anything), to correct an action outside the scope of allowable discretion, or to correct an "abuse of discretion" (*see infra,* §§721 *et seq.*). [*See* **Lovallo v. Froehlke,** 468 F.2d 340 (2d Cir. 1972)]

(2) Grant or denial of writ [§632]

As in the case of injunctions, a court may decline to grant a writ of mandamus where it believes this would be inequitable or unduly inconvenient. [**13th Regional Corp. v. Department of Interior,** 654 F.2d 758 (D.C. Cir. 1980)] Some courts have also required that the official's duty be "clear" before mandamus lies. The better rule is that the duty need not be "clear," as long as it is not discretionary. Mandamus will not issue if the plaintiff has any other adequate remedy.

c. Certiorari [§633]

In many states, the common law writ of certiorari is used to review a "judicial" or "quasi-judicial" action where there is a *record* available. However, certiorari is *not available in the federal courts* to review administrative decisions because of an early Supreme Court decision. [**Degge v. Hitchcock,** 229 U.S. 162 (1913)]

d. Habeas corpus [§634]

Habeas corpus is available where there is a *restriction on individual freedom*. For example, if a person has been illegally inducted into the armed forces, habeas corpus against the commanding officer is appropriate. Habeas corpus may also be used by aliens seeking review of exclusion orders.

e. Other methods [§635]

In appropriate situations, review may also be obtained through actions in tort against a particular officer or against the United States under the Federal Tort Claims Act (*see infra,* §661) and through suits against the government in the Court of Claims.

3. Review During Enforcement Actions [§636]

Whenever an agency must ask the court to enforce an administrative decision, the court will generally review the decision itself during the course of the enforcement action. [*See, e.g.,* **United States v. Nova Scotia Food Products Corp.,** 568 F.2d 240 (2d Cir. 1977)—court reviewed validity of regulation when it was used as the basis for an enforcement action against a fish processor]

---

e.g. **Example:** Judicial review of selective service cases generally took place after the registrant refused induction, during the government's prosecution for such a refusal. [*See* **Estep v. United States,** 327 U.S. 114 (1946)]

---

a. Distinguish—preclusion of review [§637]

In one case, however, the Court upheld a statute that *cut off review* of the validity of a price regulation during criminal proceedings for violation of the regulation. [**Yakus v. United States,** *supra,* §17] The statute provided for an *alternative method of review* of the price regulation (by means of an appeal to an Emergency Court of Appeals). However, in a practical sense, that method of review was quite inadequate because it had to be sought within 60 days after promulgation of the rule—when most persons subject to the regulation probably did not yet even know about it.

(1) Problem—no review possible

Due process is violated when a person is convicted of a crime where an element of that crime was determined in a prior administrative decision and that decision was not judicially reviewable at the time it was rendered or at the time of the criminal prosecution. [**United States v. Mendoza-Lopez,** 481 U.S. 828 (1987)—deported aliens charged with a felony after reentering the United States] In *Yakus,* the Court reserved judgment about whether Congress could cut off review of constitutional claims in an enforcement action. Later cases indicate that Congress probably cannot preclude review of constitutional claims. (*See infra,* §715.)

(2) Rationale for *Yakus*

The exigencies of wartime price control probably explain the severe *Yakus* holding. [*See* **Adamo Wrecking Co. v. United States,** 434 U.S. 275 (1978)—casting doubt on *Yakus*]

b. Right to jury trial [§638]

A defendant has a Seventh Amendment right to jury trial on the issue of liability when the government asserts in court a claim of civil penalties for violation of a regulatory statute. [**Tull v. United States,** 481 U.S. 412 (1987)—civil penalties for dumping into navigable waters] However, Congress can reserve the determination of the *amount* of the penalty to the trial judge; only the issue of liability for the penalty must go to the jury. [**Tull v. United States,** *supra*—statute allowed penalties "not to exceed" $10,000 per day; no right to jury trial on setting amount of penalty]

gilbert

	AVAILABLE IN FEDERAL COURT?	AVAILABLE IN STATE COURT?	RESULT OF REVIEW
STATUTORY PROCEDURES (*E.G.*, APPEAL TO COURT OF APPEAL IF PROVIDED BY STATUTE)	Yes	Yes	Dependent on statute
INJUNCTION AND DECLARATORY JUDGMENT	Yes, but court must have jurisdiction	Yes	Court declares agency action invalid and enjoins agency from taking such action
MANDAMUS	Yes	Yes, in most states	District court can compel a federal officer, employee, or agency to perform a duty owed to plaintiff
CERTIORARI	No	Yes, where a record is available	Court reviews "judicial" or "quasi-judicial" action
HABEAS CORPUS	Yes	Remedy available in *federal court for those in state custody*, and only where there is a violation of a constitutional right or the laws and treaties of the U.S.	Plaintiff is granted relief from the restriction on his individual freedom

(1) Distinguish—judicial enforcement not necessary [§639]

However, if the agency is empowered to assess a civil penalty in an administrative proceeding, there is no right to a jury trial. [**Atlas Roofing Co. v. Occupational Safety & Health Review Commission,** *supra,* §52]

B. Sovereign Immunity

1. In General [§640]

The doctrine of sovereign immunity stems from the ancient rule that "the King can do no wrong," and still has considerable importance in administrative law. In essence, the doctrine provides that government action is not subject to judicial review by individual suit, except when and to the extent that the *government has consented* to be sued.

2. Basis for Sovereign Immunity [§641]

There is no really satisfactory rationale for sovereign immunity. Perhaps the most intelligible basis for the doctrine has been described as follows:

> The doctrine of sovereign immunity may be controlling in some suits . . . because the relief sought would work an *intolerable burden* on governmental functions, outweighing any consideration of private harm. In such cases a party must be denied all judicial relief other than that available in a possible action for damages. [**Washington v. Udall,** 417 F.2d 1310 (9th Cir. 1969)]

a. Eleventh Amendment [§642]

In one respect, sovereign immunity is based on a specific constitutional provision, the Eleventh Amendment, which deprives *federal* courts of jurisdiction over suits against a state by citizens of a *different* state. Additionally, the Eleventh Amendment has been extended to bar jurisdiction of the federal courts over suits brought by a citizen against her *own* state. [**Hans v. Louisiana,** 134 U.S. 1 (1890)]

(1) Application—prohibits damages paid by state [§643]

The Eleventh Amendment forbids an action in federal court for damages where, even though suit is filed *against a state official*, the damages would in fact be *paid by the state*. [**Edelman v. Jordan,** 415 U.S. 651 (1974)]

Example: *Edelman* involved an action against a state officer for retroactive welfare benefits that had been denied by the state under an unlawful regulation. Since liability would fall on the state treasury, the action was barred. (The Court also held that state participation in a federal-state welfare program did not constitute consent to be sued.)

(a) **Distinguish—injunction when statute allegedly unconstitutional [§644]**
The Eleventh Amendment does not forbid an *injunctive* action ostensibly against a state official—but actually against the state—where it is alleged that the statute authorizing the official's conduct is unconstitutional or that the official's action is illegal under a federal statute. [*Ex parte* **Young,** 209 U.S. 123 (1908)]

(2) **Exception—damages actions allowed [§645]**
Under limited circumstances, the Eleventh Amendment prohibition is waived, and the plaintiff may bring suit for damages against the state.

(a) **Damages paid by individual [§646]**
A plaintiff may sue individual state officials for damages that will *not have to be paid by the state.* (Note, however, that such actions may be barred by official immunity; *see infra,* §§673 *et seq.*) [**Scheuer v. Rhodes,** 416 U.S. 232 (1974)]

(b) **Damages based on statute implementing Fourteenth Amendment [§647]**
Damage actions against a state are permitted in federal court where based on a statute implementing the Fourteenth Amendment, on the theory that the Fourteenth Amendment overrides the Eleventh Amendment. [**Fitzpatrick v. Bitzer,** 427 U.S. 445 (1976)] However, Congress must make unmistakably clear its intention to subject the states to suit. [**Dellmuth v. Muth,** 491 U.S. 223 (1989)] The power to subject states to suit under the Fourteenth Amendment is limited to measures that remedy or deter rights already guaranteed by court decisions under the Fourteenth Amendment: "There must be a congruence and proportionality between the injury to be prevented or remedied and the means adopted to that end." [**Kimel v. Florida Board of Regents,** 528 U.S. 62 (2000)—Congress lacks Fourteenth Amendment power to subject states to liability for violations of the Age Discrimination statute]

1) **Distinguish—Article I powers**
Moreover, the Court has held that Congress lacks power to abrogate the Eleventh Amendment by passing a statute under the authority of the Commerce Clause or its other Article I powers. [**Seminole Tribe of Florida v. Florida,** 517 U.S. 44 (1996)]

EXAM TIP   **gilbert**

Don't be misled by an exam question that simply attempts to use the Fourteenth Amendment to "override" the Eleventh Amendment. Remember that Congress is limited to measures that remedy or deter rights that are *already guaranteed* by court decisions that were decided under the Fourteenth Amendment—Congress has no power to expand the envelope of Fourteenth Amendment protection.

(c) Prospective relief [§648]

The Eleventh Amendment does not bar prospective relief, such as injunctions against the state, to correct violations of the Due Process or Equal Protection Clause, though compliance will be expensive. [**Papasan v. Allain,** 478 U.S. 265 (1986)] Nor does the Eleventh Amendment prevent a court from awarding *attorney's fees* to the plaintiff who successfully obtained such an injunction. [**Hutto v. Finney,** 437 U.S. 678 (1978)] However, the government is not liable for attorney's fees unless it (rather than one of its employees) is liable for damages or injunctive relief. [**Kentucky v. Graham,** 473 U.S. 159 (1985)]

(d) Waiver of Eleventh Amendment [§649]

A state can waive the protections of the Eleventh Amendment, but not by implication. Thus the state does not waive the Eleventh Amendment by consenting to actions against itself in state court or by accepting funds under a federal statute that imposes obligations on states. [**Atascadero State Hospital v. Scanlon,** 473 U.S. 234 (1985)— state not liable for discrimination against handicapped person under Rehabilitation Act of 1973]

(3) Suit in state courts [§650]

Congress *cannot* abrogate a state's sovereign immunity by adopting a law that allows suit to be brought against the states in state (as opposed to federal) court. [**Alden v. Maine,** 527 U.S. 706 (1999)—state may refuse to entertain federal statutory private party cause of action against state arising under the overtime provisions of the Fair Labor Standards Act]

3. Federal Waiver of Sovereign Immunity [§651]

By a statute enacted in 1976, the federal government waived its sovereign immunity in all suits seeking relief *other than money damages.*

a. Prior law [§652]

The 1976 statute disposed of a vast body of confusing case law which previously had governed the sovereign immunity of the federal government. Under these cases, the United States could not be sued directly, but an official who acted outside the scope of authority could be named as defendant (unless the official's action was merely in error). [*See* **Larson v. Domestic & Foreign Commerce Corp.,** 337 U.S. 682 (1949)]

b. Current law—APA provisions [§653]

The law governing the liability of the United States for claims for relief is now found in the APA.

(1) *Section 702* provides that a person suffering legal wrong because of agency action may seek judicial review by naming the United States as

defendant in an action for relief other than money damages (*e.g.*, declaratory or injunctive relief).

(2) *Section 703* provides that an action for judicial review may be brought against the United States, the agency, or the appropriate officer where statutory review procedures are absent or inadequate.

(3) *Section 704* provides that agency actions reviewable by statute "and final agency action for which there is no other adequate remedy in a court" can be judicially reviewed. This provision did not prevent the federal district court from taking jurisdiction over an action for judicial review of an agency action that might, possibly, have been brought in the Claims Court. Claims Court jurisdiction was somewhat uncertain and the remedies available there were not entirely adequate. [**Bowen v. Massachusetts,** 487 U.S. 879 (1988)]

c. Damage actions [§654]

The United States has not waived its immunity to suits for money damages, except as provided in the Tucker Act (as to contract claims) or the Federal Tort Claims Act (*see infra,* §§661 *et seq.*). The term "money damages" means compensatory relief to compensate for a suffered loss, whether the particular remedy is legal or equitable. [**Department of the Army v. Blue Fox, Inc.,** 525 U.S. 255 (1999)—U.S. immune from claim by subcontractor for equitable lien on governmental funds to compensate for plaintiff's losses] However, the term "money damages" does not include specific remedies designed to give the plaintiff the very thing to which he was entitled (such as restitution). [**Bowen v. Massachusetts,** *supra*]

4. Proper Venue in Cases Against Government [§655]

By statute, a civil action naming the United States or a federal agency or officer as defendant may be brought in any judicial district in which: (i) a defendant resides, (ii) plaintiff resides (if no real property is involved), or (iii) a substantial part of the events or omissions giving rise to the claim occurred or a substantial part of the property that is the subject of the action is situated. The summons and complaint in such an action may be served outside the judicial district in which the case is brought. [28 U.S.C. §1391(e)]

a. Prior law

Prior law required that venue of most actions against the government be laid where all defendants reside or where the cause of action arose (usually Washington, D.C.), presenting an obvious hardship to plaintiffs located elsewhere.

b. Note

This provision applies only to actions seeking nonmonetary relief. It does not apply to actions for money damages against individuals by reason of conduct in their official capacity. [**Stafford v. Briggs,** 444 U.S. 527 (1980)]

C. Tort Liability of Government

1. In General [§656]

An action in tort provides an effective form of judicial review of government activities. However, the doctrine of sovereign immunity may preclude tort liability unless the government has *waived* its immunity, or unless the *activity falls outside the area protected* by sovereign immunity.

2. Liability of State Government [§657]

Under the traditional rule, neither state and local government nor the federal government was liable for the torts of its agents.

a. Exception—"proprietary" function [§658]

However, an established exception held that if the agent was engaged in a *"proprietary"* rather than a *"governmental"* function, state or local government could be liable for such activities. This distinction created a great deal of confusion in classifying agents' activities.

b. Modern trend—immunity abolished [§659]

Today, many states have simply *abolished* governmental immunity by statute or judicial decision. [*See, e.g.,* **Muskopf v. Corning Hospital District**, 55 Cal. 2d 211 (1961); *and see* Torts Summary]

c. Civil rights acts [§660]

Local government entities can be sued for damages or other relief if their officials deny to any person under color of law, official policy, or established government custom, any rights secured by the Federal Constitution or laws. [42 U.S.C. §1983; **Monell v. Department of Social Services**, 436 U.S. 658 (1978)] However, section 1983 does not permit actions against *states, or state officials* sued in their official capacity, whether the action is brought in state or federal court, because states (or state officials sued in their official capacity) are not "persons" under section 1983. [**Will v. Michigan Department of State Police**, 491 U.S. 58 (1989)]

3. Liability of Federal Government—Federal Tort Claims Act

a. Negligent torts [§661]

Tort actions against the federal government have been authorized since 1946 under the Federal Tort Claims Act ("FTCA"). [28 U.S.C. §§1346(b), 2671 *et seq.*] This statute makes the United States liable for personal injury or property damage—caused by the negligent or wrongful acts of government employees *acting within the scope of their employment*—to the same extent that a private employer would be liable.

b. Strict liability torts [§662]

The FTCA has not been applied to *strict liability* torts. Thus, for example, the United States is not liable where the plaintiff claims injury from an ultra-hazardous activity carried on by government employees, unless negligence can be shown. [**Laird v. Nelms,** 406 U.S. 797 (1972)—damage from sonic boom]

c. Intentional torts [§663]

The following principles govern liability of the federal government for intentional torts.

(1) Committed by investigative or law enforcement officers [§664]

The FTCA was amended in 1974 to include *certain intentional torts* committed by federal investigative or law enforcement officers. Thus, a plaintiff may sue the United States for injuries arising out of an assault, battery, false imprisonment, false arrest, abuse of process, or malicious prosecution committed by such an officer. [28 U.S.C. §2680(h)]

(2) Committed by other federal employees [§665]

However, the Act expressly *exempts* the government from liability for most other intentional torts caused by federal employees, such as defamation or misrepresentation. [28 U.S.C. §2680(h)]

(a) Note—trespass

The list of exempted intentional torts does not include *trespass*, however, and some cases have held the government liable for trespasses committed by its officers.

(b) But note

Trespass liability cannot be stretched to cover claims founded primarily on strict liability (*e.g.,* ultrahazardous activity) rather than on intentional trespass. [**Laird v. Nelms,** *supra*]

d. Discretionary functions [§666]

The government is *immune* from tort liability for damages "based on the exercise or performance of or the failure to exercise or perform a discretionary function or duty" even if the discretion is abused. [28 U.S.C. §2680(a)] However, this exemption is difficult to apply in practice.

(1) High-level decisions [§667]

High-level policy decisions about how to implement a regulatory program are within the discretionary function exception. [**United States v. Varig Airlines,** 467 U.S. 797 (1984)]

---

e.g. **Example:** The decision to approve manufacturers' designs for new commercial aircraft by spot-checking the designs, rather than by checking every detail, is immune under the discretionary function exception. [**United States v. Varig Airlines,** *supra*]

> **Example:** Planning decisions concerning the methods used to bag and load fertilizer for export are discretionary functions. [**Dalehite v. United States,** 346 U.S. 15 (1953)]

(2) Low-level decisions [§668]

A decision that is taken in the course of carrying out a regulatory program may or may not be a discretionary function. If the action is not permissible under the statute or regulation, it could not be a discretionary function. If a statute, regulation, or guideline leaves the agent discretion, it is presumed that the action is grounded in the policy of the regulatory regime and thus involves a discretionary function. [**United States v. Gaubert,** 499 U.S. 315 (1991)]

> **Example—bank supervision:** Agency employees closely supervised the management of a bank. Their discretion to recommend managerial changes reflected agency policy. Therefore the government was immune from negligence liability under the discretionary function exception. [**United States v. Gaubert,** *supra*]

> **Example—driving:** Driving a car involves discretionary decisions, but that discretion is not grounded in regulatory policy. Consequently, negligent driving is *not* within the discretionary function exception. [**United States v. Gaubert,** *supra*]

> **Example—scientific judgment:** If approval of a new polio vaccine violated clearly established objective scientific standards, it would not be a discretionary function, but if the approval process required the exercise of policy judgment, it would be a discretionary function. [**Berkovitz v. United States,** 486 U.S. 531 (1988)]

e. No indemnity against government employees [§669]

Where the government is liable for the negligence of its employees under the FTCA, the government has *no* right of indemnity against the tortfeasor-employee. [**United States v. Gilman,** 347 U.S. 507 (1954)]

4. Other Bases of Federal Government Liability [§670]

Even where government liability cannot be based on the FTCA, many plaintiffs obtain relief through *private bills* enacted by Congress.

a. Claims based on "taking" of property [§671]

Additionally, relief may be obtained under the *Fifth Amendment duty* of government not to "take property" without just compensation. [*See, e.g.,* **United States v. Causby,** 328 U.S. 256 (1946)—government low-level flights over plaintiff's farm, which had an adverse effect on his livestock, held a "taking" of land for which government had to pay]

b. Statutory power to settle claims [§672]

Finally, statutes give a number of federal agencies the power to *settle* small claims without resorting to litigation.

D. Tort Liability of Government Officials

1. In General [§673]

Officials of both state and federal government (*i.e.*, judges, legislators, and agency members) are frequently, but not always, immune from tort claims or claims based on violations of constitutional rights, which arise from their activities in the line of duty.

2. Common Law [§674]

At common law, government officials were *personally liable* for torts committed in the line of duty.

e.g. Example: A state official—acting pursuant to statute—ordered the destruction of a horse infected with glanders. The owner of the horse sued the official in tort, claiming that the animal had not been sick. The jury agreed with the owner and damages were awarded. Good faith and reasonableness, and the fact that the official was carrying out a statute, were not considered a defense. [**Miller v. Horton,** 26 N.E. 100 (Mass. 1891)]

3. Modern Law—Immunities for Officials

a. Absolute immunities [§675]

Certain officials are *absolutely immune* from liability for damages, even though their conduct is tortious or violates constitutional or statutory rights.

(1) The President [§676]

The President (or a former President) of the United States is absolutely immune from damage actions for official conduct occurring during his term of office. This holding is based on his constitutional status under the separation of powers and from concern that the President not be influenced by the possibility of litigation questioning his actions in office. [**Nixon v. Fitzgerald,** 457 U.S. 731 (1982)] Note, however, that the President is not immune from all litigation. For example, he can be made to disclose documents needed for a criminal case. [**United States v. Nixon,** 418 U.S. 683 (1974)] Moreover, the President is not immune from liability arising out of *unofficial* actions. [**Clinton v. Jones,** 520 U.S. 681 (1997)—President not entitled to deferral of discovery or trial until after he leaves office for claims arising out of alleged sexual harassment occurring before he became President]

(2) Presidential aides [§677]

A presidential aide has absolute immunity if engaged in discharging a *special function so sensitive as to require a total shield.* For example, conducting diplomatic relations probably would fall within this area. However, other functions give rise only to qualified immunity (*see infra*). [**Harlow v. Fitzgerald,** 457 U.S. 800 (1982)]

(3) Judges [§678]

State and federal judges are absolutely immune from liability for actions taken in the line of duty. The theory is that a judge could not carry out judicial duties under the threat of possible liability. [**Stump v. Sparkman,** 435 U.S. 349 (1978)]

> **e.g. Example:** A trial judge ordered a child to be sterilized without even holding a hearing. Despite the fact that this decision was blatantly wrong, the judge was not held liable because he had acted under a statute granting him broad general jurisdiction. [**Stump v. Sparkman,** *supra*]

> **cf. Compare:** If the judge had acted in the clear *absence of any jurisdiction*, he would not be immune from suit. [**Bradley v. Fisher,** 80 U.S. (13 Wall.) 335 (1871)]

(a) Injunctive relief and attorneys' fees [§679]

While a judge cannot be sued for damages, a judge may be *enjoined* under 42 U.S.C. section 1983 from acting in an unconstitutional manner (such as by setting bail for offenses for which a person cannot be imprisoned). Moreover, a judge who has been subject to such an injunction is liable for a plaintiff's attorney's fees under 42 U.S.C. section 1988. [**Pulliam v. Allen,** 466 U.S. 522 (1984)]

(4) Others engaged in adjudicative process [§680]

Prosecutors, agency officials who present evidence, witnesses, and administrative law judges are all absolutely immune. [**Butz v. Economou,** *supra,* §229; **Imbler v. Pachtman,** 424 U.S. 409 (1976)] However, state public defenders are *not* absolutely immune from liability for intentional torts. [**Tower v. Glover,** 467 U.S. 914 (1984)—alleged conspiracy between public defender, judge, and prosecutor to convict plaintiff] Similarly, the members of a prison disciplinary committee who adjudicate prisoner misconduct cases have qualified, not absolute, liability. [**Cleavinger v. Saxner,** 474 U.S. 193 (1986)]

EXAM TIP	gilbert

Don't be fooled by an exam question involving a liability action against a prosecuting attorney, a judge, *and* a state public defender. Remember that while prosecutors and judges are absolutely immune from liability for damages, state public defenders are *not*.

(5) Legislators [§681]
Both federal and state legislators enjoy absolute immunity from liability.

(a) Congress [§682]
Congress is protected by the Speech or Debate Clause of the Constitution. [U.S. Const. art. 1, §6; **Gravel v. United States**, 408 U.S. 606 (1972)]

(b) State legislators [§683]
State legislators and rulemakers enjoy absolute immunity from civil liability (both from damages *and* equitable relief) for conduct in enacting laws, adopting rules, or otherwise serving in a legislative capacity.

Example: The chairman of a state legislative committee was immune from civil liability where he was charged with conspiring to "smear" a candidate by summoning him to a hearing. [**Tenney v. Brandhove,** 341 U.S. 367 (1951)]

Example: The Virginia Supreme Court has been delegated legislative power to make rules governing the practice of law. In this capacity, the justices are immune from suit. [**Supreme Court of Virginia v. Consumers Union,** 446 U.S. 719 (1980)] No doubt, the same immunity would apply to federal officials in their rulemaking function.

---

1) Exception [§684]
Legislative immunity does not extend to a *federal criminal prosecution* against a state legislator for *bribery*, and evidence of his legislative conduct can be introduced against him. [**United States v. Gillock,** 445 U.S. 360 (1980)]

b. Absolute immunity for authorized acts

(1) Statutory immunity [§685]
Federal employees are absolutely immune from any action based on a claim for personal injury or death or property damage arising out of their "negligent or wrongful act or omission" *while "acting within the scope of employment."* Such actions may be brought only against the United States under the FTCA. [Westfall Act, 2 U.S.C. §2679(b)(1)] If such an action falls within an exception to the FTCA, a plaintiff can sue neither the government employee nor the government. [**United States v. Smith,** 499 U.S. 160 (1991)—government doctor negligently delivers a child at Army hospital in Italy; FTCA excludes recovery for injuries sustained outside the country] In such cases, the U.S. Attorney's certification

that the employee was acting within the scope of his employment is judicially reviewable. [**Gutierrez de Martinez v. Lamagno,** 515 U.S. 417 (1995)]

(a) Exception—constitutional violation [§686]

This statute does not apply to a civil action against a government employee brought for a violation of the Constitution. [28 U.S.C. §2679(b)(2)(A)]

(2) Common law immunity [§687]

In a decision of uncertain scope that preceded enactment of section 2679(b), the Court held that a high government official was immune from tort liability for actions within the scope of his discretionary authority. [**Barr v. Matteo,** 360 U.S. 564 (1959)—issuance of defamatory press release is within scope of department head's discretionary authority]

c. Qualified immunity for actions violating statute or Constitution [§688]

Except for those officials who have absolute immunity because of their position (*see supra,* §§675-683), government officials do not have absolute immunity from liability for damages. They can be sued for actions that *violate statutory limits* on their authority (since they would then be outside the scope of their authority) or that *violate constitutional limits* on their authority. Note that section 2679(b) (discussed above) explicitly exempts actions for constitutional violations from its immunity provision. However, such officials have *qualified immunity.*

(1) Reasonable person test [§689]

Officials with qualified immunity are liable for damages if their actions violate *clearly established* statutory or constitutional limitations *of which a reasonable person should have been aware.* [**Butz v. Economou,** *supra,* §680—federal executive officials have only qualified immunity from liability for constitutional torts; **Harlow v. Fitzgerald,** *supra,* §677—objective test used to measure scope of immunity; **Scheuer v. Rhodes,** *supra,* §646—state officials who used military force against students]

(2) Examples of qualified immunity

(a) School officials [§690]

School board officials were held liable for denial of procedural due process in disciplining students. [**Wood v. Strickland,** 420 U.S. 308 (1975)]

(b) Military force [§691]

Parents of students killed at Kent State sued the governor of Ohio, the president of the University, and officers of the National Guard for damages. The Court held that the defendants might be immune from liability, depending on the reasonableness of their action in light of available information and the scope of their discretion and authority. [**Scheuer v. Rhodes,** *supra*]

(c) Law enforcement officers [§692]

Police officers who engage in an unlawful search are immune from liability if a reasonable person would have believed their action was lawful. Only if the action violated "clearly established" law could the officers be liable. [**Wilson v. Layne,** 526 U.S. 603 (1999)—bringing reporters into home when executing an arrest warrant violates Fourth Amendment, but right not clearly established at the time; **Anderson v. Creighton,** 483 U.S. 635 (1987)—warrantless search without exigent circumstances]

4. Legal Basis for Damage Actions

a. Federal officials—common law or constitutional torts [§693]

A federal official who is *not performing duties within the scope of authority* can be sued in tort under state law. (This was the plaintiff's theory in **Barr v. Matteo,** *supra,* which was rejected because the issuance of press releases was found to be within the official's authority.) In addition, such officials may be liable under federal law for violating constitutional rights. (This was the plaintiff's theory, accepted by the Court, in **Butz v. Economou,** *supra,* and it is preserved by section 2679(b), *supra.*)

e.g. Example: Federal law enforcement officials are liable for damages in conducting an unlawful search and seizure. The claim arises directly from the Fourth Amendment; it is not recognized by any federal statute. It complements the rights against *state* law enforcement officials under the Civil Rights Act, *infra.* [**Bivens v. Six Unknown Named Agents of the Federal Bureau of Narcotics,** 403 U.S. 388 (1971)] A claim based on *Bivens* can be brought only against the official who violated constitutional rights, not against the agency for which the official is working. [**FDIC v. Meyer,** 510 U.S. 471 (1994)]

e.g. Example: A member of Congress may be held liable for damages for sex discrimination in firing his administrative assistant. The claim arises directly from the Due Process Clause of the Fifth Amendment (or more precisely from the equal protection component of due process that has been judicially imported into the Fifth Amendment). [**Davis v. Passman,** 442 U.S. 228 (1979)] In *Davis,* the Court did not reach the critical issue of whether the action of the member of Congress was immunized by reason of the Speech or Debate Clause of the Constitution.

Example: In **Butz v. Economou**, *supra*, the plaintiff's claims for damages were based upon both the First and Fifth Amendments. Although the Court did not decide whether rights of action arose from either or both of these provisions, it seemed to assume that such rights existed.

Example: Federal prison officials may be liable under the Eighth Amendment for inflicting cruel and unusual punishment on a prisoner, even though the plaintiff could also sue the government under the FTCA (*supra*, §664). [**Carlson v. Green,** 446 U.S. 14 (1980)] Punitive damages can be obtained in an action against the individuals but not in an action against the government under the FTCA. [**Smith v. Wade,** 461 U.S. 30 (1983)—prison guard liable for punitive damages if he recklessly or callously disregards constitutional rights]

b. State officials—tort liability under Civil Rights Act [§694]

Any person who deprives a citizen of rights derived from the Federal Constitution or federal statutes *under color of state law* is liable for damages under the Federal Civil Rights Act. [42 U.S.C. §1983]

(1) Broad application [§695]

This principle has been applied to a wide variety of actions that violate constitutional rights. Examples include a suit for discharge of a city hospital employee because of religion [**Birnbaum v. Trussell,** 371 F.2d 672 (2d Cir. 1966)]; a suit by an unsuccessful liquor license applicant, alleging lack of due process and equal protection [**Hornsby v. Allen** *supra*, §114]; and a suit against police officers for ransacking a family residence without a search warrant or probable cause [**Monroe v. Pape,** 365 U.S. 167 (1961)].

(2) Negligence [§696]

Section 1983 does *not reach negligent conduct*. Thus a person injured by the negligence of government officials can recover in a state law tort action against the official (if not immune) or against the government (if permitted by state sovereign immunity law), but not in a federal court action under section 1983. [**Daniels v. Williams,** 474 U.S. 327 (1986)] It is unclear whether section 1983 reaches reckless conduct.

(3) Relation to state tort law [§697]

The relationship between section 1983 and state tort law has not been completely defined.

(a) Tort remedy supplants 1983 action [§698]

In many situations, even intentional actions by governmental officials do not give rise to a section 1983 action where there is an adequate state tort remedy. For example, a state could not deprive a prisoner of his property without first providing notice and hearing under procedural due process. However, if the state provides an adequate tort remedy against the official, no action under section 1983 is permitted. [**Parratt v. Taylor,** *supra,* §144—negligent destruction; **Hudson v. Palmer,** *supra,* §144—intentional destruction] Similarly, the state was not required to provide a hearing before paddling a student for misconduct; a state tort remedy against the disciplinarian provided an adequate substitute. [**Ingraham v. Wright,** *supra,* §144]

(b) Tort remedy does not supplant section 1983 action [§699]

Employees of a state mental hospital accepted the plaintiff's voluntary consent form committing himself to the hospital, although they knew that he was not mentally capable of giving informed consent. As a result, the plaintiff waived the due process protections available to him if he had been involuntarily committed. The Court held that the plaintiff could sue the employees under section 1983 for deprivation of liberty without procedural due process, even though there was a state tort remedy available. The employees' action was not random and unauthorized (as in *Hudson, supra*) and it would have been possible and meaningful to have provided a pre-deprivation hearing. [**Zinermon v. Burch,** 494 U.S. 113 (1990)]

(4) Local government has no immunity [§700]

A local government entity has no immunity—absolute or qualified—from suit under the Civil Rights Act. [**Owen v. City of Independence,** 445 U.S. 622 (1980)]

(a) When local government is liable [§701]

A local government entity is not automatically liable for the actions of its employees under the doctrine of respondeat superior (as is the federal government under the FTCA). Instead, a local government is liable in an action under the Civil Rights Act [42 U.S.C. §1983] only when the entity itself is the "moving force" behind the deprivation of civil rights, because action was taken pursuant to "official policy." [**City of St. Louis v. Praprotnik,** 485 U.S. 112 (1988)—city not liable where supervisor who fired plaintiff for exercising rights of free speech was not authorized to do so by city ordinance; only officials having final policymaking authority under local law can bind city]

(b) Suits in official capacity [§702]

An action against a local officer "in his official capacity" (rather than against him as an individual) is in reality a suit against the government entity that employs him. Consequently, in such cases, the rules relating to actions against government, not actions against officials, are applicable. [**Brandon v. Holt,** 469 U.S. 464 (1985)—action against police chief in his official capacity for failing to discover and discharge a dangerous police officer is a suit against the city; defendant has no qualified immunity under Civil Rights Act] There is no need to bring actions against local officers in their official capacity; local government can be sued directly.

(c) Damages available against government [§703]

When a government entity is liable under section 1983 (whether directly or in an action against an officer in his "official capacity"), it must pay compensatory damages, as well as plaintiff's attorney's fees and costs—but not punitive damages. However, individual defendants in civil rights cases can be held liable for punitive damages. [**Newport v. Fact Concerts, Inc.,** 453 U.S. 247 (1981); **Kentucky v. Graham,** *supra,* §648—government not liable for attorney's fees unless it is also liable for civil rights violations]

EXAM TIP   **gilbert**

Be careful! An exam question dealing with tort liability of the government (federal, state, or municipal) or government officials can be full of twists and turns with different facts and types of parties thrown in (*e.g.,* the President, a state senator, a U.S. senator, municipal government officials, etc.). You need to determine who can be sued (the government, the individual government official, or both). You must remember who has ***absolute immunity*** and who has ***qualified immunity***. You must also know which statute or constitutional amendment an action may be brought under (*e.g.,* the FTCA, section 1983, Eighth Amendment, common law, etc.). Finally, you must remember which test or standard to apply in each situation (*e.g.,* reasonable person, was the official acting within his scope of authority?, etc.). You may need to map out or place everything on a grid when answering this type of question to keep from becoming confused.

E. Statutory Preclusion of Judicial Review

1. In General [§704]

Section 701(a)(1) of the APA provides that agency decisions are reviewable "except to the extent that . . . statutes preclude judicial review." Thus judicial review can be precluded if a statute so requires. Preclusion of review can be complete or partial: because section 701(a)(2) uses the words "to the extent that," a decision might be reviewable as to certain issues but not others, or review might be available to certain parties but not others.

2. Presumption of Reviewability [§705]

The most important point about preclusion is that case law has established a ***presumption of reviewability***. As a result, review is foreclosed only where there is "persuasive reason" to believe that *Congress intended* this result and where there is "clear and convincing evidence" of such intent. Thus, for example, the fact that a statute makes one type of decision reviewable does not necessarily mean that Congress meant to make other decisions by the same agency nonreviewable. [**Abbott Laboratories v. Gardner,** 387 U.S. 136 (1967); **Bowen v. Michigan Academy of Family Physicians,** 476 U.S. 667 (1986)]

3. **Decisions of the President [§706]**

The President is not considered an "agency" under the APA, and therefore, the President's decisions are not reviewable under the APA for abuse of discretion. The President's decisions are, of course, subject to review for violation of provisions of the Constitution. [**Franklin v. Massachusetts,** 503 U.S. 929 (1992)—President's decision to include overseas military personnel in allocating congressional seats not reviewable for abuse of discretion but is reviewable for compliance with constitutional norms]

4. **Interpretation to Avoid Preclusion [§707]**

Frequently, Congress passes a statute that seems to preclude review. However, consistent with the presumption of reviewability, courts often interpret such statutes to afford at least limited review.

a. **Illustration—military justice [§708]**

A statute provided for an Army review board to consider dishonorable discharges and stated that its findings were "final subject only to review by the Secretary of the Army." The Court held that a dishonorable discharge based on pre-induction acts is judicially reviewable and the Army is not allowed to consider such acts in its determination. Congress did not "intend" to preclude review where a government official acted in excess of his powers. [**Harmon v. Brucker,** 355 U.S. 579 (1958)]

b. **Illustration—veterans' benefits [§709]**

A now-repealed statute precluded judicial review of the Veterans Administration ("VA") "on any question of law or fact under any law administered by the VA providing veterans' benefits." The statute provided that such decisions were "final and conclusive and no . . . court of the United States shall have power or jurisdiction to review" them. The VA denied all benefits to alcoholics. The plaintiff argued that this decision violated the Rehabilitation Act which prohibits discrimination against handicapped persons. Because the Rehabilitation Act is not a "law administered by the VA providing veterans' benefits," the Court held that review was not precluded. This is a good example of narrow interpretation of preclusion statutes. [**Traynor v. Turnage,** 485 U.S. 535 (1988)]

c. **Illustration—illegal aliens [§710]**

A statute provided amnesty for alien farmworkers illegally in this country. It also provided for a hearing with respect to applications and barred judicial review of "a determination respecting an application" except in the context of the review in the Court of Appeals of a deportation order. A class action alleged that the INS violated both constitutional and statutory provisions concerning its hearings. The Court held that Congress had not precluded this form of review because the suit attacked the entire system of hearings, not merely a particular "determination respecting an application." The plaintiffs did not seek to have an application approved—merely to insure fair procedures for determining applications.

(1) Rationale

Moreover, if the plaintiffs were compelled to wait until the applications were denied before seeking review in the Court of Appeals, they could not receive effective review of the procedural issues; the Court of Appeals would not have a proper record for evaluating them. The District Court is a better place to pursue litigation of this kind because a proper factual record can be assembled. The fact that serious constitutional issues were raised was certainly a factor in the Court's decision to hear the case. [**McNary v. Haitian Refugee Center,** 498 U.S. 479 (1991); *and see* **Bowen v. Michigan Academy of Family Physicians,** *supra*—permitting judicial review of a regulation denying benefits despite preclusion of review of the denial of individual applications]

d. Illustration—constitutional issues [§711]

Plaintiff challenged denial of veterans' benefits despite the now-repealed statute precluding review of VA benefit decisions [*see* **Traynor v. Turnage,** *supra*] The attack was constitutional: The statute gave educational benefits to veterans but not to conscientious objectors who had performed alternative service. The Court held that Congress did not intend to preclude review of constitutional issues; a statute cutting off benefits to a class could be reviewed on constitutional grounds. [**Johnson v. Robison,** 415 U.S. 361 (1974); **Webster v. Doe,** 486 U.S. 592 (1988)—preclusion of review of termination of CIA employees not intended to preclude review on constitutional grounds]

e. Illustration—conflicts of interest [§712]

Under the Westfall Act (*see supra,* §685), a personal injury action against a federal employee must be dismissed, and the federal government substituted as defendant, if the government certifies that the employee was acting within the scope of his employment. If the action then falls within an exception to the Federal Tort Claims Act, the action must be dismissed. [**United States v. Smith,** *supra,* §685] In such cases, the government has an incentive to certify that the employee was acting within the scope of employment, because neither the employee nor the federal government will be liable. Despite language apparently making certification nonreviewable ("upon certification by the Attorney General . . . any civil action . . . shall be deemed an action against the United States . . . and the United States shall be substituted as party defendant"), the Court held that the certification was judicially reviewable. Congress could not have wanted the Attorney General to act—without any hearing—as the unreviewable judge in her own case. [**Gutierrez de Martinez v. Lamagno,** *supra,* §685]

5. Absolute Preclusion of Review [§713]

At least in nonconstitutional cases, the courts will honor a statute that absolutely precludes judicial review.

a. Economic claims [§714]

The Court upheld as constitutional an absolute preclusion of judicial review under a government benefit program. [**United States v. Erika, Inc.,** 467 U.S. 207 (1982)]

b. Constitutional claims [§715]

It is likely, although the issue is not settled, that Congress *cannot* preclude review of constitutional claims. [*See* **Bowen v. Michigan Academy of Family Physicians,** *supra*—dictum]

c. Enforcement actions [§716]

It is likely, although not settled, that Congress *cannot* preclude judicial review of the validity of an agency rule in an enforcement proceeding against an alleged violator of the rule *unless* a full and fair opportunity was given to contest the rule at an earlier time. [**Adamo Wrecking Co. v. United States,** *supra,* §637]

d. Collateral attack [§717]

In **United States v. Mendoza-Lopez,** *supra,* §637, D was being prosecuted for illegally entering the country after having previously been deported. The prior deportation order was reviewable and D had waived review, but the waiver was not knowing and intelligent. For that reason, D was allowed to collaterally attack the prior order in the current criminal prosecution. It would violate due process to use that decision as an element of the crime without affording him the right to review it either previously or during the present prosecution.

6. Implied Preclusion [§718]

Despite the presumption of reviewability, the courts have occasionally *inferred a statutory preclusion of review* even though Congress did not explicitly address the preclusion issue. Generally such implied preclusion must be supported by legislative history or by the unsuitability of the decision for review.

a. Voting rights [§719]

Review is precluded where time is of the essence. For example, the Voting Rights Act allowed a state plan to go into effect after submission to the Attorney General if the Attorney General did not object within 60 days. The Court held that the Attorney General's failure to object was not judicially reviewable because Congress intended the procedure to move quickly and minimize interference with state autonomy. Moreover, the decision could be reviewed at a later time. [**Morris v. Gresette**, 432 U.S. 491 (1977)]

b. Statutory structure [§720]

The courts are increasingly willing to imply preclusion based on congressional intent. For example, where an agency fixed milk prices and the statute allowed wholesale buyers of milk to seek judicial review, the Court held that Congress impliedly precluded review by *consumers* of milk because such review would disrupt the statutory scheme. [**Block v. Community Nutrition Institute**, 467 U.S. 340 (1984)]

F. Commitment to Agency Discretion

1. In General [§721]

An action of an agency is ***not reviewable*** "to the extent that agency action is committed to agency discretion by law." [APA §701(a)(2)] If this exception applies, the court cannot set aside the agency action on the ground that it is "arbitrary, capricious, or an abuse of discretion." [APA §706(2)(A), discussed *supra*, §§603-609] Thus the APA seems to say, on the one hand, that agency discretion is not reviewable, but on the other hand, that it is reviewable.

2. No Law to Apply [§722]

The Supreme Court resolved this conflict by construing section 701(a)(2) quite narrowly. Review of discretionary action is precluded only in those "rare instances" where ***there is "no law to apply."*** [**Citizens to Preserve Overton Park v. Volpe**, *supra*, §608] There is no law to apply where the statute provides no judicially manageable standards to detect abuse. [**Heckler v. Cheney**, 470 U.S. 821 (1985)]

---

e.g. **Example:** In *Citizens to Preserve Overton Park*, a statute provided that federal funds should not be granted to construct highways through public parks if there was a "feasible and prudent" alternate route. The Secretary of Transportation nevertheless approved funding of such a highway, without stating a reason for doing so. The Court held that section 701(a) did ***not*** grant the Secretary unreviewably broad discretion. Rather, it held that actions committed to agency discretion were "a very narrow exception." By interpreting the statutory language "feasible and prudent" in a way that gave some specific content to the words, the Court found that there ***was*** law to apply.

---

a. Standards supplied by regulation [§723]

Judicially manageable standards can be supplied by legislative regulations as well as by statutes. [**McAlpine v. United States**, 112 F.3d 1429 (10th Cir. 1997)—review of decision by Secretary of Interior not to take land into Indian trust status—court reviews decision under factors supplied by regulation]

3. What Is "Committed to Agency Discretion" [§724]

Several types of administrative decisions have been held to lie entirely within the discretion of the agency, and therefore are exempt from review.

a. Decisions to enforce or prosecute [§725]

Decisions whether to prosecute or enforce a statute are *presumptively unreviewable*. Such decisions involve a complex balancing of factors within an agency's expertise—*e.g.,* should it expend resources on this case, what is the likelihood of success, does enforcement fit the agency's overall policies, etc. Yet the courts will review such decisions if Congress provides some guidelines for the agency to follow in exercising the power. [**Heckler v. Chaney,** *supra*—FDA's decision to allow use of lethal injections for capital punishment is unreviewable]

b. Intelligence officers [§726]

A statute allowed the director of the CIA to discharge any CIA employee "whenever he shall deem such termination necessary or advisable in the interests of the United States." The director discharged a homosexual employee without stating any reason. Such decisions are committed to agency discretion and thus cannot be judicially reviewed on nonconstitutional grounds (*i.e.,* that the decision was arbitrary, capricious, or an abuse of discretion). The Court relied on the word "deem" and on the peculiar needs of an intelligence service to discharge employees without judicial second-guessing. Yet the Court also held that the decision could be judicially reviewed *on constitutional grounds* (for violation of due process, equal protection, or privacy). [**Webster v. Doe,** *supra,* §711]

c. Admission of aliens [§727]

The executive branch has extremely broad authority over the admission of aliens. Although by statute, visas cannot be granted to aliens who advocate Communism, the Attorney General can waive this provision and grant a visa, and that decision (whether or not to waive the provision) is an act of discretion that is not reviewable *as long as the Attorney General* states a reason for the decision. (The Court did not discuss whether the decision would be reviewable if no reason was stated.) [**Kleindienst v. Mandel,** 408 U.S. 753 (1972)]

d. Refusal to reconsider [§728]

The courts will not review an agency decision that refuses to reopen or reconsider a prior decision on the ground that the prior decision was erroneous. This is action committed to agency discretion. However, the courts might review an agency decision refusing to reopen based upon newly discovered evidence or changed circumstances. [**ICC v. Brotherhood of Locomotive Engineers,** 482 U.S. 270 (1987)]

e. Economic decisions [§729]

Whether an applicant for a rural home loan is "creditworthy" is a decision committed to agency discretion. The court found that it is not equipped to second guess the decision of the agency's loan officer. The statute provided no meaningful standards and, on pragmatic grounds, the court thought the decision was inappropriate for judicial scrutiny. [**Woodsmall v. Lyng,** 816 F.2d 1241 (8th Cir. 1987)] Similarly, the approval of rent increases in low-income housing is an economic decision that would be inappropriate for judicial review and that would impair the ability of the agency to respond to economic conditions. [**Hahn v. Gottlieb,** 430 F.2d 1243 (1st Cir. 1970)]

f. **Unallocated appropriation [§730]**
An agency's choice of how to spend money from an unallocated congressional appropriation is not judicially reviewable because the decision is committed to agency discretion. [**Lincoln v. Vigil,** 508 U.S. 182 (1993)—decision to terminate specific Indian children's health program is nonreviewable]

Chapter Ten: Standing to Seek Judicial Review and The Timing of Judicial Review

CONTENTS

Chapter Approach

A. Standing to Seek Judicial Review   §731

B. The Timing of Judicial Review   §764

Chapter Approach

Exam questions involving judicial review very often involve questions of both standing and timing. Standing refers to whether *this plaintiff* is entitled to seek review; timing refers to whether the plaintiff is seeking review *too early*.

1. **Standing**

   In analyzing questions concerning standing, be sure to work through *both* the constitutional and prudential limits on standing:

   a. **Constitutional limits**

      A plaintiff must suffer palpable rather than abstract *injury in fact*; the challenged action must be the *cause of the injury*; if plaintiff wins, the injury *will be remedied*.

   b. **Prudential limits**

      The plaintiff must be within the *zone of interests* of the statute that is the basis for challenge. Also, the plaintiff must be vindicating his *own interests,* not those of third parties.

2. **Timing**

   A court may reject the petition for review for any of the following reasons:

   a. **Final order rule**

      If the action is *not final* but instead is part of an ongoing process, the court will not review it. But remember that courts make exceptions in cases of *irreparable injury*.

   b. **Ripeness**

      If the action is *not ripe* for immediate review but can only be reviewed in the context of an actual application of the rule, the court will not review it. You must *balance* the harm to the plaintiff from delay in review against the susceptibility of the issue to immediate review.

   c. **Exhaustion of administrative remedies**

      The court may not review the action if the plaintiff has *failed to exhaust administrative remedies*. But recall that there are numerous exceptions that must be considered in each case (*e.g.,* irreparable injury, futility, and inadequacy of the remedy). Note, however, that a court has less discretion to excuse a failure to exhaust requirement if the exhaustion requirement appears in a specific statute.

   d. **Primary jurisdiction**

      In the case of a judicial trial (rather than an appeal from an agency action), the court may apply the doctrine of *primary jurisdiction* and insist that the case be tried *in the agency* instead. Be sure to discuss the need for uniform results (which suggests all cases should be tried in the agency) and the degree to which the issue is highly technical (which again suggests agencies should try it).

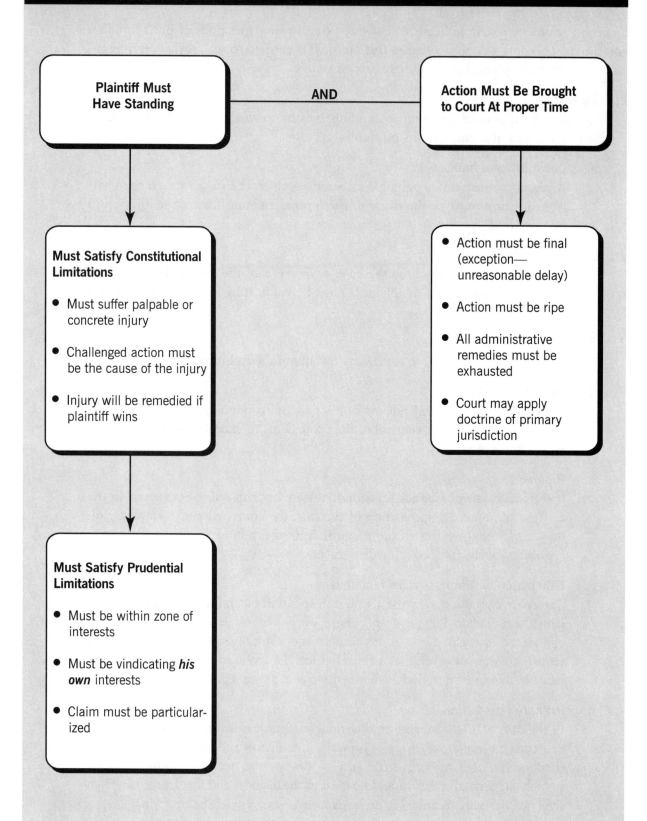

Plaintiff Must Have Standing — AND — **Action Must Be Brought to Court At Proper Time**

Must Satisfy Constitutional Limitations

- Must suffer palpable or concrete injury
- Challenged action must be the cause of the injury
- Injury will be remedied if plaintiff wins

Action Must Be Brought to Court At Proper Time

- Action must be final (exception— unreasonable delay)
- Action must be ripe
- All administrative remedies must be exhausted
- Court may apply doctrine of primary jurisdiction

Must Satisfy Prudential Limitations

- Must be within zone of interests
- Must be vindicating *his own* interests
- Claim must be particular-ized

A. Standing to Seek Judicial Review

1. Introduction [§731]

A party who wishes to obtain judicial review of an administrative decision must have standing to do so. In federal courts, standing has both constitutional and prudential limitations. The constitutional limitations derive from the fact that Article III of the Constitution grants federal courts jurisdiction only over "cases or controversies." The prudential limitations have been imposed by a number of decisions of the Supreme Court in the interest of judicial economy, fairness, accuracy, and the like.

a. Timing [§732]

The Supreme Court has held that a federal court must resolve jurisdictional issues before it may address the merits of a case. Thus, a federal court must address questions of standing before deciding substantive issues. [**Steel Co. v. Citizens for a Better Environment,** 523 U.S. 83 (1998)] However, there is no hierarchy of jurisdictional issues, so it is not improper for a court to address a ripeness question (which is a nonsubstantive, prudential timing limitation, discussed *infra*) before addressing a question of standing. [**Ohio Forestry Association v. Sierra Club,** 523 U.S. 176 (1998)]

2. Constitutional Limitations [§733]

The Supreme Court has interpreted the "case or controversy" language to require that plaintiffs have a *personal stake in the outcome of the litigation.* Most government decisions directly affect people or entities by requiring them to do or refrain from doing something. In such cases, the people or entities clearly have a stake in the outcome and standing is unlikely to be an issue. However, if agency action has affected a person or entity only indirectly or marginally, standing becomes a major issue. To have a sufficient personal stake, modern cases provide that a plaintiff must (i) suffer a palpable (as opposed to abstract) *injury in fact;* (ii) show that the challenged action is the *cause of the injury;* and (iii) show that if she wins, the *injury will be remedied.*

a. Injury in fact

(1) Background [§734]

The "injury in fact" test is a marked liberalization of the previous law on standing. Early cases recognized standing only where the plaintiff could show a violation of her "legal rights." (Study of this early law is helpful to appreciate the modern law of standing.)

(a) "Legal rights" test [§735]

Under this now outdated approach, a plaintiff was required to show that, had the government been a *private party,* its actions would have given rise to a common law cause of action.

Example: The United States Attorney General listed a charitable organization as Communist dominated, thus impairing its ability to raise funds. Had a private individual taken such action, the organization could have sued for defamation. Thus, the organization was allowed standing to seek a hearing on whether it was in fact a Communist group. [**Joint Anti-Fascist Refugee Committee v. McGrath,** 341 U.S. 123 (1951)]

Compare: A plaintiff had no standing to complain if the government competed against him or refused to contract with him, since these were not legally recognized rights at common law. [**Tennessee Power Co. v. Tennessee Valley Authority,** 306 U.S. 118 (1938)—no standing to challenge agency's licensing of plaintiff's competitor]

1) Criticism of test

The "legal rights" test insulated the government from review of many administrative decisions which in fact inflicted serious harm on private interests. In addition, the Court was often required to take a premature look at the merits of the case in order to determine whether a "legal right" had been violated.

(b) Standing granted by statute [§736]

In the 1940s, the "legal rights" test was substantially undermined by cases recognizing that Congress had the power to expand the class of persons with standing to challenge agency actions.

1) "Aggrieved persons" test [§737]

Where a statute allows "aggrieved" persons to challenge agency action, persons suffering economic harm from that action have standing to seek review even though such persons could not have satisfied the "legal rights" test. [**FCC v. Sanders Radio Station,** 309 U.S. 470 (1940)]

Example—standing of competitors: The Federal Communications Commission ("FCC") licensed B to construct a broadcasting station in an area where A was already broadcasting. A sought judicial review of the decision under a statute that allowed standing to anyone "aggrieved" by an FCC decision. Even though A would have had no cause of action at common law, the Court held that "aggrieved persons" included those who would suffer economic injury as a result of the agency's decision. [**FCC v. Sanders Radio Station,** *supra*]

2) **"Private attorney general" [§738]**

In *Sanders Radio Station,* the Court permitted the plaintiff to assert the public interest as well as its own interest. *Rationale:* A person who is financially injured by an administrative decision may be the only one sufficiently motivated to question an erroneous agency ruling. [*See* **Associated Industries of New York v. Ickes,** 134 F.2d 694 (2d Cir. 1943)]

Example: Members of the "listening public" were allowed to seek judicial review of the FCC's renewal of a broadcasting license. Also, environmental associations have been granted standing to protest the licensing of a power project. [**Office of Communication of United Church of Christ v. FCC,** *supra,* §199; **Scenic Hudson Preservation Conference v. Federal Power Commission,** 354 F.2d 608 (2d Cir. 1965)]

---

(2) Modern requirements of injury in fact [§739]

The theories articulated in the "legal wrong" and "statutory standing" cases (*supra,* §§736-738) have been reconceptualized by numerous modern cases. Under these cases, to constitute "injury in fact," an injury must be *concrete* (rather than abstract) and *particularized* (rather than generalized). While the injury is usually an economic one (such as a competitive or consumer injury), it can also be *noneconomic* (such as environmental or aesthetic). Examples include the following:

(a) Competitive injury [§740]

The Comptroller of the Currency allowed national banks to perform data processing services. This injured persons in the data processing business. Competitive injury satisfied the injury in fact requirement under section 702. [**Association of Data Processing Service Organizations v. Camp,** 397 U.S. 150 (1970)]

(b) Economic injury [§741]

Tenant farmers challenged a regulation that permitted them to assign federal benefits as security for leases. They claimed the regulation injured them because their landlords would now always demand such an assignment before leasing the land. This harm also met the injury in fact requirement. [**Barlow v. Collins,** 397 U.S. 159 (1970)]

(c) Noneconomic injury—environmental harm [§742]

Injury in fact does not require a showing of economic harm. Harm to a person's aesthetic or recreational interests is sufficient if the plaintiff alleges *specific and immediate* injury. The Court has insisted that the showings of injury be quite specific.

e.g. **Example:** Persons who allege that they currently watch whales have standing to complain of federal nonenforcement of treaties that protect whales. [**Japan Whaling Association v. American Cetacean Society,** 478 U.S. 221 (1986)]

cf. **Compare:** Plaintiff alleged that it used land for recreation in the "vicinity" of land the government planned to open for mining. This allegation of harm was not specific enough. The harm had to relate to the very parcel that plaintiff intended to use. [**Lujan v. National Wildlife Federation,** 497 U.S. 871 (1990)]

cf. **Compare:** Plaintiffs were interested in protection of endangered species in foreign countries. They alleged that they had once visited and planned to someday again visit the habitat of the species. Because their plans to return were not specific, the harm was not sufficiently imminent. Nor was their interest in seeing the animal survive (so they could see or work with it in a zoo) sufficient to establish harm with respect to a claim that projects abroad might further endanger the species. This form of harm is considered too speculative. [**Lujan v. Defenders of Wildlife,** 540 U.S. 555 (1992)]

cf. **Compare:** Plaintiff, an environmental association with a long-time concern for protection of the Sierras, sought to enjoin a ski development in the Sierras. It did not have standing. *Specific harm to specific people must be alleged.* [**Sierra Club v. Morton,** 405 U.S. 727 (1972)] However, as discussed below (*infra*, §751), an association is allowed to sue on behalf of its members if one or more of them will suffer the specific injury needed to establish standing.

(d) Noneconomic injury—deprivation of information [§743]
A sufficient injury can come from a deprivation of information from the government:

e.g. **Example:** Plaintiff claimed that he was a voter who had been deprived by the Federal Elections Commission ("FEC") of information to which he was entitled by statute and which he would have used to evaluate candidates for public office. A statute specifically gave "any person" standing to challenge FEC decisions and to seek judicial review of unfavorable FEC decisions. *Held:* Plaintiff had standing to challenge the FEC decision. His injury in fact was both concrete and particularized. [**Federal Election Commission v. Akins,** 524 U.S. 11 (1998)]

1) Comment

Akins can be read as undermining the requirement that the harm be particularized rather than generalized; after all, millions of voters suffered exactly the same injury as Akins, but the Court held that in light of the specific statute and the concreteness of the harm, injury in fact had been sufficiently alleged.

EXAM TIP   gilbert

On exams, it is important to remember that while a person will have standing only if an injury is concrete, a concrete injury can arise from harm to *aesthetic interests and environmental concerns*. But in these nonmonetary cases, you must be sure that some *actual harm to the plaintiff* is involved. For example, it is not enough for an environmentalist to allege that an agency decision will cause the "Puce Bandicoot" to become extinct; the plaintiff probably must also allege that he has watched the Puce Bandicoot in the past, has specific plans to travel to its habitat, and will be deprived of the pleasure of watching the animal in the future if the agency action is allowed to stand.

---

b. Causation and remediability [§744]

A plaintiff lacks standing unless the injury in fact is *"fairly traceable"* to the administrative action in question (the "causation" requirement) *and* the injury would *likely be remedied* by a judicial decision in his favor (the "remediability" requirement). The causation and remediability requirements often present problems when a plaintiff is suing an agency because the agency has granted *favorable* treatment to a third party. The plaintiff's injury might not be traceable only to this favorable action, and even if the court grants the requested relief, the plaintiff's injury might not be remedied.

(1) Illustration—tax exempt status

Plaintiff challenged an IRS ruling that hospitals could claim tax-exempt status even though they did not supply free medical services to the poor. Plaintiff's claim of standing was based on a denial of hospital services due to his inability to pay. The Supreme Court held that the plaintiff had no standing to sue since the denial of services might not have been *caused* by the IRS's ruling. Moreover, a change in IRS tax treatment of hospitals would not necessarily *remedy* the harm by guaranteeing the plaintiff free medical services (*i.e.*, the hospital might simply forgo its tax-exempt status). [**Simon v. Eastern Kentucky Welfare Rights Organization**, 426 U.S. 26 (1976)]

(2) Illustration—desegregation

Plaintiffs were parents of children attending public schools that were under court orders to desegregate. They alleged that the IRS had granted tax exemptions to segregated private schools. These exemptions encouraged the private schools to open and expand and thus tended to thwart the desegregation of public schools. The Court held that the plaintiffs did not have standing because they failed the causation test. The connection between the tax exemption to private schools and the desegregation of public schools was too tenuous. For example, it was not known what would happen if the exemptions were withdrawn (whether the schools would change their policy or whether parents would withdraw their children), nor was it sufficiently clear that the presence of the private schools made much difference to desegregation where the plaintiffs lived. [**Allen v. Wright,** 468 U.S. 737 (1984)]

(3) Illustration—endangered species

Agency A adopted, then revoked, a regulation requiring Agency B to consult with A about funding projects abroad that might jeopardize an endangered species. Plaintiff attacked the revocation of the rule, claiming environmental harm from destruction of the species. But B was not a party to the suit and denied that A had any authority over its actions. Because B would not be bound by a judgment against A, it is not likely that the lawsuit would remedy the injury to Plaintiff. Moreover, B played only a minor role in funding the projects; even if it did consult with A and was persuaded not to fund the project, it is not likely that the project would actually be stopped and hence unlikely that Plaintiff's injury would be remedied. [**Lujan v. Defenders of Wildlife,** *supra*, §742]

(4) Illustration—violation of reporting rules

Defendant failed to file various reporting forms about its toxic chemical storage and discharges. This violated a federal statute. Plaintiff sued under a citizen suit provision in the statute, claiming that its injury in fact was that its members had been denied information they needed to improve the local environment. However, Defendant brought its filings up to date before the action was commenced; thus the violation in the case was purely in the past. Plaintiff sought various remedies relating to the past violation of the statute, but the Court held that none of those remedies would serve to eliminate the harms caused by the late reporting. For example, Plaintiff sought civil penalties for the violation. However, because these would be paid to the United States Treasury, not to the plaintiffs, the penalties would not remedy the members' injury in fact. [**Steel Co. v. Citizens for a Better Environment,** *supra*, §732] In a later case, however, environmental plaintiffs who suffered injury in fact from mercury discharges into a river had standing to seek civil penalties that would be paid to the United States Treasury. The difference was that the plaintiffs in the second case were seeking to deter *future* misconduct, and the payment of civil penalties would be likely to deter future violations. [**Friends of the Earth v. Laidlaw Environmental Services, Inc.,** 528 U.S. 167 (2000)]

3. **Prudential Limitations [§745]**

In addition to the constitutional requirements of injury in fact, causation, and redressability, the Supreme Court has imposed prudential limitations on standing. It is important to keep in mind that because these limitations are merely prudential, Congress can eliminate the limitations by statute in order to allow persons to bring suit who otherwise would be precluded from doing so because of the prudential limitations. [*See, e.g.*, **Bennett v. Spear,** 520 U.S. 154 (1997)]

a. **Zone of interest [§746]**

A plaintiff seeking standing under the APA must establish that she arguably falls "within the zone of interests protected or regulated by the statute or constitutional guarantee in question." [**Association of Data Processing Service Organizations v. Camp,** *supra,* §740] Pursuant to this limitation, a court must carefully examine the specific provision in the statute under which the plaintiff claims its rights have been violated in order to ascertain *whether the plaintiff is among the group whose interests the statutory provision was intended to protect.* The cases have been inconsistent in their application of this test.

(1) **Lenient application [§747]**

In one case, banks were permitted to challenge a rule that allowed credit unions to sign up members from several different employers. This obviously worked to the competitive disadvantage of banks, and the Court found they were within the zone of interests. Language in the credit union statute required that employees have a "common bond of association," and this language suggested that Congress wished to limit the market in which credit unions could operate for the benefit of their competitors. [**National Credit Union Association v. First National Bank and Trust Co.,** 522 U.S. 479 (1998)] Several other cases have been similarly generous. [**Bennett v. Spear,** *supra*—provision in the Endangered Species Act requiring biological opinions was intended to protect persons who would be economically injured by actions taken to protect the habitat of endangered species; **Clarke v. Securities Industry Association,** 479 U.S. 388 (1987)—stockbrokers are within zone of interest of statute limiting bank branches]

(2) **Strict application [§748]**

In a case in which employees claimed an economic injury, however, the Supreme Court applied the zone of interests test quite strictly. [**Air Courier Conference v. American Postal Workers Union,** 498 U.S. 517 (1991)] In *Air Courier*, a statute gave the Postal Service a monopoly. A postal workers union complained that the Postal Service had allowed a new form of competition despite its statutory monopoly. This would reduce the Postal Service's need for workers, thus causing the union injury in fact. The Court held that the purpose of the monopoly statute was to give an economic advantage to the Postal Service to protect its revenue and allow it to serve all customers. Because Congress had not intended to protect postal *jobs*, the Union was outside the zone and could not sue. This decision seems far stricter than the cases discussed above.

Example: An agency failed to hold on-the-record hearings required by a particular statute. Court reporters sued the agency, claiming they were harmed economically because they had no transcripts to prepare. While the reporters were injured in fact, they were not within the zone of interests that the statute was intended to protect. Only parties to administrative action were within the zone of interests of that provision, not court reporters. [**Lujan v. National Wildlife Federation,** *supra,* §744—dictum]

---

b. Absence of nexus requirement in constitutional cases [§749]
In an action based on a constitutional violation, a plaintiff who can meet the requirements of injury in fact, causation, and remediability has standing even though there is no "nexus" (*i.e.,* logical connection) between the injury and the constitutional right being asserted. Note that such cases are brought under the Constitution rather than the APA, so the zone of interests test is inapplicable (the zone of interest test does require a "nexus" between the plaintiff's injury and the statute assertedly violated). [**Duke Power Co. v. North Carolina Environmental Study Group, Inc.,** 438 U.S. 59 (1978)]

Example: In *Duke Power Co.,* plaintiffs lived near a proposed nuclear power plant. They alleged that they would suffer injury in fact because of thermal pollution of lakes and because of low-level radioactive emissions from the plant. This gave them standing to challenge the constitutionality of a statute that limited the liability of the plant operators in the event of a catastrophic accident. The causation and remediability requirements were satisfied by a finding that if the statute were invalidated, the plant would not be built—thus preventing the alleged injuries in fact. *But note:* There was no connection between the environmental injuries and the constitutional claim (that the limitation of liability denied equal protection).

---

c. Jus tertii [§750]
In general, a person cannot assert the rights of another; the injured party must bring the lawsuit herself. This limit on third party standing is often referred to as jus tertii. [**Allen v. Wright,** *supra,* §744—A cannot sue to redress racial stigma imposed on B; **Warth v. Seldin,** 422 U.S. 490 (1975)—A cannot sue because city's exclusionary zoning harms B] The jus tertii rule is prudential rather than constitutional.

(1) Exceptions [§751]
The courts have made exceptions to the jus tertii rule. A plaintiff has

standing to assert the rights of another if the *plaintiff himself has suffered an injury* and the third party would find it difficult to assert her own rights, and the injury suffered by the plaintiff *adversely affects his relationship with the third party*. [**Singleton v. Wulff,** 428 U.S. 106 (1976)—doctor can assert patient's right to abortion]

(2) Associational standing [§752]

Associations are allowed to bring suit to redress injury to their members. Associational standing is very important because the cost of litigation against the government is so great that only well-funded and determined organizations can engage in it. Associational standing is permitted if:

(i) *Specific members would have standing* to sue in their own right;

(ii) *The interests* the association seeks to protect *are germane to its purposes*; and

(iii) *Neither the claim asserted nor the relief requested requires the participation of individual members* in the lawsuit.

[**Hunt v. Washington State Apple Advertising Commission,** 432 U.S. 333 (1977)] The third requirement means that associational standing is normally precluded in damage actions since this remedy requires individual participation. However, the third requirement is prudential—by statute Congress can authorize organizations to bring damage actions on behalf of their members. [**United Food & Commercial Workers Union v. Brown Group, Inc.,** 517 U.S. 544 (1996)]

d. Generalized grievances [§753]

A plaintiff cannot bring an action where the injury to him is generalized, rather than particularized. In other words, the class of persons harmed must be relatively small rather than extremely large. This is probably a prudential, rather than a constitutional, limitation so it can be dispensed with by a statute. [**Federal Election Commission v. Akins,** *supra*, §743—voter has standing under statute to challenge federal agency's failure to classify a group as a political association even though injury is widely shared]

4. Role of the APA [§754]

Section 702 of the APA provides: "A person suffering legal wrong because of agency action, or adversely affected or aggrieved by agency action within the meaning of a relevant statute, is entitled to judicial review thereof."

a. APA and prior law

Section 702 thus allows standing under the *"legal rights"* approach of prior law (*see supra*, §735). In addition, under the words "adversely affected or aggrieved by agency action," it incorporates the "statutory standing" approach of prior law (*see supra*, §§736-738).

b. Broad reach of APA

Section 702 is interpreted to reach the limits of Article III. It allows any person who can meet the constitutional requirements of *injury in fact, causation, and remediability* to sue. However, the statutory words "within the meaning of a relevant statute" are the source of the *prudential* requirement that the plaintiff fall within the *"zone of interests"* protected or regulated by the statute that plaintiff claims has been violated. (*See supra,* §§746-748.) [**Association of Data Processing Service Organizations v. Camp,** *supra,* §746; **Barlow v. Collins,** *supra,* §741]

5. Specificity [§755]

The plaintiff bears the burden of proof on each element of standing. If the defendant attacks the plaintiff's standing by a summary judgment motion, the plaintiff must make specific allegations as to precisely how she will be injured in fact (as well as to how she will meet the other requirements for standing). Otherwise the summary judgment motion will be granted, and the complaint will be dismissed. In addition, a plaintiff will not be allowed to challenge an entire "program," but only specific "agency action" (such as rulemaking or adjudication) that injures the particular plaintiff. [**Lujan v. National Wildlife Federation,** *supra,* §748]

---

e.g. **Example:** In **Lujan v. National Wildlife Federation,** *supra,* plaintiffs challenged the entire process of reclassification of thousands of different parcels of public land. However, they alleged specific injury in fact only with respect to a few of the parcels. The process of reclassifying the public lands is not "agency action" that can be challenged under the APA, any more than plaintiff could challenge the "weapons procurement program" of the Defense Department or the "drug interdiction program" of the Justice Department. Only specific agency action can be challenged and only by those who are harmed by the actions.

---

6. Standing in Particular Circumstances

a. Standing as a citizen or a taxpayer

(1) State law [§756]

In many states, taxpayers have standing as such to seek judicial review of the legality of state expenditures. This provides a convenient method by which a taxpayer can question many state government actions.

(2) Federal law

(a) Citizens [§757]

In *federal* court, a person's status as a citizen is *not* sufficient to create standing. There are two distinct reasons for this conclusion: (i) Standing requires allegations of some "palpable" or "concrete" injury in fact that is somehow more tangible than mere personal outrage at government action. This is a constitutional limitation derived from Article III. (ii) The plaintiff must allege some harm that is distinct to him, as opposed to injuries held in common with a large group of others (such as all the citizens of a state). This is probably a prudential limitation. [**Valley Forge Christian College v. Americans United for Separation of Church and State**, 454 U.S. 464 (1982); **Schlesinger v. Reservists Committee to Stop the War**, 418 U.S. 208 (1974)]

(b) Taxpayers

1) Background [§758]

Earlier Supreme Court cases held that the interest of a federal taxpayer in spending or appropriation measures was "too remote" to establish standing. [**Frothingham v. Mellon**, 262 U.S. 447 (1923)]

2) Establishment Clause [§759]

However, the *Frothingham* rule was later relaxed to allow a taxpayer standing to challenge a federal *spending or appropriations measure* provided the taxpayer had a *personal stake in the outcome*. This requirement is met if the plaintiff can establish a "nexus" between his status as a taxpayer and the claim sought to be adjudicated. [**Flast v. Cohen**, 392 U.S. 83 (1968)]

a) Two-pronged test [§760]

The nexus required for taxpayer standing is established *only if* (i) the challenged federal action is *based on the government's power to tax and spend* for the general welfare, *and* (ii) the government's action is challenged as contrary to a *specific constitutional limitation* on the taxing and spending power.

Example: In *Flast*, the Supreme Court allowed a taxpayer to challenge a federal program granting benefits to parochial schools as a violation of the Establishment Clause of the First Amendment. Standing was found since the aid program was enacted under Congress's general taxing and spending power *and* was alleged to violate a specific constitutional limitation.

---

b) Rule narrowly applied [§761]

Recent cases on taxpayer standing make it clear that the rule in *Flast* is to be very narrowly interpreted.

> **Example:** Pursuant to a statute relating to disposition of surplus government property, an agency donated an unneeded federal building to a church school. This action was attacked by taxpayers as a violation of the Establishment Clause. The Court held that the plaintiff lacked standing. *Flast* is inapplicable because the decision challenged was an executive rather than legislative decision and also because the constitutional power being exerted was the Property Clause [U.S. Const. art. IV, §3, cl. 2] rather than the power to tax and spend for the general welfare. [**Valley Forge Christian College v. Americans United for Separation of Church and State,** *supra*, §757]

> **Example:** A federal taxpayer challenged statutes that allowed the CIA not to publish a regular statement of its receipts and disbursements, alleging that the statutes violated Article I, Section 9, Clause 7 of the Constitution. Standing was rejected on the ground that plaintiff's attack was concerned not with the *validity* of expenditures (as required by *Flast*), but only with the *secrecy* of the expenditures. [**United States v. Richardson,** 418 U.S. 166 (1974)]

EXAM TIP	gilbert

If you see a question on your exam where a taxpayer is outraged by an agency's spending, be sure to remember the distinction between state and federal courts. Many **state courts** hold that a state taxpayer **has standing** to challenge state spending. This is **not so in federal court**. In federal court, the requirement of a concrete injury in fact is much more onerous. Mere outrage is not sufficient injury, and the injury to a taxpayer from having tax funds wasted is too remote. So far, the only exception to this rule arises where a taxpayer challenges a *spending or appropriations measure* that violates the *Establishment Clause*.

b.   Legislative standing [§762]

Members of Congress lack standing to challenge the constitutionality of legislation passed by Congress that diminishes their power vis-a-vis the President. [**Raines v. Byrd,** 521 U.S. 811 (1997)] In *Raines*, several members of Congress challenged the Line Item Veto Act, which allowed the President to veto particular appropriations without vetoing the whole bill. The Court held that their injury was neither personal to them nor sufficiently concrete to permit them to sue. Note, however, that a year after *Raines*, the President vetoed an appropriation, and beneficiaries of that appropriation successfully challenged the Line Item Veto Act. [**Clinton v. City of New York,** 524 U.S. 417 (1998); *see supra*, §25, for further discussion of this case]

c. **Statutory standing [§763]**

Congress cannot grant standing to persons who lack the necessary "concrete" injury in fact. [**Lujan v. Defenders of Wildlife,** *supra,* §744]

Example: A provision in the Endangered Species Act allows "any person" to sue to enjoin any agency alleged to be in violation of the Act. Plaintiff sued the Secretary of Interior, alleging a failure to enforce the Act against federal activities abroad that jeopardized endangered species. However, Plaintiff was unable to establish injury in fact. The statute purporting to give Plaintiff the right to sue violated the "case or controversy" limitation on the power of the federal courts. [**Lujan v. Defenders of Wildlife,** *supra*]

---

(1) Prudential limits

Congress can pass a statute that allows a plaintiff to sue despite failure to meet the *prudential* limitations on standing. [**Federal Election Commission v. Akins,** *supra,* §753] Moreover, Congress can define a specific substantive right that did not previously exist and then grant plaintiffs standing to enforce that right. [*See, e.g.,* **Trafficante v. Metropolitan Life Insurance Co.,** 409 U.S. 205 (1972)—right to live in an integrated neighborhood] For example, the Freedom of Information Act (discussed in §§483-524, *supra*) gives any person a right to obtain government documents, then gives that person a right to sue if the government fails to provide the document. Similarly, Congress can create standing for a private plaintiff who, if he wins, gets a cash bounty (the so-called qui tam action). [**Vermont Agency of Natural Resources v. United States *ex rel.* Stevens,** 529 U.S. 765 (2000)—qui tam statute assigns to private plaintiff federal government's right to sue for damages for injury done to the government] But Congress cannot provide standing for persons who lack any concrete injury. [**Lujan v. Defenders of Wildlife,** *supra*]

B. The Timing of Judicial Review

1. **In General [§764]**

Even if a plaintiff has standing to seek review of administrative action, the case must be brought to court at the right time. The action challenged must be *final,* the case must be *ripe,* and the plaintiff must have *exhausted administrative remedies.* In addition, the plaintiff must avoid the *doctrine of primary jurisdiction,* which may route the case to an agency rather than to court.

2. **Final Order Rule [§765]**

A court normally declines to review agency rulings unless they are "final." Thus various decisions made during the course of rulemaking or adjudication are not reviewable until the matter is finally concluded at the agency level. To be reviewable, the action must mark the consummation of the agency's decisionmaking process (rather than being merely tentative or interlocutory). Moreover, the action must be one by which rights or obligations have been determined or from which legal consequences will flow. [**Bennett v. Spear,** *supra,* §745]

a. Statutory requirements [§766]

The final order rule is frequently set forth in agency enabling statutes that provide for judicial review, and also in both state and federal APAs. [*See* 1981 Model State APA §5-102] APA section 704 provides:

> Agency action made reviewable by statute and *final agency action* for which there is no other adequate remedy in a court are subject to judicial review. A preliminary, procedural, or intermediate agency action or ruling not directly reviewable is subject to review on the review of the final agency action.

> Except as otherwise expressly required by statute, agency action otherwise final is final for the purposes of this section whether or not there has been presented or determined an application for a declaratory order, for any form of reconsideration, or, unless the agency otherwise requires by rule and provides that the action meanwhile is inoperative, for an appeal to a superior agency authority.

b. Leading case [§767]

The FTC issued a complaint against Oil Co. because the FTC "had reason to believe" that the statute had been violated. Issuance of the complaint was not immediately reviewable in court. Although Oil Co. had unsuccessfully moved before the FTC to dismiss the complaint (alleging that the agency had no "reason to believe" that a violation had occurred) and thus had exhausted its administrative remedy, the Court held that review was still barred by the final order rule of APA section 704. [**FTC v. Standard Oil Co. of California,** 449 U.S. 232 (1980)]

(1) Rationale

The Court indicated that intervention at this stage would deny the FTC a chance to correct its own mistakes and apply its expertise. It would lead to inefficient and perhaps unnecessary piecemeal review. It would delay ultimate resolution of the controversy. Finally, it would allow every respondent to turn the FTC from prosecutor into defendant before adjudication concludes.

c. Motions for reconsideration [§768]

Normally, if a party files a motion for reconsideration of an agency's order, the motion renders the order nonfinal. As a result, judicial review of the order is postponed until the reconsideration motion is disposed of. [**ICC v. Brotherhood** of **Locomotive Engineers,** *supra,* §728] *Exception:* This rule does not apply in deportation cases because Congress provided for separate appeals to the court of appeals of (i) decisions of the Board of Immigration Appeals ("BIA") and (ii) motions to reconsider BIA decisions. Consequently, the period for appeal of BIA decisions is not tolled despite the filing of a motion for reconsideration. [**Stone v. INS,** 514 U.S. 386 (1995)]

d.   Exception—irreparable injury [§769]

Despite section 704, courts review preliminary agency action when the *harm to the person seeking review outweighs the harm to the administrative process* from permitting such review. [*See also* 1981 Model State APA §5-103]

(1)   Health and safety [§770]

When agency action will endanger public health or safety, judicial review is immediately available.

Example: An agency refused to suspend DDT from sale as a registered pesticide pending a hearing on the matter, despite strong evidence of imminent health danger to the public. The refusal to suspend was immediately reviewable. [**Environmental Defense Fund v. Hardin,** 428 F.2d 1093 (D.C. Cir. 1970)]

(2)   Economic hardship [§771]

When agency action goes into effect pending a hearing, and would impose *severe economic hardship,* judicial review is immediately available.

Example—rate approval: Plaintiff sought review of Board's interim approval of a new shipping rate structure. It alleged that it would be driven out of business unless the new rates were enjoined pending a hearing. To protect the plaintiff from irreparable injury, the court reviewed the Board's action. [**Isbrandtsen Co. v. United States,** 211 F.2d 51 (D.C. Cir. 1954)]

Example—license suspension: An agency suspended an airline's license, thus grounding its planes, pending a hearing on revocation of the license. The airline is permitted immediate review of the suspension decision. [**Nevada Airlines, Inc. v. Bond,** 622 F.2d 1017 (9th Cir. 1980)]

(3)   Procedural disputes [§772]

Generally a dispute about proper adjudicatory procedure cannot be reviewed until the agency issues a final order. There may be an exception if the procedural flaw is so serious and so manifest that the proceeding plainly could not produce a valid agency decision. In such cases, the advantages of immediate review, in preventing a waste of private and agency resources, outweighs the disadvantage of departing from the final order rule. [**Pepsico v. FTC,** 472 F.2d 179 (2d Cir. 1972), *cert. denied,* 414 U.S. 876 (1973)—failure to join indispensable parties]

e. Exception—unreasonable delay [§773]

A court can review an *agency's failure to decide* a matter presented to it despite the final order rule.

(1) APA provisions [§774]

APA section 555(b) provides: "With due regard for the convenience and necessity of the parties and their representatives, and within a reasonable time, each agency shall proceed to conclude a matter presented to it." And section 706(1) provides that a reviewing court shall "compel agency action unlawfully withheld or unreasonably delayed." [*See* **Cutler v. Hayes,** 818 F.2d 879 (D.C. Cir 1987)—25-year delay in determining efficacy of over-the-counter drugs; agency must justify delay especially because health is at stake]

(2) Remedy usually denied [§775]

A court order to an agency to speed up processing of a matter may force the agency to act before it is prepared to do so. Moreover, it may divert limited agency resources from matters having a higher priority. Thus, the remedy is rarely granted. In deciding whether to grant this remedy, a court will consider factors such as the degree of prejudice to the plaintiff from delay and whether the plaintiff's interest concerns health or safety or whether it is merely financial. [**Heckler v. Day,** 467 U.S. 104 (1984); **Telecommunications Research & Action Center v. FCC,** 750 F.2d 70 (D.C. Cir. 1984)]

Example: The Supreme Court reversed a lower court's order to the Social Security Administration to speed up the processing of disability claims in Vermont. The Court held that this decision should be reserved to Congress (which was responsible for supplying the Administration with the resources to handle its caseload). The Court observed that the order would force the Social Security Administration to switch resources from other states to Vermont, thus making the national problem worse. [**Heckler v. Day,** *supra*]

When answering an exam question dealing with a person or organization seeking judicial review of an agency action before the agency has issued a final order, your analysis should include a discussion of the final order rule. You should explain that generally the courts will not grant judicial review of an agency action until the matter has been concluded by the agency. You should then determine whether the action occurring in the question falls under one of the exceptions to the final order rule. Courts will permit judicial review of an agency action *if the harm to the person seeking review outweighs the harm to the administrative process* from permitting the review. In deciding this issue, courts will look to see whether the agency action will *endanger the public health or safety, impose severe economic hardship on the party affected by the action, or the agency has unreasonably delayed in deciding the matter*. Even when considering these factors, remember that courts are often more inclined to review a public health or safety issue sooner than one that merely produces a financial effect. Generally, the economic harm must *truly be severe*.

3. Ripeness [§776]

The court will not review agency action unless it is "ripe" for review. The typical ripeness case involves agency action, such as a rule, that has *not yet been specifically applied* to the plaintiff. Nevertheless, the action is causing immediate problems for the plaintiff who seeks review before the agency action has actually been applied to her.

a. Purpose of requirement [§777]

The ripeness doctrine is designed to avoid litigating in the abstract—*i.e.*, before the administrative policy has been applied in a concrete way to plaintiff. *Rationale:* The reviewing court can do a better job if it sees how the administrative policy is applied in practice.

(1) Ripeness as constitutional limitation [§778]

The "ripeness" doctrine also has constitutional dimensions as part of the requirement that federal courts may hear only cases or controversies—not abstract or hypothetical matters. [*See* **Lujan v. Defenders of Wildlife**, *supra*, §763—indefinite plans to visit site where government action would jeopardize endangered species constitutes harm to plaintiff that is not sufficiently imminent to be ripe for review; **Laird v. Tatum**, 408 U.S. 1 (1972)—Army's domestic surveillance program not ripe for review where plaintiffs could not show any specific and present harm] In administrative law cases, however, the requirement is usually prudential rather than constitutional.

b. Test for ripeness [§779]

The court must consider two factors in determining whether an administrative decision is ripe for review: (i) the *"fitness of the issues"* for immediate review and (ii) the *"hardship to the parties"* that would result if the court withheld review. [**Abbott Laboratories v. Gardner**, *supra*, §705]

(1) Fitness for review [§780]

In weighing the fitness of the issues for review, the court inquires whether the questions presented are of *law*, rather than fact or discretion. Also, it considers whether either the reviewing court or the agency would *benefit from postponement* of review until the agency action or policy has assumed a final or more concrete form. In particular, it is important that the agency action be *"final."* The court also weighs the extent to which the action is *formal or informal* and whether it emanated from the top level of the agency, rather than from the staff.

---

e.g. **Example:** An FDA rule required makers of color additives to submit to an FDA inspection of their facilities and formulas. If the makers refused, the FDA would stop "certifying" the products, which would shut down the facilities. The Court found that the rule was unripe for pre-enforcement review because it could better decide the legal issues in the framework of a concrete challenge in which it could assess the FDA's enforcement problems and the risk of disclosure of trade secrets. [**Toilet Goods Association v. Gardner,** 387 U.S. 167 (1967)]

---

e.g. **Example:** The Sierra Club challenged a "forest plan" for a large forest that would permit clear-cutting trees. However, before the plan could be implemented, the Forest Service had to propose a specific site plan and allow a public hearing on that plan. The Court held that the forest plan was not ripe for review because both the court and the agency would benefit from postponement. The agency could refine the forest service plan in the context of considering a specific site plan, and the court could better consider the challenge by ruling on the legality of a specific site plan. [**Ohio Forestry Association v. Sierra Club,** *supra*, §732]

---

(2) Hardship to the parties [§781]

Plaintiffs must demonstrate hardship from a deferral of judicial review.

---

e.g. **Example:** An FDA rule required the brand name on drug labels to be accompanied *every time* it was used by the generic or common name of the chemical. If a manufacturer failed to comply with the regulation, the Attorney General could confiscate its products and seek criminal penalties. Plaintiff argued that this regulation exceeded FDA powers and sought an injunction and declaratory judgment. The hardship was that the plaintiffs were in a dilemma: either comply with the rule (which meant destroying labels and printing new ones, which was costly) or defy it (which entailed a risk of confiscation of their products as misbranded, of damages to goodwill, and even of criminal sanctions). The Court held the matter ripe for review. [**Abbott Laboratories v. Gardner,** *supra*, §779]

---

e.g. **Example:** In an earlier case, the Court held ripe FCC rules banning certain contracts between licensees and networks. The hardship from delaying review arose from the fact that the stations were canceling their contracts with the networks in reliance on the rules. A further delay would destroy the networks' business. [**Columbia Broadcasting Co. v. United States,** 316 U.S. 407 (1942)]

e.g. **Example:** In the *Sierra Club* case, *supra*, §780, the Court held that delaying review would cause no legal or practical harm to the plaintiff. Sierra Club would have to challenge numerous site plans instead of a single forest plan, which is obviously more expensive and less convenient, but the Court held this was not a sufficient showing of hardship.

(a) Benefit-creating programs [§782]

The Court distinguished duty-creating rules, as in *Abbott Laboratories,* from programs that confer benefits. Pre-enforcement review is not available to challenge regulations adopted under a benefit-creating program since the rule does not require applicants to do anything immediately and because the applicant might be rejected by the agency for some other reason. [**Reno v. Catholic Social Services, Inc.,** 509 U.S. 43 (1993)—no pre-enforcement review of rules for undocumented aliens seeking to qualify under an amnesty program]

c. Review of informal administrative action [§783]

As noted above, the *degree of formality* of the administrative action is important in determining ripeness. Early authority suggested that informal actions were never ripe for review in advance of actual application. [**International Longshoremen's Union v. Boyd,** 347 U.S. 222 (1954)—informal immigration enforcement policy; **Helco Products Co. v. McNutt,** 137 F.2d 681 (D.C. Cir. 1943)—advisory letter from FDA official] Today, the trend is in favor of reviewing informal action, such as interpretive rules and policy statements, before they are actually applied, if plaintiff shows *hardship from delay* of review and the rule is not subject to reconsideration. Note that these rules are adopted without notice and comment procedures, so the court has a less complete record on which to review the rule.

(1) Interpretive rule [§784]

The courts will review interpretive rules issued by the top level of an agency in final form upon a showing of hardship to parties who are subject to regulation. [**National Automatic Laundry & Dry Cleaning Council v. Shultz,** 443 F.2d 689 (D.C. Cir. 1971)—challenge of minimum wage ruling in letter sent by agency head]

(2) Policy statement [§785]

Policy statements are nonbinding statements indicating how discretion should be exercised. Nevertheless, the legal issues presented by policy statements can be immediately reviewed on a sufficient showing of hardship if they appear not to be subject to revision. [**Better Government Association v. Department of State,** 780 F.2d 86 (D.C. Cir. 1986)—Justice Department guidelines for fee waivers in favor of public interest groups requesting information under FOIA]

(3) Enforcement policy [§786]

The enforcement policy of an agency may be immediately reviewable where there is hardship. For example, the SEC informed management that it would "take no action" if management omitted from proxy statements a particular shareholder proposal. The issue was found to be immediately reviewable because otherwise it would not be voted on at the shareholders' meeting. [**Medical Committee for Human Rights v. SEC,** 432 F.2d 659 (D.C. Cir. 1970), *vacated as moot,* 404 U.S. 403 (1972)] However, when the "no action" letter came from SEC staff instead of the SEC, the result was contra. [**Kixmiller v. SEC,** 492 F.2d 641 (D.C. Cir. 1974)]

d. Statutory time limits for review [§787]

In many statutes, Congress requires that rules be reviewed within a short period (*e.g.,* 90 days) after adoption and *precludes any review at a later time.* Can a party be excused from seeking review during the period if the rule might not have been ripe for review during that period? The courts have held that this is no excuse, unless it is clear beyond a doubt from existing precedent that the rule would have been held unripe. Otherwise (unless the party can show that some event occurred after the period which created a new basis for challenge), judicial review is precluded after the period. [**Eagle-Picher Industries v. EPA,** 759 F.3d 905 (D.C. Cir. 1985)]

e. Statutory preclusion of pre-enforcement review [§788]

Congress can, of course, preclude pre-enforcement review. The Court found such preclusion to be implied in the Federal Mine Safety Act. [**Thunder Basin Coal Co. v. Reich,** 510 U.S. 200 (1994)]

(1) Facts

The Federal Mine Safety Act provides that miners can name representatives to participate in safety inspections. Although the miners at Coal Co.'s mine were nonunion, the miners named union officials to represent them. An agency rule permitted union officials to be representatives even at nonunion mines. Coal Co. did not wish to allow union officials into its mine. Therefore, the company challenged the legality of the regulation in district court, although the regulation had not yet been applied to Coal Co. Because the Act provided elaborate procedures whereby this issue could be litigated before the agency, and because the legislative history indicated that Congress was concerned about undue delays, the Court held that pre-enforcement review was precluded. [**Thunder Basin Coal Co. v. Reich,** *supra*]

(2) Implications [§789]

Note that Coal Co. was caught in just the type of bind that permitted pre-enforcement review in *Abbott Laboratories*: It could either allow the union representatives to participate in safety inspections (thus giving the union access to company information and a toe hold among the employees), or refuse to allow them to participate (thus opening itself up to large penalties for every day of noncompliance). *Thunder Basin* is difficult to distinguish from *Abbott Laboratories* because in the latter case, the Court allowed pre-enforcement review even though there were elaborate administrative and judicial remedies available to challenge citations for misbranded drugs. Together with **Reno v. Catholic Social Services,** *supra,* the *Thunder Basin* case may signal a judicial retreat from the *Abbott Laboratories* principle.

EXAM TIP — gilbert

Be sure that you don't confuse a question dealing with ripeness with one dealing with the final order rule. The tests may seem similar at first glance, but remember that the test for ripeness turns on two factors: (i) *the fitness of the issues for immediate review;* and (ii) *the hardship to the parties that would result if the court withheld review.* In determining whether an issue is fit for review, consider whether the questions presented are of *law* as opposed to fact or discretion, and whether the reviewing court or the agency would *benefit from postponement of review* until the agency action has become final or more concrete. Also, look to see whether the agency action is *formal or informal*, but don't forget that an *informal action may be reviewed if it results in hardship to the parties*. Other situations demonstrating hardship include actions that place a person or entity between "a rock and a hard place" (*e.g.,* compliance with the action would be very costly, but defiance would result in suspension of business or confiscation of the affected inventory), and situations where deferral of review threatens a business's actual existence.

---

4. Exhaustion of Administrative Remedies [§790]

As a general rule, judicial review is not available until the plaintiff has *exhausted all administrative remedies* whereby the controversy might be resolved at the agency level. [**Myers v. Bethlehem Shipbuilding Corp.,** 303 U.S. 41 (1938)—in a challenge to agency jurisdiction, agency must resolve question before court will decide it]

a. Purpose of exhaustion rule [§791]

The exhaustion requirement has two purposes: protecting agency autonomy and promoting judicial efficiency. [**McCarthy v. Madigan,** 503 U.S. 140 (1992)]

(1) Agency autonomy

Agencies, not courts, should have primary responsibility for the programs that Congress has charged them to administer. Exhaustion concerns apply with particular force when the action under review involves exercise of the agency's discretionary power or application of its expertise. Moreover, an agency ought to have an opportunity to correct its own mistakes before it is hauled into federal court. And exhaustion applies with special force if immediate judicial review would cause deliberate flouting of agency procedures. [**McCarthy v. Madigan,** *supra*]

(2) Judicial efficiency

Exhaustion promotes judicial efficiency because the problem may be solved at the agency level; thus the court may never have to deal with it. Moreover, exhaustion may produce a useful record for subsequent judicial consideration, which is important especially in a complex or technical factual context. [**McCarthy v. Madigan,** *supra*]

b. Exhaustion under the APA [§792]

APA section 704, which is quoted in §766, *supra*, provides that agency action is reviewable without an appeal to a superior agency authority, unless "the agency otherwise requires [such an appeal] by rule and provides that the action meanwhile is inoperative." This provision states an important exception to the doctrine of exhaustion of remedies. [**Darby v. Cisneros,** 509 U.S. 137 (1993)]

(1) Effect of *Darby* [§793]

As a result of section 704, a person adversely affected by an ALJ's decision can secure judicial review without first appealing the ALJ's decision to the agency heads—unless the agency has adopted a rule (i) requiring an appeal to the agency heads, and (ii) providing that the ALJ's decision is inoperative until the agency head appeal is completed. [**Darby v. Cisneros,** *supra*]

(2) Implications of *Darby* [§794]

Darby might mean that the doctrine of exhaustion of remedies is exclusively a creature of statute in cases brought under the APA. If so, this would suggest that the many exceptions to exhaustion (*see supra*, §§744 *et seq.*) are inapplicable. Arguably, once the agency adopts a rule of the type described in APA section 704, exhaustion of the remedy of appealing to the agency heads will be required even if one of the common law exceptions to the exhaustion doctrine would otherwise apply. [*See* **Volvo GM v. United States Department of Labor,** 118 F.3d 205 (4th Cir. 1997)—court lacks authority to excuse a failure to exhaust remedies in a case brought under the APA]

c. Effect—application of exhaustion rule may preclude review [§795]

The exhaustion rule ordinarily has the effect of *delaying* judicial review because the court orders the appellant to return to the agency and attempt to obtain relief there first. However, when the petitioner can no longer return to the agency (*e.g.*, because of failure to exercise the right of appeal within the agency or failure to raise a timely objection), application of the exhaustion rule may *preclude* judicial review.

Example: A Selective Service registrant failed to make a personal appearance before the draft board or to make an appeal from his classification. As a defense to the criminal proceeding against him for refusal to submit to induction, he alleged that he should have been classified as a conscientious objector. The Court held that his failure to exhaust the available administrative remedies precluded judicial review of the mistaken classification. [**McGee v. United States,** 402 U.S. 479 (1971)] *Note*: An earlier case *waiving* the exhaustion rule under similar circumstances [**McKart v. United States,** 395 U.S. 185 (1969)] was distinguished in *McGee*: McGee's claims were factual in nature, the expertise and discretion of the agency were involved, excusing exhaustion might lead to a flouting of the system, and the appeal could have had some effect.

---

d. **Exceptions to exhaustion rule [§796]**

The rule of exhaustion of remedies is usually a matter of judicial discretion and, in appropriate cases, the courts may rule that it does not apply. However, if a statute specifically calls for exhaustion of remedies, judicial discretion to excuse exhaustion is more narrowly circumscribed. [**Booth v. Churner,** 531 U.S. 956 (2001)—no exceptions to exhaustion rule where a statute specifically requires exhaustion] In general, administrative remedies need not be pursued if the litigant's interests in immediate judicial review outweigh the government's interests in the efficiency or administrative autonomy that the exhaustion doctrine is designed to further. Application of this balancing principle is "intensely practical . . . because attention is directed to both the nature of the claim presented and the characteristics of the particular administrative procedure provided." [**McCarthy v. Madigan,** *supra*, §791; 1981 Model State APA §5-107(3)]

(1) Irreparable injury [§797]

The most important factor is the *severity* and the *type* of plaintiff's injury. Mere litigation cost and inconvenience is not sufficient. [**Myers v. Bethlehem Shipbuilding Corp.,** *supra*, §790] However, if the economic burden would be severe and irreparable, a court may be moved to grant review.

Example: A federally regulated utility sought review of an order of a state regulatory agency that asserted that it had jurisdiction over the plaintiff. The costs of exhausting the state remedy would be very severe and would be passed on to utility customers. Moreover, it seemed plain to the court that the state agency lacked jurisdiction. Exhaustion was not required. [**Public Utilities Commission v. United Fuel Gas Co.,** 317 U.S. 456 (1943)]

(2) Futility of exhausting remedies [§798]

Exhaustion of remedies will often be waived if it would be futile to pursue the remedy because plaintiff could not possibly obtain relief.

Example: Exhaustion of remedies is not required when the administrative remedy is useless because the agency is deadlocked. [**Order of Railway Conductors v. Swan,** 329 U.S. 520 (1947)]

Example: The Selective Service System ("SSS") revoked deferments of students engaged in a constitutionally protected demonstration. The students did not exhaust remedies, but it would be futile because the head of SSS already declared that there would be no reversals. Also, irreparable injury was involved: The SSS's reclassifications chilled free speech. Thus, exhaustion was not required. [**Wolff v. Selective Service Board No. 16,** 372 F.2d 817 (2d Cir. 1967)]

(3) Inadequate remedies [§799]

An "inadequate" remedy need not be exhausted.

Example: Where the administrative remedy required presentation of a claim to Federal Savings & Loan Insurance Corporation ("FSLIC") before it is sued on in state court, the FSLIC remedy was inadequate because it contained no reasonable time limit. As a result, a claim could be "relegated to a 'black hole' from which it may not emerge before the statute of limitations" has run. [**Coit Independence Joint Venture v. FSLIC,** 489 U.S. 561 (1989)]

Example: Plaintiff was a federal prisoner suing prison guards under *Bivens* for Eighth Amendment violations. (*See supra,* §693.) He failed to exhaust internal prison remedies. The Court held that exhaustion was not required because the remedy was inadequate. First, it did not provide for money damages, so it would be useless to compel exhaustion. Second, the prison procedure had such short deadlines that many prisoners would undoubtedly fail to meet them and would thus lose their right to go to court. Third, the prison grievance process would not generate a formal factual record of the sort that would assist the court. [**McCarthy v. Madigan,** *supra*]

(4) Unauthorized procedure [§800]

Where a plaintiff contends that the administrative procedure is not authorized by the governing statute, a court may not require the plaintiff to exhaust that remedy. [**Allen v. Grand Central Aircraft Co.,** 347 U.S. 535 (1954); **Athlone Industries, Inc. v. CPSC,** 707 F.2d 1485 (D.C. Cir. 1983)]

(5) Constitutional questions [§801]

Judicial review is more likely to be available without exhaustion when the plaintiff raises constitutional issues, rather than other legal issues, since it is unlikely that the agency can grant relief on a constitutional question.

(a) Procedural issues [§802]

If a plaintiff claims there is a constitutional defect in the agency's procedure, and if this claim can be resolved by the court without factual inquiry, it may excuse a failure to exhaust remedies.

1) Application—procedural due process

Plaintiff claimed he was entitled under due process to a hearing before, rather than after, disability benefits were cut off. The constitutional issue was judicially reviewed even though the plaintiff had not exhausted remedies (by going through the post-termination hearing). Further agency proceedings would not be helpful to the court in resolving the due process issue, and further delays would be very harmful to the plaintiff. Moreover, the constitutional issue was "collateral" to (as opposed to being entwined with) the substantive issue of whether the plaintiff was entitled to benefits. [**Mathews v. Eldridge,** *supra,* §142; **Andrade v. Lauer,** 729 F.2d 1475 (D.C. Cir. 1984)—constitutional issue collateral to the merits]

(b) Civil rights statute [§803]

Under 42 U.S.C. section 1983, a federal court has jurisdiction to remedy a state's violation of constitutional rights. The plaintiff in a section 1983 action does *not* have to exhaust state administrative or judicial remedies before bringing suit. [**Patsy v. Board of Regents,** 454 U.S. 813 (1982)—victim of discrimination on basis of age and sex by state university need not exhaust state antidiscrimination remedy or university grievance procedure]

(c) But note—exhaustion required if nonconstitutional grounds [§804]

In many constitutional cases, the courts insist that remedies be exhausted. This is required because the plaintiff may prevail on a *nonconstitutional* ground, and then the court could avoid the constitutional issue.

> **e.g.** **Example—constitutionality of underlying statute:** Exhaustion is usually required when the plaintiff challenges the constitutionality of the statute that delegates authority to the agency, since the dispute may be resolved on nonconstitutional grounds. [**Aircraft & Diesel Equipment Corp. v. Hirsch,** 331 U.S. 752 (1947)] However, if the only remaining issue is a constitutional one and the decision would not be facilitated by prior agency consideration, exhaustion may not be required. [**Weinberger v. Salfi,** 422 U.S. 749 (1975)]

e. Issue exhaustion [§805]

Normally a court will review only issues that the petitioner has first raised before the agency. Thus a litigant is required to exhaust issues as well as administrative remedies. In general, this requirement makes sense because it allows the agency to consider the issue first, perhaps granting relief to the litigant and thus rendering judicial review unnecessary. Even if the agency does not grant relief, the agency's consideration of the issue will inform the court's subsequent decision. Moreover, since courts defer to administrative judgments on most issues, the agency must have the opportunity to decide the issue first so that the court will have an agency decision to defer to; allowing the litigant to raise the issue in court for the first time would permit circumvision of the deference rules. If a statute requires issue exhaustion, the court is unlikely to permit any exceptions; but if issue exhaustion is not required by statute or regulation, a court may permit exceptions that are similar to the exceptions to the exhaustion of remedies requirement. (*See supra,* §§795-799.)

(1) Application—Social Security cases

In Social Security cases, private parties are often unrepresented by counsel and may be quite unsophisticated. The hearings before an ALJ are nonadversarial; the government is not represented by counsel and the ALJ is supposed to develop the record and raise appropriate issues. Exhaustion of remedies in Social Security cases (by appealing to the Appeals Council) is required by statute, but issue exhaustion is not required by either statute or regulation. Moreover, the agency did not warn claimants that they had to exhaust all issues before the Appeals Council. Under these unusual circumstances, the Supreme Court allowed a Social Security claimant who had exhausted remedies to raise a new issue in court. [**Sims v. Apfel,** 530 U.S. 103 (2000)]

f. State law [§806]

State courts have applied the exhaustion of remedies rule even less rigorously than have the federal courts.

(1) Application—jurisdiction of agency

Charges were brought against a police officer who had the right to a hearing but sought judicial review first, contending that the state lacked jurisdiction to fire him. The court held that where the plaintiff's objection goes to the jurisdiction of the agency, he may seek review without first exhausting administrative remedies. [**Ward v. Keenan,** 70 A.2d 77 (N.J. 1949)]

(2) Application—questions of law

And exhaustion of remedies was not required by a state court with respect to questions of law. [**New Jersey Civil Service Association v. State,** 443 A.2d 1070 (N.J. 1982); **Nolan v. Fitzpatrick,** 89 A.2d 13 (N.J. 1952)]

EXAM TIP   **gilbert**

Although the exhaustion rule may appear to be overcome by its many exceptions, if an exhaustion issue comes up in an exam question, you still need to go through a *complete discussion of the rule before applying one of its exceptions*. State the purposes of the exhaustion rule (*i.e.,* agency autonomy and judicial efficiency), and then see if one of the exceptions apply.

CHECKLIST OF EXCEPTIONS TO THE EXHAUSTION RULE   **gilbert**

THE FOLLOWING MAY ALLOW FOR JUDICIAL REVIEW WITHOUT EXHAUSTION:

- ☑ Irreparable Injury (consider severity and type)
- ☑ Futility of Exhausting Remedies (*e.g.,* agency deadlocked)
- ☑ Inadequate Remedies
- ☑ Unauthorized Procedure
- ☑ Constitutional Questions
  - Procedural issues
  - Civil rights statute

---

5. Primary Jurisdiction [§807]

Frequently, both an agency and a court have jurisdiction to try a case. Plaintiff generally wants the case to be tried in court whereas the defendant wants the agency to go first. If the doctrine of primary jurisdiction is applicable, the court must allow the *agency to go first* and the matter will return to court only in connection with judicial review of the agency action.

a. Purposes of doctrine [§808]

The original purpose of the doctrine was to assure uniformity of decisions: if the matter is tried before an agency there will be a single uniform rule applied to all litigants, whereas courts might produce conflicting results for similarly situated parties. [**Texas & Pacific Railway v. Abilene Cotton Oil Co.,** 204 U.S.

426 (1907)] Later cases added an additional purpose: If the matter is highly technical, it is better to have it resolved by an expert and specialist agency rather than by an inexpert and generalist court. [**United States v. Western Pacific Railroad,** 352 U.S. 59 (1956)]

---

e.g. **Example—uniformity:** Shipper sues railroad to recover "excessive charges." A statute appeared to give shipper the choice of suing in court or before the ICC. The Court held that only the ICC has power to grant the relief. Otherwise different courts would produce different decisions about the fairness of a single railroad rate. [**Texas & Pacific Railway v. Abilene Cotton Oil Co.,** *supra*]

---

e.g. **Example—expertise:** Shipper sues railroad to find out whether bomb casings fit the high tariff rate for bombs or the lower rate for gasoline-filled drums. The Court held that the ICC must decide the case because it involves expert knowledge about the safety procedures necessary for transporting each product. [**United States v. Western Pacific Railroad,** *supra*]

---

b. **Factors militating against primary agency jurisdiction [§809]**
There is a tendency not to apply the doctrine of primary jurisdiction where the court would be a more appropriate forum. Thus, a plaintiff has been allowed a judicial, rather than administrative, trial where the issue presents a *question of law* (*e.g.,* interpretation of a contract) or seems *traditionally judicial* or *nontechnical* in nature, or where the plaintiff is *unable to use* the administrative process (*see* below).

(1) **Traditionally judicial issues [§810]**
If the controversy is one that can be better resolved by court action, the plaintiff may be allowed to seek relief in court—even though an agency also has authority over the subject of the suit.

---

e.g. **Example:** A plaintiff who was "bumped" from an airline flight because of overbooking sued the airline in a common law fraud action. Although the Civil Aeronautics Board ("CAB") had power to order airlines to cease unfair and deceptive practices, the Court refused to apply the primary jurisdiction rule and permitted the court action to continue because a CAB proceeding would not have been as effective. The CAB had no power to award damages to the plaintiff; neither could it immunize the airline from damages in any future suits. [**Nader v. Allegheny Airlines,** 426 U.S. 290 (1976)]

---

(2) **Nontechnical issues [§811]**
A court may also maintain jurisdiction over the matter where it needs no special expertise to review the administrative action.

> **Example:** A dispute between shipper and carrier turned upon the interpretation of provisions in the carrier's rate schedule, which had been approved by the ICC. The Supreme Court held that the district court could retain jurisdiction because the provisions were *nontechnical*. [**Great Northern Railway v. Merchants Elevator Co.**, 259 U.S. 285 (1922)] *But note:* The Court noted that if the tariff could not be construed without extensive evidence on railroad practices or reasonableness of rates, the matter would have to be referred to the ICC.

c. Judicial disposition of matters subject to primary jurisdiction [§812]

In cases where primary agency jurisdiction *is* found, the court must decide what to do with a case it has remanded to the agency. Should it retain the case on its docket, or should it dismiss?

(1) Disposition depends on issues involved [§813]

The answer depends on whether there will be remaining issues that the agency cannot resolve. If so, the court should retain the matter on its docket. If not, the case should be dismissed. In either event, the agency decision remains subject to judicial review.

> **Example:** The United States sued in district court to condemn certain property; one issue concerned the validity of mining claims on the property. The Supreme Court held that the Bureau of Land Management had primary jurisdiction to resolve the mining claim dispute. But it also held that the district court should retain the condemnation case on its docket for trial of the remaining issues after the Bureau resolved the claim dispute. [**Best v. Humboldt Mining Co.**, 371 U.S. 334 (1963)]

d. Specific applications of primary jurisdiction doctrine [§814]

Primary jurisdiction has had considerable impact on two areas of the law: antitrust and labor law.

(1) Antitrust regulation [§815]

Where an agency has become protective of the industry it regulates, it may not apply the antitrust laws as rigorously as would a court. Thus, if the agency has primary jurisdiction, the industry may become more or less immune from antitrust regulation.

(a) Agreements in restraint of trade [§816]

An agency may have the power to approve certain agreements in restraint of trade, thus exempting parties to the agreement from operation of the antitrust laws.

1) Application

The Federal Maritime Board ("FMB") was permitted by statute to exempt from the antitrust laws rate agreements among carriers, once the agreement was filed with the agency. One group of carriers agreed to provide lower rates to shippers who exclusively used the group's ships. Before the agreement was filed with the FMB, the United States brought a price-fixing suit. The Supreme Court held that the FMB had primary jurisdiction, even though the agreement had not yet been filed. *Rationale:* The FMB had the necessary expertise to evaluate the rate agreement in light of complex economic conditions within the merchant marine industry. [**Far East Conference v. United States,** 342 U.S. 570 (1952)]

2) Alternative—judicial review after approval

After the FMB approved the rate plan in the above example, an outside carrier sought judicial review of the FMB's action. The Court held that the FMB could *not* approve the rates, since they were contrary to the Shipping Act (rather than the antitrust laws), which prohibited retaliatory rates. [**FMB v. Isbrandtsen Co.,** 356 U.S. 481 (1958)]

(b) Application of doctrine unpredictable [§817]

It is difficult to predict when the Supreme Court will recognize primary jurisdiction in the agency and when it will allow an antitrust case to be tried first in court. The following examples reach opposite results based on the power of the agency to fashion an appropriate remedy and the legislative intent underlying the relevant statute.

Example—jurisdiction in agency: The United States brought an antitrust suit against Pan American Airways and its subsidiary for dividing routes between themselves in South America. Because the CAB had jurisdiction over unfair competition in the airline industry, the Court held that the dispute was within the primary jurisdiction of the Board. *Rationale:* Even though the CAB had no power to exempt the agreement from the antitrust laws, it could require Pan Am to divest its subsidiary. [**Pan American World Airways v. United States,** 371 U.S. 296 (1963)]

Example—jurisdiction in court: The Justice Department brought suit to set aside the acquisition of Pacific Northwest Pipeline stock by El Paso Natural Gas as a violation of the Clayton Act. While suit was pending, El Paso proposed to acquire Pacific's assets as well, and sought approval by the Federal Power Commission

("FPC"). By statute, the FPC could immunize the acquisition of assets of one pipeline company by another from the antitrust laws. The Court held that the antitrust suit pending against the stock acquisition must be tried *first*. *Rationale:* If the FPC proceeded to approve the acquisition of assets, the government's case would be adversely affected. The Court did not want to extend statutory antitrust immunity to stock acquisitions because such immunity "is not lightly implied." [**California v. FPC,** 369 U.S. 482 (1962)]

(2) Labor law [§818]

Where claims are brought in state court which involve matters arguably governed by the National Labor Relations Act ("NLRA"), the Supreme Court has held that the litigation is *preempted*—the Board's ("NLRB") jurisdiction is exclusive as to such claims.

(a) Rationale—uniformity of decisions

A comprehensive national labor policy must be administered without conflicting decisions. [**San Diego Building Trades Council v. Garmon,** 359 U.S. 236 (1959)]

> **e.g.** **Example:** A contract action brought by a union member against the union fell "arguably" within the coverage of the NLRA, and was thus preempted from state court under the *Garmon* rule, above. [**Amalgamated Association of Street, Electric Railway & Motor Coach Employees v. Lockridge,** 403 U.S. 274 (1971)]

(b) Exception—Taft-Hartley Act [§819]

However, the preemption doctrine does not apply to suits seeking to enforce provisions of a collective bargaining agreement. Such actions may be brought in federal court under section 301 of the National Labor Relations Act. [**Smith v. Evening News Association,** 371 U.S. 195 (1962)]

1) And note

Similarly, actions for breach of the union's duty of fair representation and tort actions arising from violent activity may be brought in federal court. [**Vaca v. Sipes,** 386 U.S. 171 (1967); **United Auto Workers v. Russell,** 356 U.S. 634 (1958)] (*See* further discussion in Labor Law Summary.)

(c) Note—NLRB may decline jurisdiction [§820]

In certain areas, the NLRB will not take jurisdiction where the impact of a labor practice on interstate commerce is very slight. Although state courts were originally preempted from these cases as well (leaving a "no man's land"), Congress has now provided that state courts may hear such cases.

6. Stays Pending Judicial Review [§821]

Once a court has determined that an administrative decision is reviewable, it may grant a stay to *postpone agency action pending the outcome* of its review. If it does so, the court is in effect granting a judicial reversal of the agency order until the process of review is complete.

a. APA provisions [§822]

Federal and state APAs recognize that both agencies and courts have power to order stays. [*See* APA §705; 1981 Model State APA §5-111] APA section 705 provides:

> When an agency finds that justice so requires, it may postpone the effective date of action taken by it, pending judicial review. On such conditions as may be required, and to the extent necessary to prevent irreparable injury, the reviewing court . . . may issue all necessary and appropriate process to postpone the effective date of an agency action, or to preserve status or rights pending conclusion of the review proceedings.

b. Factors considered in granting stay [§823]

In deciding whether to grant a stay pending judicial review, a court will consider the following criteria [*see* 1981 Model State APA §5-111(c)]:

(1) Likelihood of prevailing on the merits [§824]

Has the petitioner made a strong showing that she is *likely to prevail* on the merits of the appeal? Without a substantial probability of success on appeal, the court would not be justified in intruding into the normal administrative process.

(2) Irreparable injury [§825]

Has petitioner shown that without such relief she will be *irreparably injured*? Injury merely in terms of money, time, and energy may be inadequate if compensable at a later time.

(3) Effect of stay [§826]

Would the issuance of a stay *substantially harm* other parties interested in the proceedings? Since a stay is an equitable remedy, it may not be granted if one claimant is relieved only at the expense of harm to another.

(4) Public interest [§827]

Does the *public interest* suggest that no stay should be granted? This factor is especially relevant in litigation involving regulatory statutes designed to promote the public interest. [**Virginia Petroleum Jobbers Association v. FPC,** 259 F.2d 921 (D.C. Cir. 1958)]

c. Illustration—stay denied [§828]

Blue Ridge Gas applied to the FPC for authorization to distribute natural gas in Virginia. A competitor, Virginia Petroleum, sought to intervene in the FPC hearing, but its request was denied. Virginia Petroleum sought judicial review of the denial, and a stay of the FPC hearing pending review. The court denied the motion to stay. Although Virginia Petroleum was likely to prevail, it would suffer no irreparable harm; also, the question of public interest was found to be within the agency's expertise. [**Virginia Petroleum Jobbers Association v. FPC,** *supra*]

d. Illustration—stay granted [§829]

Upon reenlistment in the Army, a sergeant was investigated as to possible homosexuality. At the conclusion of hearings, the Army recommended discharge. The sergeant requested a stay of proceedings pending judicial review of the validity of the Army's evidence. The motion to stay was granted. Petitioner would suffer irreparable harm to his reputation if discharged, and he appeared to have a good chance of success on appeal. [**Schwartz v. Covington,** 341 F.2d 537 (9th Cir. 1965)]

Review Questions and Answers

Review Questions

1. A congressional statute gives the Department of the Interior the power to allow or to curtail mining within the national forests "as the best interests of all users of the national forest shall dictate." Is this an invalid delegation of legislative power? _____

2. A statute gives a state health department the power to make rules safeguarding public health. The department adopted a rule requiring bicycle riders to wear helmets. At a previous session, the legislature had considered such a measure but it had not passed. Is the rule valid? _____

3. A federal statute provides that the Librarian of Congress can adopt regulations for the proper operation of the Library. The Librarian adopts a regulation stating that the names of borrowers of books from the library will be available for sale to purchasers of lists for advertising purposes. Is the rule valid? _____

4. A statute gives the Immigration and Naturalization Service the power to adjudicate cases involving illegal aliens. The statute goes on to provide that if, after a trial-type hearing, the agency finds that the individual is illegally in the country, it can impose a range of sanctions including imprisonment. Is the statute valid? _____

5. A statute provides that the Federal Aviation Administration can assess a penalty of from $100 to $1,000 per violation for failure to adhere to federal standards for airplane maintenance. After a hearing, the agency assesses Nocturnal Airlines a $600 penalty. Is this penalty valid? _____

6. A federal statute provides for a new office to investigate and prosecute banking fraud. The Chief Justice of the Supreme Court will appoint the director who must be a member of the Senate. The director can be removed by the President for good cause, but the Senate must approve the discharge by a two-thirds vote. Finally, the Senate can veto any regulations adopted by the director.

   a. Is the provision that the director must be a member of the Senate constitutional? _____

   b. Is the provision allowing the Chief Justice to choose the director constitutional? _____

   c. Is the provision for removal of the director constitutional? _____

   d. Is the provision for veto of the director's rules constitutional? _____

7.   A federal statute provides that the President can remove certain officers only for good cause. The President removes such an officer without stating any cause. The officer sues for her salary. Will the officer win if she was:

   a.   The Secretary of the Treasury?   _____

   b.   A member of the Securities and Exchange Commission (an agency that engages in rulemaking and adjudication)?   _____

   c.   A member of the agency that operates federal prisons?   _____

8.   Ted is a clerk at the Library of Congress. His contract of employment provides no protection and he could be fired at any time. The Library proposes to fire Ted for the reason that he has been stealing books. Ted says this is not true. The government asserts that there is no right to a hearing in this situation. Is the government correct?   _____

9.   By statute, aliens are entitled to visas to work in the United States if they establish that there is a need for persons having their skills. Assume that the statute provides for no rights to a hearing. Norm wants to come to the United States to work as an engineering professor; however, his request for a visa is denied without a hearing. Is Norm entitled to a hearing?   _____

10.   A valid regulation of Nevada state prisons provides that a prisoner may be transferred between less secure and more secure prisons. Bob is transferred from a minimum security prison to a maximum security prison because the warden is concerned about his participation in prison gangs. Bob is provided with notice and an explanation of the transfer, and the right to file a written protest, but no additional protection. Bob denies he is involved with any gang.

   a.   Assume the regulation leaves such transfers purely to the warden's discretion. Is the transfer valid?   _____

   b.   Assume the regulation provides that the transfer shall not occur unless the transfer would promote the safety of the transferred prisoner or other prisoners. Is the transfer valid?   _____

11.   Mel, a junior high school student, is suspended from school for five days for fighting on the playground. He is not given any chance to explain his side of the story. Is the suspension valid?   _____

12.   A State X statute grants tenure to college professors but provides that they can be discharged for good cause. It also provides that they are entitled to no hearing upon discharge, merely an opportunity to examine their file and discuss the discharge with the dean. Karen has tenure. She is discharged for plagiarism in her research, after complaints by a fellow English professor. Karen denies that she is guilty of plagiarism.

a. Assume Karen is given no hearing but is allowed to examine her file and discuss the discharge with her dean. Is the discharge valid? _____

b. Assume Karen is suspended after being allowed to examine her file and discuss the discharge with her dean. Twenty days after her suspension, she is given a trial-type hearing in which she is allowed to cross-examine her accuser. Is the discharge valid? _____

13. City X provides housing vouchers to all homeless people so they can stay in shelters; however, vouchers will be terminated if the recipient engages in criminal activity. Suspecting Laura of selling drugs in the shelter, X cuts off her vouchers. It promises to give her a hearing within 15 days. Laura denies selling drugs. Is City X's action valid? _____

14. Jed operates a draw poker parlor in a town where gambling is legal. However, one must have a license to operate a gambling facility, and the license must be renewed each year.

a. Jed's license is not renewed because the gambling board declares that he was using shills in violation of regulations. It denies a hearing. Is Jed entitled to a hearing? _____

b. The board adopts a new rule that no poker parlor will be licensed if it is within 100 feet of a school. Jed's parlor is next to a junior high school, so his license is not renewed. Is he entitled to a hearing? _____

15. Town X adopts a land use plan under which all land in the Brentwood neighborhood is zoned agricultural. Pam, one of the 400 people who own property in Brentwood, wants to build a shopping center on her land.

a. Is she entitled to a hearing? _____

b. Town X's charter provides for petitions for variance from land use plans in the case of extreme hardship. Pam requests a variance from the land use plan, arguing that her particular parcel is completely unsuited for agriculture, so that the zoning plan would work an extreme hardship on her. The Town Council rejects her petition without a hearing. Is she entitled to a hearing? _____

16. State X operates public housing for poor people. A number of complaints have arisen in respect to the administration of this program.

a. It appears that there are no definitive standards for allocation of the scarce housing. In fact, no one is sure exactly how available apartments are allocated. Does this system violate due process? _____

b. Occasionally, the department will order a tenant shifted from one apartment to another if it is determined that the tenant has an apartment that is larger than his family needs. Would there be a constitutional right to a hearing when such an order is made? _____

17. Federal regulations require a trucker to receive a certificate of convenience and necessity before transporting goods by truck in interstate commerce. The United States Department of Transportation requires a hearing by the Surface Transportation Board before denial of such a certificate. The agency's regulations require that the trucker show, by written application, that he already owns (or has a binding contract to purchase) adequate equipment for the carriage of such goods. No oral hearing will be granted unless the written showing is made. Ken wishes to transport fertilizer between El Paso, Texas and Oklahoma City, Oklahoma. However, he does not yet own any adequate equipment, nor has he contracted to purchase any. The Board refuses to grant him a hearing and denies his application for a certificate. Must the hearing be granted? _____

18. A statute gives the Nuclear Regulatory Commission power to license new nuclear reactors. A hearing must be granted before such a license is denied. At the hearing, the private party has the burden of proof to show that its plan for a reactor is safe within NRC guidelines. Even before a hearing will be granted, the NRC requires submission of elaborate written data containing extensive scientific studies concerning safety. Idaho Power Co. wishes to build a nuclear reactor, but its application is denied without a hearing since it has failed to submit the written studies. Is the NRC's action valid? _____

19. A number of trucking lines have petitioned the Surface Transportation Board to give them certificates to carry steel between Detroit, Michigan and Gary, Indiana. Although there is apparently a need for additional service, it seems likely that only one of the applicants will receive a certificate, since that would satisfy the anticipated need. On April 1, the Board considers the first request for certification by Team Trucking Co. The certificate is granted. The application of Lerner Trucking Co. for the same route is set for June 1. Lerner attacks the grant to Team, arguing that Lerner has been denied a hearing. Is this position correct? _____

20. A federal statute provides that an agency can adopt safety standards but only "after providing for a fair hearing." The Safety Agency adopts standards for computer screens after validly following the APA provisions for informal rulemaking. Y Co., whose business will be wiped out by the new rules, requests a hearing at which it can cross-examine agency experts to show that the rule is far more drastic than needed. Is Y Co. entitled to a hearing? _____

21. A statute provides that the EPA can grant a variance from water pollution standards to an applicant upon a showing that the applicant cannot meet the standard under existing technology. The statute provides that the applicant is entitled to a "hearing" on its application.

   a. Assume the statute is federal. Do the APA hearing provisions apply to this application? _____

b.   Assume the statute is of State X, which has adopted the 1981 Model State APA. Do the state APA hearing provisions apply to this application?   _____

22.   A federal statute allows the Farm Mortgage Agency ("FMA") to grant extensions of time to farm debtors who cannot make payments on their mortgage because of a natural disaster such as a locust plague. The statute explicitly makes the decision to grant such extensions discretionary with the agency, and it says nothing about procedures that the FMA should follow in granting or denying relief. Betsy is turned down when she asks for an extension of time and the FMA refuses to grant her an oral hearing or provide an explanation of its decision.

      a.   Can a court decide that the FMA is required to provide hearings as a matter of good administrative procedure?   _____

      b.   Is Betsy entitled to an explanation of the FMA's decision?   _____

23.   KZZZ, a television station, is uncertain whether the FCC's fairness doctrine requires it to present the opposite point of view from that taken in certain commercials. It is concerned that if it fails to follow the fairness doctrine, it might find its license revoked. Therefore, it petitions the FCC for a decision as to whether the fairness doctrine applies to its case. The FCC refuses to consider the case because there is no current dispute. Is its position well taken?   _____

24.   For many years, the NLRB had decided in its adjudications that certain conduct by an employee in organizing a union was not protected by the National Labor Relations Act, and that the employer could rightfully discharge an employee who engaged in such conduct. In reliance on this policy, Big Steel Co. discharges Mel. Mel files charges that an unfair labor practice has occurred. In the adjudication of the charges, the NLRB changes its policy and declares that the previous rule was wrong. Furthermore, it awards back pay to Mel in the amount of $6,000. Big Steel Co. seeks judicial review, arguing that the change is invalid. Will the order for back pay be reversed?   _____

25.   The SEC filed a complaint against Sam, saying that he should lose his license as a stockbroker because he was negligent in giving investment advice to Mabel, a widow. Sam pointed out that the SEC had never done this before. Consequently, in Sam's case, the SEC held that a stock brokerage license could be revoked because of negligent advice but that this new rule would be prospective only; *i.e.*, it would not be applied to Sam. Later, the SEC filed a complaint against Fred for the same thing and revoked his license, citing the Sam case. Should a court reverse the decision in Fred's case?   _____

26.   The NRC is considering whether to license the construction of a new nuclear reactor. The Sierra Club seeks to intervene in the proceedings to take the position that the reactor will cause extensive thermal pollution in the ocean. The NRC statute says nothing about intervention nor does it provide for taking thermal pollution

into account in deciding whether to grant a license. The NRC denies the Sierra Club the right to intervene and the Club appeals. Will the NRC be upheld on judicial review?

27. The Medical Board in State X brings a proceeding to revoke Dr. Joe's license because he prescribed excessive amounts of barbiturates. The only evidence against Dr. Joe is offered by Mary, who said that Stella had told her that Dr. Joe would prescribe any amount of phenobarbital whenever she asked for it. Stella died as a result of an overdose of phenobarbital. Assume that Mary's statement does not meet any state law hearsay exception. The ALJ revoked Dr. Joe's license and the Medical Board adopted the ALJ's opinion.

   a.   Should the ALJ have admitted Mary's evidence?

   b.   State X follows the residuum rule. Should the court affirm the Medical Board's decision?

   c.   Assume State X does not follow the residuum rule. Can Dr. Joe argue that the proceedings violated his constitutional right to confront the witnesses against him?

28. In a proceeding to license the construction of a new nuclear reactor, the NRC administrative law judge referred to a new book on radiation safety procedures. Relying on what she had learned in this book, she rejected the application and the full agency affirmed.

   a.   Assuming that the company was not given warning that the book would be relied upon, and thus had no opportunity to contradict the information in the book, would this be acceptable?

   b.   Assuming that the administrative law judge told the company that she planned to refer to the book and take official notice of the discussion on nuclear safety therein, and the company offered no rebuttal, would evidence taken from the book be acceptable?

29. The Department of Transportation's Surface Transportation Board is considering an application by King Truck Lines to carry fertilizer between Atlanta and Miami. The price at which King wishes to carry the fertilizer is much lower than the rate now charged by railroads for the same service.

   a.   The Board states that a great deal of business would be diverted to the trucking line from the railroads and this would have a destructive effect on the finances of the competing railroads. However, no actual evidence is presented of the economic effect that the new service would have. Is the Board's conclusion supported by substantial evidence?

   b.   Suppose in this case that the trucking firm introduces evidence of three expert transportation economists to the effect that relatively little trade would be diverted from the railroads to the trucks. The evidence shows that the effect on the railroads would be insignificant, while the effect on the trucking company would be to change a failing company into a relatively successful competitor. The ICC states that it does not accept the financial analysis of these economists. Is the ICC's decision still supported by substantial evidence?

30. The FAA issues licenses for pilots. The pilot must establish that he has the requisite training and experience. Luigi applies to be a pilot but a factual issue has arisen concerning whether he has the necessary experience. His case is heard by an administrative law judge, but the agency instructs the law judge not to make any report. Instead, the agency tells Luigi that it proposes to deny the license because it finds that he has lied about his experience. After the decision becomes final, Luigi argues that he has been denied his rights under the Administrative Procedure Act since the law judge did not write a report. Is he correct?

31. A federal agency charged with monitoring coal mine safety brings charges against Acme Coal Co. for permitting illegally high concentrations of methane gas in its mine. The ultimate decisionmaker is a three-person board. The organization chart of the agency indicates that Wiley Coyote, the director of compliance, supervises a staff of investigators. Wiley is also in charge of the administrative law judges who hear cases. Acme contends that this organization is invalid.

    a.   Is Acme correct?

    b.   Would the results in this case change if Wiley were one of the agency heads?

32. The FCC charged television station KISS with fraud in its license application and proposes to revoke its broadcasting license. Ian was the FCC's investigator. Ian met with the FCC Commissioners, who decided there was probable cause to proceed against KISS. Paul prosecuted the case before Alex, the ALJ. Alex decided that KISS did not commit fraud and that its license should not be revoked. However, the FCC Commissioners reversed Alex's decision and decided to revoke the license. Are the following incidents reversible error?

    a.   The meeting between Ian and the FCC Commissioners, who ultimately decided the case.

    b.   Alex did not understand some testimony about complex engineering matters and asked Sam to help him figure out what it meant. Sam works in the FCC's engineering department and had not previously been involved in the case.

    c.   Rex, who managed another TV station, had lunch with Carla, an FCC Commissioner, while the case was under submission, and told her that KISS was a rotten broadcaster and deserved to lose its license.

33. State University brings a proceeding to expel Roy, who took part in a demonstration against the school. According to the rules of the university, a hearing board consisting of three faculty members is to hear the case, decide what happened, and fix an appropriate penalty.

    a. Roy proves that the faculty members on the board are philosophically in favor of law and order and are opposed to various sorts of radical activities and disruptions. Does this establish that they are biased? _____

    b. One of the faculty members on the hearing board was overheard making a statement prior to the hearing to the effect that Roy was a well-known troublemaker who should be gotten rid of. If Roy proves this, has he established bias? _____

    c. Assuming that the facts given in paragraph b. represent bias, can the university take the position that under the rule of necessity the board of faculty members must hear the case? _____

    d. Assume that at the hearing another member asks questions of Roy that are obviously very hostile. During the hearing, the board member makes the statement, "Frankly, I think that you are lying." Do these facts indicate that this fact finder was biased? _____

34. By statute, the State Board of Dental Examiners must pass upon the education and moral caliber of persons applying for licenses as dentists in State X. The Board finds that Martha is of poor moral character and refuses to grant her a license. Martha takes the position that the Board is unconstitutionally made up exclusively of dentists, who have a pecuniary interest against licensing her. Will this position prevail? _____

35. The Secretary of the Interior has the power to permit or curtail mining on public lands. He announces that development of oil shale resources on public lands will be permitted. A hearing will be held to decide which of various applicants will be allowed to make the development. The winning company will be chosen on the basis of its financial resources, technological skills, and environmental responsibility. The rights are very valuable, and there is a heated competition among a number of oil companies to get the award. Prior to the hearing, the president of Nevada Oil Co. took the official responsible for making the decision to dinner. Afterwards, there was some discussion about the pending case and the president of Nevada Oil talked about the fine environmental record of his company. Ultimately, Nevada Oil received the award. Can a disappointed applicant have the award reversed? _____

36. The FCC declined to renew the license of television station WXYZ on the basis that WXYZ had persistently and deliberately violated the fairness doctrine. The administrative law judge recommended that the license be terminated, and WXYZ appealed to the full Commission. Oral argument was made before the Commission. Of the seven Commissioners, two were unavoidably absent on the day of the

oral argument. Before the decision was reached, two more members resigned and their replacements were appointed. The decision to terminate the license was four votes to three. Of the four votes in the majority, two came from newly appointed Commissioners and the other two from the Commissioners who had been unavoidably absent. Is this decision valid?

37. By law, the state Insurance Commissioner has the power to set the rates for automobile insurance. The Commissioner sends a notice to Banker's Insurance Co. that its automobile insurance rates are too high and that he proposes to lower them. However, he does not indicate the grounds for his position or the level to which he believes they should be lowered. By statute, a hearing is held before an administrative law judge. At the hearing, a great deal of economic evidence is introduced by both sides concerning the company's rate structure. By statute, the report of the law judge goes directly to the Insurance Commission and cannot be examined or excepted to by the insurance company. The Commissioner decrees that the rates should be lowered 10%. On judicial review, will the court find these procedures acceptable?

38. By statute, the Director of Immigration and Naturalization has power to grant discretionary relief to persons who are otherwise deportable but who face political punishment in their home country. Tashi, who is deportable, argues that he would be subject to political persecution if he had to return to Tibet. After a hearing and the filing of briefs, the matter is ready for decision. The actual decision was reached by Ralph, one of the attorneys on the staff of the Director. However, the Director signed the decision.

    a.   Is this procedure acceptable?

    b.   Assume now that the facts stated in the previous problem are not admitted to by the Immigration Service. They are merely Tashi's contentions, which he wishes to prove. Is he entitled to take the deposition of the Director in order to establish that the Director was not familiar with the case when he made the decision?

39. The NRC must license the construction of new nuclear power plants. Following an extensive scientific study, the NRC approved an application by the Idaho Power Co. to build a new nuclear facility. Six months later, before Idaho had begun construction, the NRC reversed its decision, on the ground that the Idaho Power facility does not have sufficient safety precautions. Is the NRC prevented by the principle of res judicata from changing its mind?

40. Turnco was accused of fraud in connection with an Air Force contract.

    a.   Assume Turnco was criminally convicted of fraud. Later, the Air Force held a hearing to decide whether Turnco should be permanently barred from bidding on Air Force contracts. At the hearing, can Turnco argue that it had never committed government contract fraud (because it should have been acquitted during the criminal case)?

    b.   Assume the Air Force held a hearing and barred Turnco from bidding on future contracts. Then Turnco was criminally prosecuted. At the criminal trial, can Turnco deny that it defrauded the government?

41.   The SEC ordered revocation of Dennis's stock brokerage license because he had negligently advised a customer. Dennis appealed to the Court of Appeals for the Tenth Circuit, which reversed, holding the SEC had no power to revoke a license for this reason. The SEC decided this decision was wrong and it hopes to persuade both the Tenth Circuit and other circuits of its position in future cases. In a subsequent case, Paula, also a stockbroker, negligently advised one of her customers.

    a.   Can the SEC attempt to revoke Paula's brokerage license if Paula could appeal her case to the Tenth Circuit?

    b.   Can the SEC attempt to revoke Paula's brokerage license if Paula could appeal her case to the Ninth Circuit?

42.   John wishes to graze sheep on an Indian reservation. He telephones the Bureau of Indian Affairs in Washington and speaks to one of the attorneys who assures him that no permit is needed if he grazes the sheep less than six months a year. This advice is wrong and the Bureau seeks to evict John from Indian lands. Will it be estopped from doing so?

43.   The Naturalization Law requires that an alien live in the United States for five years of uninterrupted residence in order to be naturalized. However, short journeys out of the country would not interrupt the five years. Jane wished to take a 30-day trip to Canada and asked the Immigration and Naturalization Service whether this would break the chain of her five-year residence. A letter from the local district director told her it would not. However, when she later tried to become naturalized, the agency took the position that the director's letter was clearly wrong under all the existing statutes and she is not entitled to naturalization. Jane argued that the government should be estopped. Is she right?

44.   Josefina, a real estate broker, was told by a federal government official that she could get a commission if she negotiated a sale of some land the government wanted to sell. She worked for 500 hours and finally made a deal. However, the advice was wrong and the government is not permitted to pay a commission in this situation. Can Josefina recover a commission from the government?

45.   A federal statute empowers the Health Agency to adopt regulations concerning reimbursement of hospitals for kidney dialysis procedures performed under Medicare. After appropriate notice and comment procedure, the Health Agency publishes a

regulation on February 20, 2001, that sets reimbursement rates for services performed after January 1, 1998. Under the rule, Downey Hospital is reimbursed only $80 for a procedure that it thought would produce a reimbursement of $120. Is this regulation valid?

46. The SEC adopts a rule giving respondents in administrative cases the right to take depositions before hearings. Dean, a stockbroker accused of fraud, seeks to take the deposition of the persons accusing him but the ALJ refuses to order a deposition. Is Dean entitled to take the deposition?

47. A statute allows the Federal Reserve Board to adopt rules setting the capital requirements for banks. On February 1, the Board published a notice in the Federal Register of a proposed rule raising capital requirements for banks. It invited written comments to be submitted by February 6. Bank Two submitted 50 pages of critical comments on February 5. The Board held no oral proceedings of any kind. The final rule was published in the Federal Register on February 12, and was effective on February 13. The final rule was accompanied by a two-line statement of basis and purpose that said the rules were necessary to assure the solvency of banks. But the statement did not respond to any of Bank Two's arguments. Bank Two seeks judicial review. Decide whether the court should overturn the rule based on the following arguments:

    a. The notice gave insufficient time for the public to submit comments.

    b. The APA requires agencies to hold oral argument before adopting rules.

    c. The court should order the agency to reconsider the rule and allow cross-examination of key witnesses with respect to critical factual assumptions.

    d. The rule could not be made effective on February 13.

    e. The explanatory statement failed to respond to Bank Two's arguments.

48. Water pollution by chemicals produced in the manufacture of chrome-plated products poses a serious problem. The EPA proposes a rule that allows manufacturers to discharge not more than five parts per million (ppm) of chemical XYZ into navigable waters. During the rulemaking process, public comments persuaded the EPA that the standard was too lenient. In addition, the comments indicated that chemical ABC also posed health hazards. The final rule allows only one ppm of XYZ and ABC to be discharged. You can assume these rules are substantively valid. Decide whether a court will uphold the procedural validity of the rule in cases brought by the following plaintiffs, both of which make chrome-plated products:

    a. Company D produces XYZ in its process. It could have met the five ppm standard of the proposed rule but believes it will have to go out of business because it cannot meet the one ppm standard.

b.   Company E discharges only ABC but not XYZ. It also believes that the standard for ABC will drive it out of business. _____

49.   A section of the Federal Trade Commission Act gives the FTC power to make trade regulation rules. By a validly adopted rule, the Federal Trade Commission declares that all claims of product efficiency made in television commercials must be backed by adequate scientific studies, conducted according to prevailing scientific standards. In a television commercial, Flashy Toothpaste advertises that it will augment the user's sex appeal. There is no adequate scientific study that this will occur. The FTC brings an order against Flashy to cease and desist, claiming a violation of the rule. Flashy argues that it cannot be guilty of violating the rule, only of violating the statute, and that the FTC must consider again whether commercials must really be backed by scientific studies. Is Flashy's position well taken? _____

50.   The FTC adopts a rule requiring disclosure of whether any parts of a product were made from imported materials. The publication of the final rule in the Federal Register announces that the FTC dispensed with notice and comment procedure because the public interest required that the rule be adopted immediately without any delays. Is this rule valid? _____

51.   The INS has power to allow deportable aliens to remain in the United States if they would be subject to extreme financial hardship as the result of deportation. It publishes the following documents, in each case without any prior notice and comment. Is the document procedurally invalid?

a.   The INS publishes a document called "guidelines" instructing personnel in the field to disregard evidence that the alien has a business in the United States that would be destroyed by deportation. _____

b.   The INS publishes a document called a "ruling" in which it states that the meaning of the term "hardship" in the statute is that the alien would be reduced to extreme poverty in his native country if he is deported. _____

c.   The INS publishes a document stating that persons claiming relief under the statute must file a petition within five days after a final order of deportation. _____

52.   The SEC proposes a new rule increasing the amount of disclosure of environmental problems that must be contained in a proxy statement. The rule is highly controversial.

a.   During and after the comment period, numerous lawyers and lobbyists visited the SEC commissioners in their offices and tried to persuade the SEC to water down the new rule. The SEC did not disclose these contacts. The final rule is much less demanding than the proposed rule. Assuming environmentalists have standing to challenge the rule on judicial review, can they argue that it is procedurally invalid? _____

b.	After the new rule was proposed, the chair of the SEC resigned and the President appointed Gus, a new chair. During his confirmation hearings, Gus stated that the proposed rule was very poorly considered and that he believed that companies should be able to keep embarrassing material about environmental problems confidential. Can environmentalists argue that the final rule is procedurally invalid?

53.	The Nuclear Regulatory Commission operates a licensing scheme whereby certain laboratories having need for radioactive materials are permitted to use them under strictly limited conditions. The NRC reserves the right to inspect, at any time and without a warrant, the premises where the materials are being used. It makes such an inspection, discovers unauthorized uses of the material, and seeks to bar the laboratory from any further access to radioactive materials. Can the laboratory assert that the search was invalid?

54.	The SEC suspects that Smith Co. (a stock brokerage corporation) has been selling unregistered stock. It issues a subpoena calling for the production of all records of stock sales during 1998. The corporation resists on the following grounds. Should any of them be accepted by the court as grounds for quashing the subpoena?

a.	It violates the privilege against self-incrimination.

b.	There has been no showing of probable cause that a violation has occurred.

c.	The burden of complying with the subpoena is too great.

55.	The rules of the Small Business Administration ("SBA") require that anyone receiving an SBA loan preserve particular financial documents, in order that compliance with the loan restrictions may be ascertained. Beth is an individual who received an SBA loan for use in her business. The SBA believes that Beth spent part of the money on a personal yacht. This would be a violation of the SBA statute and also a criminal offense. The SBA orders Beth to produce particular financial records by which it can trace the use of the funds. Can Beth use her privilege against self-incrimination to avoid producing the records?

56.	A federal statute sets up a panel to investigate malnutrition in the United States. The committee has subpoena power, and it subpoenas Zeke to testify at public hearings. It wishes to show that Zeke has been selling unfit meat and produce, contrary to state and federal criminal laws. Zeke wishes to resist the subpoena on the ground that he will be unconstitutionally deprived of the right to confront and cross-examine the informants against him.

a.	Should the subpoena be quashed?

b.	The rules of the malnutrition commission preclude persons appearing before it from having counsel with them. Is this restriction valid?

57. The Secretary of the Interior is empowered to allow or curtail mining in national forest areas and adopts a new set of regulations setting forth the procedure for applying for renewals of leases already held for mining in the forests.

    a. The Secretary fails to give any public notice or to permit any public participation in the making of the new rules. Are the rules for that reason invalid? _____

    b. The Secretary fails to publish the new rules in the Federal Register. Sam, a tungsten miner, had no actual notice of the rules. He failed to file the necessary papers and his lease is declared terminated. Is the termination of Sam's lease valid? _____

58. The Civil Service Commission ("CSC") gives advice on whether political activities by federal employees would violate the Hatch Act. It sends out several hundred such letters per year. Bob is writing a book on the Hatch Act and wants copies of the letters. The Commission refuses to produce them.

    a. Is there a judicial remedy by which Bob can test the legality of the CSC's refusal to give him the documents? _____

    b. Is the CSC obligated to make public all of its private rulings? _____

    c. Must the CSC make available an index of all of these rulings? _____

    d. Can the government resist disclosure of the private rulings on the ground that they contain confidential material about federal employees submitted in confidence? _____

59. Clyde wishes to inspect a report prepared by the Defense Department concerning Middle East policy. This report has been classified "Secret" under the government's classification procedure. Clyde asserts that the material should not be secret since there is nothing in it that would jeopardize foreign policy. In an action brought to compel disclosure of the document, will Clyde prevail? _____

60. The Comptroller of the Currency requires banks to submit a large volume of confidential financial information. Jake would like to inspect the filings made by the First National Bank. Can he do so under the Freedom of Information Act if the Comptroller refuses to release them? _____

61. The Secretary of the Interior is authorized to permit or curtail mining in the national forests. His deputy for environmental protection prepares a detailed report on the effect of strip mining in the national forests, including a great deal of factual material as well as recommendations for changes in policy.

    a. The Rex Coal Co. wishes to see the report. Is it entitled to see the entire report? _____

b. Assume that the factual material in the report contains a great deal of extremely embarrassing material about government officials. Does the court have equity jurisdiction to keep the material secret even though it does not fall within an exception to the Freedom of Information Act? _____

c. Suppose the report rejected environmental complaints about a proposed mineral lease and had the effect of ending the administrative process and authorizing the lease. Must the report be disclosed? _____

62. An EPA rule establishes the amount of chemical XYZ that can be discharged into rivers. Meadow, an environmentalist, persuaded an appellate court to invalidate the rule because it was not supported by the rulemaking record. Meadow paid $100,000 in attorney's fees to obtain this result. Her attorney charged $300 per hour, but other environmental attorneys charge only $200 per hour.

a. Is Meadow entitled to recover these fees? _____

b. The EPA statute provides that a court can order the agency to pay the attorney's fees of a prevailing party "if appropriate." Is Meadow entitled to recover any part of these fees? _____

c. Under the facts given in paragraph b., is Meadow entitled to recover all of the fees? _____

63. The SEC seeks to revoke the license of Barney, a stockbroker, alleging that he cheated his customers. However, the ALJ rejects these charges and the SEC affirmed the ALJ's decision. Barney seeks to recover attorney's fees. Barney's attorney's fees were $100,000, based on charges of $300 per hour.

a. Is Barney entitled to recover attorney's fees? _____

b. If Barney is found to be entitled to recover attorney's fees, is he entitled to recover all of the fees? _____

64. Rex alleges that he is completely disabled and is entitled to Social Security disability benefits. The government has taken the position that Rex is faking. A hearing is held before an administrative law judge in the Social Security Administration. Various doctors are called to testify on the question of disability. Rex's witnesses contend that he is truly and completely disabled, but the government's witnesses testify that he is faking. The administrative law judge states that he believes Rex and finds him to be truthful. On review by the appellate board, which is ultimately responsible for the decision in the case, the decision is reversed. The board states that based on its examination of the record, Rex's testimony was not convincing. On judicial review, Rex contends that there is no substantial evidence supporting the board's decision. Is Rex correct? _____

65. The Food and Drug Administration is conducting a study of the effectiveness of vitamins. It alleges that Megavite is ineffective for curing problems of iron deficiency and lack of energy. There is a full hearing before an administrative law judge. Considerable scientific evidence has been presented on both sides. The law judge resolves the question in favor of Megavite. The Food and Drug Administration reverses, finding that on its analysis of the scientific evidence, Megavite is ineffective. Its drug certification is therefore revoked. On appeal, Megavite contends that there is not substantial evidence supporting the FDA decision. Is the decision apt to be reversed?

66. The SEC revoked the license of Morgan as a broker-dealer on the grounds that he had participated in securities fraud. By statute, judicial review is obtained in the court of appeals.

    a. In its review of the record of the SEC proceeding, is the court authorized to reweigh the evidence and find that the preponderance of the evidence is in favor of Morgan rather than the SEC?

    b. In its proceeding, the SEC staff presented evidence of statements that Morgan had made in selling the stock of a particular company. These statements were clearly not correct in every detail, and if this had been the only evidence, a reasonable person could have come to the conclusion that Morgan had engaged in securities fraud. However, Morgan introduced considerable evidence to the effect that the errors in his statements were accidental, not deliberate, and that he had reasonable cause for believing in the statements that he had made. Further witnesses indicated that the persons to whom Morgan spoke did not consider these details important in their decision to invest in the stock. In deciding whether the SEC's decision is supported by substantial evidence, can the decision be upheld by looking to the SEC staff's evidence alone?

67. The Immigration and Naturalization Service seeks to deport Sinead on the ground that she is not a citizen and that she does not qualify for any other statutory protection. Sinead contends that she is a citizen, but in an administrative proceeding the INS decides that this is not true. Sinead seeks a writ of habeas corpus in the federal district court and asserts the right to a judicial retrial of the issue of whether she is a citizen. Is Sinead entitled to a full trial on this issue?

68. A statute authorizes the SEC to adopt rules relating to disclosures in proxy statements. There is a statutory exception providing that no such rules shall relate to matters of "internal business." The SEC adopts a rule requiring disclosure of environmental problems. As part of its statement of basis and purpose, the SEC interpreted the words "internal business" and said that those words do not describe environmental problems since such problems had a substantial impact on the community. On judicial review, assume the court does not agree with this interpretation. Does it have power to overturn the rule?

69. The SEC's statute provides that it can revoke the licenses of stockbrokers for intentionally cheating customers. The SEC brings a proceeding to revoke Jake's broker's license. It found that Jake had negligently described a certain investment to a customer who had lost money as a result, and held that the statute is intended to cover negligence. There is substantial evidence supporting these findings. Must the court affirm? _____

70. The Federal Health Agency reimburses hospitals for outlays for Medicare patients. By regulation, it will pay $300 per session of kidney dialysis. Zeke, an auditor for the Health Agency in Dubuque, wrote a letter to Hospital X stating that the agency would not reimburse for kidney dialysis unless three doctors first certified the need for the procedure. This is a new interpretation of the regulation and is contrary to prior agency procedure. On judicial review, must the court follow Zeke's interpretation of the regulation if it disagrees with it? _____

71. In this question, agencies decide "ultimate questions," meaning that they apply basic facts to a statutory standard. Assume that *Chevron* is not followed, so courts have power to substitute judgment on a question of law, but must follow the substantial evidence test on a question of fact. In each situation, the court substitutes its judgment on the question of ultimate fact. Was this correct?

   a. "Security" is defined as an investment in which the management of a person's money is given to another. The SEC has a case in which the staff contends that a particular tax shelter arrangement involving oil drilling is a security. The promoters argue that it is not, since all the investors will take part in management. The SEC decides that it is a security. _____

   b. Aliens who fought in the United States Armed Forces in World War II are entitled to claim United States citizenship. Tom fought in a unit called the Philippine Scouts. During World War II the Philippines was still an American territory and the Scouts were commanded by an American officer. The Immigration and Naturalization Service has determined that the Scouts are not part of the United States Armed Forces. _____

   c. A statute provides that television stations must grant equal time to all persons running for public office if it grants time to any of them. However, there is an exception for appearances on bona fide news broadcasts. Vic, who is running for mayor, appears on a program on television that includes matters of religious news. Warren, who is running against Vic, demands equal time but the FCC decides that the program on which Vic appeared was a bona fide news show. _____

72. The Federal Highway Administrator is given statutory power to determine the routes of new highways. He is to consider such factors as cost, traffic movement, traffic safety, and minimization of the destruction of neighborhoods. The administrator approves the decision to construct an interstate highway that passes through

a certain neighborhood of Acme City. The people in the neighborhood believe that a different route would have avoided disruption of their area, but the different route would be considerably more expensive and lengthier. Is it likely that the court will set aside the administrator's decision? _____

73. The Bureau of Indian Affairs is given the power to approve or disapprove proposals for leases of Indian lands. It is instructed to consider the best interests of the Indian tribe in its decision. The Bureau approves a proposed lease, over the opposition of the tribe, to coal mining companies that wish to perform strip mining on the Indian lands. The stated reason is the nation's need for additional coal.

   a.   Is it likely that the Bureau's decision will be upheld? _____

   b.   Assume that the Secretary approves the lease in the preceding paragraph without any discussion at all of the reasons. When the tribe seeks judicial review, the Secretary's attorney attempts to supply a list of reasons that relate to the best interests of the tribe. Is this an acceptable method of making a record? _____

74. The SEC has power to suspend the license of broker-dealers who are engaged in various sorts of securities fraud. Traditionally, in cases involving a particular violation, the agency would issue a reprimand against the broker-dealer on a first offense. However, in Tina's case, it terminated her license for exactly the same conduct.

   a.   Is it likely that the reviewing court will set aside the penalty? _____

   b.   Assume that hundreds of different broker-dealers were doing exactly the same thing as Tina. However, the SEC singled her out for sanction and so far has not gone after anyone else. Will this decision be set aside by a reviewing court? _____

75. The Iowa Encyclopedia Co. has a door-to-door selling scheme in which it tells customers that encyclopedias can be placed in their home for free. All they have to do is agree to buy the yearly supplements. However, the yearly supplements are so expensive that in fact the customer ends up paying more than the regular amount for the set of encyclopedias and supplements. The FTC issues an order against Iowa Encyclopedia Co. to refrain from this practice. In addition, the FTC requires that in future sales, the company must charge the full value of its encyclopedias and must permit their purchase even if no supplement service is ordered at all. The company protests that the FTC order has gone far beyond the particular unlawful conduct originally alleged against it. Will the FTC's order withstand judicial review? _____

76. A statute gives the Interior Department power to permit or curtail mining in the national forests. The Department proposes to halt the mining of magnesium in a national forest. Clearfield Mining Co. feels that this action is an abuse of discretion

since the proposal resulted from congressional pressure. The statute says nothing about judicial review. Can Clearfield go to the United States Court of Appeals for judicial review? _____

77. If Clearfield Mining Co. (in the previous question) goes into federal district court, must it allege that more than $75,000 is in controversy? _____

78. Bob wants to get a job with the Postal Service. Unfortunately, someone else was selected for the position even though Bob feels he was better qualified. The statute appears to give the Postal Service discretion to hire the person that it feels is best qualified.

a. Bob would like to seek a writ of mandamus against the Postmaster. Can such a writ be obtained in the federal courts? _____

b. Is this an appropriate case for mandamus? _____

c. Suppose, instead, the statute provided that the Postmaster must hire the person who scores highest on a competitive exam. Bob has the highest score but the Postmaster hires someone else. Is this an appropriate case for mandamus? _____

79. The Milk Regulatory Board of Michigan passes a regulation that raises the minimum price for milk in the state to 70¢ per half gallon. A consumer seeks judicial review of this action. Can he obtain a writ of certiorari? _____

80. A statute permits the government to sue polluters in federal court for civil penalties. The statute allows the court to impose penalties of $10 to $1,000 per day for water pollution. The judge held that Blackwater Co. was liable for polluting a river and imposed the maximum penalty. Blackwater Co. asserts that it has a right to a jury trial on both issues but the judge refuses to put the issues to the jury. Should the decision be affirmed? _____

81. The law in State X prohibits suits for damages against the state for injuries caused by state employees. Liz, who was injured in an accident involving a truck operated by an employee of State X, believes that the statute is unconstitutional as a violation of due process of law. She brings an action in federal court for damages. Assume that her constitutional argument is well-founded. Can the federal court hear the case? _____

82. A statute provides that before an interstate highway can be built through a populated area, it is necessary to publish notice thereof and have a public meeting of the residents of the area. The federal highway administrator proposes to build a road through an area of Tennessee, but has failed to post a notice or call a public hearing. Residents of the area seek to enjoin construction of the road and bring an action against the administrator in the federal district court in Tennessee. The

administrator asserts that the venue of the suit is incorrect and should be brought in Washington, D.C. Is the administrator correct? _____

83. Joe, a corporal in the Marines, drove a jeep negligently and injured Anne. Joe was on duty at the time.

   a.   Can Anne sue the United States? _____

   b.   If Anne sues the United States for damages, can it get indemnity from Joe? _____

84. The Immigration and Naturalization Service conducts border searches. When Luisa sought to enter the country, she was negligently mistaken for a wanted criminal and detained for six hours by officials of the INS. Can Luisa sue the United States for damages for false imprisonment? _____

85. The Secretary of the Interior has authority over the control of predators on public lands. In response to complaints by environmentalists, the Secretary terminated the trapping and poisoning of coyotes on public lands. Ned is a sheep farmer who is entitled to graze sheep on public lands. After the Secretary's decision, several of Ned's sheep were eaten by coyotes. Ned brings a lawsuit based on a tort theory for damages against the Secretary of the Interior personally and against the United States.

   a.   The Secretary moves to dismiss Ned's suit against him for damages on the ground that he is immune from suit. Should the court dismiss the action? _____

   b.   The United States moves to dismiss the damage action against it on grounds of sovereign immunity. Should this action be dismissed? _____

86. A federal statute granting benefits to injured or disabled employees of the federal government, or to their families, provides that illegitimate children can receive no benefits. The statute provides that determinations of disability and damages shall be "final and unreviewable by any court." Fred is the illegitimate child of George, a federal employee who is injured. Fred wishes to attack the statutory denial of benefits to illegitimate children as an equal protection violation. May he do so? _____

87. The Federal Trade Commission has the power to restrain corporations from unfair methods of competition. Sweetbite Corp. sells sugary breakfast foods and advertises them heavily on television. Sweetbite gives many free trinkets to children who purchase the cereal. Goodenbland Corp. is a producer of healthy breakfast cereals. Goodenbland feels that Sweetbite's method of advertising is unfair since it preys so heavily on the susceptibility of children. However, the FTC has refused to take any action against Sweetbite. Assuming that Goodenbland has standing, can it get judicial review of the FTC's refusal to prosecute? _____

88. A statute gives the Federal Health Agency power, "in its discretion," to grant funds for the purpose of research in curing Alzheimer's Disease. The agency head decided

not to grant any funds for this purpose, because he felt that such research is a waste of money. Is the decision reviewable?

89. Dorothy objects to the Public Relations Department of the Pentagon. She feels that the daily handouts of news to reporters tend to devitalize independent investigations. Consequently, she alleges that they violate the freedom of the press under the First Amendment.

    a. Does Dorothy have standing to bring this action as a "citizen"?

    b. Does Dorothy have standing as a "taxpayer" since public money is expended in operating the Public Relations Department?

    c. Can Dorothy base her standing on the theory that she is "injured in fact"?

90. A statute empowers the Department of the Interior to either permit or curtail mining in the national forests "as the best interests of all users of the forest shall dictate." There is no provision concerning judicial review in the statute. Deepwell Corp. has been drilling for oil in a national forest under a previous Interior Department grant. The Interior Department now proposes to permit Evendeeper Corp. also to drill for oil in the same forest. Does Deepwell have standing to complain?

91. A statute requires competitive bidding for government contracts and requires the government to give the contract to the "lowest responsible bidder." Both Seaworthy Corp. and Dolphin Corp. bid on a Navy contract. Seaworthy is the low bidder, but its bid is disqualified—the government feels that Seaworthy is not responsible since it went bankrupt two years ago. Instead, the contract is given to Dolphin, which had made a higher bid. Does Seaworthy have standing to complain of this decision?

92. A federal statute permits the expenditure of federal money for the construction of monuments, as the Secretary of the Interior shall decide. The Secretary proposes to construct a monument on a particular parcel of federal property in San Francisco in honor of a composer who lived nearby.

    a. Ed, who lives across the street from the site of the monument, opposes the construction. He feels that the design of the monument will be ugly and will blight the neighborhood. His complaint is that the Secretary has failed to file an environmental impact statement, which is required before the federal government takes action having a significant effect on the environment. Does Ed have standing?

    b. Assume the plaintiff in this case were instead an association formed by persons living near the park to resist construction of the monument. Would the association have standing to protest if an individual would have had standing?

93. The Department of Transportation allows the Surface Transportation Board to adopt regulations under which interstate trucking will be deregulated. The Surface

Transportation Board adopts rules permitting trucks to carry any product they wish on the way back to their home after delivering a load that they were licensed to carry. All parties agree that these rules will make trucking more efficient by avoiding the need to return with an empty truck. However, it will undoubtedly reduce the number of persons employed as truck drivers. Can the truck drivers' union secure judicial review of this rule?

94. A federal agency adopts rules providing that magazines can receive reduced postal rates even though they contain solely advertising. The previous rules required the magazines to contain some editorial content. The authors' union attacks these rules, complaining that they will reduce employment opportunities for authors. Does the union have standing?

95. Norma applies for a license as a pilot. The license application remains with the FAA for two years and they refuse to act upon it, repeatedly stating that a hearing will be scheduled in the near future but never scheduling one. Can Norma go to court to force the FAA to act?

96. The Surface Transportation Board adopts a new regulation stating that railroads that retain boxcars belonging to other railroads for an unreasonable time must pay a penalty of $100 per day. The Nevada Railroad seeks to enjoin the new regulation on the theory that it is not authorized by statute. Will the court hear this attack now?

97. Nell is a stockbroker who has made a contract with Paul. Paul's job is to get business for Nell by joining various organizations, talking about Nell's brilliant investment advice, and signing up clients for Nell. Paul gets a commission based on a percentage of Nell's sales to clients whom Paul has found. The SEC adopts a new regulation stating that broker-dealers may not make contracts with outsiders to get business for them and share their commissions with the outsiders. Nell tells Paul that they must cancel their contract. Can Paul get judicial review of the validity of the SEC's new regulation?

98. Large Corp. and Small Corp. want to merge but fear the application of the antitrust laws. They submit an application to the antitrust division of the Justice Department, which, under an established procedure, will review the facts and issue a ruling about the proposed merger. The subordinate official in the antitrust division who is charged with making these reviews informs the corporations by letter that the merger would violate the antitrust laws and that the Attorney General might well seek to attack it. Can the corporations obtain judicial review of this ruling?

99. The SEC served notice on Stanley that it was about to begin proceedings to revoke his license as a broker-dealer, which would prohibit him from trading on behalf of others in the stock market. This action was taken as a result of certain securities frauds Stanley allegedly committed. Stanley feels that the particular conduct the SEC seeks to punish is beyond its regulatory jurisdiction.

   a.   Stanley therefore goes into federal district court, seeking an injunction against the SEC to block the hearings. Should the court hear this case?

b.   Stanley believes the SEC did not have probable cause to issue the notice although the statute requires the agency to find probable cause. He has already moved that the SEC dismiss the complaint, but it refused to do so. Can Stanley get immediate judicial review of the probable cause issue? _____

100. Under the Postal Obscenity Statute, the Postal Service has the power to seize and impound obscene matter sent through the mails. It can also prohibit persons found to have used the mails for such purposes from sending or receiving mail in the future. The Director of the Postal Service Obscenity Section states in a press release that a particular movie is certainly obscene and the Post Office plans to seize it if it goes through the mails. A print of the movie is seized in Florida. An administrative appeal procedure is provided for judging obscenity after the seizure occurs. Mel, the producer of the movie, seeks to enjoin the Postal Service to return the movie. He has not used the administrative appeal. Can this suit for injunction be heard? _____

101. Larry is a student at the Air Force Academy. He is suspected of cheating. The applicable regulations of the Academy provide that he can be given a hearing, but that he is not entitled to confront the witnesses against him. Before the hearing begins, Larry goes into federal district court, seeking to enjoin continuation of the hearing. Should the court hear this case? _____

102. A statute gives the Federal Highway Safety Agency the power to order the recall of motor vehicles for the correction by the manufacturer of safety defects. There is a hearing procedure for the purpose of making these determinations. In several cases, the exhaust system on 1981 Chryslers has leaked into the car and caused death by carbon monoxide poisoning. Roy brings a class action suit in federal district court on behalf of all purchasers of 1981 Chryslers, in which the relief sought is that the manufacturer repair the defect free of charge. Chrysler moves to dismiss the action on the ground that the Federal Highway Safety Agency should decide this issue. Should the court dismiss? _____

103. The Department of Transportation gives to the Surface Transportation Board the power to approve railroad mergers. It provides that if the Board approves a merger, the merger is exempt from attack under the antitrust laws. The Washington Railroad and the Oregon Railroad have merged and the Board is now studying the matter. The Justice Department goes into federal district court, seeking to have the merger declared a violation of the antitrust laws. The railroads move to dismiss the case. Should the motion be granted? _____

104. The legal services agency makes a grant of $1 million to a legal aid office in Portland, Oregon for legal services to the poor. However, there are many restrictions in the grant, including some that prevent the attorneys from taking criminal cases or from participating in political activity. During the term of the grant, the government learns that the attorneys have been taking criminal cases and participating in politics. Following a hearing that substantiates these charges, the grant is terminated. The office is seeking judicial review, arguing that the various restrictions imposed

are unconstitutional and that there was no substantial evidence that the attorneys were in fact engaging in prohibited conduct. Will the court grant a stay of the agency's determination pending judicial review? _____

Answers to Review Questions

1. **NO**   Although extremely vague, the standard used here brings the case within prior Supreme Court precedent, which upholds such delegations. If Congress can give the FCC power to regulate television and radio as "public convenience, interest or necessity" dictates, the delegation in the problem should clearly be upheld. [§§13-14]

2. **PROBABLY NOT**   Under *Boreali v. Axelrod,* this rule might be held ultra vires. The statute is vague and it is unclear whether this sort of a measure is a proper public health measure. The legislature's failure to deal with the problem might also suggest that it did not intend the agency to adopt a rule on the subject. Moreover, there are constitutional issues present—a legal requirement that a bike rider wear a helmet could violate substantive due process. And state courts apply the ultra vires doctrine more strictly than do federal courts. [§§30-32]

3. **POSSIBLY NOT**   The rule raises questions about the privacy rights of the users of the library and, at least, has constitutional dimensions. Under cases like *Kent v. Dulles,* a court might hold the rule ultra vires (beyond the Librarian's power under the statute) because it does not concern the proper operation of the library. The court prefers this approach rather than invalidating the statute on constitutional grounds. In effect, it forces Congress to make the ultimate decision whether it really wants the agency to have this particular power. In *Rust v. Sullivan,* however, the Court ignored this approach and held a constitutionally questionable regulation was not ultra vires; then it went ahead and rejected the constitutional attack on the rule. [§33]

4. **NO**   The courts have held that imprisonment can be imposed only by a court, not an agency. [§48]

5. **YES**   Federal agencies have the power to assess civil penalties, including a decision on the amount thereof within a statutory range. [§§49-52]

6.a. **NO**   *Buckley* and *Metropolitan Washington* make clear that Congress cannot require that a member of Congress hold any executive position. [§64]

  b. **PROBABLY NOT**   The Constitution allows Congress to adopt statutes providing that inferior officers can be appointed by the courts of law. In *Morrison,* the Court upheld a provision whereby a panel of federal court judges appointed an independent prosecutor to prosecute specific cases of wrongdoing in the executive branch. In *Freytag v. Commissioner,* the Court upheld a provision allowing the chief judge of the Tax Court to appoint special Tax Court judges. In *Mistretta,* the Court upheld a provision requiring federal judges to serve on the sentencing commission. This provision is distinguishable from all three cases. The director of an agency who will engage in important long-term executive and adjudicatory responsibilities (unlike the prosecutor in *Morrison* who worked only on one case) is not an "inferior officer" and thus must be appointed by the President. [§§65-71] Unlike *Mistretta*, the Chief's service is obligatory, not voluntary. Also, this provision threatens to involve the Chief Justice in a conflict of interest since cases brought by the director are likely to come to the Supreme Court; thus it could undermine the integrity of the judicial branch. [§§46, 65-71]

c. **NO**   *Bowsher* and *Morrison* prohibit Congress from having any role in the removal process of an officer engaged in executive functions. [§78]

d. **NO**   *Chadha* struck down all forms of legislative veto over executive action, including rulemaking, as forbidden attempts by Congress to legislate without submission to the presidential veto. This provision also violates the requirement of bicameralism—both houses of Congress must act to adopt legislation. [§§60-61]

7.a. **NO**   Under *Morrison*, the President must have unrestricted power to remove certain officers where otherwise his ability to discharge constitutional duties would be impeded. A member of the cabinet who carries out fundamental presidential policy decisions is clearly in that category. [§§72, 77-78]

b. **YES**   *Humphrey's Executor* established the validity of independent agencies to engage in rulemaking and adjudication. Congress clearly can give tenure to the members of such agencies. [§75]

c. **PROBABLY YES**   *Morrison* establishes that Congress can protect the jobs of most federal employees unless to do so would impede the President in carrying out constitutional functions. Probably the inability to fire a person engaged in managing prisons would not undermine the integrity of the executive branch by interfering with the President's ability to carry out constitutional functions. [§77]

8. **PROBABLY NOT**   The government is correct that Ted has no "property" in his job since the contract confers no protection. This is like the position of an untenured teacher, who has no due process protection. [§107] However, the reason for the firing would clearly impose a stigma on Ted since he has been accused of theft. Therefore, the firing invades his "liberty" and he is entitled to a hearing if the reason for his termination would be made available to other employers, or if the stigma would foreclose employment opportunities or otherwise cause Ted a concrete economic injury. [§§85-88]

9. **NO**   There are no due process rights for an alien seeking to enter the country. [§91]

10.a. **YES**   Under *Sandin*, imprisonment following due process criminal procedures generally extinguishes one's liberty interests during incarceration unless an administrative decision lengthens the term of confinement. [§93]

b. **YES**   Prior law required nondiscretionary standards for a warden's decision to transfer. However, under *Sandin,* the transfer does not deprive Bob of his liberty since it neither lengthens his term of confinement nor falls within certain exceptions, *e.g.,* transfer to a mental hospital. [§§93-96]

11. **PROBABLY NOT**   *Goss v. Lopez* held that a suspension of 10 days or less from high school was a deprivation of liberty and entitled the student to a conference with the disciplinarian and opportunity to state his side of the case. This case involves only a five-day suspension but probably *Goss* would be followed in this situation. [§§99, 102]

12.a. **NO**   Under *Loudermill,* if the state creates a tenured position, it cannot define the procedural protection for that position. Due process standards apply. In this situation, an oral trial-type hearing would be required, not merely a conference. [§§107, 110]

b. **YES**   *Loudermill* established that the hearing can be given after suspension if there is an adequate opportunity before suspension to show that the state had no probable cause for its action and if a full hearing is provided promptly after the suspension. [§110]

13. **PROBABLY NOT**   *Mathews* requires a three-factor balancing test to decide timing questions. Clearly Laura has a property interest; under *Goldberg* there is a property interest in welfare programs, at least as long as they are not discretionary. *Goldberg* requires a pre-termination hearing before a person is terminated from welfare because of the brutal need of the recipient. [§§103-105, 117-118] Unlike *Mathews,* which upheld post-termination hearings for disability benefit recipients, homeless persons are likely to be much needier than disability recipients. Also, the decision turns much more on credibility problems than disability cases, which are decided mostly on written medical reports. However, the state's need for immediate action is greater here than in *Goldberg* or *Mathews*—it's not just a matter of saving money, but removing somebody who might be selling drugs in shelters. This calls for immediate action. This is a close call and City X's procedure might be upheld if there is an adequate pretermination procedure to determine probable cause. [§§119-123]

14.a. **PROBABLY YES**   Although there is some authority to the effect that no due process rights attach to licenses relating to such trades as gambling or selling liquor, this is probably no longer true. Nonrenewal of a license to operate a business without a hearing denies due process. [§§111-112, 115]

b. **NO**   Even though hearings would generally be required before nonrenewal of licenses, there are no facts to be determined—the rule prevents a license from being issued and the location of the facility is not in dispute. [§§146, 149, 155]

15.a. **NO**   No hearing is required even though Pam is deprived of a potential use of her property. Under *Bi-Metallic*, no individualized (or "adjudicative") facts need to be resolved, and the proceeding involves many landowners, not just Pam. The Town obviously found generalized (or "legislative") facts about the Brentwood neighborhood, but this does not trigger due process. [§§149, 152-154]

b. **YES**   Here, as in *Londoner*, the proceeding is individualized, and individualized facts about Pam's property must be resolved. Moreover, the town charter appears to create an entitlement to a variance upon a showing of extreme hardship, so a denial of the petition is a deprivation of property. Consequently, due process would require a trial-type hearing. [§§148, 151]

16.a. **YES**   A number of cases, including *Holmes*, have held that a city violates due process when it allocates benefits like public housing without first adopting standards for how it is to be done. [§§106, 191-195]

b. **PROBABLY YES**   Since the department is bound by a standard ("larger than his family needs"), an undesired transfer will probably be treated as a deprivation of property. Probably a transfer of living quarters is significant enough so that it cannot be considered de minimis. And it would appear that issues of fact must be resolved (involving family needs) so a hearing should be required. [§§106, 147-148]

17. **NO**   Although the statute requires a hearing before denial of a certificate, the agency can, by regulations, condition the hearing upon satisfaction of certain prerequisites. If the needed preliminary showing is not made, the hearing required by statute can be denied. (*See* the *American Airlines* case.) [§155]

18. **YES**   This is a form of administrative summary judgment. The agency is entitled to ask for a written showing of scientific material so that it can determine whether there is any real issue of fact to be handled at the hearing. In the absence of such a submission, the hearing can be denied even though one is generally required by statute. This was established in the *Hynson, Westcott & Dunning* case. [§156]

19. **YES**   The ICC has violated the comparative hearing requirement of the *Ashbacker* case, holding that mutually exclusive applications must be heard at the same time. Otherwise, the effect is, as a practical matter, that the grant of the certificate to the first applicant will effectively preclude the second. [§145]

20. **NO**   Y Co. is not entitled to a hearing under due process because the standard is generalized, not individualized. Nor is it entitled to a hearing by statute; under *Florida East Coast*, the statute calls for informal, not formal, rulemaking, so no trial-type procedure is necessary. In order to require formal rulemaking, the statute must explicitly call for a hearing "on the record." [§§146-149, 153]

21.a. **PROBABLY YES**   The application is adjudication under the APA since it is a request for a license. However, the APA does not apply unless a hearing is required by an external source—either constitutional due process or a statute requiring a hearing "on the record." [§§156-160] Here, it is arguable that denial of the application would be a deprivation of property, in which case *Wong Yang Sung* would apply and would trigger the APA. [§164] Also, under *Seacoast*, the courts will presume Congress intended a "hearing on the record" when it calls for a "hearing" in cases of adjudication. Note, however, that *West Chicago* is contra. [§164]

b. **YES**

Under the 1981 Model State APA, there is no requirement of an external source that requires a hearing. A hearing is provided in all cases of adjudication. However, note that different hearing models may be applicable, such as conference or summary hearings. [§§166, 173-176]

22.a. **NO**

There is no external source here that would require any procedure, including a hearing on the record. Due process does not apply because the benefit is discretionary—hence there is no property right. A court is not at liberty to impose procedures on an agency that go beyond what the APA would require—which in this case is nothing. *See PBGC v. LTV.* [§177]

b. **YES**

APA section 555(e) requires an explanation even though it requires no hearing. [§171]

23. **NO**

The FCC could issue a declaratory order under APA section 554(e), which authorizes such orders to terminate a controversy or remove uncertainty. Like a judicial declaratory judgment, no current dispute is necessary for a declaratory order to be a proper remedy. [§§180-181]

24. **POSSIBLY YES**

Generally, the agency has the discretion to decide whether to implement a new policy by rulemaking or by adjudication. However, if the hardship caused by the retroactive effect of the decision is out of proportion to its public importance, the court will protect the employer from the consequences of the retroactive decision. This may be the case here, since the employer appears to have relied on the previous Board interpretations. There is no reason why the Board could not have changed its policy by means of a rule, rather than by adjudication; therefore, the court might reverse the back pay order. [§§186-189]

25. **NO**

In *Wyman-Gordon*, the Court held that the NLRB violated proper procedure when it adopted a purely prospective holding in adjudication. It had engaged in rulemaking, not adjudication, but had failed to follow APA rulemaking procedures. However, ironically the Court allowed the NLRB to rely on the earlier invalid case in a subsequent case, holding that the later case was an independently valid adjudication. [§196]

26. **PROBABLY NOT**

Under APA section 555(b), intervenors have a qualified right, "so far as the orderly conduct of public business permits . . . [to] appear before an agency . . . ." Therefore, it would appear that the agency might have abused its discretion in excluding the Sierra Club, a responsible spokesman for environmental issues.

The Club seems to be within the zone of interests protected by the statute. Furthermore, it seems quite possible that the Sierra Club will be able to appeal the ultimate result, assuming that it is able to argue injury in fact to its members. In the *National Welfare Rights Organization* case, it was held that anyone who has standing to appeal also has a right to intervene. For these reasons, the Sierra Club probably has a right to intervene. [§§198-200]

27.a. **YES**

The general rule in administrative law is that ALJs need not follow evidence law and can admit whatever evidence they wish if it is of the sort that reasonable persons rely on in the conduct of serious affairs. This evidence clearly meets that standard. [§§218, 221]

b. **NO**

The residuum rule requires that the decision be reversed because the only evidence in support of the critical finding is hearsay not admissible in a trial. Some states have rejected the residuum rule, and some that still follow it will allow a decision supported by hearsay alone to stand if the other circumstances are consistent with the hearsay. Under the latter standard, the decision might be affirmed. [§§219-220]

c. **PROBABLY NOT**

Although reliance on hearsay does deprive the opponent of the right to confront the declarant, and the evidence in this case was critical to the result, it is unlikely that the decision would be set aside on this ground since the declarant was unavailable. [§224]

28.a. **PROBABLY NOT**

Although an agency is free to take official notice—even of facts that are not indisputable—it must generally provide the parties with an opportunity to prove the contrary. [§§230-234]

b. **YES**

This seems to be within APA section 556(e) and therefore would be acceptable since there was reasonable opportunity to contradict the material in the book. [§§232-234]

29.a. **PROBABLY YES**

In an area such as this, the Surface Transportation Board's expertise will certainly be considered in deciding whether there is evidence to support the decision. This is an area in which the Board specializes and in which it has technical knowledge. There is a certain degree of guesswork involved in predicting the economic effect of any change, and yet this is exactly what the Board was set up to do. Direct evidence of the effect that a rate change will have is hard to come by. For these reasons, it seems that this is an acceptable use of expertise. [§§235-237]

b. **DEPENDS**

This is an area where the result is very hard to predict. Although the agency can reject the evidence of expert witnesses, it takes a substantial risk of reversal when it does so. According to *Davis & Randall*, such agency action should be upheld only if (i) the agency's criticisms of the expert are so compelling that the court feels the agency would not have been affected by anything the witness could say had he known of the agency's criticisms; and (ii) even assuming a hypothetical rebuttal by the witness, the court would have upheld the agency out of deference to its expertise. Based on the facts given in the problem, it does not appear that the agency's uncommunicated criticisms of the experts are that compelling—although it is likely that the court would defer to the agency if the experts had a chance to rebut the agency's point of view. Therefore, the outcome is hard to predict; but because the agency's rejection of the experts' opinion lacks any analysis or reasoning, it is possible that the agency decision would not be upheld. [§237]

30. **NO**

In initial license proceedings, section 557 of the APA permits the agency to dispense with the usual requirement of either a recommended or initial decision. It can issue a tentative decision itself. [§252]

31.a. **YES**

Section 554(d) of the APA provides that the administrative law judge may not be subject to the supervision of an employee who is engaged in performing investigative or prosecutorial functions. [§§260-262]

b. **YES**

The rule of section 554(d) does not apply "to the agency or a member of the body comprising the agency." [§§259, 265-266] *Note:* The 1981 Model State APA contains no exception for agency heads. [§268]

32.a. **NO**

Agency heads are permitted to meet with investigators at the preliminary stage to decide whether to go forward with the case. [§267]

b. **PROBABLY**

APA section 554(d)(1) was interpreted in *Butz v. Economou* to preclude ex parte ALJ communications with anyone in the agency, even if they were not adversaries in the case. However, the language was dictum and the point has not been squarely decided. Here the communication did not involve new evidence so it might not concern a "fact in issue" under the APA. Sam was not an adversary, and Alex needed help. This seems no worse than a judge talking to his law clerk who happens to be an expert in engineering. A court might find this was not a violation of the APA. [§§227-229]

c. **YES**

This is a violation of section 554(d). The "agency head" exception of section 554(d)(C) does not exempt this sort of communication. [§§286-287]

33.a. **NO**

Philosophical bias in favor of the law being enforced is not a ground for disqualification. (*See* the *Cement Institute* case.) [§275]

b. **YES**

Animus against a person or prejudgment of the facts disqualifies a fact finder. [§§273-274, 280]

c. **NO**

There appears to be no reason why the university could not name other faculty members to the board in order to hear this case. Consequently, the rule of necessity seems not to be a barrier to correction of the bias. [§282]

d. **NO**

A fact finder is entitled to develop attitudes during the hearing about the credibility of witnesses. Even if these are very unfavorable, it does not demonstrate bias—it merely shows that the fact finder is trying to evaluate the evidence presented. [§281]

34. **NO**   A board made up of professionals is not presumed to be biased. Only a very strong showing of actual bias, such as was made in *Gibson v. Berryhill*, would suffice. *Friedman v. Rogers* makes it clear that a facial attack will not succeed. [§279]

35. **YES**   If the hearing was required by statute, APA section 557(d) applies and the ex parte contact was clearly improper. Even if the hearing was not required by statute, it is likely that ex parte contacts are improper even in informal adjudication that determines who will receive valuable rights. [§§286-292]

36. **YES**   Oral argument is not a constitutional prerequisite. Assuming that all the members read the transcript of the oral argument, it was not necessary that they actually be present. Consequently, the decision is valid. [§§297-298, 300]

37. **PROBABLY NOT**   They are clearly contrary to the *Mazza* case in New Jersey, which held that an administrative law judge's report must be part of the record. Even if the state does not follow the strict rule in the *Mazza* case, this result might be found invalid under the second *Morgan* case. *Morgan II* held that there must be some focusing on the issues prior to the final decision. However, that case also involved extensive ex parte contact between the ultimate decisionmaker and attorneys for the department, which does not appear in our problem. Nonetheless, the requirement of some intermediate report, or at least a focusing of the issues at some point, does seem to be an enduring requirement of administrative law. [§§306-308]

38.a. **NO**   This appears to be a violation of the first *Morgan* case, which requires that he who has the statutory responsibility for decisions must hear the case, at least in the sense of being familiar with the evidence and argument. Ad hoc delegations are not permitted. (*See KFC National Management Corp.*) [§§294-295]

   b. **NO**   This would be a violation of the fourth *Morgan* case, which prevents the court from investigating the process by which the decisionmaker reached his decision. In the absence of some objectively determinable evidence that Tashi is correct, it is likely that he would receive no relief. [§§302-303]

39. **NO**   In general, the principles of res judicata are applicable to agencies. However, it seems clear that res judicata is not applicable in this case. The NRC probably did not act in a judicial capacity. In addition, Idaho Power has not yet begun construction, and presumably has not relied to any great extent on the previous decision. Res judicata would probably contravene statutory policy; the public interest in nuclear reactor safety is of enormous importance and certainly justified the Commission's change in position. [§§310-311, 322]

40.a. **NO**   Principles of res judicata and collateral estoppel apply generally in administrative law. Turnco should be precluded by collateral estoppel from relitigating the criminal case in the later administrative case. [§313]

b. **YES**
Collateral estoppel should not apply here because the government's burden of proof in the administrative hearing was merely to prove its case by a preponderance. In the criminal case, it must prove its case beyond a reasonable doubt. This difference precludes application of collateral estoppel. [§318]

41.a. **PROBABLY NOT**
Although not settled, it is likely that the SEC cannot relitigate the issue in the same circuit. It must acquiesce in the prior decision. [§315]

b. **YES**
The government is not bound by nonmutual collateral estoppel and can relitigate the issue in another circuit in hopes of producing a conflict that will enable it to get to the Supreme Court. [§314-315]

42. **NO**
Although a few lower court cases hold the government bound by estoppel, this is not a proper case. For one thing, the advice was informal; well-founded claims of estoppel usually arise from formal written advice rather than telephone conversations. Furthermore, the use of estoppel here would prejudice the rights of the Indians. In cases where the government has been estopped, no particular individuals or groups have been harmed by the estoppel. Also, it is not clear that John has detrimentally relied on the advice. There is no showing that he will lose any investment by denial of future grazing rights. [§§322-325]

43. **PERHAPS**
In immigration cases, the courts have been willing to hold the government bound by estoppel. Jane's case is much stronger than *Moser*, which so held. Also, the *Hibi* case suggests that the government can be estopped in an immigration case if it acts affirmatively to cause reliance, as it did here. However, recent estoppel cases suggest that the Court may overrule the estoppel-immigration cases. [§327]

44. **NO**
Under *Office of Personnel Management v. Richmond*, equitable estoppel can never apply against the government where the plaintiff seeks a money judgment because this would violate the Appropriations Clause of the Constitution. [§326]

45. **NO**
Absent explicit statutory authorization, legislative regulations cannot be retroactive under the *Georgetown* case. In addition, it can be argued that the regulation violates the 30-day pre-effective date provision of section 553(d). [§§338, 378]

46. **YES**
Agencies are bound by their own procedural rules, even though these rules were not required by any statute, unless the rule was adopted for agency convenience rather than protection of outsiders. [§§349-350]

47.a. **YES**
The APA does not state how long the comment period must be, but it must be sufficient for people to prepare comments and participate in the process. Five days is too short, even though Bank Two was able to prepare comments during that period. [§§365-366]

b. **NO**   The APA does not require any oral proceedings in rulemaking. [§§367-368]

c. **NO**   *Vermont Yankee* precludes courts from adding any new procedural requirements to those set forth in the APA. [§§363, 384]

d. **YES**   APA section 553(d) requires a 30-day grace period before rules become effective absent a finding of good cause for a shorter period. There was no such finding here. [§§378-379]

e. **YES**   Court decisions construe the APA to require the agency to respond in its statement of basis and purpose to material arguments made by the public in comments submitted during rulemaking. [§§372-374]

48.a. **PROBABLY NOT**   The final rule is probably a logical outgrowth of the proposed rule. A final rule does not have to be the same as the proposed rule. The agency is entitled to change it based upon the comments submitted by the public. The final rule can be either more or less restrictive as long as it is a logical outgrowth of the proposed rule, so that commenters would be placed on notice that such an outcome could occur. However, it can be argued that the final rule is so much more severe than the proposed one that Company D could not possibly have anticipated it. [§§369-370]

b. **PROBABLY YES**   Again the logical outgrowth test would suggest that Company E could not anticipate that the EPA would adopt a rule relating to its pollution problem when ABC was not even mentioned in the proposed rule. Yet the EPA was addressing the general problem of pollution from chromium manufacturing and perhaps E should have realized that all chemicals produced in manufacturing that product were up for review. [§§360, 369-370]

49. **NO**   Since the FTC has statutory power to make legislative rules, Flashy can be proceeded against for violation of the rule. The FTC does not, in an adjudicatory proceeding, have to reconsider the legal questions involved in making the rule. The rule now sets the applicable standard of conduct, not the statute. [§330]

50. **NO**   An agency can dispense with public proceedings only upon a finding that such proceedings would be impracticable, unnecessary, or contrary to the public interest. Generally, this requires a real emergency and the court carefully scrutinizes the agency's explanation. Here, the FTC failed to explain what sort of emergency required its shortcuts. Moreover, this is not a situation that appears to be a true emergency; the public could wait a little longer for disclosure to occur in order that people affected would have the right to comment on the rule. [§§396-398]

51.a. **PERHAPS**   The document might fall under the policy statement exception to the APA, which allows the guidelines to be adopted without any prior procedures. A policy statement constrains the agency's discretion but is tentative rather than definitive. These guidelines do affect a discretionary power, but they seem quite inflexible; field personnel are instructed to disregard certain evidence without any exceptions. Although courts often defer to the labels placed on rules by agencies, and this one is called a guideline rather than a rule, it may be too definitive to meet the policy statement exception. [§§408-410] However, the *Lincoln* case suggests that a rule concerning a discretionary function is a policy statement even if it is definitive. [§411]

b. **PROBABLY NOT**

This rule seems to fall under the interpretive rule exception to the APA. Courts usually follow the label placed on the rule by the agency and this is called a "ruling" rather than a "rule," which does suggest it is interpretive. It explains the meaning of a word in the statute and thus could well be interpretive. It does not appear to be legislative in either its purpose or its effect. [§§400-404]

c. **NO**

This rule seems to fall under the procedural rule exception to the APA. It does not modify substantive rights but merely explains what procedures the public must follow to take advantage of certain legal rights. [§394]

52.a. **PROBABLY NOT**

Although *Home Box Office* indicated that undisclosed ex parte contacts in rulemaking were prohibited, later cases have refused to follow it (at least in the context of a rule that applies to an entire industry) and indicate that there is no duty of disclosure of such comments, absent some statutory requirement of disclosure. Imposition of such a duty might violate *Vermont Yankee*. However, the point is not yet completely settled. [§§413, 415-418]

b. **PROBABLY NOT**

Bias standards from adjudication do not apply in rulemaking. According to one case, to disqualify a rulemaker for bias, you must offer clear and convincing evidence that he has an unalterably closed mind on the subject. This standard is designed to be almost impossible to meet and the evidence here is weaker than that found inadequate in the *Association of National Advertisers* case. [§420]

53. **PROBABLY NOT**

Although the rules of the Fourth Amendment prohibiting unreasonable searches and seizures do apply to civil investigatory searches (as shown by *Barlow's*), it appears that this case falls closer to *New York v. Burger*, which allowed a warrantless search. Like *Burger*, the defendant had a license and therefore had "consented in advance" to the inspections. Also, the search was not accompanied by any unauthorized force, and was limited only to specific items. It seems that it was essential to carry out an urgent federal purpose. On the other hand, it is not so clear that a requirement of obtaining a warrant would frustrate the search requirement. Additional facts are needed to know whether the unauthorized use of the materials could be quickly concealed. Also, a search appears to be authorized here during any hour of the day or night, which goes beyond *Burger*. [§§446, 450-454]

54.a.	**NO**	Corporations do not have this privilege. [§462]
b.	**NO**	This is not adequate grounds for quashing an agency's subpoena under the *Endicott-Johnson* case. [§440]
c.	**PERHAPS**	It is possible that the vast amount of information required here by the SEC is excessive for its regulatory purposes and that the court would scale down the request to documents relating to sales of particular stocks or to particular customers. [§443]
55.	**PROBABLY NOT**	The SBA regulations specifically require that certain records be retained. The *Shapiro* case held that Fifth Amendment protection did not apply to such records. Although the *Shapiro* doctrine was later limited by the *Marchetti* case, it would appear that Beth could not rely upon *Marchetti* here: The records required by the SBA are similar to those kept by persons in business, and the recordkeeping requirements concern a primarily noncriminal regulated activity. [§§467, 470]
56.a.	**NO**	This appears to be within the authority of *Hannah v. Larche*, which stated that investigatory panels need not allow cross-examination or afford other due process requirements. The theory in *Hannah* was that the proceedings were simply investigatory, and that the commission could not impose any sanctions for criminal or other violations. Although the *Hannah* case was limited by *Jenkins v. McKeithen*, the latter case involved an investigatory panel that was part of the criminal process; such facts do not appear in our problem. [§§473-474]
b.	**NO**	Although the Constitution does not require counsel at investigatory proceedings, APA section 555(b) provides for representation by counsel for anyone compelled to appear before an agency. [§§477-478]
57.a.	**NO**	Under APA section 553(b)(A), public participation is not required in connection with adopting rules of agency organization, procedure, or practice. [§394]
b.	**NO**	The new rules cannot be applied against Sam because they were not published in the Federal Register as required by APA section 552(a)(1). Unless a person has actual notice of unpublished regulations, he cannot be adversely affected by them. [§484]
58.a.	**YES**	The Freedom of Information Act provides that an action can be brought in the federal district court for a mandatory injunction to require the disclosure of such materials. [§§490, 495]
b.	**YES**	These appear to be "interpretations" not published in the Federal Register. If so, the agency must make all such interpretations available for public inspection and copying under APA section 552(a)(2). [§§485, 487]
c.	**YES**	If the rulings are within APA section 552(a)(2), the CSC is required to maintain an index of all of the interpretations and to make it available to the public. In addition, the index must be updated quarterly. [§488]

d. **PROBABLY YES** — Under APA section 552(b)(6), the agency need not disclose personnel and similar files, the disclosure of which would work a clearly unwarranted invasion of personal privacy. Clearly, disclosure about political activities would be a substantial invasion of privacy. But perhaps the rulings should be released to Bob with all names and identifying details removed; this would probably solve the privacy problem. [§§489, 514-517]

59. **DEPENDS** — Under the 1974 amendments to the Act, the court can review the classification to decide whether secrecy is really necessary. We do not have enough facts to predict what the judge will do. [§498]

60. **NO** — This is commercial or financial information that is privileged or confidential. However, there may be material within the report that is not confidential, and Jake is entitled to see whether it is possible to release this much without making public the confidential part. [§§501-505, 523]

61.a. **NO** — This brings into play APA section 552(b)(5)—an exemption for inter-agency or intra-agency memoranda from disclosure except to an agency in litigation with the agency. Nevertheless, the agency must disclose the factual material in the report, although the policy recommendations need not be made available. Consequently, the court will order production of part of the report. Even then, if the agency can show that disclosure of the factual material would produce an unwarranted interference in the agency's decisionmaking, possibly that material can be kept secret also; but this does not appear to be true in the instant case. [§§506-511]

b. **NO** — There is no equity jurisdiction to refuse to disclose materials that are not specifically protected from disclosure under the Act. [§§495-496]

c. **YES** — This is a decision that terminates a case and, as such, is a final opinion that must be publicized and indexed. It does not fall within the exception for intra-agency memoranda under the *Sears, Roebuck* case. [§509]

62.a. **NO** — Under the "American rule" a party is not entitled to obtain attorney's fees from her opponent, absent some exception or a statutory rule so providing. [§530]

b. **PROBABLY YES** — Meadow is a prevailing party and it is likely that her efforts served the public interest. [§§532-535]

c. **NO** — Note that under the EAJA, reimbursement of attorney's fees is limited to $125 per hour, unless a higher figure is justified by a special factor, such as the need for distinctive knowledge or skill in a particular area. In this instance, it is reasonable to conclude that environmental law is sufficiently specialized to require particular knowledge about that area of law. Therefore, Meadow is entitled to a reasonable hourly fee, which, under the facts, is $200, not $300. Moreover, the court must find that the number of hours spent by the attorney was reasonable. [§§538, 541]

63.a. PROBABLY NOT Under the Equal Access to Justice Act, he can recover fees only if the SEC's position was not "substantially justified," meaning justified to a degree that would satisfy a reasonable person. The facts given here indicate the SEC was wrong, but fail to show that its position was not "substantially justified." [§§536, 539]

b. NO Under the EAJA, reimbursement of fees is limited to $125 per hour, absent unusual facts. [§537]

64. ROBABLY YES Under the *Universal Camera* case, the administrative law judge's assessment of credibility questions is very important. When the board overturns the law judge's decision, it detracts from the substantiality of evidence supporting the board's result. The board did not see Rex testify; the administrative law judge did. Although the appellate board has the ultimate responsibility for the decision, and can reverse the law judge even though there is not a preponderance of the evidence against him, nevertheless a reversal detracts from the evidence supporting the board's decision. In a case as evenly balanced as this seems to be, the board would probably not be sustained on review. [§§556-558]

65. NO Here the fact that the administrative law judge has been reversed is of very little importance since questions of credibility are not involved. The FDA is as competent as the law judge to resolve the scientific questions presented. If a reasonable person could have come to the same conclusion, there is substantial evidence and the board's decision will stand. [§§558, 595]

66.a. NO An agency's findings of fact generally must be upheld on review if supported by *substantial evidence* on the whole record. This means that the SEC's fact findings have to be upheld if a reasonable person could have come to the same conclusion. The reviewing court is *not* allowed to reweigh the evidence and find that a preponderance of the evidence goes a different way. If a reasonable person could have come to the result reached by the agency, the court must uphold the agency even if it believes the result is wrong. [§§544, 550-554]

b. NO The "whole record" requirement of the APA requires that the reviewing court look at both sides in deciding whether a reasonable person could have come to the conclusions that the SEC did. [§553]

67. YES Under the *Ng Fung Ho* case, such a retrial on the issue of citizenship must be provided. Although this is an old case, it has never been overruled. [§§564-565]

68. PROBABLY NOT Under *Chevron*, an agency is deemed to have the power to interpret the words of its statute. Consequently, if the statute lacks a plain meaning, and if the agency's interpretation is reasonable, the court must follow it even if it disagrees. This seems to be an ambiguous statute and the SEC's interpretation appears reasonable. [§§579-582]

69. NO The SEC has erroneously interpreted the statute. It is limited to "intentionally cheating customers," yet the SEC has interpreted this to cover negligence. Here the statute has a plain meaning and despite *Chevron* the court is not obligated to accept the agency's statutory construction. [§581]

70. **NO**   *Chevron* probably should not apply here since the interpretation does not come from the agency head but from a low-level employee. As a result, the court is not bound to follow the interpretation (even if the regulation is ambiguous and Zeke's interpretation is reasonable) if the court disagrees with it. Moreover, the "weak deference" factors do not suggest the decision was correct since it is described as a new interpretation and therefore not one that the agency has followed consistently. The low level at which the interpretation was made also suggests there should be no weak deference. [§§569-577, 585-586]

71.a. **NO**   The usual indicia suggest that the court should not substitute judgment but must follow any reasonable agency application. The issue involves expertise in analyzing a business arrangement and is technical in nature; the courts probably have confidence in the SEC's impartiality; and Congress probably wanted this sort of issue to be resolved by the agency. Finally, the patterns of basic fact can have many variations, something which points to following reasonable agency applications. [§§594-596]

b. **YES**   Determinations here do not seem within the INS's specialized expertise. Often the courts suggest a lack of confidence in the agency's impartiality and competency. The basic facts are simple and would not be subject to wide variation in other cases. Finally, on issues of citizenship, great power is given to the district courts in naturalization cases. [§§599-601]

c. **PROBABLY NO**   The FCC has substantial expertise in classifying television shows and the agency's independence is well regarded. And the issue will have great variations in practice, which suggests the court should not substitute judgment. However, there are important civil liberties implications, which suggests that they should. [§§591, 595, 599-601]

72. **NO**   Such decisions are reviewed under APA section 706(2)(A) as "arbitrary, capricious, or abuse of discretion." Assuming that the Secretary has acted within his authority, the court is only permitted to set aside his decision if the administrator has failed to consider the relevant factors (or considered an irrelevant factor) or made a clear error of judgment. Since the facts do not suggest an arbitrary decision, it should be upheld. [§§603-609]

73.a. **NO**   It should be set aside as an abuse of discretion. The only factor that the Secretary is instructed to take into account is the best interests of the tribe. The factor that he considered—the need of the nation for additional coal—is not such a factor. [§§606-607]

b. **NO**   There must be a record of some sort for the court to review in order to determine whether there has been an abuse of discretion. Post hoc rationalizations by agency attorneys are not sufficient. If there are no fact findings whatsoever by the agency, the trial court is permitted to conduct a trial in which the Secretary will be questioned about his fact finding process; or it may require the Secretary to submit a statement of his reasons. [§617]

74.a. **NO** The courts have very narrow powers of review over the remedy chosen by the agency. It must be upheld unless it is "without warrant in law or justification in fact." In the *Glover Livestock* case, a penalty more severe than that previously meted out by the agency was upheld by the court. [§§618-620]

  b. **NO** Again, the courts have very narrow powers to act where the agency chooses to proceed against one person at a time rather than the entire industry. Absent additional facts showing a particular bias against Tina, the Court would probably uphold the SEC's determination as it did in the *Universal-Rundle* case. [§619]

75. **YES** The Commission has power to order relief that goes beyond the specific wrongful act charged, so that the company will not find some method of circumventing the agency's order. This is the teaching of the *Mandel Brothers* case. [§619]

76. **NO** In the absence of any statement in the statute concerning judicial review, the appropriate forum would be the federal district court in an action for injunction and declaratory judgment. Jurisdiction would be based on 28 U.S.C. section 1331. [§§623-625]

77. **NO** There is no amount in controversy requirement in actions under section 1331. [§626]

78.a. **YES** Under 28 U.S.C. section 1361, a federal court may grant a writ of mandamus. [§630]

  b. **NO** Mandamus only applies if the statute imposes a duty to act. It will not apply to merely discretionary determinations. [§631]

  c. **YES** The statute appears to impose a clear legal duty; no discretion is involved. The court will grant a writ of mandamus requiring the Postmaster to hire Bob. [§§630-632]

79. **NO** Certiorari is only available to review quasi-judicial action based on a record. Rulemaking cannot be reviewed in this manner. [§633]

80. **NO** *Tull* held that the issue of liability for civil penalties is a jury question; however, the trial judge can set the amount of penalties. Note that if the statute allows the agency to impose penalties directly, there is no right to a jury trial at all. [§§638-639]

81. **NO** Under the Eleventh Amendment, the state is immune from actions for damages brought in the federal courts either by its own citizens or by citizens of a different state. [§§642-643]

82.	**NO**	Under 28 U.S.C. section 1391(e), an action may be brought in any judicial district in which a defendant resides, the cause of action arose, the real property is situated, or the plaintiff resides (if no real property is involved). The venue of the suit was proper, either on the theory that real property is involved in Tennessee, or that the plaintiffs reside in Tennessee. [§655]
83.a.	**YES**	Actions for negligence are permitted under the Federal Tort Claims Act. [§661]
b.	**NO**	The Supreme Court in the *Gilman* case held that the United States could not require its employees to indemnify it, even though such suits by the principal against the agent would be allowed in the private law sector. [§669]
84.	**YES**	The Federal Tort Claims Act does permit damage actions for false imprisonment by law enforcement officers. [§664]
85.a.	**YES**	Under the Federal Tort Claims Act, section 2679(b)(1), an action cannot be brought against a federal official for property damages (or personal injury) arising out of the official's negligent or wrongful act or omission while acting within the scope of employment. [§685]
b.	**YES**	This action falls within the discretionary function exception of the Federal Tort Claims Act. This is a high-level policy decision about how to implement a specific program. [§§666-667]
86.	**PROBABLY YES**	*Johnson v. Robison* held that even though such a statute appeared to preclude judicial review, preclusion would apply only to denials of *specific* claims for benefits. However, an attack on the exclusion of *groups* of persons from the benefits of the statute would be allowed. The Court noted that serious constitutional questions would be raised if attacks such as these were precluded. [§§707-711, 715]
87.	**NO**	Prosecutorial discretion is an area "committed to agency discretion by law" under *Heckler v. Chaney*. Under APA section 701(a)(2), there is no "law to apply" (in the language of *Overton Park*) in deciding whom the FTC should prosecute and whom it should not. Therefore, this decision of the FTC will not be reviewable. [§§721-725]
88.	**YES**	Under *Overton Park*, the provision in the APA precluding review of the action committed to agency discretion is construed narrowly. Here there is law to apply—Congress intended to fund research on Alzheimer's. The agency's discretion concerns which proposals to fund, not to refuse to fund any at all. [§722]
89.a.	**NO**	The Supreme Court has made it clear in several cases that one's interest as a citizen in preventing unconstitutional government actions is not sufficient for standing purposes. [§757]
b.	**NO**	Although it is possible to establish standing as a federal taxpayer, the requirements are very narrowly drawn. The challenged action must involve a legislative

decision to spend for the general welfare, and the challenge must be based upon a specific constitutional limitation on the taxing and spending power. [§§758-761]

c. **PROBABLY NOT**

The "injury in fact" test drawn from the *Data Processing* case requires that the injury be concrete and palpable, not abstract. Moreover, the injury must be particularized, *i.e.*, not abstract or general to everyone. [§§733, 739, 754]

90. **YES**

It can allege an "injury in fact" in the sense that its lease will be less valuable if others also have access to the same oil. It can also establish that it is within the zone of interest protected by the statute. Its interest is not inconsistent with the purposes of the statute. [§§736, 745-747, 755]

91. **YES**

Obviously, Seaworthy is injured in fact by having lost the contract. And the statute, which requires the contract to be awarded to the "lowest responsible" bidder, seems to place all of the bidders within the zone of interests protected by the statute. [§§746-747]

92.a. **PROBABLY YES**

The aesthetic injury is an injury in fact, under the *Lujan* and *Sierra Club* cases, as long as the plaintiff alleges that he in particular will be injured. The requirement of filing an environmental impact statement (under the National Environmental Policy Act) creates a zone of interest that protects those who might be harmed by specific federal developments. [§§739, 742, 746]

b. **YES**

Associations of persons harmed have generally been allowed standing to protect the interests of their members if specific members would have standing and the interests sought to be protected are germane to the association's purposes. [§752]

93. **PROBABLY NOT**

The union probably is not within the zone of interests of the statute, as required in cases brought under the APA. The *Air Courier* case rejected standing for unions to complain about postal service deregulation. Absent some showing in the legislative history that Congress was concerned with the impact on labor, the court will probably hold that Congress was simply not concerned with this issue. [§§746-748]

94. **PROBABLY NOT**

The union probably lacks standing for two reasons. First, as in the previous problem, authors may not be within the zone of interests that the statute intended to protect or regulate. Second, there is a causation-remediability problem. Even if the magazines could not get reduced postal rates for all-advertising issues, they might still publish all-advertising issues and pay the higher rates. This case resembles *Allen v. Wright* and *Eastern Kentucky Welfare Rights*, which involved tax subsidies. The Court held that the challenged behavior might not change even if the tax subsidy were withdrawn. [§§744, 746-748]

95. **YES**

Under APA sections 555(b) and 706(1), the court has power to compel agency action that is unreasonably delayed. The court will order the agency to proceed on Norma's application. [§§773-775]

96.	**PROBABLY NOT**	This is a "ripeness" problem—the agency has not yet sought to apply the regulation and the issue is whether the court should wait until the regulation is applied in a concrete case before giving judicial review. Although an issue of law is presented (whether this particular regulation is authorized by statute), the court might well be aided by seeing how the agency defines "unreasonable" in a particular case. The likelihood that the regulation will be clarified by its application suggests it is not yet ripe for review. [§§776-780]
97.	**PROBABLY YES**	The case is ripe for review because Paul's business could be destroyed if Nell complies with the rule, as she is planning to do. This creates a serious hardship for Paul and the case will never become more ripe since Nell does not intend to contest the rule. [§781]
98.	**PROBABLY NOT**	This is an example of attempted judicial review of *informal* administrative action, which is less likely to be ripe for review than formal actions, such as the adoption of regulations. Although the trend is in favor of early judicial review of even informal action, here the showing of injury is relatively weak. It is not clear just what injury (apart from legal fees) would be incurred if the parties go ahead with their merger and then defend an attack by the government. In fact, it is not even clear from the statement whether the Attorney General will prosecute at all. [§§783-786]
99.a.	**NO**	Stanley should first exhaust his administrative remedies by raising the issue with the SEC. Even though it is a legal issue, it is one that the SEC is able to pass upon. Furthermore, the SEC might find that Stanley is not guilty of the charge, so that judicial review would be unnecessary. This seems to be a case in which none of the exceptions to the exhaustion rule apply. [§§790-803]
b.	**NO**	Review would violate the "final order" rule as held in *Standard Oil*. [§§765-766]
100.	**PROBABLY YES**	This may be a case in which exhaustion of remedies would not be required. The Postal Service press release suggests that an appeal might be futile, civil liberties are involved, and a seizure of Mel's movies could do irreparable damage to his business. [§§796-797, 800-803]
101.	**PROBABLY YES**	Exhaustion of remedies might not be required because the hearing procedure of the Air Force Academy may be constitutionally defective in denying confrontation of adverse witnesses. (However, the constitutional point is not yet finally decided.) [§§800-801]
102.	**PROBABLY YES**	The doctrine of primary jurisdiction will probably apply in this case. The issue seems to be a technical one, more within the expertise of the agency than the district court. Furthermore, it seems that Congress has evidenced a desire to centralize the determination of this sort of issue within the agency. Also, there might be a danger of inconsistency if different courts decide this issue in different

ways; however, this seems not to be a serious problem since Roy is bringing a class action, which would bind all purchasers. However, if the court sensed that the agency had not been aggressive about asserting its statutory mandate, it is conceivable that the court might refuse to dismiss the case. [§§807-808]

103. **YES**

This matter is within the primary jurisdiction of the Board. Generally, the courts have deferred to the agencies in cases where a statute clearly gives the agency power to exempt the merger from the antitrust laws; such language shows a congressional intent that the matter be passed upon by the agency. This occurs even though the agency may be less interested in preserving competitive economic conditions than the courts or the Justice Department. An additional argument for dismissal on the grounds of primary jurisdiction is the agency's expertise concerning the economic conditions of the industry, as in *Far East Conference*. [§§815-816]

104. **PROBABLY YES**

A stay seems appropriate. Irreparable injury is shown in the sense that without any money the office would have to close immediately, denying legal representation to many of its clients. Such an abrupt termination of legal services could well be contrary to the public interest. The government will argue that a stay will have the effect of forcing it to spend more money on a program that should be terminated, which is against its best interests. The court must also make a preliminary determination of the likelihood that the agency will prevail on the merits, something that is not possible from the sketchy facts given. On balance, and assuming that the office makes a reasonably good showing that it may prevail on the merits, a stay could well be granted. [§§821-827]

Exam Questions
and Answers

QUESTION I

A. Spray Corp. manufactures various aerosol products, one of which is Howl, a canned spray for driving away dogs. The United States Postal Service ("USPS") is a government corporation which, for purposes of this question, is a federal agency and has the power to adopt legislative rules. The USPS purchases dog repellent on annual contracts won by competitive bidding under a federal statute. The statute requires that contracts for federal purchases of goods and services be awarded only after competitive bidding, and the "lowest responsible bidder" must receive the contract.

The contract for dog repellent for 2001 was won by Spray Corp., the lowest bidder and the maker of "Howl." However, during that year, a number of cans of Howl sold to the USPS apparently failed to work, and several mail carriers were severely mauled by large dogs. As a result, the USPS is refusing to pay for the Howl furnished under the contract. This dispute was set for hearing by the USPS Board of Contract Appeals in March 2002.

Spray Corp. had another difficulty with the government. The Environmental Protection Agency ("EPA") determined that Spray had violated water pollution laws. The EPA recommended that Spray Corp. buy new pollution control devices. Spray Corp. did so and that matter is now closed.

In October of 2001, the USPS took several steps detrimental to Spray's interests. First, without any prior notice or hearing, it adopted a rule that would bar from bidding on a USPS contract for five years any private company that had been found in violation of water pollution laws. Secondly, the USPS announced that the bids for dog repellent needed in 2002 would be received on November 1, 2001. However, the announcement stated that Spray Corp. would not be allowed to bid on the 2002 contract because of the unsatisfactory performance of its products during the previous year. Spray admits its violation of pollution laws, but denies the power of the USPS to bar anyone from bidding on government contracts by reason of such violations. It also denies that Howl functioned inadequately during 2001.

Was Spray Corp. entitled to an immediate administrative hearing in October 2001, and, if so, of what kind?

B. Assume that Spray obtained no relief and was barred from bidding on the 2002 contract. The hearing about breach of the 2001 contract occurred before an administrative law judge in March 2002.

Testimony was heard to the effect that Howl functioned effectively in many instances involving both big and small dogs, but did not function effectively in 11 cases, all of which involved big dogs. The USPS put on as witnesses some of the mail carriers who had been bitten. They testified that they used Howl on windless days, in the correct manner, but that it was not effective. However, Spray's witnesses testified that failures of this kind could be explained by adverse wind conditions, incorrect use of the device, or the fact that the mail carrier did not see the dog coming in time to spray it. Spray also put on as witnesses several mail carriers who had successfully used Howl against large dogs. The administrative law judge believed Spray's witnesses and found the government liable for the purchase price of all Howl purchased under the 2001 contract, in the amount of $96,000.

The USPS Board of Contract Appeals reversed the administrative law judge. It found that the mail carriers who testified for the USPS had testified truthfully. It blamed the failures on the fact that Howl was simply not strong enough to stop a large dog unless used at exactly the correct range. Consequently, the appeals board found that Spray had breached its contractual warranty as to the effectiveness of its product. As a result, Spray became liable for the damages to the mail carriers that the USPS had previously paid in the amount of $83,000. In addition, the appeals board ordered Spray ineligible to bid on the USPS contracts for the next five years upon its further findings that Spray was not "responsible" and thus not an eligible bidder.

Spray is now interested in the advisability of judicial review and wants to know what the scope of review will be and what its prospects of success are. Judicial review would be in the Court of Claims and pursuant to the Administrative Procedure Act.

QUESTION II

A federal statute provides for the acquisition and preservation of historical monuments. The annual appropriation for the purpose is $5 million. The statute provides that the governor of each state shall appoint a historical monument board, which will select one or more historical sites in the state. These recommendations will be forwarded to the newly created National Historical Monuments Board ("NHMB"), which will select those most appropriate for inclusion under the act. However, at least one monument must be selected in each state.

The statute provides: "It is the intention of Congress that the funds appropriated under this act be used to acquire and preserve forever for the benefit and inspiration of the people of the United States those locations or structures at which occurred significant events in the history of the United States." However, the statute provides no rules of procedure for the state and federal boards and says nothing about judicial review.

The governor of Ohio selected three people for the Ohio monuments board. One of them was Art Ardmore, a real estate developer. The Ohio board met informally at Ardmore's home and picked as their only selection for inclusion in the monuments program the home of an amateur inventor who had discovered the pop-top beer can. This home is directly adjacent to land that Ardmore will develop as a real estate subdivision in the near future. This site selection was approved at an informal meeting of NHMB. Consequently, the purchase of the inventor's home by NHMB will be finalized in the next few months.

Several members of the Ohio state legislature disagree with that decision. They wish to have a historical monument on the Kent State campus where several students were slain by the National Guard during a demonstration. From newspaper accounts, they learned of the selection of the inventor's home as a historical monument.

After unsuccessfully petitioning the state board and NHMB, the legislators go into the federal district court in Ohio, seeking to enjoin the disbursement of federal funds for acquisition of the inventor's home and to require that federal funds be spent to acquire and maintain a site on the Kent State campus. What result and why?

QUESTION III

KZXZ is a television licensee in Fresno, California. Its management likes to present X-rated movies in late-night time slots and has paid for exclusive Central California rights to a large film library of sexually oriented films. The FCC has taken no action against KZXZ although there have been a number of viewer complaints about its programming.

The FCC has had difficulties in deciding how to meet public complaints about pornographic material on television. There is a federal criminal statute against "uttering obscene, indecent or profane language" on radio or television; however, federal attorneys have declined so far to prosecute television stations for violations of the statute. The FCC has proceeded by way of forfeitures (*i.e.,* administratively imposed fines provided for by the Communications Act) in a few cases, but the licensees paid the fines rather than litigate them. Finally, the FCC has decided upon a tentative and voluntary system of prescreening by its staff of possibly objectionable material. If the staff finds the film satisfactory, the film can appear on TV without any concern for FCC sanctions. But if the staff thinks that the film is "obscene, indecent or profane," a station showing the film knows that it risks an FCC forfeiture, referral of the matter to the Justice Department for possible prosecution, or quite possibly nonrenewal of its broadcasting license.

This new practice of prescreening has become well known in the industry and was discussed in Broadcasting Magazine, a widely read trade periodical; however, it has not been officially announced by the FCC. Many films have already been prescreened by the staff and some have been approved, some disapproved. However, there has been no public announcement of these decisions. The industry believes that the FCC is trying out the new scheme as a possible method of coping with the problem, to see whether it is feasible and how the industry and Congress will react to it.

KZXZ and its lawyers believe that the prescreening procedure is an illegal system of prior restraint, and that the procedure (or any other FCC regulation of sexually oriented programming) violates the First Amendment and is unauthorized under the Communications Act.

A. KZXZ wishes to find out what has been happening so far with the prescreenings—which films have been accepted, which ones rejected, and by what standards. It also wants to examine the communications that have passed between the staff and FCC Commissioners in connection with adopting and operating the system. Can KZXZ obtain this information and, if so, how?

B. Assume KZXZ obtained no information about the prescreenings beyond what it already knew. KZXZ brings an action in the Federal District Court for the Central District of California, seeking to enjoin further operation of the prescreening system. The FCC moves to dismiss the complaint without reaching the merits. What are the grounds of the FCC's motion and how should it be decided? (*Please do not discuss the merits of the lawsuit—i.e.,* whether the prescreening system in fact violates the First Amendment or the Communications Act.)

QUESTION IV

The FCC has been concerned with violence on television for some time but has not developed any clear policy on the subject. Television station WVIO has offered some commercials advertising a new horror movie. The commercials contain explicit pictures of gory murders, screams of agony, cries for mercy, and the like. Paul Penny, WVIO's station manager, called Terry Tripp, the FCC's general counsel, and asked whether the FCC has any rules against violence on TV. Tripp said that is a sensitive subject but that there are no definite rules. Tripp advised Penny that he need not be concerned about showing any commercials based on present law.

When WVIO's license came up for renewal, several consumer groups requested the FCC to set the matter for a hearing because of the violent commercials and the FCC did so. At the hearing, the commercial was screened. When the lights went on, the administrative law judge was visibly pale. She stated that the commercial was the most horrifying thing she had ever seen and that no station manager in his right mind would have broadcasted it, especially while children might be watching. The judge recommended that the license not be renewed on the grounds of irresponsibility of the licensee in its choice of commercials. Under the Communications Act, broadcasting licenses are granted or renewed if this would serve the public interest, convenience, or necessity.

WVIO appealed to the full FCC, which affirmed the judge. Its opinion declared that station licenses would not be renewed if a licensee showed commercials with scenes of violence unrelated to the content of the message or excessive in relation to the content of the message, especially while children might be watching. Since it declared that the violence was excessive in relation to the content of the message, it declined to renew the license, stating that the public interest would not be served by allowing so irresponsible a licensee to broadcast.

WVIO has appealed to the Court of Appeals for the District of Columbia (which is the correct court in which such appeals should be lodged). What arguments can it make in support of its appeal and how should they be resolved? (Please do *not* discuss whether the FCC's action violated the First Amendment or whether it is void for vagueness.)

QUESTION V

A federal statute has created the National Institute of Health ("NIH"), a federal agency placed in the Department of Human Resources. The agency exists for the purpose of making grants to researchers in the health sciences. The statute provides for a director of the agency, who is presently Theda Thomas. It says nothing about the procedures the agency should follow or about judicial review. The statute provides that "research funds shall be granted to those applicants whom the director decides can best contribute to the store of knowledge about the causes and cures of physical and mental disease." Every year the applications for grants far exceed the funds available to NIH.

NIH has published a booklet entitled "Guidelines for Grant Applications to NIH." The booklet states that grant applications must be submitted by February 1 and the NIH's final decisions shall be announced on June 30. The booklet sets forth a model grant application, which requires information about the proposed project and the hoped-for results, a budget of how the money will be spent, and information on the qualifications of the principal investigator (that is, the person who applies for the grant and is in charge of the project). The booklet does not state that the criminal record of the principal investigator will be considered or must be disclosed. It suggests no procedures that a rejected applicant can follow.

Boris Barnes has a Ph.D. in psychology with a long record of important research and publications concerning the use of drugs for the control of certain psychotic behavior. He is a professor of psychology at Stanford University. He wishes to do a study that would yield information on the long-term results of treatment of mental patients with a particular drug. This will be an expensive project since it requires finding patients who received the drug several years ago and studying their present condition. Barnes believes that the particular drug has a very detrimental long-term effect on patients even though good short-term results are often obtained.

Barnes filed a lengthy application with NIH to receive funds for this project on January 15. He requested a $200,000 grant. However, NIH ran a routine check with the FBI that revealed that Barnes had been convicted of income tax evasion (a federal felony) in 1987. He had served six months in prison and completed two years of probation. The tax evasion consisted of Barnes's claiming deductions on his tax return greatly in excess of what he was entitled to deduct.

Theda Thomas wrote a letter to Barnes on February 16 stating that his grant application would not be considered. The reason was "that your conviction for income tax evasion establishes to our satisfaction that there is a reasonable doubt about your integrity in financial matters; consequently, we feel that you are not qualified to administer a substantial grant. If you disagree with my conclusion, you are free to take the matter up with the Secretary of Human Resources."

After receiving this letter, Barnes did not contact the Secretary of Human Resources. Instead, he filed an action against NIH and Thomas on March 1, in the Federal District Court of the Northern District of California, seeking a declaratory judgment that NIH must consider his application along with all others and that he is entitled to an administrative hearing.

A. NIH moves to dismiss the action. What are the grounds for NIH's motion and how should the district judge rule on each ground?

B. Assume the motion to dismiss is denied and the court decides to hear the case on the merits. How should the case be decided?

QUESTION VI

A. On April 15, the FCC issued the following press release, which was well covered in all major newspapers in the country:

> As part of the government-wide campaign against misleading advertising in the mass media, the FCC announced today that it intends to utilize all available powers to inhibit and prevent misleading, distorted, and false advertising on radio and television. It announced that all licensees are responsible for reasonable verification of product claims made in commercials on radio and television. The FCC stated that it fully intended to use its powers to issue cease and desist orders, impose fines, and deny license renewals to enforce this policy.

The FCC's announcement caused considerable consternation and turmoil within the broadcasting business. Stations began to take steps to inform themselves about product claims made in commercial messages. As a result, station KASH-TV refused to accept for broadcasting several announcements advertising multiple vitamins manufactured by Wonka Vitamin Co. There had recently been publicity given to charges by a Ralph Nader task force that multiple vitamins were unsafe, ineffective, and ridiculously expensive. Consequently, KASH-TV felt that it did not wish to take the risk of running the ads.

Slick Co. is the advertising agency that produced the commercials in question for Wonka Vitamin Co. As counsel to Slick Co., advise the company about whether it could now seek a declaratory judgment to the effect that the FCC's new policy is invalid under the Constitution, the Communications Act, and the APA. (Do not consider at this stage of the question whether the FCC's policy is either properly adopted or substantively valid, merely whether Slick Co. could seek declaratory relief. Do not discuss which federal court is the appropriate one in which to bring the action.)

B. On May 10, a class action is filed in the Superior Court in Los Angeles. It is brought by Hank Harvey, on behalf of himself and all others similarly situated, in tort and contract against Wonka Vitamin Co. Harvey alleges that he has been injured by vitamin overdoses from taking the Wonka multiple vitamins. He also alleges that the vitamins have entirely failed to deal with the health problems (such as iron deficiency) for which they were advertised to be effective. He bases his class action on claims made in televised commercials.

Wonka Vitamin Co. moves to dismiss the action on the grounds that the case should be tried by the FCC under the authority of the April 15 press release. How should the court rule on this motion?

C. Station KADS ran the Wonka ad on June 6. The FCC notified KADS that it proposed to order KADS to cease and desist from running ads without conducting product verification. Its action was taken pursuant to a section of the Communications Act authorizing the FCC to issue cease and desist orders to licensees who violate any validly adopted rule.

At the hearing, the FCC provided evidence that KADS was aware of the press release, that the ads were misleading, that KADS had access to data that revealed that the ads were deceptive, and that the station had failed to try to ascertain the truthfulness of this or any other ad. The administrative law judge found in accordance with these charges and the FCC agreed. It cited the press release as its only authority. It claimed that the press release was a validly adopted rule that explained the meaning of "public interest, convenience, and necessity" (which is the statutory standard for FCC license decisions) and also that it was a policy statement explaining how the FCC would exercise discretion in the future. Will the FCC's order withstand judicial review? (Please assume that the FCC's policy concerning advertising is constitutional, and that the Communications Act would allow the FCC to impose sanctions by reason of unverified advertising if all procedural requirements were satisfied.)

QUESTION VII

The Water Pollution Control Act provides that the Environmental Protection Agency ("EPA") can adopt rules setting limits on water pollution (including thermal pollution) for entire industries "after providing a fair hearing." The limits on pollution must be achievable through the "best available technology." On January 2, the EPA published in the Federal Register a proposed rule applicable to nuclear power plants that would limit the increase in the temperature of the water used to cool the reactor to not more than five degrees Fahrenheit. The EPA did not explain how it derived the five-degree standard. The notice stated that a public meeting would be convened on March 6 to consider the proposed rule and that comments would be welcome until April 1.

At the meeting on March 6, which was attended by representatives of dozens of nuclear power plants as well as many environmental groups, the staff member who presided (not an administrative law judge) said she would not permit any cross-examination of EPA staff members and she would only listen to oral statements. The lawyer for Blue Demon Power Co. was among those who requested that staff members be cross-examined; he also spoke for 20 minutes explaining that Blue Demon's seven-year-old reactor presently heated the water by 36 degrees and could not possibly meet the five-degree limitation. Blue Demon submitted a lengthy written statement to this effect, accompanied by a scientific study showing that even with the application of the best available technology its cooling system would still heat the ocean water by 20 degrees.

On June 15, the EPA adopted a final rule that retained the five-degree test for new reactors, effective immediately. It adopted a 12-degree test for existing reactors and deferred the effective date for five years. It stated that there was no available technology that would permit such a reduction at the present time, but that research was actively continuing in the field and the various pollution control companies were rushing new models to market and that adequate equipment to meet the 12-degree standard would be available long before the effective date.

Blue Demon has discovered that the EPA relied on a staff study of the pollution control industry that stated that plenty of new equipment, suitable for limiting the heat increase to 12 degrees, would be available long before the effective date. Blue Demon believes this study is full of holes, that the proposed equipment will be unworkable for its type of reactor and would not meet the 12-degree standard for any type of reactor, and will not be ready by the effective date. It feels it could have demolished the study if cross-examination of its author had been allowed and if the study had been disclosed during the comment period.

Blue Demon has also discovered that representatives of an environmental group (Friends of the Earth) had many conversations with Sam Squid, the EPA Administrator, and the staff, both during the comment period and after it closed, urging the EPA to adopt extremely strict thermal pollution standards to preserve marine life. Blue Demon's lawyer had been unable to get an appointment with Squid or with the staff to discuss its point of view informally.

Blue Demon has also learned that Donna Flounder, an EPA staff member who worked for Friends of the Earth until November of last year, had been in charge of preparing the proposed rule and considering comments and was by far the most influential staff member on the subject. Flounder had many conversations with Squid urging him to adopt a strict limit on pollution and to disregard the critical comments submitted by Blue Demon and other operators. The EPA's final rule is an exact copy of Flounder's final memo to Squid.

Finally, Blue Demon discovered that Squid recently gave a speech to the Save the Whales Foundation in which he stated that thermal pollution from nuclear power plants was a grave threat to marine life and he intended to do all in his power to remedy the problem, consistent with economic and technological constraints.

Blue Demon properly seeks review of the rule in the appropriate United States Court of Appeals. What arguments should it raise and how should the court dispose of them?

QUESTION VIII

Congress enacted a statute to deal with the critical problem of toxic waste dump sites. Thousands of these dump sites, in use for many years, are leaking toxic chemicals, endangering large numbers of people, and poisoning ground water. The statute creates a "superfund" to which all companies producing toxic wastes must contribute (in a total amount between $4 to $6 billion) to be matched by a contribution from the United States Treasury of $5 billion; the superfund will pay for cleaning up the most dangerous dump sites.

The statute creates the Federal Toxic Waste Agency ("FTWA"), headed by an Administrator, to administer the superfund and clean-up operations. The statute gives the FTWA five years to adopt rules to fix the amount each company must pay to the superfund. This amount depends on the toxicity of the chemical wastes the firm produces, the length of time it has been in operation, and its ability to pay. The statute provides that the rules fixing liability are to be adopted in conformity with section 553 of the Administrative Procedure Act and that the Administrator, in his discretion, may permit cross-examination on disputed issues of material fact. In the event a company fails to pay the amount set forth in the rules, this sum can be collected by an action in federal district court.

The FTWA decided to approach the rulemaking task in several phases. The first phase would establish which manufacturing processes produced sufficient toxic wastes so that such manufacturers would be forced to pay into the superfund. The second phase would fix the exact liabilities.

The rules recently adopted in this first phase list PFB as a chemical, the manufacture of which produces toxic wastes. They also list QRC as a chemical, the manufacture of which does not produce toxic wastes. Sniff Chemical Co. makes PFB exclusively and concedes that making it produces highly toxic wastes. However, Sniff believes that making QRC also produces toxic wastes. Sniff appeals to the District of Columbia Court of Appeals (the correct court) complaining of the omission of QRC from the list of chemicals whose manufacture produces toxic wastes. The Administrator moves the appeal be dismissed because Sniff lacks standing. How should the court rule on this motion?

QUESTION IX

Assume the same facts as Question VIII. The FTWA undertook the second phase of rulemaking—assessing exact liabilities for superfund contribution. Because of the enormous complexity of the problem, the thousands of firms affected, and the now-pressing time schedule (only about six months remain to do the job), the Administrator announced that no cross-examination would be permitted and only written comments would be considered. The proposed rules published in the Federal Register would impose a liability of $22 million on Sniff—about one-third of its entire net worth and much more than its available cash. One day after publication of the proposed rules, Sniff appeals to the District of Columbia Court of Appeals (again the correct court) arguing that the procedures to be used in the second phase of rulemaking are legally inadequate. Assuming the court reaches the merits of this claim, how should the court rule?

QUESTION X

Assume the same facts as Questions VIII and IX. Should the court of appeals have dismissed Sniff's appeal, described in Question IX, on the grounds that it was premature?

ANSWER TO QUESTION I

A. Right to Immediate Administrative Hearing

The right to an immediate administrative hearing depends on whether there is a constitutional or statutory right to a hearing.

Rule barring bidding by pollution violators: Spray has no constitutional right to a trial-type hearing on the issue of whether the USPS may properly bar it from bidding on government contracts. The *individualized facts* required for such a hearing are missing here; the only issue is one of policy as to whether violators of the pollution laws should be allowed to bid on government contracts. Even though this rule is somewhat unusual in having a retroactive effect, and in perhaps being aimed at only a single company, there is still no right to a trial-type hearing. Moreover, the rule is questionable from a rationality point of view. It might also be ultra vires, but that is not an issue within the scope of this question.

Spray will also argue that it has a right to the notice and comment procedures provided under APA section 553. However, the USPS will argue that this particular rule falls under one of several possible exceptions. The most likely exception is that this rule relates to *public contracts* and therefore is entirely exempt from the requirements of notice and comment under section 553(a)(2). A court might construe this exception narrowly, however, holding that the rule relates to much more than public contracts; it actually represents an undertaking by the USPS to enforce the pollution laws. Therefore, it is not the simple sort of rule, merely regulating public contracts, that was contemplated by the section 553(a)(2) exception.

The USPS might also argue that this is an *interpretive rule* (interpreting the word "responsible") and thus exempt from the notice and comment procedures under APA section 553(b)(A). However, this argument should be rejected. The test is whether the agency intended to use its legislative rulemaking power.

The USPS has not labeled the rule as interpretive, and any doubt should be resolved in favor of public participation. In addition, the substantial impact of the rule suggests it is not interpretive. Finally, the rule does seem to fill a gap in the statute and definitely alters the rights of Spray to bid on contracts. For all the above reasons, the rule must be legislative rather than interpretive, and therefore requires a legislative-type hearing.

If APA section 553 applies, the USPS must give prior notice and allow public comments before putting the proposed rule into effect. In addition, the USPS must publish the rule 30 days before its effective date. Although no oral hearing is required, the provision for public comments would permit Spray to make its position on the rule clear to the USPS.

Debarment of Spray from bidding due to unsatisfactory performance: This determination does involve resolution of *individualized facts* (*i.e.,* did a particular product perform unsatisfactorily); thus, there is a constitutional right to a trial-type hearing on this matter. Moreover, a ***property interest*** of Spray is involved since it has a right to receive the contract if it is the lowest responsible bidder—this is an entitlement under *Board of Regents v. Roth*. Also, a ***liberty interest*** is arguably involved, since Spray's corporate good name has been maligned, with financial loss likely in terms of lost opportunities to sell to the government.

Is Spray entitled to an ***immediate hearing***, or can the debarment from bidding be heard at the March 2002 hearing set for the 2001 contract dispute? Ordinarily, a hearing must occur ***before*** the relevant deprivation of liberty or property, unless there is good reason to delay it. Under the three-factor formula of *Mathews v. Eldridge,* Spray's interest in an immediate hearing is strong: It will miss out on the 2002 bidding unless the error is corrected now, the risk of error by the USPS is substantial, and the government has no apparent interest in delaying the hearing.

[For extra credit, the rights of Spray at a trial-type hearing might be discussed: confrontation of adverse witnesses, the right to present its own witnesses, the right to counsel, a decision based on the record, a statement of reasons, and an independent decisionmaker.]

B. Judicial Review of the Agency Decision

Scope of review: Two decisions were reached by the USPS appeals board. The first decision—that Spray's product was not effective—seems like a pure question of fact (*i.e.,* what happened and why). The scope of review applicable to a pure question of fact is "substantial evidence on the whole record" under APA section 706(2)(E).

The second decision was that, by reason of the failure of Howl, Spray was not a "responsible bidder." This involves the application of basic facts to a statutory term. The scope of review of a mixed question is sometimes treated as a review of fact, sometimes as a review of law. Here, the issue will probably be treated as one of fact.

The court must first define the term "responsible bidder" as an issue of law. Does it mean financially responsible? Or able to turn out a reliable product? Assuming it means the latter, the factual issue is then whether a company that turns out 11 defective cans out of thousands is "responsible."

The agency would probably be a more appropriate forum for making this determination. There could be innumerable factors to consider in fitting the basic facts to this rather loosely defined standard. The USPS is the expert on product quality and its own needs, not the court; and, as far as one can tell, the court trusts this agency to make an impartial determination. It is also arguable that Congress intended to commit this sort of decision to the agency.

Similar analysis could be used to establish that the agency would be a better arbiter than the court as to the question of whether the malfunctioning cans constituted a breach of the warranty of effectiveness.

Under *Chevron*, federal courts must follow reasonable agency legal interpretations. The same principle may be applied to application questions.

The appeals board decision concerning remedy—the five-year debarment from bidding—is a matter of agency discretion, and would be reviewed under the abuse-of-discretion standard.

Prospects for success: The strongest point in Spray's favor is the fact that the administrative law judge believed Spray's witnesses, not those of the USPS. Evidently, the administrative law judge decided that Howl was used on windy rather than windless days, or that the mail carriers did not see the dogs coming in time. Where an agency reverses the administrative law judge on an issue of credibility, this undercuts the substantiality of evidence in favor of its decision. [Universal Camera Corp. v. NLRB]

On the other hand, the issues may actually turn on technical chemical analysis, rather than credibility of witnesses, where the conclusion of the administrative law judge is entitled to no special deference. Even so, it could be argued that the USPS has no expertise in considering issues relating to chemistry.

Another point in Spray's favor is that apparently there was no evidence supporting the Board's finding that the chemical was not strong enough to stop a large dog unless used at exactly the correct range. Indeed, this could be a case in which the agency could be reversed for ignoring the approach taken by the administrative law judge. [Cinderella Career & Finishing Schools, Inc. v. FTC]

However, the standard for review of the Board's decision on product effectiveness is substantial evidence. The Board's finding here appears reasonable and should be affirmed. Similarly, its finding on the application question of whether Spray is "responsible" is reviewed under the substantial test; that finding also appears reasonable. It is very unlikely that the Board's discretionary choice of remedy would be overturned.

ANSWER TO QUESTION II

Standing: To have standing to obtain judicial review of action taken by a federal agency, the plaintiff must be able to show an *injury in fact* and fall arguably within the *zone of interests* protected or regulated by the statute.

It is far from clear whether the Ohio legislators have been injured in fact. The proposed purchase by NHMB does not jeopardize any legislation with which they have been involved, nor does it interfere with the Ohio legislative process. Thus, the legislators appear to be in no different position than all other citizens who simply are unhappy with the NHMB decision, and any harm is merely "generalized." True, the legislators claim an aesthetic or environmental injury because they do not like the chosen site and would prefer another one, but this interest seems to fall short of the definite and palpable harm to particular plaintiffs that the Court was willing to accept in *Sierra Club v. Morton.* Moreover, it is necessary for the plaintiff to claim that he plans to use the very property in question in order to claim environmental injury. [Lujan v. National Wildlife Federation]

It is not possible to base the legislators' standing on the fact that they pay taxes; under *Flast v. Cohen,* taxpayer standing is appropriate only where a specific constitutional provision has been violated.

Moreover, the court might deny them standing under *Simon v. Eastern Kentucky Welfare Rights Organization* because the requirement of remediability cannot be met. A decree enjoining the NHMB from building the monument to the pop-top inventor would not at all guarantee that they could have a monument at Kent State.

However, if the legislators are somehow able to satisfy the injury in fact requirement, they probably will have no difficulty in establishing that they fall within the zone of interests protected or regulated by the statute. Since the statutory language suggests that the monuments are intended to inspire citizens, anyone who might be inspired is within the zone of interests.

Sovereign immunity: Although once a serious problem, the government has now consented to be sued for nonmonetary relief for injuries caused by the actions of federal agencies. [APA §702] Therefore, sovereign immunity would not bar an action by the legislators against the government.

Reviewability: There is no evidence that Congress intended to preclude judicial review of the selection of historical sites; therefore, the general presumption of reviewability prevails. However, the possibility remains that the decision is committed to agency discretion, and is thus unreviewable under APA section 701(a)(2).

It could well be argued that Congress meant to leave the funding decisions entirely to the discretion of the relevant state and federal agencies. Yet *Citizens to Preserve Overton Park v. Volpe* makes clear that the exemption from review of decisions committed to agency discretion is very narrow in scope. There is "law to apply" here—the sites have to "benefit and inspire" the people and have to be "locations at which occurred significant events" in United States history. This provides some framework of law—certainly as much as the "feasible and prudent" language found to be sufficient in *Overton Park.* Consequently, the decision is reviewable and is not one committed wholly to agency discretion.

Ripeness: It could be argued that the decision is not yet ripe for judicial review because the site has not yet been purchased. However, further delay in this case will not make the issues any more fit for review, and the remaining steps of actual purchase are merely mechanical. Thus, the decision does seem ripe for review.

Mandamus: Although it is possible that the court will enjoin the purchase of the pop-top site, it is most unlikely that it would issue a mandatory injunction to force acquisition of the Kent State site. This would be an unwarranted interference with the agency's discretion. Mandamus will not lie to compel an agency to take a particular discretionary action—only to compel the exercise of discretion or performance of a ministerial act. At best, therefore, the process would be started anew to choose a more favorable site.

Abuse of discretion: Even though the NHMB decision is reviewable, it would be difficult to establish that the board had considered inappropriate factors, had failed to consider appropriate factors, or had made a clear error of judgment. Surely there are people who would find the chosen site more beneficial and inspiring than Kent State, and surely people might find the invention of the pop-top beer can to be a significant historical event. Thus, the decision is probably not an abuse of discretion, although a judge might find it to be a clear error of judgment if he were sufficiently offended. However, even if not an abuse of discretion, the decision could be set aside for procedural irregularities—namely, Ardmore's participation.

Bias: Ardmore's financial interest in the site chosen is a form of pecuniary bias that would have disqualified him from an adjudicatory proceeding. However, this was not an adjudication—it was a discretionary grantmaking process. Nevertheless, it has been held that political pressure can result in grantmaking procedure being set aside [D.C. Federation of Civic Associations v. Volpe], and the same should be true where the bias stems from a decisionmaker who has a financial interest in the proceedings. All potential grantees of government funds should be entitled to an unbiased selection process. Whether this requirement is constitutional, or implied from the statute, Ardmore should be disqualified and the process started anew without him. On the other hand, this might be viewed as judicial prescription of procedures for informal adjudication not found in the APA and thus contrary to the *LTV* case.

ANSWER TO QUESTION III

A. Obtaining Information

Information as to prescreenings: Information about particular films could be subject to disclosure as "final opinions" or as "interpretations adopted by the agency" under the Freedom of Information Act. Alternatively, they could be "identifiable records" that the agency must make available to the public under APA section 552(a)(3). Therefore, KZXZ should first request the information from the FCC. If the request is denied, KZXZ should then seek a mandatory injunction from the federal district court in the district in which it resides to compel disclosure of this information.

The FCC could not prevent disclosure of the information regarding the films on the basis of the exemption for intra-agency memoranda [APA §552(a)(5)] since the results of the prescreenings were disclosed to those who submitted the films. Conceivably, the information could be exempt from disclosure under APA section 552(a)(4) as commercial information obtained from a person that is privileged or confidential, but this seems unlikely since there was no expectation that the results of the prescreenings would be kept confidential.

Communications within FCC: The memoranda between the FCC Commissioners and the staff might fall within the exception for intra-agency memos [APA §552(b)(4)], which are not available by law to outsiders. Policymaking memoranda are exempt from disclosure because the agency cannot operate "in a fishbowl," and disclosure might inhibit candid comments. However, any *factual material* contained in these memos is *not* within the privilege, and disclosure can be compelled with appropriate deletions of protected material. Thus, at least some of the comments made by the staff on how the prescreening program is working probably would be discoverable.

B.   **Motion to Dismiss:** The FCC can argue a number of grounds in support of its motion to dismiss KZXZ's complaint.

Venue: The venue is appropriate. Actions against agencies can be brought where the cause of action arose or where the plaintiff resides. [28 U.S.C. §1391(e)]

Ripeness: The FCC will contend that litigation as to its prescreening procedures should not occur until it has formalized the process and applied it to KZXZ—in other words, until the suit is "ripe for review." To determine whether a regulation that has not yet been applied to a plaintiff is ripe for review, the susceptibility of the issues to immediate review must be weighed against the hardship to the parties from delaying review. [Abbott Laboratories v. Gardner]

The issues here may well be better suited to review in the context of actual facts—after it is seen precisely how the prescreening system is functioning, whether it is sensed as mandatory or voluntary, whether the staff has developed any standards, etc. At this point, the system is still very tentative and subject to change. Moreover, it has never been formally adopted by the FCC as a final decision; nor is it "self-executing" in the sense that it would require any immediate change in anyone's behavior. Thus, the issues are *not* well suited for immediate review.

Also, the hardship to KZXZ seems relatively modest. The suit could easily wait until the procedure is firmed up by formal adoption and actual application. The system is completely voluntary, so KZXZ is probably not taking any serious risks by screening a few films on TV that have not been prescreened. (However, an argument could be made that the present uncertainty is extremely damaging, and the KZXZ would not dare, as a practical matter, to defy the FCC staff by ignoring the procedure.)

Another factor sometimes weighed is whether the public interest would be harmed or helped by immediate review. Here, prompt review might well serve the public interest by removing doubts about the validity of the system without interrupting the FCC's experiment. But this consideration is not sufficient to outweigh the unsuitability of the issues for immediate review; and, in sum, the procedure is probably not yet ripe for review.

Exhaustion of remedies: The FCC will also argue that KZXZ should exhaust its administrative remedies before seeking judicial review. The prescreening procedure is itself an administrative remedy, and it could be argued that KZXZ should not be able to litigate before submitting its films for review. After all, the films might be approved by the FCC, thus eliminating any problem. The traditional rule is to give the agency a chance to complete its procedures, without interrupting them by premature review.

However, KZXZ could counter by stating that the problem would not really be solved by submitting the films for review. The objection is to the *legality* of the procedure itself, and even if the films were approved, the objection would remain. As in *Allen v. Grand Central Aircraft Co.*, the objection is that the law does not permit the administrative remedy to exist at all. Moreover, the issues are legal, not factual, and would not be clarified by having the agency screen any particular films. Because of the substantial constitutional questions here, and the great danger of chilling the First Amendment rights involved in media programming, it would seem that an exception to the exhaustion requirement is appropriate.

Commitment to agency discretion: The agency might argue that adoption of such procedures as prescreening, in order to enforce the federal statute prohibiting obscenity on TV, was committed to its discretion. But this argument is not persuasive, since the basis of KZXZ's attack is that the procedures are unlawful, and the agency would not have discretion to adopt an unconstitutional or illegal procedure.

ANSWER TO QUESTION IV

Adoption of new policy: It can be argued that the FCC's new policy on violence in commercials should have been adopted through rulemaking instead of adjudication. This would have eliminated the harsh and unjust result of adopting the policy in a way that retroactively punishes conduct that was legal when it occurred. It also would have insured public participation so that all the pros and cons of a rule of far reaching significance could have been explored. The problem obviously is not new and unexpected, and the harm from allowing renewal of WVIO's license is slight, based on the single nonrecurring instance of broadcasting the commercials. This may well be a case like *NLRB v. Guy F. Atkinson Co.*, in which the rules of *SEC v. Chenery* and *NLRB v. Bell Aerospace Co.* would suggest that adoption of the policy through adjudication was an abuse of discretion.

Estoppel: A few cases suggest that the government can be estopped. However, it is unlikely that the FCC would be estopped by Tripp's advice to Penny. The United States Supreme

Court cases have been very negative toward estoppel claims, but have not definitively precluded them. Most of the lower court cases arise in situations in which the government is acting in a proprietary character or engaged in programs like subsidies or insurance, not in standard regulatory programs where an estoppel would cause the agency to be prevented from implementing the public interest. Penny may well have detrimentally relied on Tripp's statement, but the case would be stronger if Penny had been advised by the FCC Commissioners in an advisory opinion or an interpretive regulation and if he had gotten the statement in writing. Also, Tripp made it clear that the area was sensitive and there was no definite rule, which suggests Penny was still assuming substantial risks. All in all, estoppel is unlikely.

Validity of new policy: Although you are instructed by the question not to discuss the First Amendment or the void for vagueness doctrine, it is apparent that the policy touches on sensitive First Amendment concerns and is suspiciously vague in an area in which clearcut rules are important (regulation of expression). Since the Communications Act standard itself is very vague (public interest, convenience, necessity), a court could certainly construe the statute to prohibit the FCC from regulating violence on television. In line with cases like *Kent v. Dulles,* statutes are often construed narrowly so that agency action touching on sensitive constitutional concerns is held ultra vires. *Rust v. Sullivan* is to the contrary, however. Although the FCC's statute has been upheld as a valid delegation of legislative authority, this does not mean that the FCC has carte blanche to suppress any form of expression because it decides that public interest requires it; much clearer congressional approval might be needed for such a departure from present law.

Bias of judge: Although the judge made an unguarded comment about the case after seeing the commercial, this would not be considered a disqualifying personal bias since it arose from events at the hearing and simply was the judge's evaluation of the evidence she had seen and heard.

Remedy: It could certainly be argued that the FCC has committed a "clear error of judgment" by refusing to renew a license because of one isolated instance, particularly where the licensee had good reason to think it was valid under present law and taking into consideration the harshness of forfeiting a license in which large economic investments have been made, the questionability of the new policy, the retroactive aspects of its adoption, and the Tripp advice. However, courts have a narrow scope of review and may not substitute their own judgment for that of an agency, even where the agency's remedy is unusually harsh or severe. Generally, an agency's remedy must be upheld unless it is without warrant in law or justification in fact, or where there has been an abuse of discretion. On the other hand, if the FCC failed to explain why its remedy was unusually harsh, WVIO may be able to have the case remanded so that the FCC can rationalize its decision.

ANSWER TO QUESTION V

A. Motion to Dismiss

Sovereign immunity: Previously this would have raised difficult questions of whether Thomas had acted beyond her powers—but it has now been waived in actions against the United States (except those for money damages). Barnes need not seek money damages, but only a declaratory judgment that he is entitled to reconsideration of his application without considering the conviction; also, he might seek different administrative procedures. Neither is a claim for money damages.

Venue: Venue is appropriate under the federal statute. [28 U.S.C. §1391(e)]

Exhaustion of remedies: This is a serious problem, as Barnes has not appealed to the Secretary. Exhaustion might well be required—it would not be onerous to delay judicial review until Barnes appeals to the Secretary. His appeal might be successful, thus making judicial intervention unnecessary. On the other hand, the issues are not factual (irrelevant factor, inadequate procedure) and the facts are fully developed; moreover, the statute does not provide for appeal to the Secretary, so no congressional scheme is being flouted if the appeal is eliminated. Most significantly, under APA section 705 (which covers the related "final order" problem), agency action is final for judicial review purposes even though there has been no appeal to superior agency authority unless the agency otherwise provides by rule—and there is no NIH or DHR rule mentioned in the problem. Exhaustion thus is not required.

Ripeness: There should be no problem with ripeness since the agency has done all that it is ever going to do in Barnes's case. There is nothing tentative about its actions and nothing will be clarified by waiting for any other agency action.

Commitment to agency discretion: There should be no problem where the issue is whether the agency has considered an improper factor or whether it has provided inadequate procedures. If the ultimate issue were simply whether Barnes's application should be funded as against someone else's, and the decision turned on scientific appraisal, the decision would probably be committed to agency discretion, but such is not the case.

Preclusion of review: This is no problem since the statute does not implicitly or explicitly preclude review. Reviewability is presumed absent some strong reason for making decisions nonreviewable, and no such reason appears here.

B. Merits

Abuse of discretion: The scope of review here is whether the action is "arbitrary, capricious, or an abuse of discretion." An income tax conviction suggesting fraud in listing deductions is a relevant factor in consideration of a grant application. Giving a large federal grant certainly presupposes honesty in accounting for costs and funds; someone who greatly overstated deductions on a tax return quite possibly is not trustworthy in accounting matters. Perhaps Thomas overdid things by her decision that the grant application would not be considered at all—*i.e.*, that the tax conviction completely ruled out Barnes's application, as opposed to simply being taken into account as a negative factor. It might be reasonable to argue that a conviction over 10 years old could properly be considered, but not as a clear disqualifying factor, simply as a negative factor.

Right-privilege doctrine: In earlier days, Barnes's claim would undoubtedly have been denied since he was seeking a federal grant that would certainly be in the area of a privilege, not a right, but modern cases reject the distinction and enforce claims even for discretionary benefits if they have been wrongfully denied or denied without proper procedures.

Right to a hearing: Barnes should claim that he has a right to a hearing, although this claim is somewhat tainted by his failure to ask for one. The statute grants no right to a hearing so the APA is inapplicable, but Barnes can argue that he has been denied either liberty or property by the denial. The liberty argument is that rejection of the application because he lacks financial integrity imposes a stigma that would prevent his getting any grants in the future and this would probably terminate his scientific career. The rejection of the application, together with its stigmatic effect, meets the "stigma plus" requirement of *Paul v. Davis*. Assuming that Thomas's decision will be made known to future grantors (which is likely since grant applications ask about the applicant's history and why any prior applications had been rejected), there is a serious stigmatic effect that would justify a hearing. The property argument should be rejected: Barnes has not been deprived of anything he already has and the statute certainly is discretionary and does not suggest any entitlement.

Assuming the liberty argument is accepted, there are certainly adjudicatory facts at issue (financial integrity). Thomas might argue that the only issue is one of policy—does a prior tax conviction automatically debar an applicant for a grant—and not factual at all, which suggests no constitutional right to a hearing. Thus the decision is wrapped up with the abuse of discretion issue already discussed—if Thomas is entitled to reject applicants who have tax convictions out of hand, there is obviously nothing to hold a hearing about. If she is entitled to treat convictions as a negative factor in considering financial integrity but not as a disqualifying factor, a hearing that explores all elements of Barnes's financial integrity would be appropriate.

Rulemaking-adjudication: It can be argued that the new policy—that tax convictions automatically debar an applicant—should have been adopted by rulemaking, not on a case-by-case basis. This would give the public an opportunity to have input in the decision and allow NIH to adopt a rule that would cover all crimes and thus give fair warning so that applicants would not suffer the stigma of rejection. But there is really no serious retroactive harm visited on grant applicants in the sense of *NLRB v. Guy F. Atkinson Co.* (a financial penalty); their application has simply been rejected. Moreover, NIH may not have anticipated the problem and the problem of judging financial disqualifications may not be susceptible to codification in rule form. This argument should be rejected. Moreover, even if rulemaking were employed, the agency would not have to use a public hearing because the rule would probably be an interpretive rule or a policy statement [APA §553(b)(A)] and also because rules relating to grants are excepted from the notice-comment rules [APA §553(a)(2)].

ANSWER TO QUESTION VI

A. Slick's Action

Standing: Slick has been "injured in fact," since its commissions depend on whether commercials are screened. However, there is a serious problem with the "zone of interests" test. Although several cases have been lenient in applying the zone of interests requirement, under *Air Courier Conference v. American Postal Workers Union,* the court looks only to the particular statute under which the challenge is based (the Communications Act here) and looks for evidence that the statute was intended to protect or regulate the plaintiff. It seems unlikely that the act was intended to protect advertising agencies; it is exclusively concerned with the interests of viewers and broadcasters. Absent leniency by the court or some evidence in the legislative history of concern for advertisers, Slick probably lacks standing. Moreover, there is a problem with causation and remediability; their commercial may not be screened even if the policy is struck down. This seems unduly speculative, however, since the commercials were rejected exclusively because of the FCC's policy.

Ripeness: This is a serious issue since the policy has been stated only in a press release, not a rule, and informality of statement suggests the issue is not ripe. It is not at all clear what is the meaning of reasonable verification or how the FCC will in fact carry out the policy. Waiting until the policy is applied may facilitate judicial review. On the other hand, the harm to Slick is immediate and it and many other advertisers and advertising agencies will undoubtedly be harmed (and stations will lose much revenue) before the policy is clarified, if it ever is. Also, the policy was issued by the FCC itself, not by the staff, which offsets its informality. Thus the *Abbot Laboratories v. Gardner* balance seems to point toward immediate review.

B. Harvey's Action

Primary jurisdiction: If primary jurisdiction is applicable, the trial should occur at the FCC, not in Superior Court. However, it seems clear that primary jurisdiction should not be applied here, simply because the FCC does not take cases brought by individuals and does not award damages to individuals. It does have powers to penalize broadcasters, for example, by cease and desist orders or civil penalties or license nonrenewals, but none of these would be very helpful to Harvey's class. In addition, the FCC has little or no expertise in considering tort or contract actions, and there is no problem of lack of uniformity from conflicting court decisions (the class action will definitively dispose of these claims). None of the reasons for primary jurisdiction are applicable.

C. KADS's Action

Rulemaking: The key issue on KADS's appeal is whether the press release qualifies as a validly adopted rule, since the Act only permits cease and desist orders for violation of a validly adopted rule. The press release does seem to state a rule as this term is defined in APA section 551(4)—a statement of general applicability and future effect designed to implement, interpret, or prescribe law or policy. However, was it "validly adopted"? Generally, APA section 553 requires prior notice, opportunity to comment, and a 30-day pre-publication period for a rule, and the FCC did none of this. But these requirements do not apply to interpretive rules or policy statements and the FCC must be contending that the rule is interpretive (*i.e.*, it explains the meaning of "public interest . . ." etc.) or a policy statement (*i.e.*, it explains how the FCC will exercise discretion).

Courts usually defer to agency descriptions that a rule is "interpretive," but the FCC never claimed this status for the rule at the time it was adopted. It is more plausible to argue it is a "policy" statement since the press release did describe it as a policy and did describe how the FCC intends to exercise discretion in the future. However, it is not a policy statement unless it is tentative; if it is a definitive statement of how the agency will exercise discretion, it must be adopted as a legislative rule. [Note that the Supreme Court in *Lincoln v. Vigil* may have undercut the tentative requirement for policy statements.] The language of the statement does appear to be quite inflexible. Moreover, the action against KADS appears to confirm that the FCC treats the product-claim statement as a rule, not a policy statement, since it is now seeking a sanction based directly on it.

In any event, it seems unlikely that the Communications Act requirement that a cease and desist order be based on a validly adopted rule means an interpretive rule or a policy statement. Surely the Act meant that cease and desist orders can only be based upon legislative rules, adopted after appropriate public input, stating a definite legal requirement that a broadcaster would understand is binding. An interpretive rule or policy statement could well be a valid way of warning the industry how the Commission will conduct its licensing operations, but would not be binding on the industry and thus not sufficient under the statute for a cease and desist order.

Adjudication: An agency can adopt a new rule through adjudication, as in *SEC v. Chenery* and *NLRB v. Bell Aerospace Co.*, and validly apply it to the parties to the adjudication, provided that the choice of adjudication rather than rulemaking was not an abuse of discretion. Here, the choice of adjudication would probably be upheld since there is no real hardship to KADS (it is ordered to cease and desist, not to pay a penalty) and no surprise (they had fair warning through the press release). Moreover, the problem is difficult and might well be susceptible to case-by-case development. However, the trouble is that cease and desist orders can only be imposed for violation of a rule and this probably means a rule adopted through rulemaking, not a rule adopted as part of adjudication. However, this point is arguable and the FCC could contend that a rule adopted as part of adjudication could be the basis for a cease and desist order.

Even if the FCC could adopt its "rule" through adjudication, there is a possibility of applying the *NLRB v. Wyman-Gordon Co.* case. That case held that an invalidly adopted rule could not serve as the sole basis for decision in a subsequent adjudication. The argument here is that the FCC relied exclusively on the press release as authority in the KADS case as opposed to deriving the principle from the statute, and the press release could only be used that way if it was a legislative rule and it was never adopted as such. The FCC would argue that it had created its rule in the KADS case and was not relying solely on the press release—as occurred in *Wyman-Gordon* in which the court affirmed the subsequent adjudication because it had not simply relied solely on the prior invalid rule.

In summary, even if the FCC did properly concoct its new principle through an adjudication, it probably could not issue a cease and desist order except in reliance upon a prior validly adopted legislative rule and that does not exist here.

ANSWER TO QUESTION VII

Hearing: The key point in this question is whether a trial-type hearing is required. The APA only requires a trial-type hearing in adjudication or rulemaking if the underlying statute requires one. Here the statute calls for a "fair hearing." Under *United States v. Florida East Coast Railway,* this undoubtedly means only a legislative-type hearing, not a trial-type hearing. The magic words "on the record" are missing from the statute and, since the proceeding is undoubtedly general rulemaking and not adjudication, the statute would not be construed to require a trial-type hearing. Cases like *Seacoast Anti-Pollution League v. Costle,* which do require a trial-type hearing, are inapplicable since this is rulemaking, not adjudication. Generally, on-the-record formal rulemaking does not work well and no court will interpret a statute to require that it occur. Consequently, only the requirements of APA section 553 are applicable here—meaning no administrative law judge has to be involved and no cross-examination is required. (It is not clear whether the legislative-type hearing conducted by the EPA was required by the statute or whether even that could have been omitted—but this is irrelevant.) Even if the court thinks cross-examination would have been useful, *Vermont Yankee Nuclear Power Corp. v. Natural Resources Defense Council* prevents it from tampering with the agency's chosen procedure as long as the APA is satisfied.

Notice: The EPA's notice in the Federal Register was very sketchy. For example, the final rule that distinguishes between new and existing reactors was not foreshadowed in the notice. However, the final rule seems to meet the "logical outgrowth" test. It is close enough to the notice so that this variance would not invalidate the rule; only a radically different final product—as to which no warning was given to the industry—would induce a court to set the rule aside. However, the EPA also has to disclose important staff studies to the industry to permit comment under *Portland Cement Association v. Ruckelshaus*. The cases make clear that important factual data on which the agency relies must be disclosed to permit adversarial comment and the EPA failed to do so. On this ground the court should invalidate the rule and require a new notice and comment cycle. Blue Demon will not be able to cross-examine the author (unless the EPA decides to allow cross-examination during the new comment period) but should be able effectively to criticize the study in writing.

Best available technology: Blue Demon argues the rule is substantively invalid since the statute requires that the limit be achievable through the best available technology and the EPA has admitted that none is "available." However, the EPA interprets "available" to mean available before the rule goes into effect. It would seem that the court should not set aside the rule. Under *Chevron*, the EPA's reasonable statutory interpretation of an ambiguous provision should be sustained. Absent a strong reason to disagree with the agency (such as clear legislative history), the court must go along with the agency if it is a doubtful question.

Factual basis for the rule: Rules are reviewed under the arbitrary-capricious standard of APA section 706(2)(A), which requires the court to understand the agency's data base and methodology and make sure that all material comments were considered. The EPA has to explain its reasoning, the alternatives chosen and rejected, and generally indicate that it has taken a hard, thorough look at the problem. Although the EPA has disagreed with Blue Demon, this is not dispositive as long as the agency had adequately considered and responded to its objections. Here, the staff study on which the agency relies does adequately support the rule. So far as can be seen here, the EPA has considered all comments, and adjusted the final rule to deal with them together with the other information before it. It is not for the court to resolve conflicts in the evidence. However, the court cannot do its job adequately because the staff study was never made available to Blue Demon and other objectors to attack; perhaps their attacks would indeed have demolished the study and rendered it inadequate to support the rule. Thus the court will not decide the issue of whether the rule is arbitrary and capricious for lack of factual support but will instead require a new notice-comment cycle in which the study can be attacked by objectors.

Ex parte contacts: Formerly, under *Home Box Office, Inc. v. FCC* the contacts by Friends of the Earth with Squid are improper. At the very least, Squid should have written memos about the conversations and placed them in the record. However, later cases have disagreed with *Home Box Office* (or at least limited it to rules that involve conflicts between different segments of an industry for a valuable privilege) and ex parte contacts in rulemaking generally are now permissible. Thus the ex parte rule is very questionable now. (Note that the ex parte rule of APA section 557(d) is inapplicable to informal rulemaking, but it does apply to formal rulemaking, so that the question of what the statute requires, discussed above, is critical for this issue also.) Certainly, Squid's conduct in seeing environmentalists off the record but refusing to see reactor operators falls short of minimum standards of fairness, but probably does not violate existing law unless *Home Box Office* makes a comeback. (Due process would certainly preclude such ex parte contacts in adjudication but is inapplicable to the determination of legislative facts in general rulemaking.)

Flounder: The fact that Flounder worked for an environmental group before coming to the EPA raises no problem unless she has some more concrete conflict of interest than simply having worked for a group that desires strict environmental standards. She is entitled to have contacts with Squid off the record because separation of functions provisions of APA section 554(d) do not apply in rulemaking. There is nothing wrong with Squid having copied Flounder's final memo. The facts do look suspiciously like *Morgan v. United States II,* which involved general ratemaking and invalidated rates in part because of ex parte contacts by staff with decisionmaker, but that case clearly does not apply to general rulemaking such as occurred here, under either due process or the APA, absent some statute requiring adjudicatory standards to apply.

Squid's speech: Under *Association of National Advertisers v. FTC,* Squid is entitled to make speeches indicating a strong predisposition about legislative facts or policies. The bias cases like *Cinderella Career & Finishing Schools v. FTC* and *American Cyanamid Co. v. FTC* do not apply to rulemaking. As long as his speeches do not disclose an unalterably closed mind, they do not raise any statutory or constitutional issue. Squid's speech here does not show a closed mind—he says he is willing to consider economic and technical constraints—and the court will surely find that he is capable of considering the evidence and issues fairly.

ANSWER TO QUESTION VIII

Under federal law, Sniff has no standing to seek judicial review either as a "citizen" or as a "taxpayer" (taxpayer standing is limited strictly to disputes about congressional spending decisions alleged to be limited by an explicit constitutional provision—*Flast v. Cohen*). Consequently, to establish standing Sniff must establish "injury in fact" (required by the case or controversy requirement of Article III). This means a concrete, particularized injury.

Since Sniff is seeking judicial review of agency action, it must also meet the prudential limitation of the "zone of interest" test imposed under the APA. The question does not state whether the statute imposes any unusual standing provisions so Sniff must bring itself within section 702 of the APA.

Any competitive or environmental injury will suffice to meet the "injury in fact" test. Sniff's claim of financial or competitive injury requires some imagination, for it is not apparent how it is really injured by the FTWA's rule that QRC is not toxic. The problem does not say that QRC and PFB compete for the same markets. Perhaps Sniff is arguing that if QRC is classified as a toxic chemical, its own financial liability to contribute to the superfund as a PRC producer will be less because there will be more chemical producers who are required to contribute to the superfund. Although somewhat speculative, Sniff's argument seems no weaker than that of the plaintiff in *Barlow v. Collins* (who was injured because a regulation would have allowed benefits to be pledged as security, which would have meant that landlords would always require such security).

Sniff must also confront the causation and remediability components of the Article III standing test. The injury must be fairly traceable to the regulation and must likely be remedied by a favorable decision. *Simon v. Eastern Kentucky Welfare Rights Organization* held that indigent hospital users had no standing to challenge a regulation that removed the requirement that hospitals serve indigents in order to receive a tax exemption. Although plaintiffs had been denied service, the change in regulatory policy may not have caused this denial; similarly, a change in the regulation might not secure them service. Here it is equally arguable that adding QRC as a toxic might not make any difference at all in Sniff's ultimate contribution. However, since Sniff's injury in fact was based on the possibility that QRC's inclusion would decrease its own contribution, it would follow that adding QRC would remedy this injury. Thus as long as Sniff's rather speculative injury is considered an injury in fact, it would seem that it can avoid the causation and remediability requirements. By definition, QRC's exclusion caused its injury and its inclusion would remedy that injury.

It also seems likely that Sniff can meet the zone of interest test. The test requires that Sniff is among the group whose interests the statute was intended to protect. Note that the courts have applied this test inconsistently. Under the standard applied in *Air Courier*, a strict application of the zone of interest test would probably deny Sniff standing. However, several recent cases have used a more lenient standard (*e.g., Bennett v. Spear*). Applying this standard, Sniff may indeed fall within the zone of interest since contributions are to be equitably apportioned among all contributors, and Congress thereby intended to "protect" Sniff from an inequitable assessment.

ANSWER TO QUESTION IX

Sniff's objections to the rulemaking procedure are both statutory and constitutional.

Statutory arguments: The statute clearly calls for informal rulemaking under APA section 553. There is no indication that formal, on-the-record rulemaking is required. A statute that permits discretionary cross-examination calls only for informal rulemaking. [Association of National Advertisers v. FTC] All the requisites for informal rulemaking have been met by the FTWA so far, *i.e.*, notice to the public and invitation for written comments.

Under the circumstances, it would be difficult to argue that the FTWA abused its discretion by proposing to dispense with cross-examination. An immensely complex problem, with a huge number of interested parties, and a very tight time schedule, all militate strongly against the use of slow, inefficient trial-type procedures.

In addition, *Vermont Yankee Nuclear Power Corp. v. Natural Resources Defense Council* strongly indicates that courts are not to second-guess agencies by requiring procedures (such as cross-examination) that the agency has decided not to employ. Otherwise, an agency would employ the most cumbersome procedures in every case to avoid the risk of being reversed on a procedural point.

Constitutional argument: Sniff's constitutional argument is considerably stronger. Under *Londoner v. Denver,* trial-type procedures are required by due process when there is a deprivation of liberty or property turning upon an individualized determination of facts. Dictum in *Vermont Yankee* can also be cited to support this contention; the court noted that trial-type procedure can be required when "a very small number of persons are exceptionally affected, in each case upon individual grounds."

Here, the FTWA's proposal that Sniff pay $22 million turned in part on the toxicity of its chemical wastes, the length of time it has operated, and its ability to pay. These are individualized factors (like determination of benefit in *Londoner*); in particular, a company's ability to pay is clearly an adjudicative fact. Consequently, although many producers are affected (contrary to the *Vermont Yankee* dictum that trial procedures would be required only if a very small number of persons are affected), the fact that the determination will be based on individualized grounds suggests that procedural due process is required.

Since Sniff can claim that it will be deprived of property, because of an individualized factual determination, it can claim the usual requisites of a trial-type hearing—which would include confrontation and cross-examination. Under *Wong Yang Sung v. McGrath,* where a hearing is constitutionally required, the APA adjudicatory procedures come into play—including the hearing requirements under section 556. However, Wong Yang Sung is no longer interpreted to require an elaborate trial-type hearing in all due process cases.

However, the realities of this proceeding (involving many companies, time pressure, and great complexity) suggest that less procedure may be required. After all, the various facts relating to Sniff (such as ability to pay) can be determined from documents; confrontation of witnesses is not necessary and, as far as we know, credibility is not at stake. In these circumstances, it might well be decided that cross-examination will not be granted—at least not without a strong, particularized showing by Sniff of just why it is needed (which is exactly what Sniff should be prepared to make). Absent such a showing, an agency might justifiably suspect that the demand for cross-examination is motivated largely by a desire to delay an onerous assessment.

[A good answer should assess the due process claim under the multi-factor formula of *Mathews v. Eldridge.* While Sniff's property interest in resisting the assessment is very substantial, the risk of error in dispensing with cross-examination is relatively small, and the burden on the government would be very substantial. Again, it might well be that some form of individualized hearing short of a full-fledged trial would satisfy due process.]

ANSWER TO QUESTION X

The FTWA should argue that Sniff should exhaust administrative remedies, that its claim is not yet ripe for review, and that immediate review violates the final order rule.

On the exhaustion point, the FTWA argues that Sniff should first go through the rulemaking procedure by commenting on the proposed rule. Perhaps it will prevail on the merits (by cutting down its assessment) or perhaps cross-examination will be granted if Sniff makes a strong showing of why it would be needed. In either case, no appeal would then be necessary.

However, other arguments suggest exhaustion should not be required. Like the *Allen v. Grand Central Aircraft Co.* case, the claim here is that the agency is about to subject Sniff to an unauthorized procedure. It can be argued that is unfair to force Sniff to submit to a constitutionally defective procedure. Moreover, there is a very serious risk of harm to its credit standing by reason of the large assessment and Sniff also is concerned about the substantial costs it will have to undergo in participating in an allegedly defective procedure.

Some additional factors that would influence a court to excuse exhaustion of remedies are: (i) an issue of constitutional law is presented; (ii) there is a great deal at stake for Sniff; (iii) a court is more expert than an agency in deciding questions of procedural due process; (iv) it is very unlikely that the agency will grant cross-examination after its announcement that it will not do so; and (v) the procedure may well be invalid.

On the other hand, a reviewing court might well suspect that Sniff is out merely to delay the inevitable, which would cause it to be less sympathetic. On balance, the court is likely to hear the appeal without requiring exhaustion.

The FTWA might also make a ripeness argument. Even if the rulemaking proceeding in fact fixes a $22 million liability against Sniff, Sniff will not have to pay anything until the FTWA brings an enforcement action against it in district court. At that time, a trial will occur; there will be cross-examination; and perhaps the federal district judge will reexamine the correctness of the $22 million assessment, although this is certainly not clear from the statutory scheme. The argument that judicial review is premature because the agency has not yet applied a rule to a private party is a ripeness claim.

For many of the same reasons that Sniff could avoid the exhaustion requirement, it can argue that its claim is now ripe for review. The issues are fit for immediate review; the question of whether cross-examination is required is strictly legal and constitutional, not factual, and can be easily evaluated by the court right now. The decision to deny cross-examination was formal, not informal, and it emanated from the top level of the agency, not from the staff. Sniff can argue that it needs immediate review because the assessment threatens it with bankruptcy. All things considered, under the *Abbott Laboratories v. Gardner* criteria, it is reasonable to find the appeal ripe for immediate judicial review.

Similarly, this question could be analyzed under the "final order rule." The FTWA's action denying cross-examination is not "final" at the present time—only proposed. Thus it can be argued that it should be judicially reviewed together with the rules when they are ultimately adopted. The final order rule vindicates the policy that a matter should not be brought piecemeal to appellate courts since this would contribute to delay and confusion. The final order rule is set forth in many statutes and also in APA section 704. Although there are exceptions to the final order rule of extreme hardship, as in *Isbrandtsen Co. v. United States,* it is hard to see how the denial of cross-examination imposes extreme hardship on Sniff at present. As the decision in *FTC v. Standard Oil Co. of California* shows, the courts deciding issues under the final order rule tend to reason along the same lines that are used in exhaustion and ripeness cases; thus, it is likely that the final order rule will not be applied if the court decides not to require exhaustion and also finds that the appeal is ripe.

Table of Cases

A

ABF Freightlines, Inc. v. NLRB - **§620**

AEP Chapter Housing Association v. City of Berkley - **§278**

ATX Inc. v. Department of Transportation - **§285**

Abbott Laboratories v. Gardner - **§§705, 779, 781, 789**

Acker v. United States - **§563**

Action for Children's Television v. FCC - **§416**

Adamo Wrecking Co. v. United States - **§§637, 716**

Addison v. Holly Hill Fruit Products - **§339**

Aetna Insurance Co. v. Lavoie - **§277**

Air Courier Conference v. American Postal Workers Union - **§748**

Aircraft & Diesel Equipment Corp. v. Hirsch - **§804**

Alaska Professional Hunters Association v. FAA - **§405**

Alden v. Maine - **§650**

Allen v. Board of Barber Examiners - **§28**

Allen v. Grand Central Aircraft Co. - **§800**

Allen v. Wright - **§§744, 750**

Allentown Broadcasting Co. v. FCC - **§557**

Allentown Mack Sales & Service, Inc. v. NLRB - **§560**

Allison v. Block - **§191**

Altschuller v. Bressler - **§219**

Alyeska Pipeline Service Co. v. Wilderness Society - **§530**

Amalgamated Association of Street, Electric Railway & Motor Coach Employees v. Lockridge - **§818**

Amalgamated Meat Cutters v. Connally - **§18**

American Airlines v. CAB - **§155**

American Bus Association v. United States - **§410**

American Cyanamid Co. v. FTC - **§274**

American Farm Lines v. Black Ball Freight Service - **§350**

American Hospital Association v. NLRB - **§§155, 189**

American Medical Association v. United States - **§369**

American Textile Manufacturers Institute v. Donovan - **§§19, 32**

American Trucking Association v. EPA - **§9**

Amoco Oil Co. v. EPA - **§426**

Amos Treat & Co. v. SEC - **§266**

Anaconda Co. v. Ruckelshaus - **§359**

Anderson v. Creighton - **§692**

Andrade v. Lauer - **§802**

Andreson v. Maryland - **§466**

Ardestani v. Immigration & Naturalization Service - **§540**

Arizona v. California - **§16**

Arizona Grocery Co. v. Santa Fe Railway - **§351**

Armstrong v. Commodity Futures Trading Commission - **§246**

Arnett v. Kennedy - **§110**

Arthur Young & Co., United States v. - **§472**

Asbury Park v. Department of Civil Service - **§299**

Ashbacker Radio Corp. v. FCC - **§145**

Associated Fisheries of Maine, Inc. v. Daley - **§347**

Associated Industries of New York v. Ickes - **§738**

Association of Data Processing Service Organizations v. Camp - **§§740, 746, 754**

Association of Data Processing Service Organizations v. Federal Reserve System - **§616**

Association of National Advertisers v. FTC - **§420**

Atascadero State Hospital v. Scanlon - **§§612, 649**

Atchinson, Topeka & Santa Fe Railway v. Pena - **§588**

Atchinson, Topeka & Santa Fe Railway v. Wichita Board of Trade - **§320**

Athlone Industries, Inc. v. CPSC - **§800**

Atkins v. Parker - **§153**

Atlas Roofing Co. v. Occupational Safety & Health Review Commission - **§§38, 52, 639**

Auer v. Robbins - **§§382, 590, 593**

Austin v. Shalala - **§38**

Automotive Parts & Accessories Association v. Boyd - **§373**

B

B.F. Goodrich Co. v. DOT - **§362**

Bakalis v. Golembeski - **§274**

Baltimore Department of Social Services v. Bouknight - **§468**

Baltimore Gas & Electric Co. v. Natural Resources Defense Council - **§615**

Banker's Life & Casualty Co. v. Cravey - **§115**

Barlow v. Collins - **§§741, 754**

Barr v. Matteo - **§§687, 693**

Barry v. Barchi - **§§112, 130**

Bell v. Burton - **§128**

Bellis v. United States - **§462**

Bennett v. Spear - §§745, 765

Berger v. United States - §280

Berkovitz v. United States - §668

Best v. Humboldt Mining Co. - §813

Bethel School District v. Fraser - §36

Better Government Association v. Department of State - §785

Bi-Metallic Investment Co. v. State Board of Equalization - §152

Birnbaum v. Trussel - §695

Bishop v. Wood - §§87, 109

Biswell, United States v. - §454

Bivens v. Six Unknown Named Agents of the Federal Bureau of Narcotics - §§693, 798

Block v. Community Nutrition Institute - §720

Blum v. Stenson - §541

Board of Regents v. Roth - §§85, 86, 107

Booth v. Churner - §796

Borden, Inc. v. Commissioner of Public Health - §612

Boreali v. Axelrod - §32

Bowen v. Georgetown University Hospital - §§338, 339, 590

Bowen v. Massachusetts - §§653, 654

Bowen v. Michigan Academy of Family Physicians - §§705, 710, 715

Bowsher v. Synar - §77

Bradley v. Fisher - §678

Brandon v. Holt - §702

Braswell v. United States - §465

Brinkley v. Hassig - §282

Brock v. Roadway Express, Inc. - §127

Buckhannon Board & Care Home, Inc. v. West Virginia Department of Health and Human Resources - §533

Buckley v. Valeo - §64

Bunker Hill Co. v. EPA - §427

Bureau of National Affairs v. Department of Justice - §493

Burlington Northern Railroad v. Office of Inspector General - §81

Butz v. Economou - §§229, 680, 689, 693

Butz v. Glover Livestock Co. of Texas - §618

C

CAB v. United Airlines, Inc. - §442

CNA Financial Corp. v. Donovan - §505

Califano v. Sanders - §628

California v. FPC - §817

California Bankers Association v. Shultz - §442

Camara v. Municipal Court - §§447, 448, 449, 451

Camp v. Pitts - §§423, 425

Carlson v. Green - §693

Carlton v. Department of Motor Vehicles - §224

Carroll v. Knickerbocker Ice Co. - §219

Carson-Truckee Water Conservation District v. Secretary of Interior - §534

Carter v. Carter Coal Co. - §29

Castillo-Villagra v. INS - §§233, 234

Causby, United States v. - §671

Chamber of Commerce v. OSHA - §402

Chamber of Commerce v. USDA - §531

Chamberlain v. Kurtz - §§491, 500

Checkosky v. SEC - §381

Chemical Waste Management, Inc. v. EPA - §164

City of West Chicago v. NRC - §164

Chevron, USA v. Natural Resources Defense Council - §§164, 579, 582, 583, 584, 585, 586, 587, 589, 591, 594, 595, 599, 601

Chief Probation Officers v. Shalala - §405

Chocolate Manufacturers Association v. Block - §369

Christensen v. Harris County - §§586, 588

Chrysler Corp. v. Brown - §505

Chrysler Corp. v. United States - §§37, 138, 328

Cinderella Career & Finishing Schools, Inc. v. FTC - §§274, 559

Citizens Committee of Georgetown v. Zoning Commission - §241

Citizens to Preserve Overton Park v. Volpe - §§179, 304, 425, 605, 608, 722

City of Burlington v. Dague - §541

City of Riverside v. Rivera - §541

City of St. Louis v. Praprotnik - §701

City of West Chicago v. NRC - §164

Civil Service Commission v. National Association of Letter Carriers - §36

Clardy v. Levy - §165

Clark-Cowlitz Joint Operating Agency v. FERC - §188

Clarke v. Securities Industry Association - §747

Cleavinger v. Saxner - §680

Cleveland Board of Education v. Loudermill - §§110, 124, 125

Clinton v. City of New York - §§26, 762

Clinton v. Jones - §676

Codd v. Velger - §87

Coit Independence Joint Venture v. FSLIC - §799

Collord v. Department of the Interior - §§165, 540

Colonnade Catering Corp. v. United States - §454

Columbia Broadcasting Co. v. United States - §781

Commodity Futures Trading Commission v. Schor - §43

Connecticut v. Doehr - §134

Consolidated Edison Co. v. NLRB - §552

Couch v. United States - §§464, 469, 472

Critical Mass Energy Project v. Nuclear Regulatory Commission - §503

Crowell v. Benson - §§43, 566, 567

Cutler v. Hayes - §774

D

D.C. Federation of Civic Associations v. Volpe - §§285, 419

DCP Farms v. Yeutter - §§284, 285

Dalehite v. United States - §667

Daniels v. Williams - §696

Darby v. Cisneros - §§792, 793, 794

Davis v. Passman - §693

Davis & Randall, Inc. v. United States - §238

DeFries v. Association of Owners - §545

Degge v. Hitchcock - §633

Dellmuth v. Muth - §647

Department of Defense v. Federal Labor
Relations Authority - §516

Department of the Air Force v. Rose - §§499, 518

Department of the Army v. Blue Fox, Inc. - §654

DeRieux v. Five Smiths, Inc. - §398

Dickinson v. Zurko - §555

Director, Office of Workers' Compensation v. Greenwich
Collieries - §212

Dixon v. Alabama State Board of Education - §100

Dixon v. Love - §129

Doe v. United States - §463

Dole v. Service Employees Union - §439

Donovan v. Dewey - §454

Duke Power Co. v. North Carolina Environmental Study
Group, Inc. - §749

Dunlop v. Bachowski - §§241, 243

E

EPA v. Mink - §511

Eagle-Picher Industries v. EPA - §787

Ed Taylor Construction Co. v. Occupational Safety and
Health Review Commission - §256

Edelman v. Jordan - §643

Edmunds v. United States - §66

Edward De Bartolo Corp. v. Florida Gulf Coast Council -
§591

Endicott Johnson Corp. v. Perkins - §440

Envirocare of Utah, Inc. v. Nuclear Regulatory Commission - §200

Environmental Defense Fund v. EPA - §267

Environmental Defense Fund v. Hardin - §770

Erika, Inc., United States v. - §714

Escalera v. New York City Housing Authority - §106

Estep v. United States - §636

Ethel Corp. v. EPA - §613

Ettinger v. Board of Medical Quality Assurance - §214

Ex Parte - See name of party

Excelsior Underwear - §196

F

F.A. McDonald Co. v. Industrial Commission - §237

FAA v. Robertson - §500

FBI v. Abramson - §521

FCC v. ITT World Communications - §528

FCC v. Sanders Radio Station - §§737, 738

FCC v. Schreiber - §§480, 481

FCC v. Station WJR - §297

FDA v. Brown & Williamson Tobacco Corp. - §581

FDIC v. Mallen - §§126, 154

FDIC v. Meyer - §693

FMB v. Isbrandtsen Co. - §815

FTC v. American Tobacco Co. - §434

FTC v. Atlantic Richfield Co. - §444

FTC v. Cement Institute - §275

FTC v. Cinderella Career & Finishing Schools, Inc. - §276

FTC v. Grolier, Inc. - §507

FTC v. Mandel Brothers, Inc. - §619

FTC v. Miller - §437

FTC v. Standard Oil Co. of California - §767

FTC v. Texaco - §312

FTC v. Texaco, Inc. - §442

FTC v. Universal-Rundle Corp. - §619

FTC Line of Business Report Litigation, In re - §443

Fahey v. Mallonee - §119

Far East Conference v. United States - §816

Farrar v. Hobby - §533

Federal Crop Insurance Corp. v. Merrill - §326

Federal Election Commission v. Akins - §§743, 753, 763

Federal Open Market Committee v. Merrill - §§496, 513

Federal Power Commission v. Hope Natural Gas Co. -
§563

Federal Radio Commission v. Nelson Brothers - §14

Field v. Clark - §7

Fisher v. United States - §§463, 469, 472

Fitzpatrick v. Bitzer - §647

Flagstaff Broadcasting Federation v. FCC - §320

Flast v. Cohen - §§759, 760, 761

Florida East Coast Railway, United States v. - §§153,
163, 334

Florida Power & Light Co. v. United States - §365

Foote's Dixie Dandy, Inc. v. McHenry - §323

Ford Motor Co. v. Milhollin - §573

Forsham v. Harris - §492

Franklin v. Massachusetts - §706

Franz v. Board of Medical Quality Assurance - §231

Freytag v. Commissioner - §§34, 68, 71

Friedman v. Rogers - §279

Friends of the Earth v. Laidlaw Environmental Services,
Inc. - §744

Frink v. Prod - §546

Frothingham v. Mellon - §§758, 759

Fuentes v. Shevin - §132

G

Gagnon v. Scarpelli - §§97, 143

Gamble-Skogmo, Inc. v. FTC - §301

Gaubert, United States v. - §668

General Electric Co. v. EPA - §§37, 138, 328

General Motors Corp. v. Ruckelshaus - §402

Gibson v. Berryhill - §279

Gilbert v. Babbitt - §267

Gilbert v. Homan - §126

Gillock, United States v. - **§684**

Gilman, United States v. - **§669**

Goldberg v. Kelly - **§§104, 118, 122, 135, 140, 141, 142, 143, 242, 259**

Gonzales-Riviera v. INS - **§482**

Goss v. Lopez - **§§99, 102, 139**

Granfinanciera, S.A. v. Nordberg - **§39**

Gravel v. United States - **§682**

Great Northern Railway v. Merchants Elevator Co. - **§811**

Green v. Bock Laundry Machine Co. - **§581**

Greene v. Babbitt - **§267**

Greene County Planning Board v. Federal Power Commission - **§531**

Greenholtz v. Inmates of Nebraska Complex - **§98**

Griggs v. Duke Power Co. - **§578**

Grimaud, United States v. - **§§8, 47**

Grolier, Inc. v. FTC - **§265**

Grumman Aircraft Corp. v. Renegotiation Board - **§504**

Guardian Federal Savings & Loan Association v. FSLIC - **§410**

Guentchev v. INS - **§246**

Gutierrez de Martinez v. Lamagno - **§§685, 712**

H

Hahn v. Gottlieb - **§729**

Hannah v. Larche - **§§473, 479**

Hans v. Louisiana - **§642**

Harlow v. Fitzgerald - **§§677, 689**

Harmon v. Brucker - **§708**

Harry and Bryant Co. v. FTC - **§335**

Heckler v. Campbell - **§155**

Heckler v. Cheney - **§§722, 725**

Heckler v. Community Health Services - **§326**

Heckler v. Day - **§775**

Helco Products Co. v. McNutt - **§783**

Helvering v. Mitchell - **§50**

Hewitt v. Helms - **§94**

Hoctor v. United States Department of Agriculture - **§403**

Holly Farms Corp. v. NLRB - **§588**

Holmes v. New York City Housing Authority (1970) - **§§106, 191**

Holmes v. New York City Housing Authority (1968) - **§21**

Home Box Office, Inc. v. FCC - **§§415, 416, 417**

Hornsby v. Allen - **§§114, 695**

Hortonville Joint School District v. Hortonville Educational Association - **§276**

Hoska v. Department of Army - **§223**

Hudson v. Palmer - **§§144, 698, 699**

Hudson v. United States - **§51**

Humana of South Carolina v. Califano - **§393**

Humphrey's Executor v. United States - **§75**

Hunt v. Washington State Apple Advertising Commission - **§752**

Hunt Foods & Industries, Inc. v. FTC - **§443**

Hutto v. Finney - **§648**

I

ICC v. Brimson - **§433**

ICC v. Brotherhood of Locomotive Engineers - **§§728, 768**

INS v. Chadha - **§60**

INS v. Hibi - **§327**

INS v. Lopez-Mendoza - **§482**

Idaho Farm Bureau Federation v. Babbitt - **§375**

Imbler v. Pachtman - **§680**

Independent U.S. Tank Owners Committee v. Dole - **§373**

Industrial Union Department v. American Petroleum Institute - **§§19, 32**

Ingraham v. Wright - **§§144, 698**

International Longshoremen's Union v. Boyd - **§783**

International Paper Co. v. Federal Power Commission - **§510**

Isbrandtsen Co. v. United States - **§771**

J

J.W. Hampton & Co. v. United States - **§9**

Janis, United States v. - **§482**

Japan Whaling Association v. American Cetacean Society - **§742**

Jay v. Boyd - **§91**

Jenkins v. McKeithen - **§474**

John Doe Agency v. John Doe Corp. - **§519**

Johnson v. Robison - **§711**

Joint Anti-Fascist Refugee Committee v. McGrath - **§735**

Ju Toy, United States v. - **§565**

K

KFC National Management Corp. v. NLRB - **§295**

Kastigar v. United States - **§461**

Keating v. Office of Thrift Supervision - **§471**

Kent v. Dulles - **§33**

Kentucky v. Graham - **§§648, 703**

Kentucky Department of Corrections v. Thompson - **§98**

Kimel v. Florida Board of Regents - **§647**

Kissinger v. Reporters Committee for Freedom of the Press - **§492**

Kixmiller v. SEC - **§786**

Kleindienst v. Mandel - **§727**

Koniag, Inc. v. Andrus - **§§200, 283**

L

La Casa del Convaleciente v. Sullivan - **§404**

Laird v. Nelms - **§§662, 665**

Laird v. Tatum - **§778**

Landon v. Plasencia - **§92**

Landry v. FDIC - **§68**

Larson v. Domestic & Foreign Commerce Corp. - **§652**

Lassiter v. Department of Social Services - **§143**

Lechmere, Inc. v. NLRB - **§592**

Liberty Homes v. Department of Industry - **§429**

Lichter v. United States - **§16**

Lincoln v. Vigil - **§§394, 411, 730**

Lincoln Dairy Co. v. Finigan - **§47**

Link v. NLRB - **§436**

Londoner v. Denver - **§§151, 384**

Lopez v. Heckler - **§315**

Louisiana Association of Independent Producers v.
Federal Energy Regulatory Commission - **§290**

Lovallo v. Froehlke - **§631**

Lujan v. Defenders of Wildlife - **§§742, 744, 763, 778**

Lujan v. G & G Fire Sprinklers - **§144**

Lujan v. National Wildlife Federation - **§§742, 744, 748,
755**

M

McAlpine v. United States - **§723**

McCarthy v. Madigan - **§§791, 796, 799**

McCarthy v. Sawyer-Goodman Co. - **§235**

McGee v. United States - **§795**

McGraw Electric Co. v. United States - **§298**

McHugh v. Santa Monica Rent Control Board - **§§44, 53**

McKart v. United States - **§795**

McLaughlin v. Union Oil Co. - **§281**

McNary v. Haitian Refugee Center - **§710**

McPherson v. Employment Division - **§§594, 595**

Mackey v. Montrym - **§129**

Madison v. Alaska Department of Fish & Game - **§569**

Marcello v. Bonds - **§§165, 269**

Marchetti v. United States - **§470**

Marcus v. Director, Office of Workers' Compensation
Programs - **§272**

Market Street Railway v. Railroad Commission - **§236**

Marshall v. Barlow's, Inc. - **§§452, 454**

Marshall v. Cuomo - **§263**

Marshall v. Jerrico Inc. - **§§84, 278**

Martin v. Occupational Safety and Health Review
Commission - **§§256, 590**

Massman Construction Co. v. TVA - **§290**

Mathews v. Eldridge - **§§120, 121, 122, 135, 142, 802**

Mayberry v. Pennsylvania - **§280**

Mazza v. Cavicchia - **§308**

Mead v. Arnell - **§61**

Mead Corp., United States v. - **§§574, 587**

Mead Data Central, Inc. v. United States Department of
the Air Force - **§§497, 511**

Medical Committee for Human Rights v. SEC - **§786**

Megdal v. Oregon State Board of Dental Examiners -
§§22, 192, 194

Memphis Light, Gas & Water Division v. Craft - **§§103,
137**

Mendoza, United States v. - **§314**

Mendoza-Lopez, United States v. - **§§637, 717**

Metropolitan Washington Airports Authority v. Citizens for
the Abatement of Aircraft Noise - **§64**

Mid-Tex Electric Cooperative v. Federal Energy Regulatory
Commission - **§399**

Miller v. Horton - **§674**

Miller v. Johnson - **§591**

Milwaukee Metropolitan Sewerage District v. Wisconsin
Department of Natural Resources - **§166**

Missouri Coalition for the Environment v. Joint Committee
on Administrative Rules - **§61**

Mistretta v. United States - **§§19, 26, 45**

Mitchell v. W.T. Grant Co. - **§133**

Mobil Oil v. FPC - **§616**

Monell v. Department of Social Services - **§660**

Monroe v. Pape - **§695**

Morgan, United States v. ("Morgan IV") - **§§302, 303,
304, 425**

Morgan v. United States (1938) ("Morgan II") - **§§306,
307, 308**

Morgan v. United States (1936) ("Morgan I") - **§§294,
295, 296, 302, 303**

Morris v. Gresette - **§719**

Morrisey v. Brewer - **§97**

Morrison v. Olson - **§§67, 70, 72, 73, 74, 77**

Morrison-Knudson Co. v. O'Leary - **§566**

Morton v. Ruiz - **§§21, 191, 484, 572**

Moser v. United States - **§327**

Motor Vehicle Manufacturers Association v. State Farm
Mutual Auto Insurance Co. - **§§376, 610, 612**

Muskopf v. Corning Hospital District - **§659**

Myers v. Bethlehem Shipbuilding Corp. - **§§790, 797**

Myers v. United States - **§§73, 77**

N

NLRB v. Bell Aerospace Co. - **§§187, 188**

NLRB v. Donnelley Garment Co. - **§276**

NLRB v. Food Store Employees Union - **§618**

NLRB v. Hearst Publications, Inc. - **§§596, 597, 600,
601**

NLRB v. Kentucky River Community Care, Inc. **§§211,
582**

NLRB v. Mackay Radio & Telegraph Co. - **§307**

NLRB v. Pittsburgh S.S. Co. - **§281**

NLRB v. Robbins Tire & Rubber Co. - **§520**

NLRB v. Sears, Roebuck & Co. - **§§507, 509, 510**

NLRB v. Thompson & Co. - **§557**

NLRB v. Wyman-Gordon Co. - **§196**

Nader v. Allegheny Airline - **§810**

National Automatic Laundry & Dry Cleaning Council v.
Shultz - **§784**

National Black Media Coalition v. FCC - **§§361, 369**

National Credit Union Association v. First National Bank
and Trust Co. - **§747**

National Petroleum Refiners Association v. FTC - **§340**

National Treasury Employees Union v. Von Raab - **§457**

National Welfare Rights Organization v. Finch - **§201**

Nationsbank of North Carolina v. Variable Annuity Life
Insurance Co. - **§589**

Nevada Airlines, Inc. v. Bond - **§771**

New Jersey Civil Service Association v. State - **§806**

New York v. Burger - **§454**

Newport v. Fact Concerts, Inc. - **§703**

Ng Fung Ho v. White - **§§565, 567**

Nixon v. Fitzgerald - **§676**

Nixon, United States v. - **§512**

Nolan v. Fitzpatrick - **§806**

North American Cold Storage Co. v. Chicago - **§119**

North Carolina v. Chas. Pfizer & Co. - **§318**

Northern Arapahoe Tribe v. Hodel - **§398**

Northern Pipeline Co. v. Marathon Pipe Line Co. - **§§39,
567**

Nova Scotia Food Products Corp., United States v. -
§§363, 373, 374, 636

O

O'Bannon v. Town Court Nursing Center - **§117**

Office of Communications of the United Church of Christ
v. FCC - **§§199, 738**

Office of Personnel Management v. Richmond - **§326**

Ohio Bell Telephone Co. v. Public Utilities Commission -
§233

Ohio Forestry Association v. Sierra Club - **§§732, 780**

Ohio Valley Water Co. v. Ben Avon Borough - **§§562,
563, 565**

Oklahoma Press Publishing Co. v. Walling - **§441**

O'Leary v. Brown-Pacific-Maxon, Inc. - **§§598, 601**

Order of Railway Conductors v. Swan - **§798**

Owen v. City of Independence - **§700**

PQ

Pacific Gas & Electric Co. v. FPC - **§§410, 577**

Pacific Legal Foundation v. Goyan - **§531**

Pacific States Basket & Box Co. v. White - **§612**

Packard Motor Car Co. v. NLRB - **§§600, 601**

Pan American World Airways v. United States - **§816**

Panama Refining Co. v. Ryan - **§§11, 566**

Papasan v. Allain - **§648**

Papish v. University of Missouri - **§100**

Parham v. J.R. - **§139**

Parklane Hosiery Co. v. Shore - **§313**

Parratt v. Taylor - **§§144, 698**

Patsy v. Board of Regents - **§803**

Paul v. Davis - **§88**

Penasquitos Village, Inc. v. NLRB - **§558**

Pennsylvania Industrial Chemical Co., United States v. -
§328

Pension Benefit Guaranty Corp. v. LTV Corp. - **§§177,
178, 179, 241, 607, 608**

People v. Scott - **§454**

Pepsico v. FTC - **§772**

Perry v. Sindermann - **§§89, 108**

Pierce v. Underwood - **§§537, 539**

Pierce Auto Lines, United States v. - **§244**

Pillsbury Co. v. FTC - **§283**

Portland Audubon Society v. Endangered Species
Committee - **§288**

Portland Cement Association v. Ruckelshaus - **§§361,
614**

Portmann v. United States - **§324**

Professional Air Traffic Controllers' Organization v. Federal
Labor Relations Authority - **§§278, 292**

Public Citizens Health Research Group v. FDA - **§502**

Public Utilities Commission v. United Fuel Gas Co. -
§797

Pulliam v. Allen - **§679**

R

Radio Officers' Union v. NLRB - **§554**

Railroad Commission v. Rowan & Nichols Oil Co. - **§563**

Raines v. Byrd - **§762**

Red Lion Broadcasting Co. v. FCC - **§§182, 184**

Renegotiation Board v. Bannercraft Clothing Co. - **§§483,
495**

Renegotiation Board v. Grumman Aircraft - **§509**

Reno v. Catholic Social Services, Inc. - **§§782, 789**

Retail, Wholesale & Department Store Clerks Union v.
NLRB - **§188**

Rhoa-Zamora v. INS - **§234**

Richardson v. Perales - **§222**

Richardson, United States v. - **§761**

Rock Royal Cooperative, United States v. - **§29**

Rodway v. USDA - **§374**

Rust v. Sullivan - **§§33, 591**

Rybachek v. EPA - **§375**

S

SEC v. Chenery Corp. (1947) - **§§187, 190**

SEC v. Chenery Corp. (1943) - **§§187, 245**

SEC v. Jerry T. O'Brien - **§445**

St. Joseph Stock Yards Co. v. United States - **§§562,
563, 565**

San Diego Building Trades Council v. Garmon - **§818**

San Luis Obispo Mothers for Peace v. Nuclear Regulatory
Commission - **§305**

Sandin v. Conner - **§§93, 95**

Sangamon Valley Television Corp. v. United States - **§414**

Save the Dolphins v. Department of Commerce - **§493**

Scenic Hudson Preservation Conference v. Federal Power
Commission - **§753**

Schechter Poultry Corp. v. United States - §§12, 566

Scheuer v. Rhodes - §§646, 689, 691

Schlesinger v. Reservists Committee to Stop the War - §757

Schwartz v. Covington - §829

Seacoast Anti-Pollution League v. Costle - §§164, 225

Sealed Case, *In re* - §512

See v. Seattle - §451

Seminole Tribe of Florida v. Florida - §647

Sepulveda v. Block - §398

Shalala v. Guernsey Memorial Hospital - §402

Shapiro v. United States - §§467, 468, 469, 470

Shasta Minerals & Chemical Co. v. SEC - §438

Shaw's Supermarkets, Inc. v. NLRB - §320

Shell Oil Co. v. EPA - §370

Ship Creek Hydraulic Syndicate v. State of Alaska - §241

Shively v. Stewart - §204

Siegert v. Gilley - §88

Sierra Club v. Costle - §§288, 416, 419

Sierra Club v. Morton - §742

Simon v. Eastern Kentucky Welfare Rights Organization - §744

Sims v. Apfel - §805

Singleton v. Wulff - §751

Skidmore v. Swift & Co. - §§570, 571, 574, 586

Skinner v. Railway Labor Executives' Association - §456

Smith v. Evening News Association - §819

Smith v. Wade - §693

Smith, United States v. - §§685, 712

Sniadach v. Family Finance Corp. - §132

Solid Waste Agency of Northern Cook County v. Army Corps of Engineers - §590

Spanish International Broadcasting Co. v. FCC - §794

Stafford v. Briggs - §655

Stauffer Chemical Co., United States v. - §312

Steadman v. SEC - §213

Steel Co. v. Citizens for a Better Environment - §§732, 744

Steffel v. Thompson - §624

Sterling Drug, Inc. v. FTC - §486

Stivers v. Pierce - §§279, 281

Stone v. INS - §768

Storer Broadcasting Co., United States v. - §155

Stump v. Sparkman - §678

Supreme Court of Virginia v. Consumers Union - §683

T

Tax Analysts & Advocates v. IRS - §487

Telecommunications Research & Action Center v. FCC - §775

Tennessee Power Co. v. Tennessee Valley Authority - §735

Tenney v. Brandhove - §683

Texas & Pacific Railway v. Abilene Cotton Oil Co. - §808

13th Regional Corp. v. Department of Interior - §632

Thomas v. Union Carbide Agricultural Products, Inc. - §43

Thomas Jefferson University v. Shalala - §593

Thunder Basin Coal Co. v. Reich - §§788, 789

Thygesen v. Callahan - §20

Todd & Co. v. SEC - §29

Toilet Goods Association v. Gardner - §780

Topanga Association for a Scenic Community v. Los Angeles - §244

Tower v. Glover - §680

Trafficante v. Metropolitan Life Insurance Co. - §763

Traynor v. Turnage - §§709, 711

Trinity Broadcasting Co. v. FCC - §138

Trujillo v. Employment Security Commission - §220

Tull v. United States - §638

Tumey v. Ohio - §277

U

USA Group Services, Inc. v. Riley - §391

Unbelievable, Inc. v. NLRB - §531

United Auto Workers v. Russell - §819

United Autoworkers of America v. NLRB - §320

United Food & Commercial Workers Union v. Brown Group, Inc. - §752

United States v. - *see name of other party*

United States Department of Justice v. Reporters Committee for Freedom of the Press - §§514, 515

United States Department of Labor v. Kast Metals Corp. - §394

United States *ex rel.* Knauff v. Shaughnessy - §91

United Steelworkers of America v. Marshall - §421

Universal Camera Corp. v. NLRB - §§553, 556, 557

University of Missouri v. Horowitz - §101

University of Tennessee v. Elliott - §317

Utah Construction & Mining Co., United States v. - §311

V

Vaca v. Sipes - §819

Valley Forge Christian College v. Americans United for Separation of Church and State - §§757, 761

Varig Airlines, United States v. - §667

Vaughn v. Rosen - §497

Vermont Agency of Natural Resources v. United States *ex rel.* Stevens - §763

Vermont Yankee Nuclear Power Corp. v. Natural Resources Defense Council - §§363, 384

Vietnam Veterans of America v. Secretary of the Navy - §352

Virginia Petroleum Jobbers Association v. FPC - §§827, 828

Vitarelli v. Seaton - §349

Vitek v. Jones - §§96, 139, 143

Volvo GM v. United States Department of Labor - §794

WX

WWHT, Inc. v. FCC - **§383**

Walters v. National Association of Radiation Survivors - **§142**

Ward v. City of Monroeville - **§278**

Ward v. Keenan - **§806**

Warder v. Shalala - **§406**

Warth v. Seldin - **§750**

Washington v. Harper - **§96**

Washington v. Udall - **§641**

Washington Post Co. v. Department of Health & Human Services - **§§487, 517**

Waukegan v. Pollution Control Board - **§50**

Webster v. Doe - **§§711, 726**

Weinberger v. Hymson, Westcott & Dunning, Inc. - **§156**

Weinberger v. Salfi - **§804**

Weiner v. United States - **§76**

Western Pacific Railroad, United States v. - **§808**

White v. Roughton - **§§21, 106, 191**

Whitman v. American Trucking Associations - **§§9, 19, 582**

Will v. Michigan Department of State Police - **§660**

Willner v. Committee on Character & Fitness - **§113**

Wilson v. Layne - **§692**

Wisconsin v. Constantineau - **§88**

Withrow v. Larkin - **§§259, 276**

Wolff v. McDonnell - **§96**

Wolff v. Selective Service Board No. 16 - **§798**

Wong Wing v. United States - **§48**

Wong Yang Sung v. McGrath - **§§90, 165, 269, 540**

Wood v. Strickland - **§690**

Woodby v. INS - **§214**

Woodsmall v. Lyng - **§729**

Wright v. Central DuPage Hospital Association - **§40**

Wyman v. James - **§449**

Y

Yakus v. United States - **§§15, 17, 637**

Young, *Ex parte* - **§644**

Z

Zemel v. Rusk - **§33**

Zinermon v. Burch - **§699**

Table of Citations

CITATIONS TO THE ADMINISTRATIVE PROCEDURE ACT

Section	Text Reference	Section	Text Reference	Section	Text Reference
504	§540	552b(c)(5)	§529	555(c)	§§170, 430
551	§159	552b(c)(6)	§529	555(d)	§§170, 205, 430, 476
551(4)	§§159, 338, 354, 357	552b(c)(7)	§529	555(e)	§§171, 241, 380
551(5)	§§159, 355	552b(c)(8)	§529	556	§158
551(6)	§§159, 164	552b(c)(9)	§529	556(b)	§§271, 272
551(7)	§§159, 164	552b(c)(10)	§529	556(c)(6)	§208
551(8)	§164	552(e)	§492	556(c)(7)	§208
551(14)	§§289, 290	553	§353	556(c)(8)	§208
552	§483	553(a)	§393	556(d)	§§212, 216
552(a)(1)	§484	553(b)	§360	556(e)	§§225, 232, 308
552(a)(2)	§§485, 486, 488	553(b)(A)	§§394, 400, 408	557	§§158, 288
552(a)(2)(A)	§509	553(b)(B)	§396	557(b)	§§249, 250
552(a)(3)	§490	553(c)	§§364, 372	557(c)	§§239, 247, 308
552(b)	§§497, 525	553(d)	§§365, 378	557(d)	§288
552(b)(1)	§498	553(d)(3)	§396	557(d)(1)	§286
552(b)(2)	§499	553(e)	§380	558(c)	§172
552(b)(3)	§500	554	§§158, 269, 540	701(a)	§722
552(b)(4)	§501	554(a)	§161	701(a)(1)	§704
552(b)(5)	§§486, 506, 507, 511	554(b)	§197	701(a)(2)	§§601, 704, 721, 722
552(b)(6)	§514	554(d)	§§260, 261, 262, 263, 300, 301	702	§§628, 653, 754
552(b)(7)	§519			703	§653
552(b)(8)	§523	554(d)(A)	§264	704	§§653, 767, 792
552(b)(9)	§524	554(d)(B)	§264	705	§821
552b(a)(1)	§526	554(d)(C)	§264	706	§§544, 555, 569
552b(a)(2)	§527	554(d)(1)	§229	706(1)	§774
552b(c)(1)	§529	554(d)(2)	§253	706(2)(A)	§§381, 602, 611, 721
552b(c)(2)	§529	554(e)	§§181, 182, 185	706(2)(E)	§551
552b(c)(3)	§529	555(b)	§§169, 199, 478, 479, 774		
552b(c)(4)	§529				

Index

A

ABUSE OF DISCRETION
choice between adjudication and rulemaking, §§187-189
declaratory orders, §185
review of agency discretion, §603

ACADEMIC DISMISSALS, §101
See also Due Process

ACCOUNTANT-CLIENT PRIVILEGE, §472
See also Obtaining information and attorney's fees

ADJUDICATION
See also Formal adjudication
defined, §§159-160
rulemaking distinguished, §359
when hearing required, §§147-154

ADJUDICATIVE POWERS, DELEGATION
See Delegation of adjudicative powers

ADJUDICATORY DECISIONMAKING, §§248-328
administrative law judge, §§248-255
    independence of, §§253-255
        APA provisions, §254
        central panel, §253
        in-house, §253
        splitting agencies, §256
agency head exception, §§265-268
    advisors to, §267
basis for, §§294-305
binding effect on, §§309-328
    consistency, duty of, §320
    equitable estoppel, §§321-328
        apparent authority, §322
        federal law, §§324-328
            civil or criminal sanctions, §328
            immigration cases, §327
            money judgment cases, §326
        state law, §323
    res judicata, §§310-319
        exceptions, §§316-319
            full and fair opportunity to litigate, §318
            statutory policy, §317
        generally, §311
        nonmutual collateral estoppel, §§313-315

preclusion against government, §312
familiarity with record requirement, §§294-305
    defects in decisionmaking, §305
    delegation of decisionmaking, §295
    intermediate review boards, §296
    Morgan case, §294
    oral argument, failure to hear, §§297-299
        credibility in issue, §299
    proving violation of, §§302-305
        abuse of discretion, §304
        no questioning of decisionmaker, §302
    unavailability of examiner, §§300-301
improper influences on, §§257-292
    bias or prejudice, §§270-282
        APA provision, §§271-272
        conduct at hearing, §281
        defined, §270
        economic, §§277-279
        effect of complaint, §271
        exposure to facts, §276
        hostility toward party, §§280-281
        institutional interest, §278
        prejudgment of facts, §§273-274
        prejudgment of law or policy, §275
        press releases, §276
        professional licenses, §279
        rule of necessity, §282
        timing of challenge, §272
    combination of functions, §§258-269
        APA, §§260-268
        deportation hearings, §269
        due process, §259
        lower level staff, §259
        prosecuting employee, §262
        staff members, §263
        supervision by ALJ, §261
    pressure on fact finder, §§283-292
        congressional interference, §§283-285
        ex parte communications, §§286-292
        judicial review, §292
        White House staff, §288
intermediate decision requirement, §§306-308
types of decisions, §§249-252

initial, §250
    recommended, §251
    tentative, §252

ADMINISTRATIVE LAW JUDGE ("ALJ")
See Adjudicatory decisionmaking

ADMINISTRATIVE PROCEDURE ACT ("APA")
admissible evidence, §§215-217
ALJ's report, §308
alternative dispute resolution, §§207-210
bias, §§270-272
burden of proof, §§211-214
combination of functions, §§260-269
decisions, types of, §§249-252
declaratory orders, §§181-185
delegation doctrine, §23
discretionary actions, §§602-604, 721-722
ex parte contacts, §§286-291
exceptions to informal rulemaking, §§392-393, 396,
    400, 407-408
exclusive record rule, §§225, 232, 235
exhaustion of remedies, §792
final order rule, §§766, 769, 774
findings and reasons requirement, §§239-241
Freedom of Information Act, §§206, 484-492, 497-501,
    506-509
government liability, §653
hearing
    formal adjudication, §§158-166
    notice, §197
hearsay, §§215-217
independence of ALJs, §§253-255
informal adjudication, §§167-179
informal rulemaking, §353
intervention, §§198-199
obtaining information, §430
open meetings, §§525-529
personal privacy, §514
prospective application of rule, §§338, 357
public parties in rulemaking, §§364-371
publications required, §§377-378, 484-493
right to counsel, §§478-479
right to petition, §380
rule defined, §§354-359
rulemaking preferred, §§193-195
settlement, §207
standing, §754. *See also* Standing
statement of basis for rule, §372
statutory preclusion of judicial review, §704
stays pending review, §§821-829
subpoena power, §§205, 430, 476
substantial evidence test, §§544, 551
substitute ALJ, §§300-301

ADMINISTRATIVE SUMMARY JUDGMENT, §156

ADMISSIBLE EVIDENCE
See Proof

ADVISORY OPINIONS
ripeness, §§783-786

AGENCIES
delegation doctrine. *See* Delegation of legislative power
executive controls, §§63-83
independent, §75
legislative controls. *See* Delegation of legislative power
ultra vires acts, §§30-33

AGGRIEVED PERSONS TEST, §737
See also Standing

AGREEMENTS IN RESTRAINT OF TRADE, §816

ALIENS
admission, §727
deportation. *See* Deportation
exclusion, §§90-92

ALTERNATE DISPUTE RESOLUTION, §§207-210
See also Formal adjudication

ANTITRUST, §§815-816

APPLICATION QUESTIONS, §§594-601
See also Judicial review

APPOINTMENT POWER, §§63-68

APPOINTMENTS, §58

APPROPRIATIONS, §56

ASCERTAINMENT OF FACTS, §7

ATTORNEY-CLIENT PRIVILEGE, §472

ATTORNEY'S FEES, §§530-541
See also Obtaining information and attorney's fees

AUTHORIZED ACTS, §§685-687
See also Government officials' tort liability

B

BANK REGULATION, §523

BEN AVON RULE, §§562-563
See also Judicial review

BIAS, §§270-282, 420
See also Adjudicatory decisionmaking; Rulemaking

BUSINESS INSPECTIONS, §§450-454

C

CERTIORARI, §633

CHECKS AND BALANCES, §3

CIVIL LIBERTIES, §33
See also Delegation of legislative power

CIVIL PENALTIES, §§49-53

CIVIL RIGHTS ACTIONS
exhaustion of remedies, §802

liability of government officials, §§660, 694-703. *See also* Government officials' tort liability

COMBINATION OF FUNCTIONS, §§258-269
See also Adjudicatory decisionmaking

COMMERCIAL SECRETS, §§501-505

COMPARATIVE HEARINGS, §145

CONFERENCE HEARINGS, §175

CONFRONTATION OF WITNESSES, §139
See also Due process

CONGRESSIONAL INTERFERENCE, §§283-285

CONSTITUTIONAL FACTS
See Ben Avon rule

CONTROLS OVER ADMINISTRATIVE ACTION
See also Delegation of Adjudicative powers; Delegation of legislative power

executive, §§63-83
  appointment power, §§63-68
    inferior officers, §§65-68
    no congressional participation, §64
    special prosecutors, §67
  executive orders, §81
  fiscal power, §79
  gubernatorial veto, §83
  inspector generals, §82
  organizational power, §80
  removal power, §§72-78
    good cause, §§73-77
      independent agencies, §75
      independent counsel, §74
      legislative courts, §76
      without cause, §77
  rulemaking, §81
judicial, §§66-71
  court martial judges, §66
  inferior officers, §69
  special prosecutors, §70
  special Tax Court judges, §71
legislative, §§55-62
  Administrative Conference of U.S., §62
  appointments, §58
  appropriations, §56
  Congressional Review Act, §59
  federal standing committees, §54
  investigations, §55
  legislator intervention, §62
  no legislative veto, §§60-61
  ombudsmen, §62
  state review committees, §57

COUNSEL, RIGHT TO
See Right to counsel

COURT OF CLAIMS, §635

CREDITORS' REMEDIES, §§131-134

CRIMINAL SANCTIONS, §§47-48, 328

D

DAMAGES ACTIONS
against government officials, §§693-703
sovereign immunity, §§643-647, 651-654, 660

DECLARATORY JUDGMENTS, §§624-629

DECLARATORY ORDERS, §§180-185
APA, §181
judicial review, §§184-185

DELEGATION DOCTRINE
See Delegation of adjudicative powers; Delegation of legislative power

DELEGATION OF ADJUDICATIVE POWERS, §§34-53
appointment of judges to nonjudicial duties, §45
generally, §34
penalties, §§47-53
  civil, §§49-53
  criminal, §§47-48
private rights, §§39-44
  as ancillary claims, §43
public rights, §38
state courts, §§40, 44
vagueness, §§35-37

DELEGATION OF LEGISLATIVE POWER, §§4-33
See also Controls over administrative action
delegation doctrine
  early cases, §§6-9
  generally, §§4-5
  today, §§19-20
judicial formulas for review of, §§6-33
  ascertainment of facts, §7
  filling in details, §8
  fixing a standard, §9
  National Industrial Recovery Act, §§10-12
    "hot oil" case, §11
    Schechter Poultry case, §12
  post-NIRA cases, §§13-18
    broad delegations upheld, §13
    economic stabilization, §17
    fair prices, §15
    Meat Cutters case, §18
    no standards, §16
    public interest, §14
Line Item Veto Act invalid, §25
state law, §§20, 22, 28
substitutes for delegation doctrine, §§21-24
  duty to adopt regulations, §§21-23
  narrow statutory construction, §24
  state law, §22
to federal judges, §26
to private parties, §§27-29
ultra vires acts, §§30-33

OSHA rules, **§32**

passports, **§33**

vs. constitutional issues, **§33**

DEPORTATION

combination of functions, **§269**

due process, **§90**

jurisdictional facts, **§565**

DISABILITY BENEFITS, §§122-123

DISCOVERY, §§204-206

See also Formal adjudication

DISCRETIONARY FUNCTIONS, §§666-668

See also Government tort liability

DRIVER'S LICENSE, §§128-129

DUE PROCESS, §§84-156

deprivation of, **§117**

elements of hearing, **§§135-145**

balancing test, **§135**

basis for decision, **§141**

comparative hearings, **§145**

confrontation of witnesses, **§139**

impartial decisionmaker, **§140**

minimum requirements, **§136**

notice, **§137-138**

fair warning, **§138**

right to counsel, **§§142-143**

issues requiring hearing—rulemaking vs. adjudication,
§§146-156

adjudication, **§§147-149**

generalized facts–no hearing, **§149**

individualized facts–hearing, **§148**

administrative summary judgment, **§156**

legislative preemption, **§155**

rulemaking—adjudication distinctions, **§§150-154**

rulemaking—no hearing, **§146**

liberty, **§§85-102**

aliens, **§§90-92**

deportation, **§90**

exclusion, **§91**

temporary absence, **§2**

deprivation of constitutional rights, **§89**

physical liberty, deprivation of, **§§93-98**

parole, **§§97-98**

prisoners' rights, **§§93-96**

probation, **§97**

school, **§§99-102**

academic dismissals, **§101**

college expulsion, **§100**

high school suspension, **§102**

stigma, **§§86-88**

property, **§§103-116**

government employment, **§§107-110**

de facto tenure, **§108**

licenses, **§§111-116**

welfare, **§§104-106**

public housing, **§105**

purpose of due process requirement, **§84**

timing of hearing, **§§118-134**

balancing test, **§§120-123**

creditors' remedies, **§§131-134**

absolute rule, **§132**

exigent circumstances, **§134**

judicial determination, **§133**

emergency exception, **§119**

employment discharge, **§§124-127**

general rule—before deprivation, **§118**

licenses, **§§128-130**

welfare and disability benefits, **§§122-123**

E

ECONOMIC BIAS, §§277-279

See also Adjudicatory decisionmaking

ECONOMIC HARDSHIP, §771

See also Final order rule

ECONOMIC STABILIZATION, §§17-18

ELEVENTH AMENDMENT, §§642-650

See also Sovereign immunity

EMPLOYMENT TERMINATION

See also Due process

government job, **§§107-110**

notice and hearing, **§§124-127**

ENTITLEMENTS

as related to residuum rule, **§219**

ENVIRONMENTAL IMPACT STATEMENTS, §346

See also Rulemaking

EQUAL ACCESS TO JUSTICE ACT

See Obtaining information and attorney's fees

ESTABLISHMENT CLAUSE

See also Standing

taxpayer standing, **§§759-761**

ESTOPPEL

equitable, **§§321-328**

apparent authority, **§322**

federal law, **§§324-328**

civil or criminal sanctions, **§328**

immigration cases, **§327**

money judgment cases, **§326**

state law, **§323**

nonmutual collateral, **§§300-302**

EVIDENCE

See Proof

EX PARTE COMMUNICATIONS

by outsiders to agency adjudicators, **§§286-292.** *See
also* Adjudicatory decisionmaking

defined, **§289**

effect, **§291**

interested person, **§287**

judicial review, §292

by public to rulemaker, §§413-418. *See also* Rulemaking

EXCLUSIVE RECORD PRINCIPLE, §§225-238

See also Formal adjudication

EXECUTIVE CONTROLS

See Controls over administrative action

EXHAUSTION OF ADMINISTRATIVE REMEDIES,
§§790-804

See also Judicial review APA, §§792-793

exceptions to rule, §§795-803

   civil rights, §803

   constitutional questions, §§800-804

   deadlock, §797

   futility, §797

   inadequate remedies, §798

   irreparable injury, §796

   unauthorized action, §799

in general, §790

issue exhaustion, §805

preclusion of review effect, §794

purpose of rule, §791

state law, §806

EXPERTISE, §§235-238

See also Proof

F

FEDERAL STANDING COMMITTEES, §54

FEDERAL TORT CLAIMS ACT, §§661-669

See also Government tort liability

FIFTH AMENDMENT, §§459-471

See also Obtaining information

FILLING IN DETAILS, §8

See also Delegation of legislative power

FINAL ORDER RULE, §§765-775

See also Judicial review

"final" defined, §765

irreparable injury exception, §§769-772

   economic hardship, §771

   health and safety, §770

   procedural disputes, §772

nonfinal orders, §768

statutory requirements, §766

unreasonable delay exception, §§773-775

FINDINGS AND REASONS, REQUIREMENT OF,
§§239-247

See also Formal adjudication

APA, §§239-240

constitutional, §242

purpose, §243

sufficiency of findings, §244

FISCAL POWER, §79

FISHING EXPEDITIONS, §434

See also Obtaining information and attorney's fees

FIXING A STANDARD, §9

FOREIGN AFFAIRS, §393

FORMAL ADJUDICATION

See also Adjudicatory decisionmaking

adjudication vs. rulemaking, choice of, §§186-196

   abuse of discretion, §§187-189

   appropriate matters for adjudication, §190

   broad agency discretion, §186

   required rulemaking, §§191-196

      no rules by adjudication, §196

   retroactivity factor, §188

alternate dispute resolution, §§207-210

   when used, §210

applicability of APA, §§158-166

   adjudication defined, §§159-166

      general vs. particular applicability, §160

      external source for hearing, §§161-166

         Constitution, §165

         state APA, §166

         statute, §§162-164

declaratory orders, §§180-185

   agency interpretive guidance, §180

   APA, §181

   judicial review, §§184-185

discovery, §§204-206

   Freedom of Information Act, §206

   subpoena power, §205

evidence, §§215-224

   admissibility, §§215-217

   hearsay alone, reliance on, §§218-224

      constitutional problem, §224

      federal rule, §222

      judicial review, §223

      residuum rule–state courts, §§219-221

exclusive record principle, §§225-237

   assistance to fact finder, §§227-229

   official notice, §§230-233

   physical inspections, §226

   use of expertise, §§235-237

findings and reasons requirement, §§239-247

   adoption by agency heads, §246

   APA, §§239-240

   based on record, §245

   constitutionally required, §242

   formal and informal adjudications, §241

   parties' proposed findings, right to, §247

   purpose, §243

   sufficiency of, §244

intervention, §§198-203

   criteria for, §200

   discretion of agencies, §199

   purpose, §198

   standing, relation to, §200

notice, §197

   prehearing process, §§197-210

preponderance of evidence, §213
 proof, burden of, §§211-214
settlement, §§207-210
statutory right, §157
 APA, §§239-240

FOURTH AMENDMENT, §§440-442, 446
See also Warrants

FREEDOM OF INFORMATION ACT, §§225, 483-524
See also Obtaining information and attorney's fees
agencies covered, §492
APA, §§484-496
exceptions, §§497-524
 bank regulation, §523
 commercial secrets, §§501-505
 government commercial information, §513
 inter- or intra-agency memoranda, §§506-513
  executive privilege, §§508, 512
  government trade secrets, §513
 internal matters, §499
 law enforcement, §§519-522
 national security, §498
 natural resources, §524
 personal privacy, §§514-517
 statutory exemptions, §500
generally, §483
interpretations, §§485, 487
invasion of privacy deletions, §489
memoranda, §486
opinions, §§485-486
policy statements, §485
procedure for requests, §§490-496
 agencies and records covered, §§492-493
 attorney's fees, §491
 judicial enforcement, §§494-496
 quarterly index, §488

FUTILITY, §797
See also Exhaustion of administrative remedies

G

GENERALIZED FACTS, §149
See also Notice and hearing

GOVERNMENT EMPLOYMENT, §§107-110
See also Due process

GOVERNMENT IN THE SUNSHINE ACT, §§525-529

GOVERNMENT OFFICIALS' TORT LIABILITY, §§673-703
absolute immunities, §§675-687
 authorized acts, §§685-687
  common law, §687
  statutory, §§685-686
 judicial, §§678-680
  injunctions and attorney's fees, §679
 legislators, §§681-684
 President, §§676-677

  aides, §677
  prosecutorial, §680
 Civil Rights Act, §§694-703
 damage actions, legal basis for, §§693-703
  constitutional torts, §693
  federal officials, §693
  state officials (Civil Rights Act), §§694-703
   broad application, §695
   local government, §§700-703
    damages available, §703
    no immunity, §700
    suits in official capacity, §702
    when liable, §701
 judges, §§678-679
 qualified immunities, §§688-692
  law enforcement officers, §692
  military force, §691
  reasonable person test, §689
  school officials, §690
  statutory or constitutional violations, §§688-692

GOVERNMENT TORT LIABILITY, §§656-670
federal government, §§661-670
 Federal Tort Claims Act, §§661-669
  discretionary functions, §§666-668
  indemnity, §669
  intentional torts, §§663-665
  negligence, §661
  strict liability, §662
 small claims settlement, §672
 taking of property, §671
state government, §§657-660
 abolition of immunity, §659
 civil rights acts, §660
 proprietary functions, §658
 traditional rule, §657

GUBERNATORIAL VETO, §83

GUN DEALERS, §484
See also Obtaining information and attorney's fees

H

HABEAS CORPUS, §634

HEARING
See Notice and hearing

HEARSAY, §§215-224
See also Proof

HOME INSPECTIONS, §§427-429

"HOT OIL" CASE, §11

HOUSING
See Public housing

I

IMMUNITY
See Government officials' tort liability

IMPROPER INFLUENCES, §§257-292
See also Adjudicatory decisionmaking

INDEMNITY, §669

INDEPENDENT AGENCIES, §75

INDIVIDUALIZED FACTS, §148
See also Notice and hearing

INFORMAL ADJUDICATION
APA, §§167-176
    federal, §§167-172
        enforcement of subpoenas, §170
        explanation of denial, §171
        gap in coverage, §167
        licensing provisions, §172
        no hearing on record, §167
        right to appear, §169
    model state APA, §§173-176
        appropriate hearing required, §173
        conference adjudicative hearings, §175
        emergencies, §174
        summary adjudicative proceedings, §176
judicial innovation, §§177-179
requirement of findings and reasons, §241

INFORMAL LETTER, §783

INFORMAL RULEMAKING
See Rulemaking

INFORMATION
See Freedom of Information Act; Obtaining information
        and attorney's fees

INJUNCTION, §§624-629

INJURY IN FACT TEST
See Standing

INTENTIONAL TORTS, §§663-665

INTERMEDIATE REVIEW BOARDS, §296

INTERPRETIVE RULES, §§400-407
See also Rulemaking

INTERVENTION, §§198-203
See also Notice and hearing
purpose of, §198
relation to standing, §§200-203

INVASION OF PRIVACY, §489
See also Freedom of Information Act

INVESTIGATIONS, §55

IRREPARABLE INJURY
exhaustion of remedies, §796
final order rule, §§769-772

JK

JUDICIAL FORMULAS FOR REVIEW, §§6-34
See also Delegation of legislative power

JUDICIAL IMMUNITY, §§678-680
See also Government officials' tort liability

JUDICIAL NOTICE
See Official notice

JUDICIAL REVIEW
declaratory orders, §§184-185
exhaustion of administrative remedies, §§790-804. *See also*
        Exhaustion of administrative remedies
ex parte communications, §292
final order rule, §§765-775. *See also* Final order rule
formulas, §§6-34. *See also* Delegation of legislative
        power
government officials. *See* Government officials' tort
        liability
government tort liability. *See* Government tort liability
means of obtaining, §§621-639
    nonstatutory, §623
        certiorari, §633
        Court of Claims, §635
        habeas corpus, §634
        injunction and declaratory judgment, §§624-629
        mandamus, §§630-632
        tort actions, §635
    review during enforcement action, §§636-639
        jury trial, §638
    statutory, §§621-622
negotiated rulemaking, §390
petitions to institute rulemaking, §§381-383
primary jurisdiction in agency, §§807-820. *See also*
        Primary jurisdiction in agency
ripeness, §§776-789. *See also* Ripeness
scope of
    agency exercise of discretion, §§602-620
        arbitrary-capricious test, §§603-611
            abuse of discretion, §603
            APA standard, §§603-604
            policy determinations in legislative rules,
                §§610-611
            proper procedure, §609
            reasonableness, §608
            relevant factors basis, §607
            scope of agency authority, §606
        nonreviewable cases, §602
        record for review, §617
        remedies, limited review, §§618-620
        review of facts, §§612-616
            agency expertise, §615
            hard look scrutiny, §613
            statutory standard–substantial evidence, §616
    application of law to fact, §§594-601
        analysis of, §601
        reasonableness test, §§595-598
            federal rule, §§596-598
        substitution of court's judgment, §§599-600
        ultimate question generally, §§594-595

committed to agency discretion, §§602, 721-730
  aliens, admission of, §727
  decisions to prosecute or enforce, §725
  economic decisions, §729
  intelligence officer, discharge of, §726
  no law to apply, §§722-723
  not reviewable, §§602, 721
  refusals to reconsider, §728
  unallocated appropriations, §730
legal interpretations of agency, §§568-593
  Chevron rule–strong deference, §§579-592
    automatic delegation, §584
    clarity of statute, §581
    constitutional issues, §591
    formal adjudication, §588
    informal adjudication, §589
    interpretative rules, §586
    legislative rule, §§579-582
    plain meaning, §592
    policy statements, §586
    reasonableness of interpretation, §581
    ruling letters, §587
  decisions of law, §§568-593
  traditional rule–weak deference, §§569-578
questions of basic fact, §§543-567
  constitutional facts, §§561-563, 567
    Ben Avon rule, §§562-563, 567
     exceptions, §563
     present status, §567
  defined, §543
  jurisdictional facts, §§564-567
    deportation cases, §565
    present status, §567
    workers' compensation, §566
  standards, §§544-549
    any basis in fact, §547
    clearly erroneous, §545
    not reviewable, §548
    preponderance of evidence, §546
    substantial evidence, §544
sovereign immunity, §§640-655. *See also* Sovereign immunity
standing, §§731-763. *See also* Standing
statutory preclusion, §§704-720
  absolute preclusion, §§713-717
  APA, §704
  constitutional questions, §§711, 715
  implied preclusion, §§718-720
    voting rights, §719
  interpretation to avoid, §§707-712
    conflicts of interest, §712
    constitutional issues, §711
    illegal aliens, §710
    military justice, §708
    veterans' benefits, §709
    presidential decisions, §706

  presumption of reviewability, §705
stays, §§821-829. *See also* Stays pending judicial review
  timing, §764

JUNKYARDS, §454

JURISDICTIONAL FACTS, §§564-567
See also Judicial review
deportation, §565
workers' compensation, §566

JURY TRIAL, §638

JUS TERTII, §§750-752. *See also* Standing

L

LABOR LAW
policymaking, §§188-189
primary jurisdiction, §§818-820

LAW ENFORCEMENT, §§519-522, 654, 691

LEGAL RIGHTS TEST
See Standing

LEGISLATIVE FACTS, §§149, 152
See also Notice and hearing

LEGISLATIVE POWER
See Controls over administrative action; Delegation of legislative power

LEGISLATIVE VETO, §§60-61
See also Controls over administrative action

LEGISLATORS
control of agency actions, §62
immunity, §§681-684
pressure on agencies, §§283-285

LIBERTY
See Due process

LICENSES, §§111-116, 128-130, 172
See also Due process

LOCAL GOVERNMENT, §§700-703
See also Government officials' tort liability

M

MANDAMUS, §§630-632

***MEAT CUTTERS* CASE, §18**

MEMORANDA, §486

MILITARY, §393

N

NATIONAL INDUSTRIAL RECOVERY ACT, §§10-12

NATIONAL SECURITY, §498

NATURAL RESOURCES, §524

NEGLIGENCE, §§661, 696

NEGOTIATION, §§207-210
See also Formal adjudication; Rulemaking

NOTICE AND HEARING
comparative hearings, §145
due process, §§84-156. *See also* Due process
form of hearing, §§135-247
    general requirements, §§135-145
        basis for decision, §138
        confrontation, §139
        impartial decisionmaker, §140
        notice, §137
        right to counsel, §§142-143
    formal adjudication. *See* Formal adjudication
    informal adjudication. *See* Informal adjudication
    intervention, §§198-203
    issues requiring hearing, §§146-156
        adjudication vs. rulemaking, §§146-156
        application, §§150-154
        generalized facts, §149
        individualized facts, §148
        adjudicative facts, §148
        administrative summary judgment, §156
        legislative facts, §§149, 152
        remedies for violations, §§380-383
    rulemaking
        concise statement, §373
        exceptions to informal rulemaking requirements, §392
            agency management or personnel, §393
            agency organization, §394
            foreign affairs, §393
            general policy statements, §§408-410
            good cause, §§395-399
            interim-final rules, §399
            interpretive rules, §§400-407
            military, §393
            procedural rules, §394
            public property, §397
            right to petition, §380
            tentative ruling, §§410-411
        notice
            disclosure of data, §§361-363
            negotiated rulemaking, §388
            public comment insufficient, §370
            revisions after notice, §§369-371
            timing, §§365-366
        on the record requirement, §224
        right to petition, §380
    time of hearing, §§112, 118-134
        balancing test, §§120-121
        emergencies, §119
        termination of existing rights, §§122-134
            disability benefits, §§122-123
            discharge from employment, §§124-127
            general rule, §118
            licenses, §§112, 128-132

            repossession by creditors, §§131-134
            welfare payments, §§122-123

O

OBTAINING INFORMATION AND ATTORNEY'S FEES,
§§430-531
agency acquisition of information, §§430-457
    APA, §430
    constitutional protection, §458
    methods, §430
    physical inspections, §§446-457
        warrant requirement, §§446-452
            business property, §§450-454
                OSHA inspections, §452
            homes, §§447-448
            probable cause, §448
            welfare visit exception, §449
        warrantless exceptions, §§453-454
            gun dealers, §454
    physical tests, §§455-457
        accountant-client privilege, §472
        attorney-client privilege, §472
        due process, §§473-476
            accusatory proceedings, §474
            notice and hearing, §473
            right to subpoena, §§475-476
            APA, §476
        Fifth Amendment privilege, §§459-471
            immunity, §461
            scope, §§462-471
                private papers, §§463-466
                    search warrant, §466
                production of child, §468
                records of criminal activity, §470
                required records, §467
                simultaneous criminal investigation, §471
                tax records, §469
        right to counsel, §§477-481
            APA, §478
            scope of right, §§479-481
        unlawful searches, §482
    subpoena power, §§431-445
        adjudicative, §444
        burdensomeness, §443
        early view, §§432-434
        First Amendment, §439
        fishing expeditions, §434
        fourth amendment, §§440-442
        modern view, §§435-442
        reasonableness, §§441-442
        relevance, §442
        scope of, §§436-438
        third parties, §445
attorney's fees, §§530-541
    amount of award, §541

Equal Access to Justice Act, §§536-540

general rule, §530

statutory only, §§532-535

Freedom of Information Act, §§483-524. *See also*
Freedom of Information Act

Government in the Sunshine Act, §§525-529

OCCUPATIONAL SAFETY AND HEALTH ADMINISTRATION, §32

inspections, §452

OFFICIAL NOTICE, §§230-234

See also Proof

OMBUDSMEN, §62

ON THE RECORD REQUIREMENT, §225

OPINION, §486

ORDER, §159

ORGANIZATIONAL POWER, §80

P

PAROLE, §§97-98

See also Due process

PASSPORTS, §33

PERSONS ADVERSELY AFFECTED

See Injury in fact

PHYSICAL INSPECTIONS, §§226, 446-457

See also Obtaining information

PHYSICAL TESTS, §§455-457

POLICY STATEMENTS, §§408-411

See also Rulemaking

PREDECISION MEMORANDA, §§508-510

PRESUMPTION OF REVIEWABILITY, §705

See also judicial review

PRIMARY JURISDICTION IN AGENCY, §§807-820

See also Judicial review

agency proceeds first, §807

antitrust, §§814-817

factors against, §809

nontechnical issues, §811

traditionally judicial issues, §810

judicial disposition, §§812-813

labor law, §§818-820

purposes, §808

unpredictable application, §817

PRISONERS' RIGHTS, §§93-98

PRIVATE ATTORNEY GENERAL, §738

PRIVATE PAPERS, §463

PRIVATE PARTIES, DELEGATION TO, §§28-30

PROBATION, §§97-98

PROFESSIONAL LICENSES, §§111-116, 130

PROOF, §§211-237

admissible evidence, §§214-217

APA, §208

model state APA, §209

burden of proof, §§211-214

hearsay, §215

admissibility, §215

APA, §216

model state APA, §217

reliance on hearsay alone, §§218-224

due process, §224

federal courts, §222

residuum rule, §§219-223

state courts, §§219-221

official notice, §§230-234

expertise, §§235-237

conjecture, §237

lack of reasons, §238

prediction, §§235-236

generally, §230

opportunity to contradict, §§232-234

what can be noticed, §231

standard of proof, §§212-214

PROPERTY

See Due Process

PROPERTY, TAKING OF, §671

PROPRIETARY FUNCTIONS, §658

See also Government tort liability

PROSECUTORIAL IMMUNITY, §680

See also Government officials' tort liability

PUBLIC HEALTH, §§119, 448

PUBLIC HOUSING, §§105-106

PUBLICATION, §377

See also Rulemaking

Q

QUALIFIED IMMUNITY, §§688-692

QUARTERLY INDEX, §488

QUESTIONS OF BASIC FACT, SCOPE OF REVIEW OF

See Judicial review

R

REGULATORY ASSESSMENTS, §345

See also Rulemaking

REMOVAL POWER, §§73-78

congressional participation, §78

for cause, §§73-77

presidential, §72

REPLEVIN, §132

RES JUDICATA, §§310-319

See also Adjudicatory decisionmaking

RESIDUUM RULE, §§219-223

See also Proof

RETROACTIVE RULES, §§338-339

See also Rulemaking

REVIEW COMMITTEES, §57

RIGHT TO COUNSEL

agency seeking information, §§447-481

APA, §478

hearing, §143

parole revocation, §97

RIGHT TO PETITION, §§380-383

See also Rulemaking

RIPENESS, §§776-789

constitutional limitation, §778

informal administrative action, §§783-786

    enforcement policy, §786

    hardship from delay, §783

    interpretive rule, §784

    policy statements, §785

purpose, §§777-778

test, §§777-782

    fitness for review, §780

    hardship to parties, §§781-782

    Sierra Club, §§780-781

time limits for review, §787

statutory preclusion–preenforcement review, §§788-789

RULE, §§159, 354

RULE OF NECESSITY, §282

RULEMAKING

choice between adjudication and rulemaking, §§186-196

    abuse of discretion, §§187-189

    prospective adjudication, §196

    required rulemaking, §§191-195

        duty to adopt, §§191-192

        model state APA, §§193-195

    subject matter for adjudication, §190

construction of statutes, §340

controls on,

    executive, §§83, 344-347

        environmental impact statements, §346

        impact on small business, §347

        regulatory assessment–executive order, §345

        Regulatory Flexibility Act, §347

    judicial, §§30-33, 342. *See also* Controls over

        administrative action

    legislative, §§54-62, 343. *See also* Controls over

        administrative action

defined, §§159, 385

formal, §334

impartiality of rulemaker, §§412-421

    bias, §420

    ex parte contacts, §§413-418

        agency rules, §417

        Home Box Office rule, §415

        model state APA, §418

        no separation of functions rule, §421

        Sangamon rule, §414

informal process, §§353-411

    adjudication distinguished, §359

    applicability of APA, §§353-359

        characteristics of rule, §§357-358

        definitions, §§354-356

    delayed effective date, §§378-379

    disclosure of data, §§361-363

    exceptions to informal requirements, §§392-411

        categorical, §393

            good cause, §§395-399

            contrary to public interest, §398

            impracticable, §398

            interim-final rules, §399

            unnecessary, §397

        interpretative rules, §§400-407

            "actually interprets," §403

            binding on agency, §406

            inconsistent interpretations, §405

            intent analysis, §402

            results in new law, §404

        policy statements, §§408-411

            defined, §409

            tentativeness test, §§410-411

                Lincoln case, §411

        procedures, §394

    imposition of additional procedures, §384

    judicial remedies, §§381-383

        in general, §381

        refusal of petition, §§382-383

    Negotiated Rulemaking Act, §§386-391

        judicial review, §390

        when used, §387

    petition, right to, §380

    notice, §360. *See also* Notice

    public participation, §§364-368

        timing, §§365-366

    publication, §377

    revisions to rule, §§369-371

        logical outgrowth test, §369

    statement of basis and purpose, §§372-376

        adding material to record, §375

        concise and general, §373

        post hoc rationalizations, §376

        response requirement, §374

    interference by legislature or executive, §419

legal effect of rules, §§349-352

    legislative, §351

    nonlegislative, §352

    procedural, §§349-350

        rules of convenience, §350

policymaking, as technique for, §§336-337

procedures, §§332-335

formal, §334

hybrid, §335

informal, §333

no procedural due process, §332

record, §§422-429

exclusive record rule, §§423-427

exceptions, §§424-427

expert testimony, §427

lack of administrative findings, §425

new evidence, §426

model state APA, §428

state law, §429

retroactive rules, §§338-339

types of rules, §§329-331

legislative rules, §330

nonlegislative rules, §331

S

***SCHECHTER POULTRY* CASE, §12**

SCHOOL SUSPENSIONS, §§99-102

See also Due process

SEARCHES AND SEIZURES, §482

See also Obtaining information and attorney's fees

SELF-INCRIMINATION, §§459-471

See also Obtaining information and attorney's fees

SEPARATION OF POWERS, §§1-3

SOVEREIGN IMMUNITY, §§640-655

Eleventh Amendment basis, §§642-650

and commerce or Article I powers, §649

damage actions allowed, §§645-647

Fourteenth Amendment override, §647

prospective relief, §648

state court suits, §650

state-paid damages prohibition, §§643-644

waiver by state, §649

federal waiver, §§651-654

APA, §653

damages actions, §654

in general, §640

venue, §655

SPLITTING AGENCIES, §256

STANDING, §§731-763

APA, §754

case and controversy requirement, §§731-733

citizens, §§756-757

constitutional limitations, §§733-744

injury in fact, §§734-744

legal rights test outdated, §§734-735

modern requirements, §§739-744

causation and remediability, §744

competitive injury, §740

concrete and particularized, §739

economic, §741

noneconomic, §§742-743

deprivation of information, §743

environmental harm, §742

legislative standing, §762

prudential limitations, §§745-753

generalized grievances, §753

jus tertii, §§750-752

associational standing, §752

nexus not required, §749

zone of interests test, §§746-748

application, §§747-748

specificity–burden of proof, §755

statutory standing, §763

taxpayers, §§758-761

Establishment Clause, §§759-761

test, §§760-761

STANDING COMMITTEES, §54

STAYS PENDING JUDICIAL REVIEW, §§821-829

See also Judicial review

APA, §822

effect, §826

factors considered, §§823-827

effect of stay, §826

irreparable injury, §825

likelihood of prevailing on merits, §824

public interest, §827

illustrations, §§828-829

STIGMA

See Due process

STRICT LIABILITY, §662

SUBPOENA POWER, §§431-445

See also Obtaining information

"SUBSTANTIAL EVIDENCE" TEST, §§550-560

See also Judicial review

SUMMARY PROCEEDINGS, §175

T

TAFT-HARTLEY ACT, §819

TAKING OF PROPERTY, §671

TAX RECORDS, §469

TAXPAYERS, §§756-761

See also Standing

TORT LIABILITY OF GOVERNMENT

See Government tort liability

TORT LIABILITY OF GOVERNMENT OFFICIALS

See Government officials' tort liability

U

ULTRA VIRES ACTS, §§31-34, 748

See also Delegation of legislative power

UNREASONABLE DELAY, §§773-775

See also Final order rule

V

VAGUENESS, §§36-38

VENUE, §655
See also Sovereign immunity

VOTING RIGHTS, §719

WXY

WARRANTS, §§418-457
See also Obtaining information and attorney's fees
requirements for warrantless inspection, **§454**

WELFARE BENEFITS, §§104-106, 122-123
See also Due process

WELFARE INSPECTIONS, §449

WORKERS' COMPENSATION, §566

Z

ZONE OF INTERESTS, §§746-748
See also Standing

Notes

Notes

Notes

Notes

Notes

Notes

Notes

Notes

Notes

Notes